web publisher's
design guide
for Macintosh
2nd Edition

web publisher's
design guide
for Macintosh
2nd Edition

Mary Jo Fahey

CORIOLIS GROUP BOOKS

Publisher:	**Keith Weiskamp**
Managing Editor:	**Paula Kmetz**
Production Manager:	**Nomi Schalit**
Production:	**Nicole Colon**

Web Publisher's Design Guide For Macintosh, 2nd Edition
Copyright © 1997 by The Coriolis Group, Inc.

Limits of Liability and Disclaimer of Warranty

The author and publisher of this book have used their best efforts in preparing the book and the programs contained in it. These efforts include the development, research, and testing of the theories and programs to determine their effectiveness. The author and publisher make no warranty of any kind, expressed or implied, with regard to these programs or the documentation contained in this book.

The author and publisher shall not be liable in the event of incidental or consequential damages in connection with, or arising out of, the furnishing, performance, or use of the programs, associated instructions, and/or claims of productivity gains.

Trademarks

Trademarked names appear throughout this book. Rather than list the names and entities that own the trademarks or insert a trademark symbol with each mention of the trademarked name, the publisher states that it is using the names for editorial purposes only and to the benefit of the trademark owner, with no intention of infringing upon that trademark.

The Coriolis Group, Inc.
An International Thomson Publishing Company
14455 N. Hayden Road, Suite 220
Scottsdale, Arizona 85260
602/483-0192
FAX 602/483-0193
http://www.coriolis.com

Printed in the United States of America
10 9 8 7 6 5 4 3 2 1

Preface

**Author:
Mary Jo Fahey**

This is an exciting time for digital artists. Many new tools are available for creating digital artwork, and several are related to creating Web pages: HTML style sheets that make text formatting easier; NetObjects Fusion, a hot new Web page layout tool for artists who don't like HTML tags; client-side image maps, a superior way to create image maps that frees you from image map scripts on the server; frames; forms; VRML, the language that describes 3D space on the Web; shortcuts for creating art with Fractal Design Painter; GIF animation; background sound for Web pages; and streaming video. Even as this second edition of *Web Publisher's Design Guide For Macintosh* goes to press, numerous new trends and developments are continuing to emerge. Because the new trends are so numerous, Chapter 1 is now called *Web Watching And Planning*. Included in that chapter is information about resources that enable digital artists to follow these changes as they occur.

This second edition is more interactive than the first. Many of the artists who have contributed samples have also generously provided art files, which can be found on the companion CD-ROM.

I hope you like the second edition of *Web Publisher's Design Guide.* Send me an email message and let me know how you like the book!

Mary Jo Fahey

mjfahey@interport.net

http://www.echonyc.com/~art

Contents

Chapter 1
Web Watching And Planning   1

Web watching: Internet magazines (online and print) and user group SIGs 3

Web watching: Windows 95 and Webtv   4

Options for running Windows 95 software on your Macintosh 5

New trend to watch: CD-ROMs that augment a print publication or a Web site   7

The Net magazine's director of CD-ROM development, Tom Hale, shares tips on creating a hybrid CD-ROM   8

New trend to watch: offline browser software that automatically downloads Web content   9

New trend to watch: Web site analysis software   10

The Reuters Web sites   11

David Reinfurt's tips on planning a Web site   16

Wayfinding principles in Web site design   22

Chapter 2
Navigation   27

The Mobius Gallery   29

Principles of Web site navigation   33

Information design and Web site "map making"   41

Create a table with HTML to hold navigation buttons and text links   42

Internet cafe owner John Scott shares tips on creating frames 54

Chapter 3
NetObjects Fusion   69

A new Web page layout tool for designers   71

Chapter 4

Style Sheets And New HTML Text Tags 95

Microsoft style sheets offer formatting features such as point size, page margins, and leading 97

Formatting text in columns with Netscape's new <MULTICOL> tag 119

Controlling font color and family with the <FONT> tag (Netscape Navigator or Internet Explorer) 122

Microsoft's plan to add fonts to the Web: Free TrueType now and Web page font embedding in the future 124

Chapter 5

Online Tools 127

Convert a Pantone RGB value to a Web page color code with the BBS Color Editor 129

Searching the Web on Yahoo! search 137

Extending your Yahoo! search to other search engines 139

NetSite assistance from Netscape 140

Add information about your site to Yahoo! and other search engines 142

Locating, downloading, and decompressing shareware from the Web 144

Chapter 6

Photography 147

Mark Elbert's notes on Web graphics 149

Pixel depth 155

Saving your image: GIF or JPEG? 158

GIF and the LZW compression patent 161

HTML tags and page markup 162

The moveable grid for pictures and text 165

Using HTML to move page elements horizontally 166

Using HTML to move page elements vertically 173

Creating a banner graphic or splash screen 178

Linking a thumbnail GIF to an external JPEG 188

Wrapping text around a photo 192

Controlling text wrap with HTML   198

Fading an image into the browser background   202

Create a tiled background   204

Create a full-bleed photo background with larger tiles   206

Creating a silhouette on an image background   207

Creating a drop shadow in Photoshop   213

Jane Greenbaum's tips on creating a drop shadow in
   Painter 4.0   221

Creating a blue duotone with Photoshop   232

Creating a Super Palette with DeBabelizer   236

Chapter 7
Client-Side Image Maps 239

A virtual walking tour of NY's World Financial
   Center   241

Finding coordinates for clickable regions with
   Photoshop   244

Creating a client-side image map HTML file   248

Use PhotoGIF with Photoshop to create a transparent
   GIF   258

Use Fetch to upload files to a provider's server   262

Chapter 8
Video   265

Marc Thorner's tips on using VivoActive Producer to create streaming video   267

Experiment with Apple's QuickTime Plug-in, and embed a
   QT movie on a Web page   269

Use Premiere's Movie Analysis Tool to learn about data
   rate and compression settings   273

Steven McGrew's tips on capturing and compressing   276

Creating a link to a movie on your Web page   278

Pick the best palette for an 8-bit color QuickTime movie
   using DeBabelizer's Super Palette, and create a script to
   remap your movie   284

File conversion: Converting QuickTime files to AVI   294

File conversion: Converting AVI movies to QuickTime
movies   297

File conversion: Preparing QuickTime files for
Windows   293

Chapter 9
Sound   299

Web sites with sound   301

The compact MIDI file format   310

Set Netscape's Preferences to download music files   311

Greg Hess' tips on adding a background sound to a Web
page   313

Creating a link to sound files on your Web page   318

Creating sound effects with clip media   324

File conversion: AU to AIFF or WAV to AIFF   326

Mixing clip music with sound effects in SoundEffects   327

Recording and mixing sound in SoundEffects   330

File optimization: Resample and downsample sound files for
playback on the Web   333

File conversion: Preparing sound files for other
platforms   336

Chapter 10
GIF Animation And Shockwave   337

Curtis Eberhardt's GIF animation   339

Animation and interactive Web games that use Shockwave,
Java, live video, and QTVR   341

Curtis Eberhardt's tips on creating GIF animation frames in
Photoshop   349

Curtis Eberhardt's tips on assembling a GIF animation in
GIFBuilder   355

Curtis Eberhardt's tips on creating an HTML file to test your
GIF animation   358

GIF Wizard at Raspberry Hill   360

Create an interactive animation with Macromedia
Director   364

Creating a Director movie for use with the Shockwave
Director Internet Player   381

Compressing a Director movie with Afterburner   390

Chapter 11
VRML World Building 391

VRML on the Internet   393

The NYVRMLSIG's Coney Island Project   406

Alex Shamson's tips on creating a VRML model in Virtus
WalkThrough Pro   418

Open your WRL file in a VRML browser   452

Open a VRML file in a word processor and alter the
PerspectiveCamera   454

Embed a VRML window in a Web page   458

Chapter 12
Forms   461

The Slappers Web site   463

Using NetObjects Fusion to create a client-side image
map   466

Before you design a form for your Web site...   473

Using NetObjectsFusion to design a form (with a
MAILTO for routing data)   476

Index 485

Acknowledgments

The *Web Publisher's Design Guide, Second Edition* was made possible thanks to a large number of people who contributed their time and their talents. Special thanks to:

Keith Weiskamp, president of the Coriolis Group and other members of The Coriolis Group, including Paula Kmetz, Project Editor; Nomi Schalit, Book Production Manager; Nicole Colon, Typesetter; and Michael Peel, Production Assistant.

Peju Alawusa, Antonio Antiochia, Antonio Arenas, Elaine Arsenault, Don Barlow, Brian Behlendorf, Gavin Bell, Nick Bodor, Travis at BoxTop, Richard Boyd, Catherine Burns, Peggy Burton, Teri Campbell, Melissa Caruso, Harry Chesley, Peter Chowka, Tom Cipolla, Michael Clemens, Tom Cunniff, Frank DeCrescenzo, Diana DeLucia, Chris Dolan, Matt Dominianni, Juanita Dugdale, Curtis Eberhardt, Frauke Ebinger, Mark Elbert, Ron Elbert, Kevin Ellis, Michael Erde, Merry Esparza, Guillermo Esparza, John Farrar, David Filo, David Fry, Frank Gadegast, Gail Garcia, Steven Garson, Beth Gilbrech, Aaron Giles, Andrew Green, Jane Greenbaum, Lauren Guzak, DJ Hacker, Tom Hale, Maynard Handley, Patrick Hennessey, Stacy Horn, Tim Hunter, Grant Hurlbert, Regina Joseph, Trevor Kaufman, Rod Kennedy, Priti Khare, Iva Kravitz, Fred Krughoff, Ken Krupka, Shirley Lew, Robert Liu, Robert Lord, Charles Marelli, Steve Margolis, Paul Marino, Greg Marr, Peter Marx, JimMatthews, Steve McGrew, Kevin Mitchell, John Nardone, OkeyNestor, Pauline Neuwirth, Dan O'Donnell, Matt O'Donnell, John Olinyk, Patricia Pane, Tony Parisi, Jeff Patterson, Mark Pesce, Dave Pola, Berta Ponzo, David Reinfurt, Alberto Ricci, Alicia Rockmore, Larry Rosenthal, Barry and Jackie Ryan, Kleber Santos, John Scott, Bill Scott, Brandee Amber Selck, Alex Shamson, Ashley Sharp, Alex Sherman, Chuck Shotton, David Smith, Christina Sun, Barbara Tanis, John Tariot, David Theurer, Marc Thorner, Jack Waldemaier, Robert Weideman, Heini Withagen, Jerry Yang, and Jon Zilber.

Digital media specialist featured in this chapter:

Tom Hale is director of CD-ROM development at Imagine Publishing located in Brisbane, CA. Imagine publishes The Net, PC Gamer, Boot, Ultra Game Players, Next Generation, *and* Mac Addict *magazines.*

cdrom@net-usa.com

Artist featured in this chapter:

David Reinfurt is a multidisciplinary graphic designer with a B.A. in Visual Communications from the University of North Carolina. David specializes in interaction design.

reinfurt@ideo.com

Chapter 1

Web Watching And Planning

Offline Web browsing facilitated by CD-ROMs is one of many new trends for Web designers to watch. This chapter highlights important resources for Web trend watching and includes several examples of new trends.

The most significant new Web development that will affect planning is the impending browser war between Netscape and Microsoft. Regardless of which company wins the browser war, Macintosh Web artists cannot ignore the software development that is taking place on the Windows platform. Because some software may never be developed for the Macintosh platform, this chapter includes tips on how to run Windows 95 software on Macintosh hardware.

Although it's tempting to begin your Web page creations with graphics, in this chapter David Reinfurt makes us aware of key project elements to have in place before the graphics begin.

Web watching: Internet magazines (online and print) and user group SIGs

Summary: Graphic designers who keep up with changes on the Web will be better equipped to create content for their clients.

Above: Interactive Week, *published by Ziff-Davis, is both a print and online publication (http://www.zdnet.com/intweek).* ***Above right:*** *Web Week, published by Mecklermedia, is both a print and online publication (http://www.webweek.com).*

Above: Internet World, *published by Mecklermedia, is both a print and online publication (http://www.iworld.com).*

B y investigating new trends, graphic designers can assist their clients in planning content strategy for their Web site. Resources include:

1. Online publications.
a. *Webweek* and *Interactive World*, published by Mecklermedia.

b. *Interactive Week*, published by Ziff-Davis.

2. Print publications.
Magazines that provide in-depth product reviews and identify emerging trends on the Internet include:

a. *The Net*, published by Imagine Publishing, includes a hybrid CD-ROM with Web tools, software demos, movies, animation, and other large files which are difficult to download (http://www. thenet-usa.com).

b. *WebTechniques*, a Miller Freeman publication, contains an excellent HTML column written by Laura Lemay, author of *Teach Yourself Web Publishing and HTML in a Week, published by Sams.net.*

c. *PC Novice*, by Peed Corporation, contains a plain-language introduction to PCs.

3. User group SIGs (special interest groups).
User groups represent a tradition that has existed for two decades. Call a local computer store or university computer center for information about local user group meetings.

Web watching: Windows 95 and Webtv

Summary: *Macintosh artists should be aware of Web-related trends on the Macintosh, PC, and the new Webtv boxes.*

Above: *ActiveX animation on Spike Lee's site available through Microsoft's Internet Explorer browser window.*

Above: *New Webtv boxes are now available from Philips Magnavox and Sony Electronics are priced from $329 to $349. The Webtv Internet provider service is $19.95 per month for unlimited access.*

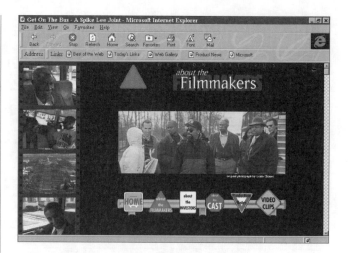

Graphic designers cannot assume that Macintosh Web pages are the same as PC Web pages. For example, Spike Lee's Web site (http://blackamericaonline.com/bus/index.html) opens with ActiveX animation that cannot be seen on the Macintosh platform at this time. Rather than wait for Macintosh software to be developed, graphic designers should consider adding Windows 95 hardware to their studio. *(Note: See "Options for running Windows 95 software on your Macintosh" in this chapter.)*

Webtv is an inexpensive portable Web-viewing box, which makes Web viewing and email possible on a TV set. The small, lightweight boxes are available from Philips Magnavox and Sony Electronics. *(Note: Local access phone numbers are listed on the Webtv site at http://www.webtv.net.)* The $330-$350 unit uses a proprietary browser, and Web viewing is made possible through Webtv Internet provider service. A 33.6 Kbps modem is built in, and an optional cordless keyboard is available at the electronics retailers for $50-60. The unit also contains a PS/2 keyboard socket, a smartcard slot, and a 96-pin I/O port which Webtv plans to enable for a printer (800-469-3288).

Although the Webtv browser cannot see frames or VRML at this time, updates to the Web browser are expected. Graphic designers who create Web content for the home market should consult the HTML guidelines on the Webtv site (http://www.webtv.net).

Options for running Windows 95 software on your Macintosh

Summary: Running Windows 95 software on a Macintosh computer can get you acquainted with PCs and keep you up-to-date on important developments.

By adding a board with a Pentium processor to your Macintosh, your computer becomes a dual processor that can run software for both platforms. The flip between operating systems is controlled with keys on the keyboard. In addition to a processor, the card must contain its own memory and its own sound. A port that hooks to a modem is optional on some cards because the PC card may share the Mac modem.

Although a second computer is an option that should be considered, a dual processor solution is about half the price of new 166 MHz Pentium machines. A PC card is also several hundred dollars cheaper than reconditioned Pentiums that are now being sold through outlet stores for major hardware manufacturers, such as Dell and Micron. The companies that sell Windows 95 enabling hardware and software for Macintosh include:

1. Apple Computer.

Apple's Power Macintosh 7200/120 PC compatible computer is equipped with a pre-installed Pentium 586/100 MHz card. Industry benchmarks compare the speed of the 586/100 MHz card to that of a Pentium 75 MHz. The card may also be installed in any PCI-based Power Macintosh system. J & R Computer World in New York City sells this system for $2,295.

2. Orange Micro.

Orange Micro makes two varieties of Orange PC cards: one for NuBus-based Macintosh computers and another for PCI-based machines. The cards come with one parallel port and two serial ports for adding PC peripherals. Windows 95 must be purchased separately for $142.

Card	Speed	8 MB	16 MB	32 MB
Model 320 (NuBus)	133 MHz	$738	$852	$1,080
Model 340 (PCI)	133 MHz	$1,040	$1,128	$1,356

Orange Micro cards are available from Orange Micro at
714-779-2772 and Mac Powerhaus at 800-615-3183.
*(Note: Look for Orange Micro's home page at http://www.
orangemicro.inter.net.)*

3. Reply Corporation.

Reply Corporation (800-955-5295) manufactures the PC
cards that Apple adds to the 7200/120 MHz Power Mac. The
card is slightly less expensive than Orange Micro's. Windows
95 and sound are bundled, but the cards do not come with the
ports necessary to hook up PC peripherals. A port adapter
can be purchased separately. *(Note: Look for Reply
Corporation's home page at http://www.reply.com.)*

Card	Speed	40 MB
NuBus	100 MHz	$700
PCI	166 MHz	$1,115

*(Note: Smaller memory configurations at lower prices are
also available for Reply Corporation's PC cards. A 40 MB
memory configuration is listed to give readers an approximate idea of price. A card for the 6100, 7100, and 8100
Power Macs is approximately $800 to $900.)*

4. Insignia Solutions.

Insignia has created a software emulation program that is
the least expensive alternative for running Windows 95
software. Speed is entirely dependent on the Macintosh
machine's processor. J & R Computing in New York City
sells Insignia's SoftWindows software for approximately
$400. *(Note: Look for Insignia Solutions' home page at
http://www.insignia.com.)*

New trend to watch: CD-ROMs that augment a print publication or a Web site

Summary: CD-ROM is a convenient media for high-bandwidth content. Publishers at The Net *magazine assume that anyone who is buying an Internet magazine also has a CD-ROM drive. The magazine editors have copied simple HTML files to the CD-ROM, which can be opened in a reader's Web browser.*

Internet Explorer
1c.

1d.

1e.

W ho said HTML files need to be "served" from a file server? Digital media experts at *The Net* magazine have created a clever CD-ROM disk that gets distributed with their magazine and allows HTML files to be viewed online or offline (http://www.thenet-usa.com).

1. Steps to open *The Net's* CD-ROM.

a. Connect to the Web with your PPP connection.

b. Open *The Net's* CD-ROM.

NETPOWER
1a.

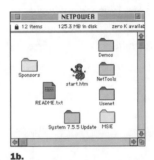

1b.

c. If you do not have a Web browser software program, launch or install Microsoft's Internet Explorer browser, which is included on *The Net's* CD-ROM.

d. Select Open File from the File pull-down menu.

e. In the dialog box that follows, select Start.htm, and click on Open.

f. *The Net* magazine's CD-ROM interface will open in the browser window.

1f.

The Net magazine's director of CD-ROM development, Tom Hale, shares tips on creating a hybrid CD-ROM

Summary: The Net *magazine's CD-ROM disk is a valuable supplement to the magazine, providing tools and helpful links for readers.*

start.htm

Hybrid CD-ROMs can be played on both Macintosh and PC hardware. Although Tom Hale at *The Net* magazine admits that it's challenging to create content that is identical for both platforms, one CD-ROM is more efficient than two separate disks. In this section, Tom has identified tips for Web developers who are considering a CD-ROM supplement for their Web site.

1. HTML files work cross-platform.
HTML files are perfect for a hybrid CD-ROM because the Web is a cross-platform digital medium. However, it's still challenging to create content that will be useful for a variety of PCs and Macintosh computers.

2. Put all large files on the CD-ROM.
The Net magazine puts all art, movies, animation, and demo software on the CD-ROM and puts text on the Web site. This shift solves all bandwidth problems, and the Web site becomes a vehicle to distribute fresh content that's easy to download.

3. Web tools are a valuable addition.
Web tools are distributed each month, so readers do not need to download the software themselves. Shareware and demo software programs are usually large, and downloading is time consuming. Tools are valuable, and readers will want to keep the CD-ROM near their computer.

4. Future add-ons to the CD will include chat.
As *The Net* magazine's Web site and CD-ROM evolve, live interactive chat between editors and readers is an interesting addition that's planned.

New trend to watch: offline browser software that automatically downloads Web content

Summary: Offline browsers act as spiders or Web agents that automatically deliver fresh Web pages to your hard drive by topic.

Several new Internet utilities help collect, organize, and save Web pages or entire sites for offline viewing or CD-ROM mastering.

1. Macintosh offline browsers.

a. *Web Buddy*, by Dataviz, PowerMac and 68 K versions, $50 (http://www.dataviz.com).

b. *Freeloader*, by Freeloader, Inc., free (http://www.freeloader.com).

c. *Web Whacker*, by Forefront, requires System 7.1 or greater, $69.95.

d. *BackWeb*, by BackWeb, Inc., Macintosh OS, free (http://www.backweb.com).

2. PC Offline browsers.

a. *Web Buddy*, by Dataviz, Windows 3.x, Windows 95, and Windows NT versions, $50 (http://www.dataviz.com).

b. *Freeloader*, by Freeloader, Inc., Windows 3.x, Windows 95, and Windows for Workgroups versions, free (http://www.freeloader.com).

c. *Web Whacker*, by Forefront, requires Windows 95, $69.95 (http://www.ffg.com).

d. *Surfbot 3.0*, by Surflogic LLC, Windows 95 and Windows NT versions (http://www.surflogic.com).

e. *WSmart Bookmarks*, by First Floor, Windows 3.x, Windows 95, and Windows NT versions, $24.95 (http://www.firstfloor.com).

f. *Net Attache Light*, by Tympani Software, Windows 3.x, Windows 95, and Windows NT versions, free for noncommercial, personal use (http://www.tympani.com).

g. *Milktruck*, by Traveling Software, Windows 95 and Windows NT versions, free for noncommercial, personal use (http://www.travsoft.com).

h. *BackWeb*, by BackWeb, Inc., Windows 3.x, Windows 95, and Windows NT versions, free. A BackWeb server is available for Unix, NT, and proxy servers (http://www.backweb.com).

New trend to watch: Web site analysis software

Summary: *Broken links and image references are easier to manage with Web site analysis tools.*

Web site analyzers let you see what's working on any Web site and solve the problems associated with restructuring a Web site, moving files, updating a Web site, renaming pages, or deleting files that are still in use.

1. Adobe SiteMill for Macintosh.

Adobe SiteMill reads an existing Web site and automatically finds and summarizes the errors found. The software includes Web page authoring features found in Adobe's HTML editor, Adobe PageMill. SiteMill can be run on any Macintosh running System 7 or higher with at least 3 MB of free memory and a color display. Price is $199.95 (http://www.adobe.com). Features include:

a. automatically fixes all links throughout a site when folders are renamed, moved, or deleted.

b. shows warnings for unreachable or unused resources.

c. displays all resources, page titles, and folders.

2. InContext WebAnalyzer for Windows.

Like Adobe's SiteMill, InContext WebAnalyzer identifies broken links and problem resources. However, unlike Adobe SiteMill, which fixes broken links automatically, WebAnalyzer must be integrated with an external HTML editor to repair links. The software requires Windows 95 and at least 8 MB of RAM. Price is $129.95 (http://www.incontext.com). Features include:

a. identifies broken links and images.

b. is compatible with popular Web browsers.

c. can be integrated with popular HTML editors for Web page repair.

The Reuters Web sites

Summary: *In this chapter on planning, the Reuters sites provide an excellent Web site development model. Built by a professional graphic designer for a client who understands online information technology, these sites represent perfect "Web craftsmanship."*

Note: *Two Twelve Associates is a multi-disciplinary design firm specializing in environmental graphics, print, and interactive design. The firm is located at:*
596 Broadway, Suite 1212
New York, NY 10012-3234
212-925-6885.

Few people wander around the Web without a purpose. Travelers usually search and navigate with the help of signs, just as they do on the street.

For several decades, signs in architectural spaces have been designed by a group of graphic designers known as *environmental designers*. Just as graphic design has evolved in the print medium, so have the visual aesthetics and formulas used in environmental graphics. For example, environmental designers have adopted the architect's phased approach to project development, which includes planning, schematics, design, and production.

Environmental graphic designers now know a great deal about effective organization of space and use of environmental elements. In fact, one graphic design firm specializing in environmental graphics is uniquely positioned to offer advice on "planning a Web site." The underlying principles of helping people "find their way" are as appropriate for virtual spaces as they are for real spaces.

Two Twelve Associates.

Using the principles of "wayfinding," the graphic designers at Two Twelve Associates have been designing spaces for almost 20 years. *Wayfinding* is the study of peoples' movements and their relationship to space. It's also the process of reaching a destination, which involves problem solving. Two Twelve Associates has used wayfinding design to plan spaces for clients such as the South Street Seaport, the Central Park Zoo, the Baltimore Light Rail Subway, the Baltimore Waterfront Promenade, the City of New York Department of Parks and Recreation, and the Metropolitan Transportation Authority.

Recently, David Reinfurt, a graphic designer with Two Twelve, designed and built the two Web sites for Reuters, shown in this chapter. David's skill as an environmental

1.

graphic designer and his insight into how to plan a project will help Web designers organize their own sites.

1. Reuters News Machine.

For business people suffering from "information overload," Reuters News Machine offers what might be called an electronic clipping service called *my.news*. For a fixed monthly fee, a computer user can predefine the categories of news they wish to receive, and Reuters will deliver all related stories. The service also offers general news, sports news, business news, offbeat news (alt.news), and an area called *news.talk*, dedicated to online discussions about current events.

a. **News content groups.** Up-to-the-minute reports from the Reuters bureaus around the world are organized into four "content" groups. Users can click on a category and then review a list of headline/synopsis items. Each news headline is a link to the full story. Content groups include:

- **news**, which contains general news items from around the world.

- **business**, which includes stories shaping the economic and business news.

- **sports**, which contains the latest sports stories.

- **alt.news**, which includes "offbeat" news.

1a.

1b.

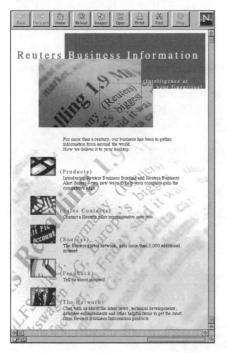

2.

Tip: The Reuters Business Information Products site has full-bleed images, which have been ghosted to a light gray and white and used to cover the background. This effect is achieved with the <Body Background = "filename.gif"> tag at the top of the HTML document:

```
<body background=
"filename.gif"></body>
```

b. News functions. This consists of two unique "news tools" and a news discussion area where you can participate in news discussions with people around the world.

- **News.search** is a powerful search tool that responds to a keyword search, gathering news items on any topic you choose.

- **My.news** is the Web equivalent of an electronic clipping service allowing you to predefine news categories of interest. The news stories are automatically delivered to your computer several times a day.

- **News.talk** is an area containing news "threads," which are followed by people all over the world. Users exchange their views by posting messages to a particular thread in response to a news item.

2. Reuters business information products.

Reuters Business Information site was created to support two new Reuter's online business services: *Reuters Business Briefing* and *Reuters Business Alert*. These two online, user-definable news retrieval services offer news gathered from more than 2,000 sources and delivered up to 15 times a day to a subscriber's PC or server.

Reuters Business Briefing is a server-based product that can assemble news in one central location and distribute it on an enterprise-wide basis via Lotus Notes.

Reuters Business Alert is a smaller, workstation or LAN-based news-gathering service designed for PCs running Microsoft Windows.

a. Products. A mouse click on the Products button will take visitors to pages that describe both of the Reuters business information products.

2a.

```
<img src="filename.gif"
border=0>
```

b. Sales Contacts. The Sales Contacts button (Figure 2b1) will branch to a map of the United States. Clicking on a state (Figure 2b2) will bring up a silhouette image of the sales rep for that state (Figure 2b3), and, if the browser has a built-in sound player, the rep's "hello" will be heard.

2b1.

2b2.

2b3.

c. Sources. If visitors are interested in knowing the sources for news, a Sources button will branch to a section that will display the information onscreen.

2c.

d. Feedback. The Feedback button (Figure 2d1) branches to a questionnaire. A multiple-choice format with checkboxes makes the form (Figure 2d2) easy to use.

2d1.

2d2.

e. The Network. The Network button takes visitors to an area that changes most frequently. It includes product announcements and a "faq"—or frequently asked questions—section.

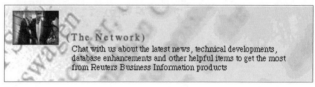

2e.

David Reinfurt's tips on planning a Web site

Summary: *The essential early steps in the Web site development process do not involve graphics; they require the creation of an underlying structure.*

1. Assemble the team.

For a graphic design firm, the Web development team includes client members as well as members from the graphic design firm, including:

a. **A manager, client.** This person has the authority to make decisions and is most likely a member of the firm's marketing team. Ideally, this team member is very familiar with the Web and can be relied upon for content ideas.

b. **Writer/marketing specialist, client.** In Reuters' World Wide Web terminology, this person is known as an editor. Analogous in some ways to a managing editor, this member contributes content ideas and has an on-going role in the life of the Web project. Ideally, this team member is very familiar with the Web.

c. **A technical specialist, client.** This member is responsible for making the Web pages and the server work. The team might look to an Internet provider to fill this role. Ideally, this person is familiar with the Macintosh, PC, and Unix platforms.

d. **Graphic designers, graphic design firm.** Depending on the size of the project, two designers may be involved. A senior designer directs in artistic areas, and a junior designer is involved in production.

e. Information Designer, graphic design firm. This member has a writing background and will review the marketing content to see if it is appropriate for the Web. For example, marketing content created for print is often too wordy; an information designer will know how to edit the content for Web pages. This member should be very familiar with the Web.

2. Develop a concept.

Developing a concept usually involves a brainstorming session, which may last an entire week. At this stage, a rough content list consisting of bullets should be developed. This information will be refined and organized in a schematic process, as outlined next. To help facilitate the flow of ideas in brainstorming sessions:

a. Tour the Web. Analyze what's possible, and examine well-implemented sites. Because the Web is large and changes frequently, each team member should have a connection and be able to search the Web independently.

b. Consider sources for content. Although a firm's existing collateral materials may be repurposed for a Web site, ideally the site should have new content.

c. Develop an underlying paradigm or metaphor. One of the most important elements to consider during initial brainstorming sessions is the underlying paradigm:

- Is it a bookstore?

- Is it a record store?

- Is it a catalog?

- Is it a public relations vehicle?

The Reuters development team decided the News Machine site would be an online news source, somewhere between newspaper and television, and the Business Information Products site would be a public relations vehicle.

3. Develop a schematic (on paper).

While the writers develop copy, the graphic designers develop a minimal schematic. Copy, in the form of diagram labels, is used to identify the components of the Web site (Figure 3a).

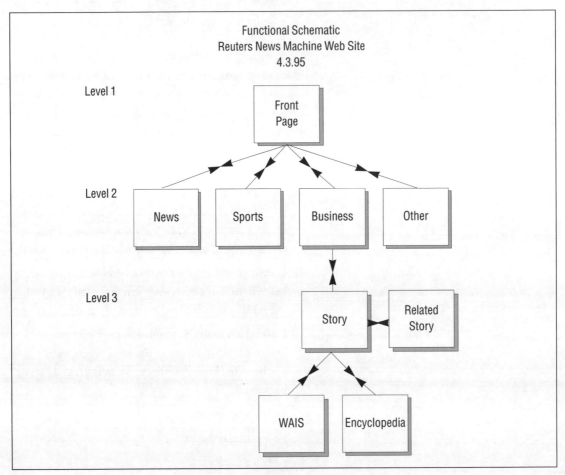

3a.

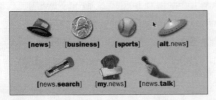

3b.

Level 1 contains the site's components as described in wayfinding design. (See *Wayfinding principles in Web site design* later in this chapter.) In this model, the components are the four news content areas and three news functions. Although these are not shown on the minimal schematic, they show up as text in the schematic prototype and as glyphs, or identifying icons, in the graphic design phase (Figure 3b).

Level 2 contains the destinations described in wayfinding design. In this model, destinations include types of news. (News, sports, business, and other fields are page names, which were modified and rearranged later in the project.)

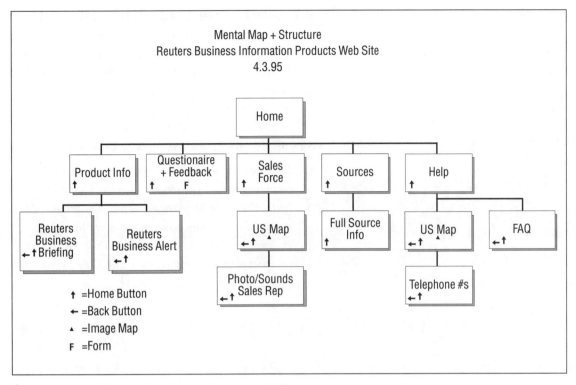

Mental Map + Structure
Reuters Business Information Products Web Site
4.3.95

4a.

4. Plan navigation.

The arrows on the schematic diagrams roughly describe navigation. Later, sets of glyphs are developed to help users navigate (represented schematically in Figure 4a and implemented in Figure 4b). Other navigation aids include links to a help screen and a site map.

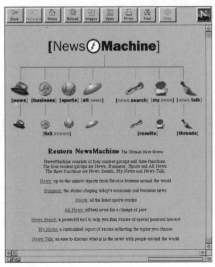

4b.

Tip: Make sure text copy is proofread carefully. Fun, "amateur" Web pages are not harmed much by typos, but professional business sites riddled with typos can have an unprofessional appearance.

5. Create a schematic prototype (no graphics).

A schematic prototype consists of text-only Web pages. Although text is boring to look at, it focuses a team's attention on content before graphics enter the picture. For the graphic design firm, a schematic prototype can be used to get client approval before moving on to the next phase. The prototype should follow the earlier schematic and contain easy-to-read copy developed for quick consumption.

a. **Easy-to-read chunks.** The content should consist of plain language organized into chunks of four to five items. For example, in the News Machine project, the graphic design elements on the Reuters "front page" evolved much later in the project. Early in the project, the front page was represented with text items, such as:

- News
- Sports
- Business
- Other

b. **Analyze the information.** Carefully plan how information is presented. Web visitors should:

- **Understand where they are at all times.** At the prototype stage, locations were identified with text labels. Much later, matching graphic design elements were created as location identifiers on every page. In the Business Information pages, the page backgrounds identify a visitor's location.
- **Understand the "destinations" built into a site.** Although the decision to provide visitors with some facility to see all destinations at all times was made at the prototype stage, the toolbar did not take shape until later in the graphic design stage. In the News Machine site, a toolbar on every page includes all the destinations available to a visitor.
- **Understand what action will take them to a destination.** At the prototype stage, text links were used as navigation links. Buttons and other graphic design elements were added later. For example, in the News

Machine site, a click on a small icon will give a larger icon at the top of the next page. This reinforces that the action is correct.

c. **Streamline the copy.** Because it is likely that Web visitors will do more scanning and glancing than reading from left to right, the content should be refined to contain essential information, conveyed in keywords.

6. Begin the graphic design process.

If planning is phase one, then graphic design is phase two. During this second phase, the development team meets regularly to review the design direction. As in print, the design cycle is an interactive process. During this phase, the graphic designers carefully review the visual elements and constantly ask themselves, How can I improve this? Does this work? Are the visual elements easy to understand?

The work that goes into the planning phase does not end when graphic design begins. During the graphic design phase, the designer must constantly look back at the planning work accomplished in phase one and ask, Does the project's design match the original project plan? Is it clear? Are the ideas easy to understand?

Wayfinding principles in Web site design

Summary: Wayfinding principles, used to help people "find their way," offer important guidelines for Web site developers. These ideas will become even more valuable as Web sites develop into 3D spaces.

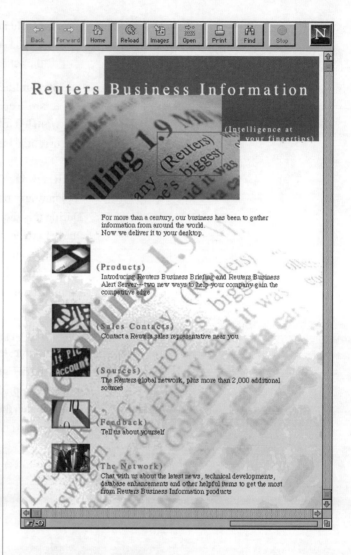

1. What is wayfinding?

Introduced to environmental design in the late 70s, the term *wayfinding* describes spatial behavior. It includes the decision making, decision execution, and information processing involved in reaching a destination. Although the term initially referred to the process of reaching a physical destination, wayfinding principles may also be used for navigating Web sites. At the most basic level, wayfinding consists of *cognitive mapping* and *spatial problem solving*, defined next.

a. **Cognitive mapping.** The process of forming a mental image of a physical layout.

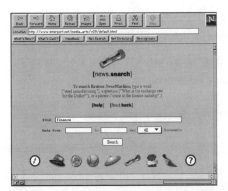

2a.

2b.

b. Spatial problem solving. Behavior, usually decision making, needed to make a journey or reach a destination.

2. Wayfinding decisions.

Wayfinding decisions are hierarchically structured in a *decision plan*, which consists of one or more wayfinding decisions broken down into smaller decisions. For example:

a. Decision to use Reuters news.search. If the news.search page in the Reuters News Machine site is a destination, smaller wayfinding decisions required would include:

- Get on the Web.

- Use a bookmark or open the URL associated with the Reuters News Machine site.

- Select news.search from the Reuters home page. You would then see the screen shown in Figure 2a.

If news.search were not an option available on the Reuters home page, the list of decisions would include whatever actions would be necessary to get to the destination or the news.search page.

b. Decision to contact a Reuters Sales Representative. If the Sales Contacts page in the Reuters Business Information Products site is the destination, the smaller wayfinding decisions would be:

- Get on the Web.

- Use a bookmark or open the URL associated with the Reuters Business Information Products site.

- Select Sales Contacts from the Reuters home page.

- Scroll to the map of the United States.

- Click on a state.

- Record the name and phone number of the Reuters salesperson, as shown in Figure 2b.

3. Wayfinding conditions.

Wayfinding conditions result in a Web visitor's arrival at your site. Different visitors will have different reasons for viewing your site.

4a.

4b.

4c.

a. The Web visitor is exploring. The visitor has no particular goal or destination in mind.

b. The Web visitor has an objective. The Web visitor is seeking specific information.

4. The wayfinding design process.

Although wayfinding principles are applied throughout the entire planning and graphic design process, it is interesting to examine the details of the wayfinding design process.

a. Identification of components. In the News Machine project, identifying components was an essential part of the design process because it meant naming the four content areas and three functions. Identifying the types of news (news, business, sports, and alt.news) took place in the planning phase and again in the design phase. Notice the change in the names from the schematic to the graphic design phase.

b. Grouping of components into destinations. In the News Machine site, Web visitors move from a front page to a destination page with news headlines and a news synopsis under each headline. Although it may contain further links, a page that contains news is considered a destination.

c. Linking of components. A toolbar with elements small enough to fit on every page means a Web visitor can branch to every section from every page.

5. Wayfinding design.

Wayfinding design involves themes that can be adapted and applied to Web site development.

a. Decision diagram. A decision diagram is a list of decisions a visitor has to make to navigate a site. Although this step was not used in the two Reuters projects, there was a conscious effort to review the number of steps a visitor needs to take to get to a destination. As in space planning for physical sites, visitors should take as few steps as possible to get to Web destinations.

b. Graphics as landmarks. Web site pages should have related graphics that act as a masthead, but multiple mastheads should not be identical. In the Reuters Business Information site, the masthead graphic varies slightly from page to page. The backgrounds also act as visual landmarks.

5b.

5c.

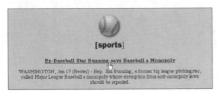

5c.

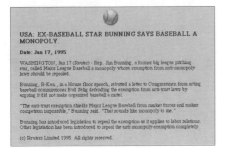

5c.

5b, 5c.

c. Redundancy. In the Reuters News Machine site, the glyphs, or identifying icons, are repeated to remind Web visitors where they are at all times. Although the size varies, this reoccurring graphic assures that a Web visitor is not lost. In the Reuters Business Information Product example, notice how David repeated the identifying button image in the background graphic.

d. Color. Although color was not used as a landmark in either Reuters site, it can be used as an effective identifier to help a Web visitor navigate.

e. Iteration. Web designers should anticipate from 5 to 20 cycles of change in the development of a Web site. Focus groups, alpha testers, beta testers, and a questionnaire on the Web site are all vehicles for gathering feedback from the people who travel the site.

6. Conclusion.

Although a planning phase can be rigorous, it represents a time-tested model that adds a solid foundation to a project. Experience has shown that the project model that includes thorough planning withstands change much more than a project with little planning.

Artist featured in this chapter:

Merry Esparza is an illustrator and painter who specializes in 3D computer illustration and interactive computer graphics.

merry@interport.net

http://www.users .interport.net/~merry/ mobius.html

Internet cafe owner:

John L. Scott is Webmaster and co-owner of alt.coffee, an Internet cafe in New York City's East Village.

jetsam@flotsam.com

http://www.altdotcoffee .com

Chapter 2

Navigation

In this chapter on navigation, Merry Esparza introduces us to both 2D and 3D navigation on the Web. Although 3D "worlds" are relatively new, the technology does exist, and it's changing the way Web visitors move around. For example, text links and inline links on a Web page are replaced by new navigation controls in 3D space. The new 3D browsers include network anchors, rubber bands, and node pointers that help Web travelers move by hyperlinking through 3D worlds.

John Scott, an Internet cafe owner, demonstrates how frames can be used to navigate a Web site. Follow step-by-step instructions on how to assemble a frame document using art from the cafe's Web site. *(Note: Look for John Scott's images in an alt.coffee folder on the CD-ROM in the back of this book.)*

The Mobius Gallery

Summary: An art gallery in cyberspace provides a model for learning how to plan and develop navigation controls for your Web site.

1. The Mobius Gallery site.

Designed by computer artist Merry Esparza (merry@interport.net), the Mobius Gallery site (http://www.users.interport.net/~merry/mobius.html) provides a showcase for Merry's artwork and Guillermo Esparza's paintings and sculpture. A Web site is a unique and advantageous space for artists to set up their own exhibit—it's international, art does not need to be physically transported, and the site can be easily updated.

a. **Sculpture.** To display Guillermo's work, Merry photographed his paintings and sculpture and scanned the images into Photoshop. *La Magdalena*, shown on this page, is a cast stone high-relief figure, created by Guillermo in 1994. The original is in The National Museum of Catholic Art and History in New York City.

b. **Painting.** Although images of Guillermo Esparza's paintings can be seen on the Web, electronic duplicates can never totally render his original work, which can be found inside many New York City churches. His projects have included wall murals, domes, sanctuary paintings, and sanctuary statues. Geographically spread out, they can be easily brought together in one place—a Web site.

Above: Merry Esparza's splash screen for the Mobius Gallery site.

Above: Merry created a 3D cube for her logo.

Above: Three-dimensional mural created for Empyrean, an interactive computer strategy game.

c. **Graphics** is the section of the Web site containing Merry's computer illustration. One of her specialties is optical illusion art, reflected in the site's splash screen. Merry explains that the Mobius Gallery's opening screen is designed to "reflect the relationship between the viewer and the work of art." In the image, Merry superimposes *inverted perspective* on *linear perspective*. Linear perspective establishes depth by using actual or suggested lines that intersect in the background. This creates a space where objects diminish in size relative to distance from the viewer's eye. Combined are elements of inverted perspective, a concept used in Byzantine art. In inverted perspective, objects that are farthest away appear larger than elements in the foreground.

Merry's work in three-dimensional art has also led to a series of murals she created for Empyrean, her computer strategy game. Merry built a prototype game in Macromedia Director and is currently talking with game developers about building an interactive game for the Web. As Merry explains, "by 1996, cable modems will provide enough bandwidth for game developers to by-pass CD-ROMs and develop exclusively for the Web."

2. Future 3D graphics on the Mobius site.

Merry's work in 3D graphics overlaps new developments in Web technology. As a result, she sees the Mobius Gallery as a test site for interesting new software programs. Examples include:

a. **VRML and 3DMF.** Merry plans to develop a 3D version of the Mobius Gallery, which Web visitors could navigate with 3D browsers such as the Duet Development Corporation's Walkabout 3D World Browser (Figure 2a). Three-dimensional spaces also have the potential for typed conversation between visitors or between Guillermo, Merry and visitors. In June 1996, Black Sun Interactive (http://www.blacksun.com) announced CyberHub, a server software program that adds multiuser capabilities to any Web site. The software is highly scalable and can support virtual communities ranging from 10 to thousands of simultaneous users.

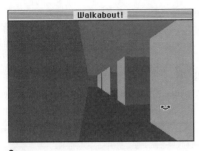

2a.

Above: Duet Development Corporation's 3D World browser and Model is a QuickDraw 3D software application that allows you to navigate and walk about in 3D worlds.
Below: Realtime voice communication is available over the Internet from Electric Magic (http://www .emagic.com). A mouse click on a virtual phone link inside a 3D space could place a realtime (voice) phone call over the Internet from anywhere in the world.

NetPhone 1.2.1 †

For more direct chat with sound, realtime voice communication over the Internet is available from Electric magic (http://www.emagic.com). With a mouse click on a "virtual" phone link inside the Mobius Gallery, a realtime phone call could be placed to either Guillermo or Merry Esparza from anywhere in the world. Although still relatively crude compared to telephone technology, parties can converse by alternately talking over the computer's microphone. (*Note: On the IBM PC, a product called Internet Phone from Vocaltec works in a similar way.*)

3D "walkthrough" environments can be built with Strata's new Strata Studio Pro and Virtus Corporation's Virtus Walkthrough Pro. The developments that make walkthrough worlds on the Web possible are two new cross-platform 3D file formats with built-in features designed for Web travel. VRML (Virtual Reality Modeling Language), sponsored by Silicon Graphics, and 3DMF (3D Meta File), from Apple Computer, will soon become as familiar to Web artists as GIF and JPEG.

Software application programs that are VRML- and 3DMF-savvy will have a selection on the File menu for saving a 3D image as a VRML or 3DMF file. Applications will also have built-in features that enable artists to specify the location of a *network anchor* or *hotspot*. Network anchors are clickable spots in a 3D world that hold URL information. When clicked, the Web visitor hyperlinks or travels to a related Web site.

b. **Apple's QuickTime VR.** For Web visitors to see gallery rooms from a 360-degree perspective, Merry is planning QuickTime VR (virtual reality) movies for the Mobius site. 3D panels can be rendered for a 360-degree panoramic image and stitched together using Apple's QuickTime VR Authoring Tools Suite. Using Apple's QuickTime VR Player, visitors can twist, turn, twirl, zoom, and pick up 3D objects in a 3D environment. In the future, the QuickTime VR experience will include

Tip: Image maps, with clickable regions in an inline image, may also be thought of as a Web navigation device. Client-side image maps, covered in the Client-Side Image Maps chapter, are easier to build than server-dependent image maps.

music and hyperlinks to other Web sites; Apple has only just begun to develop the QuickTime VR format.

c. **Animated 3D graphics for the Director Internet Player.** Merry sees potential for animated tours with music, sound effects, and interactivity using shockwave, Macromedia's Director Internet Player technology.

Principles of Web site navigation

Summary: *For the past few decades, print, radio, and television have been considered the three mass market media. Recently, the Web has been described as the fourth mass market medium. This very different new medium allows viewers to interact and "navigate."*

Graphic designers who have started to design Web pages have the privilege of shaping the newest media—the media predicted to influence the way we work, play, think, and learn. Because of its rapid growth, the Web will evolve in ways we cannot anticipate. Although many changes are expected to occur in the next few years, several underlying principles are likely to remain.

1. Hypermedia.

The Web is a hypermedia system developed in 1989 by Tim Berners-Lee, a software engineer at the Center for European Particle Physics. Hypermedia is interactive information that has no beginning and no end. Although *home pages* are starting points, Web pages should be thought of as non-linear. Links found on each page jump to other Web pages, providing a random sequencing of information. Viewers can navigate through an information base in a variety of ways, depending on the links they follow—and the information base can be spread out all over the world.

Hypermedia is a term invented in the 1970s, but the concept dates back to 1945. Read on for a bit of history.

a. Vannevar Bush and the Memex system. In 1945, 30 years before anyone thought of a personal computer, computer scientist Vannevar Bush described a Memex—a system that provided *associative indexing*, or the ability to string together information meaningful to an individual user. Bush envisioned a system with text and graphics that could be viewed either sequentially or by following a user's trail of associative thinking.

b. Ted Nelson and the word *hypermedia*. In the 1970s, Ted Nelson, author of Dream Machines, introduced the term *hypermedia*. He saw hypermedia as a two-way medium in which computer users are creators as much as they are consumers. Apple Computer has promoted this idea since their 1987 introduction of HyperCard, a user-friendly hypermedia "authoring" toolkit.

c. Two-way communication is attracting big business. Although CD-ROMs and kiosks have hypermedia characteristics, most are read-only. The potential for two-way communication is much stronger on the World Wide Web. As a result, commercial interests are focused on the Web's marketing potential. From a marketing point of view, tomorrow's virtual worlds can attract the curious Web explorers, and dynamic database engines can measure and track a visitor's every response.

2. Active explorer vs. passive observer.

An underlying theme in every form of hypermedia is the viewer as an active explorer. As a traveling participant in the media, the viewer is given the option of deciding where to go and how to get there. Viewers move around to navigate and interact with an information base.

a. Two-dimensional HTML. The two-dimensional Web page formed from HTML tags is becoming less of a page and more of a background for multimedia player windows and new animation technologies built into the browser's page. Examples include the Director Internet Player, the new 3D browsers, and Hot Java, an interactive 3D animation technology that can enhance a browser page with multimedia presentations or launch small *applets* in the form of interactive floating windows. All of these new developments have been built with viewer participation in mind.

b. **Three-dimensional VRML and 3DMF.** In VRML and 3DMF worlds, there are no passive observers. Navigation in 3D implies moving through a space or handling objects. Software engineers involved in the development of 3D worlds have invented built-in anchors, or hotspots. This means a click on an object in a 3D world will hyperlink a Web visitor to another world.

3. The home page.

Regardless of how a Web site is organized or how many pages a site has, the starting point is referred to as the *home page*. Although Web visitors can travel directly to any page on a Web site, it's the home page address that usually gets published or promoted.

4. Navigating with URLs.

URLs, or Uniform Resource Locators, are addresses used to locate information on the Web. URLs can be used to locate Web documents, FTP files, Gopher files, news files, or other Web resources as they're developed. Navigation on the Web means opening a link that contains a URL. This can be accomplished by using a browser's Open command and typing in the URL or by clicking on a link that contains a URL. A URL stores information in three ways.

a. **Protocol information** is the first part of the URL. For example, Stanford University's Sumex-aim Macintosh software archive has two public mirror sites at Apple Computer. Accessing one requires the FTP protocol typed into the Open Command's dialog box, and the other requires an http protocol, as follows:

ftp://mirror.apple.com/mirrors/Info-Mac.Archive/
http://mirror.apple.com

In Italy, the Sumex-aim Macintosh software archive is mirrored on a Gopher site, as follows:

gopher://gopher.cnuce.cnr.it/11/pub/info-mac

The protocol provides a clue concerning what type of information request is sent from the *client* (browser software) to a server (any computer on the Internet). HTTP (Hypertext Transfer Protocol) is the most common protocol found on the Web because it is used to request Web documents from HTTP servers. FTP (File Transfer Protocol) is used to access files on an FTP server, and a Gopher protocol is used to access a Gopher server.

b. Domain name information is the part of the URL that follows the protocol. For example, the Yahoo! search engine created by David Filo and Jerry Yang can be found at http://www.yahoo.com, where www.yahoo.com is the domain name.

Early Internet addressing assigned addresses to machines, or *hosts*. Later, Domain Name Service (DNS) addressing was implemented, and addresses now refer to domains and not physical machines. A domain is considered to be an entity that can be a person or an organization.

Although it's implied that the domain name reflects the name of the organization managing the physical Web server, or host, many Internet providers allow their clients to use their own domain names on server space they lease. On behalf of a client, a provider can apply to InterNIC, an organization that registers and maintains a database of domain names used on the Internet (http://www.internic.net/ds). InterNIC is the result of a cooperative agreement with the National Science Foundation, AT&T, and Network Solutions, Inc. The registration process takes about a week, and the application procedure is handled through email (http://www.internic.net/ds). Once InterNIC approves a domain name, the provider receives a notification via email.

c. **Directory and file name information** follows the domain name and provides additional information about the location of a file or directory. If a file name is present in an URL, it has a three or four letter extension and will occur in the position furthest to the right. The names to the left of the file name, separated by slashes, are directory names. For example, the Arizona Macintosh Users Group in Phoenix Arizona runs a Sumex-aim Macintosh mirror archive at:

ftp://ftp.amug.org/pub/mirrors/info-mac

Info-mac is the name of a directory. The User's Group has an index document to the mirror site available at:

http://www.amug.org/index.html

Index.html is the name of a document.

5. 2D navigational structures.

a. **Linear slide shows.** The simplest Web sites are developed as linear slide shows in which one page is

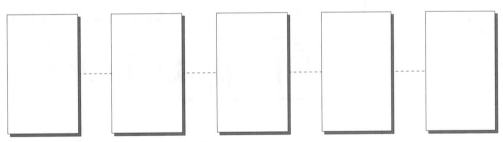

5a.

equivalent to the next, without a top-down structure. For example, small sites with one or two dozen pages can be arranged with simple navigation buttons to move ahead or back.

b. Hierarchical tree. Large sites should be organized into branches, or grouped areas. Visitors can choose to follow a branch that interests them, which may bring them to a fork and then to a related group of pages. However, hypermedia experts have known for some time that when allowed to cross from one branch to another without first going back "up the tree," viewers get lost. In Figure 5b, notice there are no interconnecting lines between branches. In order to navigate from one major branch to another, a visitor must follow a branch back to the starting point.

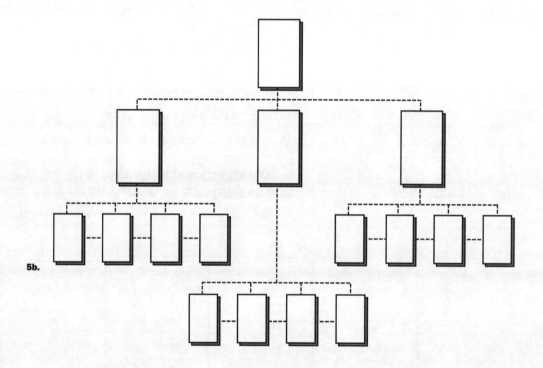

5b.

Sculpture

6a.

6. 2D navigation controls.

a. Text links. Text links are the most common form of links on a browser page. The color of the text link indicates the type of link.

- **Link text** is blue by default in the Netscape browser, indicating that a different Web page can be accessed with a click on the highlighted text. Link text is not necessarily underlined because viewers may turn underlining on or off in the Preferences dialog box.

Merry Esparza's button link with a border.

6b1.

The same graphic with the border turned off.

6b2.

The color of text links can be changed by Web page designers by using a hexadecimal RGB value added to the <BODY> tag. (*Note: See* Convert a Pantone RGB value to a Web page color code with the BBS Color Editor *in the* Online Tools *chapter.*)

- **Visited link text** is purple by default in the Netscape browser, indicating that the link has been followed.

- **Active link text** is red by default in the Netscape browser, indicating that the link is open.

b. **Inline graphics as links (buttons or arrows).** Inline graphics are graphics that are loaded on the browser page along with text. When inline images are defined as links, the Netscape browser outlines the graphic with a border coded with the same colors as text links (Figure 6b1). By default, a blue border indicates the link has not been followed, purple indicates the link has been followed, and red indicates the link is open. This border can be turned off with a BORDER=0 attribute added to the image <IMG> tag (Figure 6b2). For example:

```
<IMG SRC="button1.gif" BORDER=0>
```

7. Creating 2D navigation controls with HTML.

HTML text links and inline graphic links are both created with the HTML link tag <A>…</A>. Inside the link tag, you'll need:

a. **The name of a file or URL to link, which will be specified with the HREF attribute inside the link.**
For example:

```
<A HREF="toc.html">
```

b. **The text or graphic that will act as the hotspot.**
Examples:

```
<A HREF="toc.html">Sculpture
<A HREF="toc.html"><IMG SRC="optica.gif">
```

c. **An ending link tag.**

Following are some examples of completed links:

```
<A HREF="toc.html">Sculpture</A>
<A HREF="toc.html"><IMG SRC="optica.gif"></A>
```

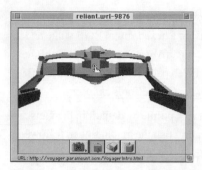

8a.

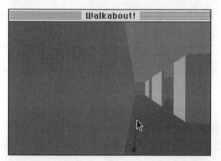

8b.

8c1.

8c2.

8. 3D navigation controls.

a. VRML's *network anchors* are encountered in a VRML 3D browser window when the viewer's mouse passes over a link which, when clicked, will hyperlink the viewer to another Web site.

b. Walkabout *rubber bands* were invented by the Duet Development Corporation when they built the Walkabout 3D World Browser. The rubber bands provide a means to move forward and control navigation speed. Stretching the rubber band a small amount provides slow navigation; stretching it a large amount provides greater speed.

c. QuickTime VR's *node pointers* are encountered in a QuickTime VR movie player window when the viewer's mouse passes over a link which, when clicked, will move the viewer to another movie node.

9. Creating 3D navigation controls with VRML and 3DMF.

Because VRML and 3DMF are both file formats, 3D software applications that support VRML and 3DMF export or save 3D rendered images as VRML or 3DMF files.

An extra feature that will be important for creating 3D worlds is the ability to add network anchors in a VRML or 3DMF file. These are in the form of URLs, which, when clicked, will hyperlink a Web visitor to another part of the Web.

Information design and Web site "map making"

Summary: Preliminary structural sketches are an important part of the hypermedia development process.

Above: *3D murals created for Empyrean, Merry Esparza's interactive computer strategy game.*

1. Flowcharting.

Flowcharts, or program maps, are essential to the hypermedia design process. Merry used a sketchbook to create ideas for her interactive computer game. Sketches can lead to new ideas, which the information designer or illustrator can refer to in the schematic.

2. Interactive storyboarding.

For large projects with production teams, storyboards provide a convenient means to communicate development ideas to an entire team. Some companies find it helpful to create wall maps, which show the function and approximate layout of all the graphic components.

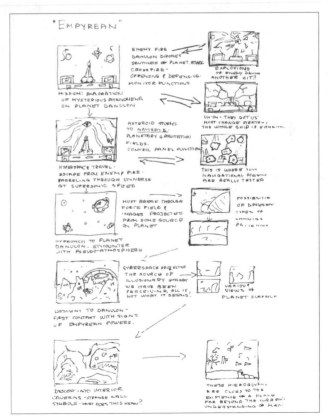

2.

Create a table with HTML to hold navigation buttons and text links

Summary: *Tables created with HTML tags can form an invisible grid that can hold text or graphics.*

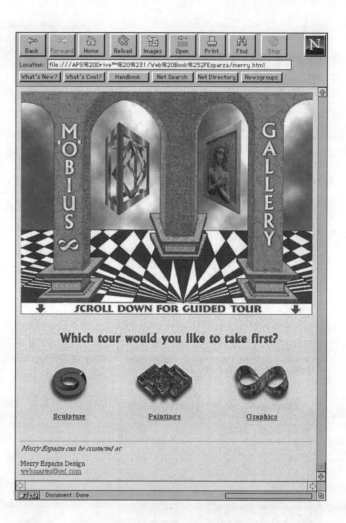

1a.

Table tags are an important part of Netscape's extensions to HTML. Table cells can be used to form columns of text, which are otherwise impossible to create with HTML. For the Mobius Gallery home page, Merry discovered that a table offers a convenient way to line up button graphics and text links—each is in a separate table cell with the borders turned off.

1. Use Photoshop to crop button graphics.
Because the button graphics will occupy table cells, crop them into identical-sized rectangles, using Photoshop's Info palette.

   a. Open Photoshop, and select Open from the File pull-down menu.

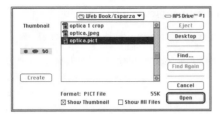

1b.

b. Select a graphic in the dialog box that appears, and click on Open.

c. Select Show Info from the Window|Palettes pull-down menu.

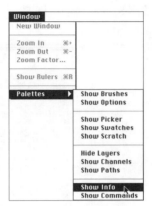

1c.

1d.

d. The Info Palette will appear as a floating palette in the Photoshop work area. Click on the Info Palette's pop-up menu to select Palette Options.

e. Click on the Mouse Coordinates Ruler Units pop-up menu to select Pixels. Click on OK.

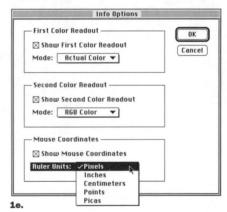

1e.

1f.

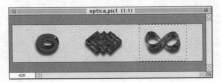

1g.

f. Select the rectangle marquee in the Photoshop Toolbox.

g. Drag a selection rectangle around your graphic.

h. Note the Width and Height measurements in the Info Palette—you'll need these measurements to crop your other button graphics.

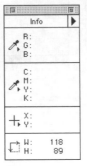

1h.

i. When you're satisfied with the selection rectangle, select Crop from the Edit pull-down menu.

j. You will need to repeat these steps for all of your button graphics.

1i.

1j.

2a.

2b.

2. Save the graphic.

a. Select Save As from the File pull-down menu.

b. Type in a file name and add GIF as an extension.

c. Press on the Format pop-up box, and select CompuServe GIF. Click on Save.

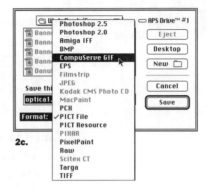

2c.

SimpleText

3. Open SimpleText.

Use SimpleText or a word processor. If you use a word processor, be sure to save the document as Text Only.

4. Create a new HTML document.

Start a new document with the following markup tags:

```
<HTML>
<HEAD>
<TITLE>Mobius Gallery</TITLE>
</HEAD>
```

5.

5. Add a BODY BACKGROUND tag.

Merry used a small tile with a paper texture for the Mobius Gallery background. When you list a GIF or JPEG image in the BODY tag with a BACKGROUND attribute, Netscape and Internet Explorer will automatically tile it to fill the background.

```
<HTML>
<HEAD>
<TITLE>Mobius Gallery</TITLE>
</HEAD>
<BODY BACKGROUND="paper.jpeg">
</BODY>
</HTML>
```

6.

6. Add an image tag.

The IMG tag contains a *source*, or SRC parameter, which contains the name of an image file. In this example, the image is the splash screen that Merry designed for the Mobius Gallery (Figure 6).

```
<HTML>
<HEAD>
<TITLE>Mobius Gallery</TITLE>
</HEAD>
<BODY BACKGROUND="paper.jpeg">
<IMG SRC="Gallery3.jpeg">
</BODY>
</HTML>
```

7. Add a table tag.

The <TABLE>…</TABLE> tag is the principle tag used to begin and end a table.

```
<HTML>
<HEAD>
<TITLE>Mobius Gallery</TITLE>
</HEAD>
<BODY BACKGROUND="paper.jpeg">
<IMG SRC="Gallery3.jpeg">
<TABLE>
</TABLE>
</BODY>
</HTML>
```

8. Add a table row tag.

Use a table row tag <TR> each time you define a new row. (*Note: Merry used this tag twice in her HTML document because her table has two rows.*)

```
<HTML>
<HEAD>
<TITLE>Mobius Gallery</TITLE>
</HEAD>
<BODY BACKGROUND="paper.jpeg">
<IMG SRC="Gallery3.jpeg">
<TABLE>
<TR>
</TABLE>
</BODY>
</HTML>
```

Tip: An HTML specification is currently under development that will add typographic controls to HTML with style sheets. For more information, stay tuned to http://www.w3.org/hypertext/WWW /Arena/style.html.

9. Add table header tags.

The table header tag <TH>…</TH> is used to define text or graphics that will appear in data cells. In this sample, Merry used the table header tag to define a row of images followed by a row of text. (*Note: The table header tag <TH>…</TH> is very similar to the table data tag <TD>…</TD>. Although both function the same, the table header tag has a default BOLD FONT and a default ALIGN=CENTER, which was useful in this sample.*)

```
<HTML>
<HEAD>
<TITLE>Mobius Gallery</TITLE>
</HEAD>
<BODY BACKGROUND="paper.jpeg">
<IMG SRC="Gallery3.jpeg">
<TABLE>
<TR>
<TH><A HREF="toc.html"><IMG SRC="optical.gif"></A></TH>
<TH ><A HREF="toc2.html">
     <IMG SRC="optica2.gif"></A></TH>
<TH><A HREF="toc3.html"l><IMG
     SRC="optica3.gif">
</A></TH>
</TR>
<TR>
<TH><A HREF="toc.html">Sculpture</A></TH>
<TH><A HREF="toc2.html">Paintings</A></TH>
<TH><A HREF="toc3.html">Graphics</A></TH>
</TABLE>
</BODY>
</HTML>
```

10. Use the WIDTH attribute to widen cells.

The default width of each of the table cells caused the entire table to look too narrow (Figure 10a). By experimenting with the WIDTH attribute in the table header tag, Merry was able to widen the table across the page (Figure 10b).

```
<HTML>
<HEAD>
<TITLE>Mobius Gallery</TITLE>
</HEAD>
<BODY BACKGROUND="paper.jpeg">
<IMG SRC="Gallery3.jpeg">
<TABLE>
<TR>
<TH WIDTH=160><A HREF="toc.html">
     <IMG SRC="optical.gif"></A></TH>
<TH WIDTH=160><A HREF="toc2.html">
     <IMG SRC="optica2.gif"></A></TH>
<TH WIDTH=160><A HREF="toc3.html">
     <IMG SRC="optica3.gif"></A></TH>
</TR>
<TR>
<TH WIDTH=160><A HREF="toc.html">Sculpture</A></TH>
<TH WIDTH=160><A HREF="toc2.html">Paintings</A></TH>
<TH WIDTH=160><A HREF="toc3.html">Graphics</A></TH>
</TR>
</TABLE>
</BODY>
</HTML>
```

10a.

10b.

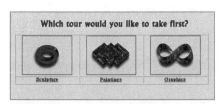

11a.

11b.

11. Use the BORDER attribute to turn borders off.

By default, the table header tag and the image tag add borders that Merry needed to turn off (Figure 11a). Use the BORDER attribute in both tags to make the borders disappear (Figure 11b).

```
<HTML>
<HEAD>
<TITLE>Mobius Gallery</TITLE>
</HEAD>
<BODY BACKGROUND="paper.jpeg">
<IMG SRC="Gallery3.jpeg">
<TABLE BORDER=0>
<TR>
<TH WIDTH=150><A HREF="toc.html">
     <IMG SRC="optical.gif" BORDER=0></A></TH>
<TH WIDTH=150><A HREF="toc2.html">
     <IMG SRC="optica2.gif" BORDER=0></A></TH>
<TH WIDTH=150><A HREF="toc3.html">
     <IMG SRC="optica3.gif" BORDER=0></A></TH>
</TR>
<TR>
<TH WIDTH=150><A HREF="toc.html">Sculpture</A></TH>
<TH WIDTH=150><A HREF="toc2.html">Paintings</A></TH>
<TH WIDTH=150><A HREF="toc3.html">Graphics</A></TH>
</TR>
</TABLE>
</BODY>
</HTML>
```

12. Add line breaks.

The line break tag <BR> adds space below the table.

```
<HTML>
<HEAD>
<TITLE>Mobius Gallery</TITLE>
</HEAD>
<BODY BACKGROUND="paper.jpeg">
      <IMG SRC="Gallery3.jpeg">
<TABLE BORDER=0>
<TR>
<TH WIDTH=150><A HREF="toc.html">
<IMG SRC="optical.gif" BORDER=0></A></TH>
<TH WIDTH=150><A HREF="toc2.html">
     <IMG SRC="optica2.gif" BORDER=0></A></TH>
<TH WIDTH=150><A HREF="toc3.html">
      <IMG SRC="optica3.gif" BORDER=0></A></TH>
</TR>
<TR>
<TH WIDTH=150><A HREF="toc.html">Sculpture</A></TH>
<TH WIDTH=150><A HREF="toc2.html">Paintings</A></TH>
<TH WIDTH=150><A HREF="toc3.html">
Graphics</A></TH>
</TR>
</TABLE>
<BR>
<BR>
</BODY>
</HTML>
```

Tip: Providing a signature area aids in interactive design by encouraging viewers to send comments, questions, or suggestions about your Web site.

13. Add the signature area.

It's customary to add a signature area at the bottom of each Web page. This area contains contact information separated from the rest of the page with a horizontal rule <HR>.

```
<HTML>
<HEAD>
<TITLE>Mobius Gallery</TITLE>
</HEAD>
<BODY BACKGROUND="paper.jpeg">
        <IMG SRC="Gallery3.jpeg">
<TABLE BORDER=0>
<TR>
<TH WIDTH=150><A HREF="toc.html">
<IMG SRC="optica1.gif" BORDER=0></A></TH>
<TH WIDTH=150><A HREF="toc2.html">
        <IMG SRC="optica2.gif" BORDER=0></A></TH>
<TH WIDTH=150><A HREF="toc3.html">
        <IMG SRC="optica3.gif" BORDER=0></A></TH>
</TR>
<TR>
<TH WIDTH=150><A HREF="toc.html">Sculpture</A></TH>
<TH WIDTH=150><A HREF="toc2.html">Paintings</A></TH>
<TH WIDTH=150><A HREF="toc3.html">Graphics</A></TH>
</TR>
</TABLE>
<BR>
<BR>
<HR>
<ADDRESS>
Merry Esparza can be contacted at:<BR>
Merry Esparza Design<BR>
</ADDRESS>
<A HREF="mailto:webmaster@ref.com">
        webmaster@ref.com</A>
</BODY>
</HTML>
```

14. Summary of HTML tags used in this section.

The tags you see in this list (in alphabetical order) reflect the HTML3.2 specification.

<A>...</A>

Referred to as an *anchor*, this tag uses the HREF attribute to link to an external file. For example:

```
<A HREF="toc.html">Sculpture</A>
```

(Note: The HTML file name must include the path name if the file is located in another directory.)

<ADDRESS>...</ADDRESS>

The address tag provides a means of signing your Web page. The information inside is specially formatted and provides Web visitors with information about who created the page and who they can contact. This tag occurs at the bottom of a Web page, in a section known as the *signature*.

(Note: It is customary to add an email address to the signature and to use a MAILTO URL. By building a link with an email address and by adding the MAILTO URL to the HREF attribute, viewers get an empty email form with the address already filled out whenever they click on the link.)

<BODY>...</BODY>

A tag used to open and close the body of a document.

A tag used to break a line. This tag does not require an ending tag.

<HEAD>...</HEAD>

A tag used to open and close the header portion of a document.

<HTML>...</HTML>

A tag used to open and close an HTML document.

<HR>

A tag used to create a horizontal rule. This tag does not require an ending tag.

Tip: Derrick Smith, a Visual Basic pro-
grammer from Provo, Utah, collabo-
rated with artist Frank Decrescenzo and
built a popup navigation menu for the
Slappers Web site using Microsoft's
ActiveX. Look for details about
Slappers, a new, flat drumstick in the
Forms *chapter.*

<IMG>

Used to refer to an image, this tag uses the SRC="…"
attribute, which represents the the URL
(location) of the image. For example:

```
<IMG SRC = "optica3.gif">
```

This tag also uses the BORDER attribute, which can be
used to turn off the border around a graphic used in a link.
For example:

```
<IMG SRC="optica3.gif BORDER=0>
```

<TABLE>…</TABLE>

A tag used to describes the beginning and end of a table.
This tag uses the BORDER attribute to control the width of
the border. For example:

```
<TABLE BORDER=0> or
<TABLE BORDER=1>
```

<TD>…</TD>

A tag used to describe the contents of a table cell. *(Note:
In Netscape, the contents of the Table Data cell are
ALIGN=LEFT.)*

<TH>…</TH>

A tag used to describe the contents of a table header cell.
*(Note: The contents of the table header cell are bold and
center—aligned by default.)* Both the table data <TD> and
the table header <TH> tags accept the WIDTH attribute.
For example:

```
<TD WIDTH=160>
<TH WIDTH=160>
```

<TITLE>…</TITLE>

A tag used to describe the title of a document, which
shows up inside a browser's title bar.

<TR>…</TR>

A tag used to describe a table row.

Internet cafe owner John Scott shares tips on creating frames

Summary: Use a two-frame layout to create a table of contents window and a window to display linked documents. By organizing a Web site's content in this way, frames become a navigation device.

The frame layout has become very popular on the Web. Much like panes in a window, this layout allows you to divide a page into rectangular frames. You can:

- specify a unique HTML document to fill each frame
- create independent links in a frame
- create links in one frame to change content in another frame

John Scott, who owns an Internet cafe in New York's East Village, used a two-frame layout on the cafe's Web site. The first frame acts as an index or table of contents containing links to content that is displayed in the second frame.

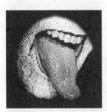

Above: John Scott used small JPEG images as links in the first frame. With its own scroll bar and links to content in the second frame, this frame acts as an index or table of contents.

1. Overview.

To create his document, John created three separate HTML documents.

a. Defining frame document, or compound document

b. First frame document

c. Second frame document

The next three sections provide step-by-step examples of how each of these component documents are assembled. *(Note: If you wish to follow the steps in this section, you may use the images provided in the alt.coffee folder on the CD-ROM in the back of this book.)*

First frame

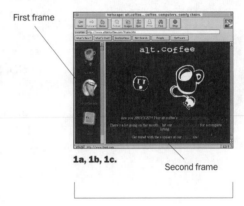

1a, 1b, 1c.

Second frame

Defining frame document

2. Create the defining frame document.

The defining document, or compound document, uses the <FRAMESET> tag to open and close a set of frames. This tag replaces the <BODY> tag in an HTML document and defines the number and size of frames on a page. Web designers will notice that a frame document *never* has a <BODY> tag.

Inside the <FRAMESET> tag, John used the <FRAME> tag to define each frame. Following the <FRAMESET> tag, he added the <NOFRAMES> tag to display content viewable by browsers that do not support frames.

a. Open SimpleText. Use SimpleText or your word processor. If you use a word processor, be sure to save the document as Text Only.

Above: The "Links" graphic inside the alt.coffee table of contents frame.
Below: A click on the Links graphic displays a "Links" content page. Designed for Web newbies, "Links" contains a sampling of interesting places to visit.

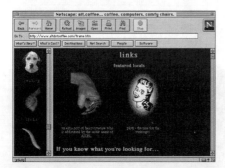

b. Create a new HTML document. Start a new document with the following markup tags:

```
<HTML>

<HEAD>

<TITLE>alt.coffee... coffee. computers. comfy
  chairs.

</TITLE>

</HEAD>
```

c. Add a <FRAMESET> tag. Inside a <FRAMESET> tag, a COLS attribute may be used to create columns, or a ROWS attribute may be used to create rows. Although both can be used in the same <FRAMESET>, it is best to keep the number of frames to a minimum. *(Note: Frame documents with too many frames have a history of making browsers crash.)* In this example, John used the COLS attribute to create a two-frame layout.

Column width may be set with an equal sign followed by an absolute pixel value, percentage values between 1 and 100, or a relative scaling value where an asterisk represents the remaining space.

Examples:

```
<FRAMESET COLS="30%,70%>
<FRAMESET COLS="120,*">
```

In the following source code, John Scott used an absolute pixel value for the first frame followed by an asterisk that causes the second frame to fill the remaining space. *(Note: There is no space after the comma.)*

```
<HTML>

<HEAD>

<TITLE>alt.coffee... coffee. computers. comfy
  chairs.

</TITLE>

</HEAD>

<FRAMESET COLS="120,*">
```

d. Add a <FRAME> tag. A <FRAME> tag defines a single frame. For his two-column frame layout, John needed two <FRAME> tags. Inside a <FRAME> tag, he added:

- NAME attribute, which lets you assign a unique name to a frame. Name a frame and then refer to it by name with the BASE tag and TARGET attribute in content frame documents. This directs content into a frame. *(Note: See* Create the first frame document *for an example of how the BASE tag and TARGET attribute are used.)*

- SRC attribute, which refers to the source HTML document.

- NORESIZE attribute, which prevents visitors from dragging the divider bar to resize a frame.

- MARGINWIDTH and MARGINHEIGHT attributes, which allow you to specify the distance from the edge of a frame to the content inside the frame.

- SCROLL attribute allows you to control whether the scroll bar appears in a frame. Set this to either auto, yes, or no. The default for this attribute is auto. This means the scroll bar appears if the content extends beyond the edge of the frame.

First frame (and other content frames) contains an <A HREF="doc.htm" BASE TARGET ="name"><IMG SRC="image.jpg"> </A> tag

2d.

Second frame

Defining frame document contains a <FRAME NAME="name" SRC="doc.htm"> tag

Above: The Info graphic inside the alt.coffee table of contents frame. *Below:* A click on the Info graphic displays an Information content page. This page is designed to hold detailed information about the cafe.

Notice John's two <FRAME> tags reside within the <FRAMESET> tag:

```
<HTML>

<HEAD>

<TITLE>alt.coffee... coffee. computers. comfy
  chairs.

</TITLE>

</HEAD>

<FRAMESET COLS="120,*">

<FRAME NAME="menu" SRC="menu.htm"
  NORESIZE MARGINWIDTH="0"
  MARGINHEIGHT="0" SCROLL="yes">

<FRAME NAME="main" SRC="home.html-ssi" NORESIZE
  MARGINWIDTH="0"
  MARGINHEIGHT="0" SCROLL="yes">

</FRAMESET>
```

e. Add a <NOFRAMES> tag. For "frames-challenged" browsers, John added a <NO FRAMES> tag. His message inside this tag directs visitors to the Netscape site for a Navigator download.

```
<HTML>

<HEAD>

<TITLE>alt.coffee... coffee. computers. comfy
  chairs.

</TITLE>

</HEAD>

<FRAMESET COLS="120,*">

<FRAME NAME="menu" SRC="menu.htm"
  NORESIZE MARGINWIDTH="0"
  MARGINHEIGHT="0" SCROLL="yes">

<FRAME NAME="main" SRC="home.html"
  NORESIZE MARGINWIDTH="0"
  MARGINHEIGHT="0" SCROLL="yes">

</FRAMESET>

<NOFRAMES>
```

Above: The Flotsam graphic inside the alt.coffee table of contents frame.
Below: A click on the Flotsam graphic displays a list of links to Shockwave and other entertainment pages created by Larry Rosenthal, owner of Cube Productions, Inc.

```
<H1 ALIGN=CENTER<BLINK>Frame
ALERT!</BLINK></H1>

<P>

This document is designed to be viewed using
  <B>Netscape 2.0</B>'s

Frame feature. If you are seeing this message, you
  are using a frame <I>challenged</I> browser.

<P>

Please, try our <A HREF="http://www.altdotcof
  fee.com/
  home.html-ssi">un-framed</A> page or...

<P>

a <B>Frame-capable</B> browser can be downloaded
  from

<A HREF="http://home.netscape.com/">Netscape
  Communications</A>. </P>

</NOFRAMES>
```

f. Add an ending tag. Complete the HTML document by adding an ending tag.

```
</HTML>
```

g. Save the file. Save the document in SimpleText or your word processor. If you're using a word processor, save the text as Text Only. Give the file an .HTM extension.

3. Create the first frame document.

The first frame document or table of contents page may contain either text or graphic links to content on the rest of the site. John used small images as links.

a. Open SimpleText. Use SimpleText or your word processor. If you use a word processor, be sure to save the document as Text Only.

b. Create a new HTML document. Start a new document with the following markup tags:

Above: *Premiere World is the cosponsor of Cyberchill, a monthly Internet social event that meets at alt.coffee. alt.coffee is also a sponsor and the event is free to interested cafe-goers. For details about upcoming Cyberchill meetings, check the Premiere Word link on the alt.coffee home page at http://www.altdotcoffee.com.*

```
<HTML>

<HEAD>

<TITLE>icon menu for alt.coffee</TITLE>

</HEAD>
```

c. Add background color and text color. *(Note: See the Online Tools chapter for details concerning color codes.)*

```
<HTML>

<HEAD>

<TITLE>icon menu for alt.coffee</TITLE>

</HEAD>

<BODY BGCOLOR="#000000" TEXT="00827F"
  VLINK="#00827F" ALINK="#FF006E">
```

d. Add a center tag. To make sure the links in the table of contents column are centered, use a <CENTER> tag.

```
<HTML>

<HEAD>

<TITLE>icon menu for alt.coffee</TITLE>

</HEAD>

<BODY BGCOLOR="#000000" TEXT="00827F"
  VLINK="#00827F" ALINK="#FF006E">

<CENTER>
```

e. Add an anchor tag. In this example, John's first image in the first frame is a link to the alt.coffee home page. Whenever there's any other content displayed in the second frame, a click on this link will display the home page content. To create this link, add:

- an HREF attribute and the name of the external file.

- BASE and TARGET attributes to direct content into a named frame. *(Note: See* Creating a defining frame document *for an example of naming a frame.)*

- an image tag with a SRC attribute referencing an icon, a BORDER=0 attribute to turn off the border around the icon, and an ALT attribute referencing text for browsers that cannot see images.

Above: tHUNK, a digital entertainment site on the Web, is produced by Cube Productions, Inc., a New York-based new media firm. Cube owner Larry Rosenthal is a 3D world builder and new media designer who also chairs the NYVRMLSIG, which meets at alt.coffee. For details about the NYVRMLSIG, check the tHUNK link on the alt.coffee home page.

```
<HTML>
<HEAD><TITLE>icon menu for alt.coffee</TITLE>
</HEAD>
<BODY BGCOLOR="#000000" TEXT="#00827F"
  VLINK="#00827F" ALINK="#FF006E" >
<CENTER><A HREF="home.html" BASE
  TARGET="main"><IMG SRC="home_icon.jpg" BORDER=0
  ALT="HOME"></A></CENTER>
```

f. Add line breaks.

```
<HTML>
<HEAD><TITLE>icon menu for alt.coffee</TITLE>
</HEAD>
<BODY BGCOLOR="#000000" TEXT="#00827F"
  VLINK="#00827F" ALINK="#FF006E" >
<CENTER><A HREF="home.html" BASE
  TARGET="main"><IMG SRC="home_icon.jpg"
  BORDER=0 ALT="HOME"></A></CENTER>
<BR><BR>
```

g. Add centered, decriptive text beneath the icon. *(Note: Add more line breaks beneath the new text.)*

```
<HTML>
<HEAD><TITLE>icon menu for alt.coffee</TITLE>
</HEAD>
<BODY BGCOLOR="#000000" TEXT="#00827F"
  VLINK="#00827F" ALINK="#FF006E" >
<CENTER><A HREF="home.html" BASE
  TARGET="main"><IMG SRC="home_icon.jpg"
  BORDER=0 ALT="HOME"></A></CENTER>
<BR><BR>
<CENTER>h o m e</CENTER><BR><BR><BR>
```

Above: *3D world builder Larry Rosenthal created the 3D scenes for alt.coffee's Palace site at toulouse.flotsam.com. In addition to virtual scenes of the real cafe, a back door leads from the alt.coffee back room to an elaborate underground lounge accessible through a door on a virtual subway platform (look for dragons).*

h. Add more images and text to the first frame. By continuing to add small image links with line breaks to the first frame document, the document will form a vertical table of contents. *(Note: Due to space constraints, only two of the seven alt.coffee icon links are listed. If you are creating your own frame document with the images provided on the CD-ROM in the back of this book, you may follow these sample links to create the remaining links in the table of contents frame. Notice that the HTML in each new link is the same, except for the icon file name and the descriptive text.)*

```
<HTML>

<HEAD><TITLE>icon menu for alt.coffee</TITLE>

</HEAD>

<BODY BGCOLOR="#000000" TEXT="#00827F"
  VLINK="#00827F" ALINK="#FF006E" >

<CENTER><A HREF="home.html" BASE
  TARGET="main"><IMG SRC="home_icon.jpg" BORDER=0
  ALT="HOME"></A></CENTER>

<BR><BR>

<CENTER>h o m e</CENTER><BR><BR><BR>

<CENTER><A HREF="talk.htm" BASE
  TARGET="main"><IMG SRC="talk.jpg"
  BORDER=0 ALT="ALT.COFFEE TALK"></A></CENTER>

<BR><BR>

<CENTER>alt.coffee talk</CENTER><BR><BR><BR>
```

i. Add the ending tag.

```
</HTML>
```

j. Save the file. Save the document in SimpleText or your word processor. If you're using a word processor, save the text as Text Only. Give the file an .HTM extension.

Above: Late in 1996, alt.coffee was the first stop on BlackSun International's virtual scavenger hunt. BlackSun built VRML versions of several Internet cafes across the country and contestants were asked to search for "cyberium crystals" hidden in each of the cafes. The first contestant to find crystals at all the cafes won a trip to Spain.

4. Create documents for the second frame.

A content document is similar to any ordinary HTML document. The document described below is the alt.coffee home page, which links to the icon at the top of the table of contents frame. *(Note: This document is saved as ASCII text on the CD-ROM in the back of this book.)*

a. Open SimpleText. Use SimpleText or your word processor. If you use a word processor, be sure to save the document as Text Only.

b. Create a new HTML document. Start a new document with the following markup tags:

```
<HTML>

<HEAD>

<TITLE>alt.coffee... coffee. computers. comfy
    chairs.

</TITLE>

</HEAD>
```

c. Add a background color and a text color to the document.

```
<HTML>

<HEAD>

<TITLE>alt.coffee... coffee. computers. comfy
    chairs.

</TITLE>

</HEAD>

<BODY BGCOLOR="#000000" TEXT="#FFFFFF">
```

d. Add text and images. In this example, John used the following elements:

- Font tag to change text size using the SIZE attribute, setting the font size relative to the base font size.

  Example:

  ```
  <FONT SIZE=+1>
  ```

  This sets the font one size larger than the base font.

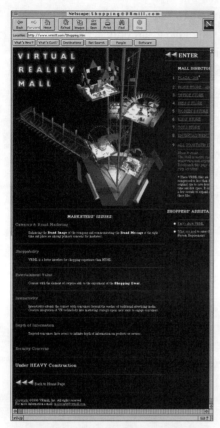

Above: *3D world builder Alex Shamson has been creating VRML models since 1994. His Virtual Reality Mall at http://www.vrmill.com/Shopping.htm resides on the alt.coffee server.*

- Anchor tag with a BASE TARGET="_TOP" attribute to make a linked page open in a new browser window. Alternatively, you can make a browser open a new window if you make the TARGET the name of a frame that doesn't exist.

Examples:

```
<A HREF="http://www.blacksun.com/cyberroute96
.html" BASE TARGET="_TOP">
```

or

```
<A HREF="http://www.blacksun.com/cyberroute96
.html" BASE TARGET="new">
```

A new window will open in front of the current page, which will be left on the screen.

- Paragraph tag with an ALIGN=CENTER attribute making text centered on a page. Options are LEFT, CENTER, and RIGHT.

- MAILTO URL, which is used in an email link and usually placed at the bottom of a page. Viewers who click on a link containing a MAILTO URL will get an empty email form with the address filled out.

```
<HTML>

<HEAD>

<TITLE>alt.coffee... coffee. computers. comfy
  chairs.

</TITLE>

</HEAD>

<BODY BGCOLOR="#000000" TEXT="#FFFFFF">

<P ALIGN=CENTER>

<IMG SRC="words.jpg" BORDER=0>

<P ALIGN=CENTER>

<IMG SRC="dance.gif" BORDER=0>

<P ALIGN=CENTER>

<FONT  SIZE=+1>Are you <I>SHOCKED</I>?
```

Above: *3D world builder Larry Rosenthal is chairman of New York's VRMLSIG, which meets at alt.coffee. His tHUNKWORLD VRML may be accessed through links on the alt.coffee server.*

Play alt.coffee's <A HREF = "http://www.altdot-
coffee.com/shock.htm">animated
homepage</A>...</FONT>

<P ALIGN=CENTER>

<FONT SIZE=+1>There's a lot going on this
month... hit our <A HREF="/CALENDER.HTM">calen-
der of events</A> for a complete listing.

<P ALIGN=CENTER>

<FONT SIZE=+1>Get wired with the regulars at our

<AHREF="http://www.altdotcoffee.com/palace.htm">

Palace</A> site!</FONT>

<P ALIGN=CENTER>

<A HREF="http://www.blacksun.com/cyberroute96

.html" BASE TARGET="_TOP"><IMG SRC="logo.gif"
ALT="cyberroute 96"
BORDER=0></A>

<P ALIGN=CENTER>

<FONT SIZE=+2>Enter this <A
HREF="http://www.blacksun.com/cyberroute96.html"
BASE TARGET="_TOP">virtual scavenger hunt</A>
and <FONT COLOR="#FFFF00">WIN</FONT> a trip
SPAIN!</FONT>

<P ALIGN=CENTER>

<A HREF="/altcoffe.wrl">vrml.coffee</A> |

<A HREF="/palace.htm">Palace</A> |

<A HREF="/links.htm">Links</A> |

<A HREF = "/reality.htm">Reality</A> |

<A HREF = "/info.htm">Info</A>

<P ALIGN=CENTER>

<A HREF = "http://www.flotsam.com" BASE
TARGET="_TOP">Visit flotsam.com</A> |

Above: An anchor tag with a BASE TARGET="_TOP" attribute, created in an HTML document intended to be frame content, makes a linked page open a new window. An example is the link shown above, which opens a page containing information about BlackSun's Scavenger Hunt.

```
<A HREF = "http://www.premiereworld.com"
   BASE TARGET="_TOP">Go to PremiereWorld</A> |

<A HREF="http://www.thunk.com" BASE
   TARGET="_TOP">Tune into tHUNK!WORLD</A>

<P ALIGN=CENTER>

You are victim number 45 today and number 25408
   since Tuesday, October 29, 1996 11:52:23!

<P ALIGN=CENTER>

Any questions? Comments? E-mail me... <A
   HREF="MAILTO:jetsam@flotsam.com">webmaster
   @altdotcoffee.com</A>

<P ALIGN=CENTER>

<FONT SIZE=-2>All Rights Reserved. No commercial
   usage of any part of this Website permitted
   without the written permission of alt.coffee,
   Inc.  &copy;1995</FONT>
```

e. **Add the ending tags.**

```
</BODY>
</HTML>
```

f. **Save the file.** Save the document in SimpleText or your word processor. If you're using a word processor, save the text as Text Only. Give the file an .HTM extension.

g. **Test the frame document.** Open Netscape or Microsoft's Internet Explorer browser. Open your document by selection Open File from the File pull-down menu.

Above: *A link to the Word.com site accessed on the alt.coffee "Links" frame.*

5. Summary of HTML tags used in this section.

The tags you see in this list (in alphabetical order) reflect the HTML 3.2 specification:

<A>...</A>

Referred to as an *anchor*, this tag uses the HREF attribute to link to an external file. For example:

```
<A HREF="http://www.blacksun.com/cyberroute96
.html" BASE TARGET="_TOP"><IMG SRC="logo.gif"
ALT="cyberroute 96" BORDER=0></A>
```

(Note: The HTML file name must include the path name if the file is located in another directory. See Create the first frame document *for details concerning the attributes used in John's anchor tag.)*

<BODY>...</BODY>

A tag used to open and close the body of a document. This tag uses the BGCOLOR attribute to add color to the browser background, using standard color names and hexadecimal RGB triplet information in the form:

```
<BODY BGCOLOR=Blue>
<BODY BGCOLOR="#ffffff">
```


A tag used to break a line. This tag does not require an ending tag.

<FONT SIZE=VALUE>...</FONT>

A tag ued to change the default font size. Values range from 1 to 7. The tag can also be written with a preceding + or - to indicate a size that is relative to the basefont.

<FRAME>...</FRAME>

A tag used to define a single frame. For example:

```
<FRAME NAME="menu" SRC="menu.htm" NORESIZE
MARGINWIDTH="0" MARGINHEIGHT="0" SCROLL="yes">
```

(Note: See Create the defining frame document *for details concerning the attributes John used inside the* <FRAME> *tag.)*

Above: *A link to the Seattle CAM accessed on the alt.coffee Links frame. This view of Seattle is live and is updated every minute.*

<FRAMESET>…</FRAMESET>

A tag used to define a set of frames. For example:

```
<FRAMESET COLS="120,*">
```

(Note: See Create the defining frame document *for details concerning the attributes John used inside the* <FRAMESET> *tag.)*

<H2>…</H2>
<H3>…</H3>

Tags used to enlarge text, as to indicate a heading. Lower numbers indicate larger type, and the options range from <H1> through <H6>.

<HEAD>…</HEAD>

A tag used to open and close the header portion of an HTML document.

<HTML>…</HTML>

A tag used to open and close an HTML document.

<IMG>

Used to refer to an image, this tag uses the SRC="…" attribute, which represents the URL (location) of the image. This tag also uses the BORDER attribute, which can be used to turn off the border around a graphic used in a link. For example:

```
<IMG SRC="home_icon.jpg" BORDER=0>
```

<NOFRAMES>…</NOFRAMES>

A tag used to add text that viewers can see if they are using a browser that can't read frame code.

<P>…<P>

A tag used to indicate a new paragraph. Unlike the <BR> tag, this tag adds line spacing. An ending tag is optional.

<TITLE>…</TITLE>

A tag used to describe the title of a document, which shows up inside a browser's title bar.

Chapter 3

Artist featured in this chapter:

Peju Alawusa is a graphic designer at Simon & Schuster in New York City and has a degree in Advertising and Design from the Fashion Institute of Technology.

peju_alawusa@ prenhall.com

http://members.aol.com/ alawusa/intro.html

NetObjects Fusion

NetObjects Fusion is a new Web page design tool for graphic designers who wish to avoid HTML tags. Page elements may be imported and placed on a page much like they're placed in a page layout software program.

NetObjects Fusion builds HTML tags in the background (tables). The software is particularly useful for creating large sites because it provides centralized control over links as they're updated.

In this chapter, new media artist Peju Alawusa builds her own site and demonstrates NetObjects Fusion features by creating her resume. Additional NetObjects Fusion features may be found in Chapter 12. Artist Frank DeCrescenzo uses NetObjects Fusion to build a site with image maps and a form.

A new Web page layout tool for designers

Summary: *A Web page layout tool is now available for artists who really don't like HTML tags. It's called* NetObjects Fusion, *created by NetObjects, Inc. (http//www.netobjects.com).*

NetObjects, Inc. was founded in November 1995 by Rae Technology and Studio Archetype (formerly Clement Mok Design). NetObjects Fusion is a unique new Web page layout tool that provides the ability to create Web pages without HTML tagging.

1. 30-day software trial.
Download a 30-day trial version of NetObjects Fusion from http://www.netobjects.com. Documentation is available as an optional download. The software is only available for one 30-day trial and cannot be reinstalled.

2. Hardware and software requirements.
NetObjects Fusion is available for Power Macintosh or Windows 95/NT. To run the software on a Macintosh, you must have:

- A Power Macintosh with a CD-ROM drive.

- 10 MB of disk space for a minimum installation, or 60 MB of disk space for a complete installation.

- 16 MB of RAM (24 MB is recommended).

- System 7.1.2 or greater (System 7.5 is recommended).

- Web browser software (an HTML 3.x complient browser).

Peju Alawusa's tips on creating Web pages with NetObjects Fusion

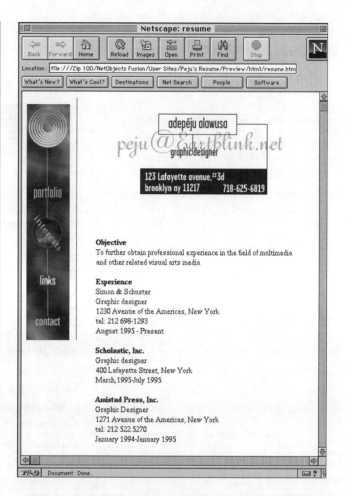

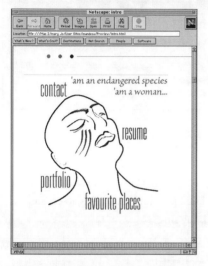

Above: *Peju Alawusa's home page contains an image map she created in NetObjects Fusion. To see her site on the Web, visit*
http://members.aol.com/alawusa/intro .html.

NetObjects Fusion

1a.

Peju's resumé is one of the pages she created for her Web site at *http://members.aol.com/alawusa/intro.html.* In much the same way a designer creates a page in a page layout program, Peju positioned the page elements as draggable elements, and NetObjects created the HTML tags. *(Note: If you wish to follow this example step-by-step, look for Peju's art files on the companion CD-ROM.)*

1. Start NetObjects Fusion.

a. Start NetObjects Fusion.

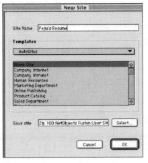

1b.

b. A New site dialog box will appear on your screen. *(Note: If the New Site dialog box did not appear, select New Site from the File pull-down menu.)*

c. Click on the Select button.

d. In the dialog box that follows, select a folder where you would like to save your site, and click on Save. *(Note: If you do not select your own folder, NetObjects Fusion will store the site in a User Sites folder inside the NetObjects Fusion folder.)*

1c.

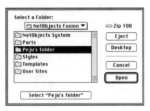

1d.

e. The path name to the folder you selected will be displayed in the Save Site field on the New Site dialog box, as shown in Figure 1e. A set of Autosites and Page Templates accompany the NetObjects Fusion software. A list of AutoSites, Tutorials, and Page Templates are displayed on the New Site dialog box.

f. Type a name for your site in the field labeled *Site Name* at the top of the New Site dialog box, and click on OK. The site name will serve as a file name, which is given a .NOD extension. The site name will also be used as the subfolder name that stores the NOD file and the site's assets.

1e, 1f.

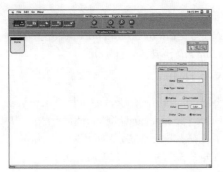

1g.

2a.

2b.

g. A NetObjects Fusion Site screen will be displayed. *(Note: The Site view will be where you create pages and a structure for your site.)*

2. Review the default preferences.

A review of the NetObjects Fusion default preferences will help you understand how the software works.

a. Select Preferences from the Edit pull-down menu.

b. A Preferences dialog box will appear, with the General Preferences tab selected at the top of the dialog box.

c. The default settings on this tab section include:

- **Autosave.** Your site will be saved automatically.

- **Window maximized at Startup.** Your opening screen will be a consistent size when you launch the software.

- **Preview Entire site.** Pressing the Preview button will launch your selected Web browser and display the entire site.

- **WYSIWYG layout in Netscape browser.** This optimizes your site in the Netscape browser.

d. Click on the Layout Preferences tab at the top of the Preferences dialog box.

2e.

e. The Layout Preferences page will be displayed. The default settings on this tab section include:

- **Times.** The default proportional font.

- **Courier.** The default monospace font.

- **Background Image Offset.** Although this is not selected at startup, setting the background image offset in pixels will add a border to the page display. Leave this unchecked.

- **Snap to Grid.** The default setting is off. Click to add a checkmark, and page elements will align with the page grid.

3. Select a browser for Web page previews.

Select your Web browser in the Preferences dialog box. With a browser selected on your hard drive, NetObjects Fusion will be able to preview your page.

a. Click on the General Preferences tab at the top of the Preferences dialog box.

b. Click on the Select Browser button.

c. In the dialog box that follows, locate the folder that contains your browser software, and click on Open.

d. In the dialog box that follows, select your browser software, and click on Open.

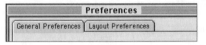

3a.

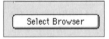

3b.

3c.

3d.

e. The browser will be listed below Current Browser in the Preferences dialog box.

3e.

4. Create Web pages and label them.

a. In NetObjects Fusion's Site view, locate the New Page button at the top of the screen. Notice that the home page icon is highlighted, indicating that it is selected.

Highlighted home page icon   New Page button

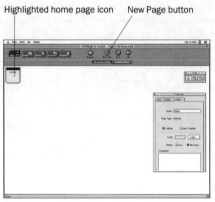

4a.

4b.

b. Click on the New Page button four times.

c. This will create four "child" pages beneath the home page, as shown in Figure 4c. (*Note: A triangle will appear at the bottom of the home page icon, indicating that it is a parent. Triangles on the side of a page icon indicate the page is a sibling. Pages may be repositioned at any time by dragging them.*)

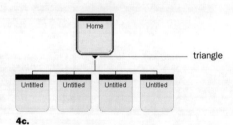

triangle

4c.

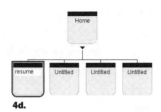

4d.

d. Click on the word *Untitled* in the first child page you created, and type:

`resume`

Press the Tab key to move the highlighted outline to the second child page you created, and type:

`portfolio`

Press the Tab key to move the highlighted outline to the third child page you created, and type:

`interest`

Press the Tab key to move the highlighted outline to the fourth page you created, and type:

`links`

e. Click to select the page labeled *portfolio,* and click on the New Page button twice. Peju labeled the two new child pages *advertising* and *misc*.

f. Click to select the page labeled *interest*, and click on the New Page button three times. Peju labeled the three new child pages *muzik, poetry,* and *literature*.

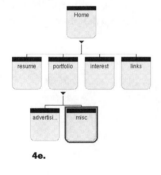

4e.

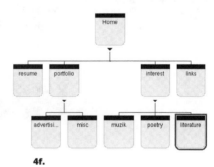

4f.

g. Peju changed the label on the home page to Intro. *(Note: When you're building a large site, the display of page icons may be collapsed by clicking on the small triangles beneath the parent page icons.)*

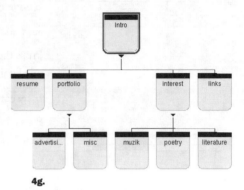

4g.

5. Change views, and add art to a page.

The NetObjects Fusion Page view is the layout area where Web pages are created.

a. In the Site view, double-click on the page labeled *resume*.

b. NetObjects Fusion's Page view will be displayed. Notice that the screen contains a default page banner labeled *resume*.

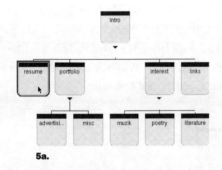

5a.

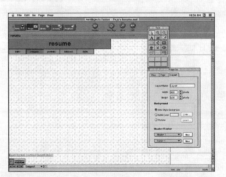

5b.

5c.

c. Select the Selection Tool.

d. Click to select the page banner, and press the Delete key to delete it.

e. Click to select the set of default navigation bars, and press the Delete key to delete the row.

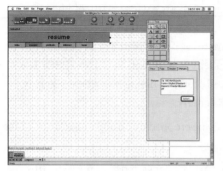
5d.

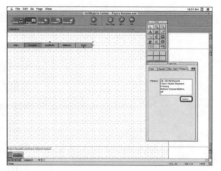
5e.

f. Drag the page divider that separates the header from the body, and move it up to make more room.

g. Select the Picture Tool.

h. Draw a picture box at the top of the page, as shown in Figure 5h.

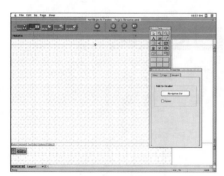
5f.

5g.

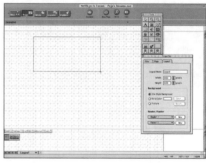
5h.

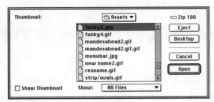

5i, 5j.

i. When you release the mouse button, an Open File dialog box will appear.

j. Use the File List window in the Open File dialog box to locate your art or Peju's image called *resname.gif*. Click on Open. Interesting features related to how NetObjects Fusion handles images include:

- The software supports a wide variety of image formats, including BMP, PICT, PCX, Photoshop, TGA, and Uncompressed TIFF. NetObjects Fusion will convert these alternative formats to GIF or JPEG. The software will present a dialog box where you may select JPEG or GIF.

- Pictures may be cropped by changing the shape of the bounding box.

- GIF images may be converted to tranparent GIFs inside the NetObjects Fusion software. The software's Transparency Tool may be used to select the color to make transparent.

k. The art will fill the picture box you've drawn, as shown in Figure 5k.

l. Repeat Steps 5g through 5k to import Peju's other image, called *funky3.jpg*, as shown in Figure 5l.

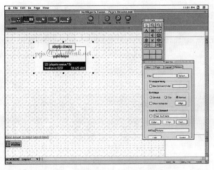

5k.

5l.

6. Use the Draw Tool to create a rule.

6a.

a. Select the Draw Tool.

b. Draw a vertical rule along the length of Peju's second image, as shown in Figure 6b.

c. (Option) Use the Properties dialog box to alter the color or weight of the rule.

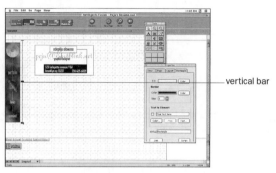

vertical bar

6b.

7. Add text to a page.

7a.

a. Select the Text Tool.

b. Draw a text box, as shown in Figure 7b.

c. When you release the mouse button, you will see a blinking cursor in the upper-left corner of the text box. Type:

```
Objective
```

7b.

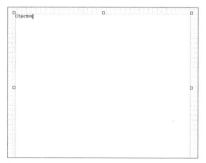

7c.

d. Drag-select the word *Objective*.

e. Click on the bold button in the Properties dialog box.

7e.

7d.

7f.

7g. through 7n.

f. Press Return, and type:

To further obtain professional experience in the field of multimedia and other related visual arts media.

g. Press Return, and type:

Experience

Notice a Return adds a line break and line spacing.

h. Drag-select this word, and add boldfacing.

i. Hold down the Shift key, press Return, and type:

Simon & Schuster

Notice that a Shift + Return adds a line break without line spacing.

j. Hold down the Shift key, press Return, and type:

Graphic designer

k. Hold down the Shift key, press Return, and type:

1230 Avenue of the Americas, New York

l. Hold down the Shift key, press Return, and type:

tel: 212-698-1293

m. Hold down the Shift key, press Return, and type:

August 1995-Present

n. Peju added the remaining text.

8a.

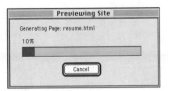

8b.

8. Preview the Web page.

a. Click on the Preview button.

b. A preview status bar will be displayed.

c. NetObjects Fusion will launch your selected browser and display your page. *(Note: For details on how to select a browser in the NetObjects Fusion Preferences, see Steps 3a through 3e.)*

d. Select Quit from the Netscape File pull-down menu to put the browser away. *(Note: Leave the browser open if you have plenty of RAM memory.)*

8c.

8d.

9. Edit the text.

Remove the line spacing beneath the word *Objective*.

a. Click before the letter *T* in the line of text below the word *Objective*. This will insert your cursor in the text.

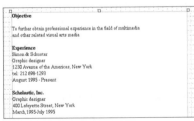

9a.

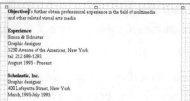
9b.

b. Press the Delete key to close up the space.

c. Hold down the Shift key, and press Return.

d. A line break will be added with no extra line spacing.

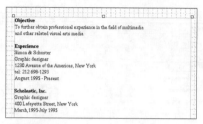
9c, 9d.

e. Repeat Steps 8a through 8d to re-preview the page.

9e.

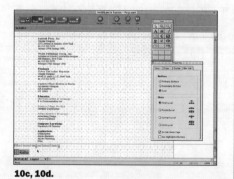
10c, 10d.

10b.

10. Remove the default links in the footer.

a. Scroll to the bottom of the page.

b. Select the Selection Tool.

c. Click on the default text links in the Footer, as shown in Figure 10c.

d. Press the Delete key to delete the text links.

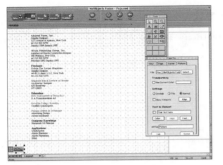

10e, 10f.

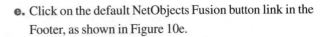

e. Click on the default NetObjects Fusion button link in the Footer, as shown in Figure 10e.

f. Press the Delete key to delete the button link.

11. Lengthen the page.

a. Click on the Layout tab at the top of the Properties dialog box.

b. The Layout page of the Properties dialog box will be displayed.

c. Click on the up arrow next to the field labeled *Height*. Add 100 pixels to the height of the page by clicking on the up arrow.

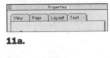

11a.

11b.

12. Add a text link to the body.

a. Select the Text Tool.

b. Drag a text box inside the body of the page, as shown in Figure 12b.

c. When you let go of the mouse, you'll see a cursor inside the text box.

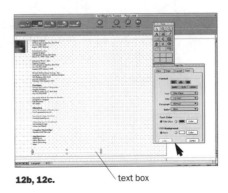

12a.

12b, 12c. text box

12d.

d. (Option) Select the Zoom Tool.

e. (Option) Click on the new text box with the Zoom Tool to zoom in.

f. Type:

    Top Page

12f.

12g.

g. Click on the Text tab at the top of the Properties dialog box.

h. The Text page of the Properties dialog box will be displayed.

i. Click on the Center button in the Properties dialog box.

12i.

12h.

j. The text will be centered in the text box.

12j.

13. Create a link.

Text and pictures can be linked to any other point on the Web or any point within your site. Link segments of text, elements you draw, pictures, or areas inside pictures in the form of an image map. NetObjects Fusion has three types of links.

These include:

- **Page Links.** This type of link leads to pages within your site. If you move the page within the site or change the name of the page, the link follows. Peju created this type of link at the bottom of her resume to link to the top of the page.

- **Smart Links.** This type of link is based on the relative position of a page, not a name. Use this type of link when there are many layers or branches in your site. Entire branches may be moved and the links will be maintained.

- **External Links.** This type of link points to other pages on the Web. A URL is required in this type of link.

a. Drag-select the words *Top Page*.

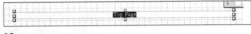

13a.

13b.

b. Click on the Link button in the lower-left corner of the Properties dialog box.

c. A Link dialog box will be displayed.

d. Click in the field labeled *Page Name,* and type:

resume

13c, 13d.

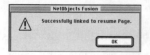

13e.

e. A status dialog box will be displayed, notifying you of a successful link.

f. The words *Top Page* will have an underline, indicating the text is now a link.

13f.

14. Peju's Web site.

Peju used the techniques described in this section to complete the remaining pages on her site. Using NetObjects Fusion's built-in commands for building the site's structure and links, Peju found that her site was easy to construct.

When the pages were complete, Peju staged the site, or tested the pages, on her local hard drive. When she was satisfied with the results, she published the site by using NetObjects Fusion's built-in FTP software to transfer the files to her provider's server. The steps to stage and publish a site are described in the next sections. Look for Peju's complete Web site on the companion CD-ROM and at *http://members.aol .com/alawusa/intro.html.*

15. Stage your site.

When you have completed your Web site, you're ready to publish it or create the HTML pages you'll need for the Web. Staging is considered to be a step prior to final publishing. Preview displays a page in HTML format. Although staging or publishing is similar to previewing a page, an FTP client built into NetObjects Fusion may be used to upload your files to any remote server.

During staging, NetObjects Fusion collects all the files associated with your site—both external and those generated by NetObjects Fusion. NetObjects Fusion refers to these files as assets, which may include the following elements:

- images

- sounds

- video

- applets

- plug-ins

a. Before you stage your site, build a folder for the site somewhere on your hard drive or locate the host name, the directory name, your user name, and the password for the remote server where you'd like to stage your site.

15b.

b. Click on the Publish button.

c. The Publish site will be displayed.

d. Click on Settings.

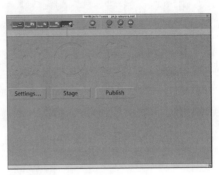

15c, 15d.

e. A Configure Publish dialog box will be displayed. The Local radio dial is the default selection in the Location section of the dialog box. In this sample, Peju used the local hard drive to stage a Web site.

f. Click on the Select button in the Location section of the dialog box.

15e.

15f.

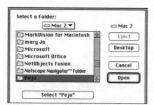

15g.

15h.

g. In the dialog box that follows, select the folder on your hard drive where you would like to stage your site, and click on Open.

h. Click on the OK button at the base of the Configure Publish dialog box.

i. Click on Stage button on the Publish site.

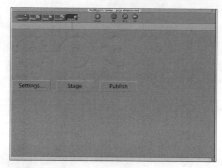

15i.

j. A status bar will be displayed.

k. When the staging is complete, a Staging Is Complete dialog box will be displayed. Click on OK.

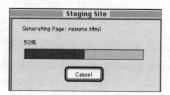

15j.

15k.

16. Test your site with your browser.

a. Launch Netscape or the Internet Explorer browser.

Netscape Navigator™

16a.

16b.

16c.

b. Select Open File from the File pull-down menu.

c. In the dialog box that follows, locate the folder where your files have been staged, and click on Open.

d. In the dialog box that follows, select your site's home page, and click on Open.

16d.

e. Your home page will be displayed in a browser window.

f. Test your site.

g. Select Quit from the File pull-down menu to put away the browser.

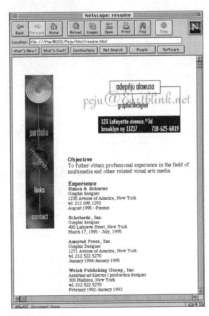

16e.

16g.

17. Publish your site.

When you are satisfied that everything in your site functions properly, you're ready to publish it.

17b.

a. Before you publish your site, locate the host name, the directory name, your user name, and the password for the remote server where you'd like to publish your site.

b. Click on the Publish button.

c. The Publish site will be displayed.

d. Click on Settings.

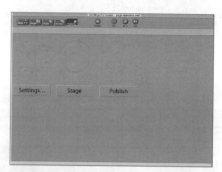

17c, 17d.

e. A Configure Publish dialog box will be displayed.

f. Click on the Remote radio button, and click on the Configure button.

17e, 17f.

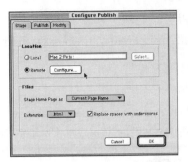

17g.

g. A Remote dialog box will be displayed. *(Note: If you do not know the following information to add to the Remote dialog box, contact the Internet service provider who manages your Web server.)*

h. In the field labeled *Remote Host*, type the name of your server.

i. In the field labeled *Base Directory*, type the path name of the remote HTML folder where you wish to transfer your files.

j. In the field labeled *CGI Directory*, type the path name of the CGI directory.

k. In the field labeled *User Name*, type your user identification.

l. Click on Remember Password.

m. In the field labeled *Password*, type your password, and click on OK.

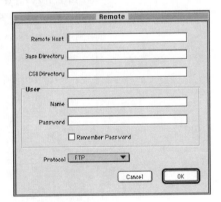

17h through 17m.

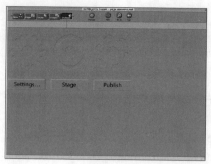

17n.

n. Click on the Publish button in the Site view.

o. A status bar will be displayed with a message that reads:

opening an ftp connection

transferring files

p. When the publishing is complete, a Publishing Is Complete dialog box will be displayed. Click on OK.

17p.

(Note: You may also move your newly published pages to your Web site with Jim Mathew's Fetch. Fetch is a Macintosh FTP shareware utility. Publish to your hard drive and then move the contents of the Preview folder to your directory on your provider's Web server. For further details on how to use Fetch, see Use Fetch to upload your files to a provider's server *in the* Client-Side Image Map *chapter).*

Writer and media specialist featured in this chapter:

Peter Barry Chowka is a journalist, medical-political analyst, lecturer, and consultant. For over two decades, his work in print, broadcasting, still photography, nonfiction films, and now the Internet has documented the promise of nontoxic, innovative, and tradition-al approaches to healing. Chowka has been a con-sultant to network televi-sion and the U.S. Congress and was appointed to the first advisory panels of the NIH Office of Alternative Medicine.

pbc@usa.net

http://members.aol.com/ mediumcool

Chapter 4

Style Sheets And New HTML Text Tags

In this chapter, writer Peter Barry Chowka shares information on how to use style sheets to simplify HTML tagging in text-heavy documents. Peter's 1994 interview with Linus Pauling is format-ted for viewing in Microsoft's Internet Explorer browser, the first browser to include cascading style sheets (CSS1) as defined by the World Wide Web Consortium. The Internet Explorer browser broke ground with this powerful new feature, which is expected to be added to Netscape's Navigator in version 4.0. *(Note: The World Wide Web Consortium, or W3C, is a standards organiza-tion that oversees the evolution of HTML.)*

Also covered in this chapter are Netscape's new <MULTICOL> tag, which formats text in newspaper-like columns, and the <FONT> tag's new attributes, which can control a font's color and typeface.

In less than a year, Microsoft plans to introduce a new form of embedded font technology they've codeveloped with Adobe Systems. Pages with embedded fonts will include font data that travels with a page—freeing a Web viewer from the need to pre-install fonts. The technology will be implemented in the Internet Explorer browser, and the two firms will present an *OpenType* proposal to the World Wide Web Consortium.

Microsoft style sheets offer formatting features such as point size, page margins, and leading

Summary: By the Spring of 1997, both Microsoft's Internet Explorer browser and Netscape's Navigator version 4.0 will provide extensive style sheets. With desktop publishing—like controls, Web authors will no longer need workarounds like the <BLOCKQUOTE> tag for margin indents.

Above right: *Peter Barry Chowka's interview with Linus Pauling formatted with style sheets built into Microsoft's Internet Explorer browser.* **Above:** *Peter's file opened up in Netscape Navigator version 3.0. Netscape will not have style sheets added until version 4.0.*

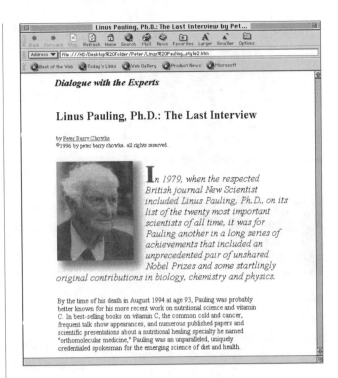

For type to look good on a page, text line length should not extend across the entire width of a document. With a shorter line length, the reader does not have to work to visually keep track of type as he/she reads from left to right.

Until now, designers who wanted to apply this principle to a Web page had to use tags that were never intended to indent text. Examples include the <BLOCKQUOTE> and <DL> tags.

Style sheets built into Microsoft's Internet Explorer browser now offer a designer powerful controls over formatting characteristics such as margins, point size, and leading. Netscape's Navigator will soon have similar controls built into version 4.0 of the software.

In this section, Peter Barry Chowka—journalist, medical-political analyst, and consultant—demonstrates how to format a page with style sheets built for Microsoft's Internet Explorer browser. The steps he uses to format his interview with the late Dr. Linus Pauling offer an ideal model for

Above: *Peter's photograph of Linus Pauling during his first interview with the Nobel laureate, who was then 79, in his office at the Linus Pauling Institute for Science and Medicine in Menlo Park, California, in 1980. Peter recalls, "It's always humbling to spend time with an individual of Pauling's stature. But I came away from that first of many encounters with Pauling enjoying a new respect for the man, based not only on his intellect but his highly engaging, accessible, down-to-earth, feisty, enthusiastic, and energetic reaction to meeting me and to my many questions. The bright twinkle in his eye on that summer day is, I hope, captured in the photo above."*

designers to follow. *(Note: Look for the Linus Pauling interview on the CD-ROM in the back of this book and at http://members.aol.com/mediumcool.)*

1. What is a style sheet?

A *style sheet* is a system that lets you define formatting characteristics such as font size, font style, font color, font weight, leading, margins, and indents in summary form at the top of an HTML document or in a separate style sheet file. This eliminates the need for complex tagging throughout a document and provides an efficient method to make changes, because the formatting information is organized in one place.

Although Microsoft is the first to build style sheets into its browser, the concept is not unique to Microsoft. Style sheets for Web browsers have been defined by the World Wide Web Consortium (W3C), and Microsoft's implementation follows the cascading style sheet (CSS1) mechanism found in the W3C proposal. *(Note: For details about the W3C style sheet proposal, see http://www.w3.org/pub/WWW/TR/WD-css1.html.)*

2. Frequently asked questions.

Although style sheets offer a greater amount of control over page layout, many designers may be concerned about using HTML features that are new. Here are answers to popular questions:

a. Are style sheets appropriate for every HTML document? As in print, style sheets make sense when documents have a large amount of text. The mechanism requires fewer tags in the text and greater control over changes. However, designers may also be interested in style sheets for smaller documents because of the point size and leading controls.

b. If I use style sheets designed for the Internet Explorer browser, what will the page look like in Netscape's Navigator? Handan Selamohlu, who wrote *A User's Guide to Style Sheets* for Microsoft's Developer Network (http://www.microsoft.com/workshop/author/

Above: A photo Peter took during a videotaped documentary interview he produced in 1989 with Pauling and Ewan Cameron (right), the Scottish physician whose promising work in the early 1970s with vitamin C and terminal cancer patients inspired Pauling to become more involved in the field of vitamin C, antioxidant nutrients, and nontoxic cancer therapies. Peter remembers Dr. Cameron, who before his death was medical director of the Linus Pauling Institute, as an intellectually impressive and highly engaging clinician. In 1979, the two doctors co-authored the popular book, Vitamin C and Cancer.

howto/css-f.htm) has invented a trick for designers who are creating pages for multiple browsers. Until Netscape implements style sheets, embed your style definitions within a comment tag. *(Note: For details on how to implement this step, see* Creating the Linus Pauling interview *in this chapter.)*

c. Will style sheets support the Postscript screen fonts popular among graphic designers? For information concerning the Adobe/Microsoft *OpenType initiative* incorporating Type 1 and TrueType data for Web pages, see *Microsoft's plan to add fonts to the Web: Free TrueType now and Web page font embedding in the future* at the end of this chapter.

d. If a Web viewer does not download and install a font specified by a style sheet, what will the browser display? A browser that cannot read style sheets or the <FONT FACE> tag will display the default typeface.

e. Are there any tags that will override formatting created by a style sheet? Yes. Inline style tags override style sheet summaries arranged at the top of a document or in a separate style sheet file.

The style sheet summary block arranged at the top of a document is referred to as an *embedded style sheet* and a style sheet organized in a separate file is called a *linked style sheet.* In total, there are three forms of style sheets that follow precedence rules:

- inline style tags override embedded style definitions. *(Note: For an example of how an inline style tag can be used to override an embedded style tag, see* Creating the Linus Pauling interview *in this chapter.)*

- inline style tags override linked style definitions.

- embedded style definitions override linked style definitions.

f. Where can I learn more about Microsoft style sheets? See Microsoft's *Style Sheet Showcase* at http://www.microsoft.com/gallery/files/styles/default .htm, *Style Sheets: A Brief Overview for Designers*

Above: *In 1983, Pauling invited Peter to his remote ranch overlooking the Pacific Ocean near Big Sur, California, for a day-long visit and another extensive recorded interview. Peter writes, "I was honored to be able to observe Pauling in his favorite place, inspired by the majesty of the Pacific, surrounded by books and scientific papers representing the many high-level projects he was involved in. Pauling graciously accommodated my many requests to photograph him, and one of my favorites (above) was taken that afternoon on his deck with the stormy ocean just yards away."*

at http://www.microsoft.com/workshop/design/des-gen/ss/css-des.htm, and *A User's Guide to Style Sheets* at http://www.microsoft.com/workshop/ author /howto/css-f.htm.

g. Can style sheets be transferred to another HTML document? A style sheet may be saved as a .CSS document and then linked to any number of Web pages on your Web site. *(Note: Microsoft's implementation of style sheets is new, and at the time of this writing, I could not get style sheet linking to work. As a result, this topic will not be included in this chapter.)*

3. Style sheet properties.

The style sheets built into Microsoft's Internet Explorer browser offer a wonderful shift away from awkward workarounds such as the <BLOCKQUOTE> tag for margins. In this system, style sheet properties such as margin-left and margin-right get added to familiar HTML tags. *(Note: For details on style sheet tag syntax, see* Adding style sheet properties to a tag *in the next section.)* The style sheet properties that have been implemented in version 3.0 of the Microsoft Internet Explorer browser include:

a. font-size may be set in points, inches, centimeters, pixels, or a percentage value that is evaluated based on the default point size (pt, in, cm, px, or %).

b. font-family sets a typeface name. Alternative family names or generic family names may be specified for systems that don't support a designer's choice of typeface names. Generic family names include serif, sans serif, cursive, fantasy, and monospaced.

c. font-weight sets the thickness of type. Examples include extra light, light, demi-light, medium, demi-bold, bold, and extra bold. Weights depend on the weights allowed in a user's system.

d. font-style sets italic text. Although the W3C draft also includes small caps, Internet Explorer only supports normal and italic.

e. line-height sets leading or the distance between the baselines of type. Leading may be specified in points,

Above: Included in Microsoft's Web Gallery at http://www.microsoft.com/ gallery are links to pages containing useful information about style sheets.

inches, centimeters, pixels, or a percentage value (pt, in, cm, px, or %). Internet Explorer adds spacing before lines and not after lines.

f. color may be specified as a named color or as a hexadecimal red-green-blue triplet.

g. text-decoration allows you to use underlined and strike-through text. W3C also supports overline and blink, which have not been added to the Internet Explorer browser.

h. margins may be specified in points, inches, centimeters, or pixels (pts, in, cm, or px). Internet Explorer 3.0 allows negative values for margin-left, margin-right, and margin-top for special effects or "outdents."

i. text-align sets text as left, right, or center-aligned.

j. text-indent sets, indentation in points, inches, centimeters, or pixels (pts, in, cm, or px). Internet Explorer 3.0 allows negative values for text-indent, providing for special effects or "outdents."

k. background (color or images) may be used on any elements by specifying a color name, an RGB triplet, or an image's URL.

4. Adding style sheet properties to a tag.

There are two methods for placing style information within a document.

a. Inline style tags are adaptations of familiar HTML tags. Style definitions get added to an HTML tag by using the STYLE attribute.

Examples:

```
<H1 STYLE="margin-left: 0.5 in; margin-right:
0.5 in">
```

or

```
<P STYLE="margin-left: 0.5 in; margin-right:
0.5 in">
```

Above: Microsoft is offering free TrueType fonts on their site at http://www.microsoft.com/truetype/ fontpack/default.htm for both Macintosh and Windows computers. (Note: For details concerning Microsoft's free TrueType offer, see Microsoft's plan to add fonts to the Web: Free TrueType now and Web page font embedding in the future *in this chapter.)*

b. An embedded style sheet gets added to the top of a document using the <STYLE>...</STYLE> tag. Use this tag between the <HTML> tag and the <BODY> tag. The <STYLE> tag's TYPE attribute specifies the Internet Media type as "text/css." This allows browsers that do not support this Media type to ignore style sheets. Use the comment tag to enclose the style definitions that get added inside the <STYLE>...</STYLE> tag as plain text. By enclosing the style definitions in a comment tag, browsers that do not support style sheets will not read style definitions as plain text.

Example:

```
<STYLE TYPE="text/css">

<!--

H1 {color: #FF5200; font-size: 40 pt; font-family:
Verdana, Arial, Helvetica, sans-serif}

P {color: #D1D1D1; font-size: 13 px; font-family:
Verdana, Arial, Helvetica, sans-serif}

-->

</STYLE>
```

5. Option: Grouped formatting.

a. If the formatting specifications are the same for several tags, group the tags into one tag. In the following example, H1, H2, and H3 all have the same style definitions:

Example:

```
<STYLE TYPE="text/css">

<!--

H1, H2, H3 {color: #FF5200; font-size: 40 pt;
font-family: Verdana, Arial, Helvetica, sans-serif}

-->

</STYLE>
```

Above: *Check http://www.microsoft .com/truetype/iexplor/quick.htm for a useful three-step guide to adding typography to your Web pages.*

b. Formatting specifications may also be abbreviated. Notice in the following example that the word *font* occurs only once.

Example:

```
<STYLE TYPE="text/css">

<!--

H1 {font: 40 pt Verdana, Arial, Helvetica,
sans-serif}

-->

</STYLE>
```

6. Option: Classes.

a. Use classes to create variations for a single HTML tag. Follow a tag name with a period and a class name. Any number of classes are allowed. *(Note: See* Creating the Linus Pauling interview *for details on how to create tags with classes.)*

Example:

```
<STYLE TYPE="text/css">

<!--

BODY {margin-left: 0.5in; margin-top: 0.5in}

BODY.main {font-size: 12pt; font-weight: light;
line-height: 14pt; margin-left: 1in; margin-right:
1in; margin-top: 1in}

BODY.callout {font-size: 18pt; font-weight: light;
line-height: 22pt; margin-left: 2in; margin-right:
2in}

BODY.references {font-size: 10pt; font-weight:
light; line-height: 12pt; margin-left: 1in; margin-
right: 1in}

-->

</STYLE>
```

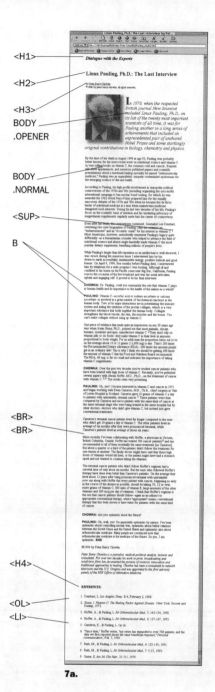

<H1>
<H2>
<H3>
BODY
.OPENER

BODY
.NORMAL

<SUP>

B

<H4>

<OL>
<LI>

7a.

b. It is not necessary to repeat the tag name. Classes may be abbreviated with a period and a class name.

Example:

```
<STYLE TYPE="text/css">

<!--

BODY {margin-left: 0.5in; margin-top: 0.5in}

.main {font-size: 12pt; font-weight: light; line-height: 14pt; margin-left: 1in; margin-right: 1in; margin-top: 1in}

.callout {font-size: 18pt; font-weight: light; line-height: 22pt; margin-left: 2in; margin-right: 2in}

.references {font-size: 10pt; font-weight: light; line-height: 12pt; margin-left: 1in; margin-right: 1in}

-->

</STYLE>
```

7. Creating the Linus Pauling interview.

a. Use a manuscript or create thumbnails to mark up text with tags you think you'll need. In this example, Peter used:

- H1, H2, H3, and H4 to mark the subheads in his manuscript. This provides an opportunity for quick changes in the style sheet header after the style block is in place at the top of the HTML document.

- Two <BR> tags between paragraphs because the <P> tag adds too much leading. *(Note: There should be no more than what appears to be a single line space between paragraphs.)*

- To create variations in body text, Peter used classes in the <BODY> tag using the words *.normal* and *.opener*. He then used the <DIV> tag to divide the document according to class.

Above: Check http://www.microsoft .com/truetype/faq/faq8.htm for a list of frequently asked questions (FAQ) concerning Microsoft's free TrueType fonts.

Example:

```
<DIV class=normal>
```

and

```
<DIV class=opener>
```

Peter could then control the properties of normal and opener text in the style block at the top of the page to make changes in type style and weight.

b. Open SimpleText. Use SimpleText or your word processor. If you use a word processor, be sure to save the document as Text Only.

c. Create a new HTML document. Start a new document with the following markup tags:

```
<HTML>

<HEAD>

<TITLE>Linus Pauling, Ph.D.: The Last Interview by

Peter Barry Chowka

</TITLE>

</HEAD>
```

d. Create a style block at the top of the document. Use the <STYLE>…</STYLE> tag between the <HTML> tag and the <BODY> tag. Use the <STYLE> tag's TYPE attribute to specify the Internet Media type as "text/css".

```
<HTML>

<HEAD>

<TITLE>Linus Pauling, Ph.D.: The Last Interview by

Peter Barry Chowka

</TITLE>

</HEAD>

<STYLE TYPE="text/css">
```

e. Add a comment tag. Until Netscape implements style sheets, embed your style definitions in a comment tag. *(Note: See* Style sheet properties *and* Adding style sheet properties to a tag *for details on style definitions.)*

```
<HTML>

<HEAD>
```

Tip: *In May 1996, Microsoft announced news of their* OpenType Initiative. *Also known as* TrueType Open Version 2, *OpenType is an extension of Microsoft's TrueType Open format, adding support for Adobe Type 1 data. This font technology represents a merger of Adobe's and Microsoft's font technologies, offering a unified system for font handling across platforms.*

```
<TITLE>Linus Pauling, Ph.D.: The Last Interview by
Peter Barry Chowka
</TITLE>
</HEAD>
<STYLE TYPE="text/css">
<!--
```

f. Add tags and style properties to the style block.

```
<HTML>
<HEAD>
<TITLE>Linus Pauling, Ph.D.: The Last Interview by
Peter Barry Chowka
</TITLE>
</HEAD>
<STYLE TYPE="text/css">
<!--
BODY {margin-left: 1in; margin-right: 1.5in}

.opener {font-size: 20 pt; font-weight: extra light;
font-style: italic; line-height: 22pt; font-family:
Times New Roman; margin-left: 1in; margin-right:
.8in}

.normal {font-weight: extra light; font-style:
normal; font-size: 14 pt; line-height: 16pt; font-
family: Times New Roman}

.references {font-weight: extra light; font-style:
normal; font-size: 14 pt; line-height: 15pt;
font-family: Times New Roman; margin-left: 1.2in;
margin-right: .8in}

B {font-weight: extra bold; font-style: normal;
font-size: 14 pt; line-height: 16pt; font-family:
Arial}

H1 {font-weight: extra light; font-style: italic;
font-size: 20 pt; line-height: 22pt; font-family:
Times New Roman}

H2 {font-weight: extra bold; font-style: normal;
font-size: 24 pt; line-height: 26pt; font-family:
Times New Roman}
```

Tip: Adobe and Microsoft will submit a proposal for Web page font embedding using OpenType to the World Wide Web Consortium committee on style sheets. The proposal suggests that font data should travel with a document, freeing the user from the need to download and install fonts.

```
H3 {font-weight: extra bold; font-style: normal;
font-size: 12 pt; line-height: 14pt; font-family:
Times New Roman}
```

```
H4 {font-weight: extra bold; font-style: normal;
font-size: 12 pt; line-height: 14pt; font-family:
Times New Roman}
```

g. **Close the comment tag.**

```
<HTML>

<HEAD>

<TITLE>Linus Pauling, Ph.D.: The Last Interview by
Peter Barry Chowka

</TITLE>

</HEAD>

<STYLE TYPE="text/css">

<!--

BODY {margin-left: 1in; margin-right: 1.5in}

.opener {font-size: 20 pt; font-weight: extra light;
font-style: italic;  line-height: 22pt; font-family:
Times New Roman; margin-left: 1in; margin-right:
.8in}

.normal {font-weight: extra light; font-style:
normal; font-size: 14 pt; line-height: 16pt;
font-family: Times New Roman}

.references {font-weight: extra light; font-style:
normal; font-size: 14 pt; line-height: 15pt;
font-family: Times New Roman; margin-left: 1.2in;
margin-right: .8in}

B {font-weight: extra bold; font-style: normal;
font-size: 14 pt; line-height: 16pt; font-family:
Arial}

H1 {font-weight: extra light; font-style: italic;
font-size: 20 pt; line-height: 22pt; font-family:
Times New Roman}

H2 {font-weight: extra bold; font-style: normal;
font-size: 24 pt; line-height: 26pt; font-family:
Times New Roman}
```

Tip: The TrueType fonts Microsoft distributes on their site may be used in applications other than HTML author-ing programs. (Note: The fonts have been optimized for on-screen display.)

```
H3 {font-weight: extra bold; font-style: normal;
font-size: 12 pt; line-height: 14pt; font-family:
Times New Roman}

H4 {font-weight: extra bold; font-style: normal;
font-size: 12 pt; line-height: 14pt; font-family:
Times New Roman}

-->
```

h. **Close the style block.**

```
<HTML>

<HEAD>

<TITLE>Linus Pauling, Ph.D.: The Last Interview by
Peter Barry Chowka

</TITLE>

</HEAD>

<STYLE TYPE="text/css">

<!--
BODY {margin-left: 1in; margin-right: 1.5in}

.opener {font-size: 20 pt; font-weight: extra light;
font-style: italic; line-height: 22pt; font-family:
Times New Roman; margin-left: 1in; margin-right:
.8in}

.normal {font-weight: extra light; font-style:
normal; font-size: 14 pt; line-height: 16pt; font-
family: Times New Roman}

.references {font-weight: extra light; font-style:
normal; font-size: 14 pt; line-height: 15pt;
font-family: Times New Roman; margin-left: 1.2in;
margin-right: .8in}

B {font-weight: extra bold; font-style: normal;
font-size: 14 pt; line-height: 16pt; font-family:
Arial}

H1 {font-weight: extra light; font-style: italic;
font-size: 20 pt; line-height: 22pt; font-family:
Times New Roman}
```

Tip: The TrueType fonts available on Microsoft's site have enlarged character sets due to multi-language support. The character sets contain 652 characters covering Western, Central, and Eastern European writing systems.

```
H2 {font-weight: extra bold; font-style: normal;
font-size: 24 pt; line-height: 26pt; font-family:
Times New Roman}

H3 {font-weight: extra bold; font-style: normal;
font-size: 12 pt; line-height: 14pt; font-family:
Times New Roman}

H4 {font-weight: extra bold; font-style: normal;
font-size: 12 pt; line-height: 14pt; font-family:
Times New Roman}

-->

</STYLE>
```

i. Add a background color to the document.

```
<HTML>

<HEAD>

<TITLE>Linus Pauling, Ph.D.: The Last Interview by
Peter Barry Chowka
</TITLE>

</HEAD>

<STYLE TYPE="text/css">

<!--

BODY {margin-left: 1in; margin-right: 1.5in}

.opener {font-size: 20 pt; font-weight: extra light;
font-style: italic;  line-height: 22pt; font-family:
Times New Roman; margin-left: 1in; margin-right:
.8in}

.normal {font-weight: extra light; font-style:
normal; font-size: 14 pt; line-height: 16pt;
font-family: Times New Roman}

.references {font-weight: extra light; font-style:
normal; font-size: 14 pt; line-height: 15pt;
font-family: Times New Roman; margin-left: 1.2in;
margin-right: .8in}

B {font-weight: extra bold; font-style: normal;
font-size: 14 pt; line-height: 16pt; font-family:
Arial}
```

```
H1 {font-weight: extra light; font-style: italic;
font-size: 20 pt; line-height: 22pt; font-family:
Times New Roman}

H2 {font-weight: extra bold; font-style: normal;
font-size: 24 pt; line-height: 26pt; font-family:
Times New Roman}

H3 {font-weight: extra bold; font-style: normal;
font-size: 12 pt; line-height: 14pt; font-family:
Times New Roman}

H4 {font-weight: extra bold; font-style: normal;
font-size: 12 pt; line-height: 14pt; font-family:
Times New Roman}

-->

</SYYLE>

<BODY BGCOLOR="#ffffff">
```

j. **Add text, an image, and HTML tags.** *(Note: The text shown in this section is for demonstration purposes only. Readers may find Peter Chowka's full interview in an HTML file on the CD-ROM at the back of this book.)*

```
<HTML>

<HEAD>

<TITLE>Linus Pauling, Ph.D.: The Last Interview by
Peter Barry Chowka

</TITLE>

</HEAD>

<STYLE TYPE="text/css">

<!--

BODY {margin-left: 1in; margin-right: 1.5in}

.opener {font-size: 20 pt; font-weight: extra light;
font-style: italic;  line-height: 22pt; font-family:
Times New Roman; margin-left: 1in; margin-right:
.8in}

.normal {font-weight: extra light; font-style:
normal; font-size: 14 pt; line-height: 16pt;
font-family: Times New Roman}
```

```
.references {font-weight: extra light; font-style:
normal; font-size: 14 pt; line-height: 15pt;
font-family: Times New Roman; margin-left: 1.2in;
margin-right: .8in}

B {font-weight: extra bold; font-style: normal;
font-size: 14 pt; line-height: 16pt; font-family:
Arial}

H1 {font-weight: extra light; font-style: italic;
font-size: 20 pt; line-height: 22pt; font-family:
Times New Roman}

H2 {font-weight: extra bold; font-style: normal;
font-size: 24 pt; line-height: 26pt; font-family:
Times New Roman}

H3 {font-weight: extra bold; font-style: normal;
font-size: 12 pt; line-height: 14pt; font-family:
Times New Roman}

H4 {font-weight: extra bold; font-style: normal;
font-size: 12 pt; line-height: 14pt; font-family:
Times New Roman}

-->

</STYLE>

<BODY BGCOLOR="#ffffff">

<H1>

Dialogue with the Experts

</H1><BR><BR>

<H2>Linus Pauling, Ph.D.:

The Last Interview

</H2>

<BR>

by <A HREF="http://members.aol.com/realmedia">Peter
Barry Chowka</A><BR>

&#169;1996 by peter barry chowka. all rights
reserved.<BR><BR><BR><DIV CLASS=OPENER>

<IMG SRC="Pauling_2a.jpg" ALIGN=LEFT><IMG SRC
="cap5.gif" STYLE= "background: white">n 1979, when
the respected British journal <I>New Scientist
```

</I>included Linus Pauling, Ph.D., on its list of the twenty most important scientists of all time, it was for Pauling another in a long series of achievements that included an unprecedented pair of unshared Nobel Prizes and some startlingly original contributions in biology, chemistry and physics.</DIV>

<DIV CLASS=NORMAL>

By the time of his death in August 1994 at age 93, Pauling was probably better known for his more recent work on nutritional science and vitamin C. In best-selling books on vitamin C, the common cold and can-cer, frequent talk show appearances, and numerous published papers and scientific presentations about a nutritional healing specialty he named "orthomole-cular medicine," Pauling was an unparalleled, uniquely credentialed spokesman for the emerging science of diet and health.

According to Pauling, his high-profile involvement in unpopular political controversies of the 1950s and '60s (including organizing the successful interna-tional campaign to ban nuclear bomb testing, for which he was awarded the 1962 Nobel Peace Prize) pre-pared him for the equally rancorous debates of the 1970s and '80s when he became the de facto leader of nutritional medicine at a time when mainstream medi-cine denigrated such interests. During the last two decades of his life, Pauling's focus on the scientif-ic basis of nutrition and his unstinting advocacy of megavitamin supplements regularly made him the cen-ter of controversy.

Even after his death, the controversies continued. Journalist Lee Dembart, reviewing two new biogra-phies of Pauling, calls the scientist an "embarrass-ment" and an "eccentric crank" for his interest in vitamin C.

k. Add a superscript tag. *(Note: Peter's style block containing style definitions has not been repeated here.)*

```
<H1>

Dialogue with the Experts

</H1><BR><BR>

<H2>Linus Pauling, Ph.D.: The Last Interview

</H2>

<BR>

by <A HREF="http://members.aol.com/realmedia">Peter
Barry Chowka</A><BR>

<SUP>&#169;</SUP>1996 by peter barry chowka. all
rights reserved.<BR> <BR><BR>

<DIV CLASS=OPENER>

<IMG SRC="Pauling_2a.jpg" ALIGN=LEFT><IMG SRC
="cap5.gif" STYLE= "background: white">n 1979, when
the respected British journal <I>New Scientist
</I>included Linus Pauling, Ph.D., on its list of the
twenty most important scientists of all time, it was
for Pauling another in a long series of achievements
that included an unprecedented pair of unshared Nobel
Prizes and some startlingly original contributions
in biology, chemistry and physics.</DIV><BR><BR>
<DIV CLASS=NORMAL>

By the time of his death in August 1994 at age 93,
Pauling was probably better known for his more recent
work on nutritional science and vitamin C. In best-
selling books on vitamin C, the common cold and can-
cer, frequent talk show appearances, and numerous
published papers and scientific presentations about
a nutritional healing specialty he named "orthomole-
cular medicine," Pauling was an unparalleled,
uniquely credentialed spokesman for the emerging
science of diet and health.

<BR><BR>

According to Pauling, his high-profile involvement
in unpopular political controversies of the 1950s and
```

Linus Pauling, Ph.D.: The Last Interview

by Peter Barry Chowka
©1996 by peter barry chowka. all rights reserved.

In 1979, when the respected British journal New Scientist included Linus Pauling, Ph.D., on its list of the twenty most important scientists of all time, it was for Pauling another in a long series of achievements that included an unprecedented pair of unshared Nobel Prizes and some startlingly original contributions in biology, chemistry and physics.

Above: *Because the opener text is italic, the* New Scientist *should be formatted in a Roman or Normal style, emphasizing that it is the name of a publication.*

Linus Pauling, Ph.D.: The Last Interview

by Peter Barry Chowka
©1996 by peter barry chowka. all rights reserved.

In 1979, when the respected British journal **New Scientist** included Linus Pauling, Ph.D., on its list of the twenty most important scientists of all time, it was for Pauling another in a long series of achievements that included an unprecedented pair of unshared Nobel Prizes and some startlingly original contributions in biology, chemistry and physics.

Above: *The only inline tag that worked to transform the type style of the words* New Scientist *at this time was* <B STYLE= "font-style: normal">.

'60s (including organizing the successful international campaign to ban nuclear bomb testing, for which he was awarded the 1962 Nobel Peace Prize) prepared him for the equally rancorous debates of the 1970s and '80s when he became the de facto leader of nutritional medicine at a time when mainstream medicine denigrated such interests. During the last two decades of his life, Pauling's focus on the scientific basis of nutrition and his unstinting advocacy of megavitamin supplements regularly made him the center of controversy.

`<BR><BR>`

Even after his death, the controversies continued. Journalist Lee Dembart, reviewing two new biographies of Pauling, calls the scientist an "embarrassment" and an "eccentric crank" for his interest in vitamin C.`<SUP>1</SUP>`

l. Add the ending tags.

`</BODY>`

`</HTML>`

m. Save the file. Save the document in SimpleText or your word processor. If you're using a word processor, save the text as Text Only. Give the file an .HTM extension.

n. Test the style sheet document. Open Netscape or Microsoft's Internet Explorer browser. Open your document by selecting Open File from the File pulldown menu.

8. Style change: Override a style.

In the opener text, the type style of the British journal *New Scientist* should be normal text to emphasize that it is a publication. This can be accomplished with an inline tag that will override the embedded style.

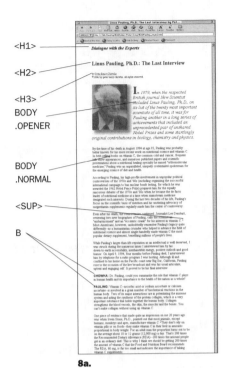

<H1>

<H2>

<H3>
BODY
.OPENER

BODY
.NORMAL

<SUP>

B

8a.

a. **Locate the words *New Scientist* in the opener text.**

```
<H1>

Dialogue with the Experts

</H1><BR><BR>

<H2>Linus Pauling, Ph.D.: The Last Interview

</H2>

<BR>

by <A HREF="http://members.aol.com/realmedia">Peter
Barry Chowka</A><BR>

<SUP>&#169;</SUP>1996 by peter barry chowka. all
rights reserved.<BR> <BR><BR>

<DIV CLASS=OPENER>

<IMG SRC="Pauling_2a.jpg" ALIGN=LEFT><IMG SRC
="cap5.gif" STYLE= "background: white">n 1979, when
the respected British journal New Scientist included
Linus Pauling, Ph.D., on its list of the twenty most
important scientists of all time, it was for Pauling
another in a long series of achievements that includ-
ed an unprecedented pair of unshared Nobel Prizes and
some startlingly original contributions in biology,
chemistry and physics.</DIV>
```

b. **Add an inline tag.**

```
<H1>

Dialogue with the Experts

</H1><BR><BR>

<H2>Linus Pauling, Ph.D.: The Last Interview

</H2>

<BR>

by <A HREF="http://members.aol.com/realmedia">Peter
Barry Chowka</A><BR>

<SUP>&#169;</SUP>1996 by peter barry chowka. all
rights reserved.<BR> <BR><BR>
```

Tip: For details concerning Microsoft's free TrueType offer, see Microsoft's plan to add fonts to the Web: Free TrueType now and Web page font embedding in the future *in this chapter.*

```
<DIV CLASS=OPENER>

<IMG SRC="Pauling_2a.jpg" ALIGN=LEFT><IMG SRC
="cap5.gif" STYLE= "background: white">n 1979, when
the respected British journal <B STYLE="font-style:
normal">New Scientist</B>included Linus Pauling,
Ph.D., on its list of the twenty most important sci-
entists of all time, it was for Pauling another in a
long series of achievements that included an unprece-
dented pair of unshared Nobel Prizes and some star-
tlingly original contributions in biology, chemistry
and physics.</DIV>
```

9. Style change: A font change in a headline.

Changes in the style definitions inside your style block are easy to make. In this example, try changing Times New Roman to a sans serif face in the <H2> tag. Start by locating the <H2> tag in the style block.

a. Locate the tag and style definition you'd like to change in the style block.

```
<HTML>

<HEAD>

<TITLE>Linus Pauling, Ph.D.: The Last Interview by
Peter Barry Chowka

</TITLE>

</HEAD>

<STYLE TYPE="text/css">

<!--

BODY {margin-left: 1in; margin-right: 1.5in}

.opener {font-size: 20 pt; font-weight: extra light;
font-style: italic; line-height: 22pt; font-family:
Times New Roman; margin-left: 1in; margin-right:
.8in}

.normal {font-weight: extra light; font-style:
normal; font-size: 14 pt; line-height: 16pt; font-
family: Times New Roman}
```

Tip: Microsoft's OpenType initiative will include Adobe's CFC compression technology and Microsoft's AGFA compression schemes, allowing for faster font downloading to Web pages.

```
.references {font-weight: extra light; font-style:
normal; font-size: 14 pt; line-height: 15pt;
font-family: Times New Roman; margin-left: 1.2in;
margin-right: .8in}

B {font-weight: extra bold; font-style: normal;
font-size: 14 pt; line-height: 16pt; font-family:
Arial}

H1 {font-weight: extra light; font-style: italic;
font-size: 20 pt; line-height: 22pt; font-family:
Times New Roman}

H2 {font-weight: extra bold; font-style: normal;
font-size: 24 pt; line-height: 26pt; font-family:
Verdana,Arial,Helvetica}

H3 {font-weight: extra bold; font-style: normal;
font-size: 12 pt; line-height: 14pt; font-family:
Times New Roman}

H4 {font-weight: extra bold; font-style: normal;
font-size: 12 pt; line-height: 14pt; font-family:
Times New Roman}

-->

</STYLE>
```

b. Make a change in a style definition. Add sans serif font alternatives to the <H2> tag. For example, add the words *Arial*, *Helvetica*, and *sans serif*. Helvetica or some other sans serif face will be added if Arial is not available on the end-user's system.

```
<HTML>

<HEAD>

<TITLE>Linus Pauling, Ph.D.: The Last Interview by
Peter Barry Chowka

</TITLE>

</HEAD>

<STYLE TYPE="text/css">

<!--
```

```
BODY {margin-left: 1in; margin-right: 1.5in}

.opener {font-size: 20 pt; font-weight: extra light;
font-style: italic;  line-height: 22pt; font-family:
Times New Roman; margin-left: 1in; margin-right:
.8in}

.normal {font-weight: extra light; font-style:
normal; font-size: 14 pt; line-height: 16pt; font-
family: Times New Roman}

.references {font-weight: extra light; font-style:
normal; font-size: 14 pt; line-height: 15pt;
font-family: Times New Roman; margin-left: 1.2in;
margin-right: .8in}

B {font-weight: extra bold; font-style: normal;
font-size: 14 pt; line-height: 16pt; font-family:
Arial}

H1 {font-weight: extra light; font-style: italic;
font-size: 20 pt; line-height: 22pt; font-family:
Times New Roman}

H2 {font-weight: extra bold; font-style: normal;
font-size: 24 pt; line-height: 26pt; font-family:
Verdana,Arial,Helvetica}

H3 {font-weight: extra bold; font-style: normal;
font-size: 12 pt; line-height: 14pt; font-family:
Times New Roman}

H4 {font-weight: extra bold; font-style: normal;
font-size: 12 pt; line-height: 14pt; font-family:
Times New Roman}

-->

</STYLE>
```

Formatting text in columns with Netscape's new <MULTICOL> tag

Summary: Use Netscape's new <MULTICOL> tag to format large amounts of text into multiple column format.

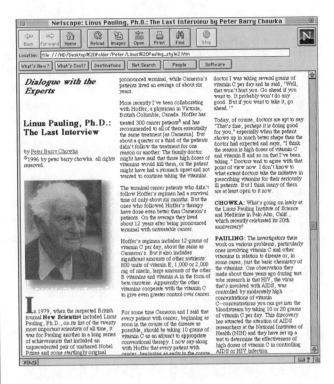

Netscape's new <MULTICOL> tag adds newspaper-like columns to a Web page, which is a practical method of formatting very long articles. In this example, Peter Chowka's Linus Pauling interview fills three columns, as defined by the tag's COLS attribute.

1. Add <MULTICOL> after <BODY>.

Decide how many columns you need, and add a column number to the tag in the form of an attribute.

Example:

```
<MULTICOL COLS=3>
```

a. Insert the <MULTICOL> tag.

```
<HTML>

<HEAD>

<TITLE>Linus Pauling, Ph.D.: The Last Interview by

Peter Barry Chowka

</TITLE>

</HEAD>
```

Above: Peter Chowka's Linus Pauling interview. Notice that the opening initial cap causes leading difficulties in the second column.

```
<BODY BGCOLOR="#ffffff">

<MULTICOL COLS=3>
```

b. Add two line breaks after the image. Linus Pauling's image now needs two line breaks inserted after the image tags and the ALIGN=LEFT attribute deleted. Recall that the image aligned on the left side of the text in the style sheet example.

```
<HTML>

<HEAD>

<TITLE>Linus Pauling, Ph.D.: The Last Interview by

Peter Barry Chowka

</TITLE>

</HEAD>

<BODY BGCOLOR="#ffffff">

<MULTICOL COLS=3>

<H1>

Dialogue with the Experts

</H1><BR><BR>

<H2>Linus Pauling, Ph.D.:

The Last Interview

</H2>

<BR>

by <A HREF="http://members.aol.com/realmedia">Peter

Barry Chowka</A><BR>

&#169;1996 by peter barry chowka. all rights

reserved.<BR><BR><BR>

<IMG SRC="Pauling_2a.jpg">

<BR><BR>
```

Above: *The <MULTICOL> tag makes all columns the same width unless you set the overall width with the WIDTH attribute. Use a pixel value or a percentage. In this example, the WIDTH attribute is set to 300 pixels:*
<MULTICOL COLS=3 WIDTH=300>

Above: *In this example, the WIDTH attribute is set to 85%:*
<MULTICOL COLS=3 WIDTH=85%>

c. **Add a closing <MULTICOL> tag.**

```
</MULTICOL>
```

d. **Add the ending tags.**

```
</BODY>
</HTML>
```

e. **Save the file.** Save the document in SimpleText or your word processor. If you're using a word processor, save the text as Text Only. Give the file an .HTM extension.

f. **Test the three-column document.** Launch Netscape, and open your document by selecting Open File from the File pull-down menu.

Controlling font color and family with the <FONT> tag (Netscape Navigator or Internet Explorer)

Summary: *Use the <FONT> tag's new attributes to control type color and type family.*

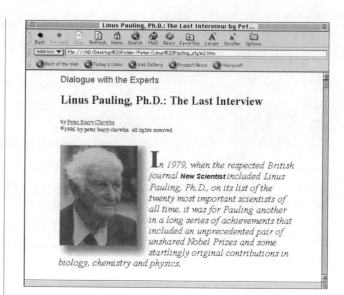

The <FONT> tags recent COLOR and FACE attributes may be used to control typography on your Web pages. In the Linus Pauling interview, the tag and its attributes may be used to alter the font color and family in the article's headlines. (*Note: The <FONT> tag and attributes may be applied to any part of a line.*)

1. Alter the headline color.

To change the color of the headline *Dialogue with the Experts*, an RGB hexadecimal triplet is needed for the <FONT COLOR=> tag.

The Linus Pauling image is a Photoshop duotone that adds a violet shade to what was originally a black and white scan. The Photoshop eyedropper revealed that the shade corresponds to Pantone 667 CV, which the Best Business Solution Online Color editor translates into a hexadecimal triplet value of #584886 using the R=88, G=72, and B=134 data taken from Photoshop. (*Note: See* Convert a Pantone RGB value to a Web page color with the BBS Color Editor *in the* Online Tools *chapter.*)

```
<HTML>

<HEAD>

<TITLE>Linus Pauling, Ph.D.: The Last Interview by

Peter Barry Chowka
```

***Tip:** For RGB hexadecimal triplet values for your <FONT COLOR=> tag, visit Best Business Solution's Online Color Editor at http://www.bbsinc .com.*

```
</TITLE>
</HEAD>
<BODY BGCOLOR="#ffffff">
<H1><FONT COLOR="#584886">
Dialogue with the Experts
</FONT></H1><BR><BR>
<H2>Linus Pauling, Ph.D.:
The Last Interview
</H2>
<BR>
by <A HREF="http://members.aol.com/realmedia">Peter
Barry Chowka</A><BR>
&#169;1996 by peter barry chowka. all rights
reserved.<BR><BR><BR>
```

2. Alter the headline face.

```
<HTML>
<HEAD>
<TITLE>Linus Pauling, Ph.D.: The Last Interview by
Peter Barry Chowka
</TITLE>
</HEAD>
<BODY BGCOLOR="#ffffff">
<H1><FONT FACE="VERDANA,ARIAL,HELVETICA SIZE="5"
COLOR=#584886">
Dialogue with the Experts
</FONT></H1><BR><BR>
<H2>Linus Pauling, Ph.D.:
The Last Interview
</H2>
<BR>
by <A HREF="http://members.aol.com/realmedia">Peter
Barry Chowka</A><BR>
```

Microsoft's plan to add fonts to the Web: Free TrueType now and Web page font embedding in the future

Summary: *The Microsoft/Adobe font technology merger represents a unique contribution to Web-based typography.*

webfonts.sit.1

Are you sick of designing with Times Roman? Typographic enhancements to HTML are on the way. To solve the Web's font problems, Microsoft has developed a new font file format with Adobe Systems.

1. Solution requires downloading (for now).

Although Microsoft and Adobe have developed a publicly available font specification that promises to improve the quality of type on the Web, their solution requires developers and end-users to have screen fonts installed in their computers. Microsoft is distributing free fonts from their Web site. These include the fonts currently supplied with Windows 95 (Times New Roman, Courier New, and Arial) and a set of fonts currently supplied with the Windows version of Internet Explorer 3.0 (Arial Black, Impact, Comic Sans MS, and Verdana). Other fonts available on the site include Trebuchet and Georgia.

The OpenType format supports both Type 1 and TrueType fonts, and the format is backwardly compatible with all existing TrueType and Postscript fonts.

2. Designing with fonts.

Although there is a TrueType rasterizer built into Windows 95, Windows NT, and the Macintosh, for now, screen fonts must be installed in an individual user's computer in order for the fonts to be displayed. Macintosh and Windows Web designers interested in using fonts need to distribute any fonts they use for Web viewers to download. Microsoft's free TrueType fonts have been designed for this purpose and font downloads are provided on the Microsoft site for both platforms.

Using fonts already bundled with Windows 95 and the Windows version of Internet Explorer version 3.0 increases the likelihood that the fonts will be displayed because the fonts are already installed.

Above: *In this example, the headline* Dialogue with the Experts *was formatted with :*

```
<FONT FACE="VERDONA,ARIAL,HELVETICA"
SIZE="5">Dialogue with the
Experts</FONT>
```

Web page developers on both platforms may use font alternatives in the <FONT> tag. Netscape's Navigator and the Internet Explorer browser will search through the fonts available on an end-user's system and load what is available. If none of the fonts are available, the browser loads the default typeface. *(Note: The <FONT> tag requires an ending </FONT> tag.)*

Example:

```
<FONT FACE="VERDONA,ARIAL,HELVETICA" SIZE="4">
```

3. Embedded fonts (the future).

Microsoft is currently developing an embedded font technology that will free Web viewers from needing to install fonts on their computer. Font information will travel with a document. Microsoft and Adobe have plans to submit a proposal for font embedding (using OpenType) to the World Wide Web Consortium. If the proposal is endorsed by W3C, the initiative will become a standard method to use fonts on the Web. Even if the proposal is not endorsed by W3C, Microsoft plans to add this font compression technology to the Internet Explorer browser.

Chapter 5

Online Tools

This chapter introduces valuable resources for the Web artist who uses the Web as a current and convenient source of information. The chapter begins with a color editor tool from a company in Houston called Best Business Solutions (BBS). Web artists who need hexadecimal codes for their HTML tags to color a background or text can use this editor in conjunction with Photoshop as a translation tool.

Also covered in this chapter are search engines, which have become popular online tools for finding information on the Web. Yahoo! search, originally created by David Filo and Jerry Yang from Stanford University, not only provides an easy-to-use search engine but it facilitates a way to extend the search to other search engines. To promote your site, you'll want to submit information about your pages to all of the search engines, and this chapter shows you how to begin the submission process at Yahoo!.

Convert a Pantone RGB value to a Web page color code with the BBS Color Editor

Summary: *Visit Best Business Solutions' Web page, enter the RGB value of a desired Pantone shade (gathered from Photoshop), and watch the BBS Color Editor display the color and generate the required HTML code for your Web page.*

Adobe Photoshop™

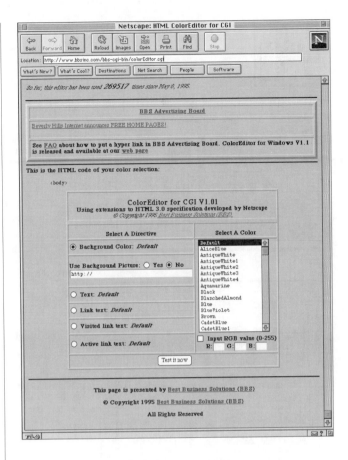

Best Business Solutions' Web page is an essential tool for graphic designers who want to add color to a Web page. You can access the tool, called the BBS Color Editor, at http://www.bbsinc.com/bbs-cgi-bin/colorEditor.cgi.

Adding color to a Netscape background or text requires placing a hexadecimal red-green-blue triplet in an HTML document tag. For example, to color a background white, the tag would appear like this:

```
<BODY BGCOLOR="#ffffff">
```

The BBS Color Editor has an extensive list of color names that were created by BBS. When I wrote and asked them if RGB color information (Photoshop, 0-255) could be translated into the HTML hexadecimal triplets needed for the HTML tags, they wrote back and said they had added an RGB field to their Color Editor! Graphic designers can obtain an RGB value for any shade they use in Photoshop

1a.

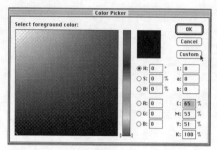

1b.

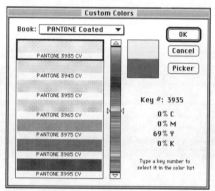

1d.

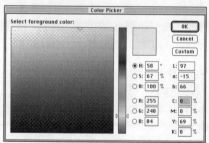

1e.

(Pantone, Toyo, Trumatch), type the RGB values into the Color Editor, and the Editor displays the desired shade on screen and generates the hex code for an HTML document, as shown in the following table.

The Pantone shades used in this example are:

Item	Pantone #	RGB Value	Hex Code
Background	3935CV	R=255 G=248 B=84	#fff854
Text	302	R=0 G=56 B=80	#003850
Linked text	1685CV	R=114 G=41 B=22	#722916
Visited link text	172CV	R=246 G=37 B=0	#f62500
Active link text	355	R=0 G=140 B=60	#008c3c

1. Find desired shade(s) in Photoshop.

Decide which Pantone you'd like to use for the background, text, link text, visited link text, and active link text. Locate the RGB values of these shades:

a. Click on the Foreground color swatch in the Toolbox.

b. Click on Custom.

c. Click on the pop-up box in the Custom Color dialog box to select a color model.

d. Scroll to select a shade.

e. Click on Picker.

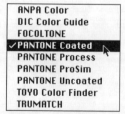

1c.

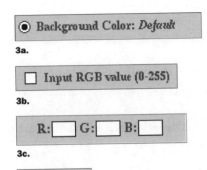

2.

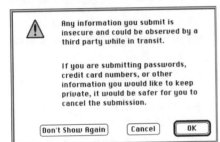

3a.

3b.

3c.

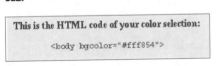

3d1.

3d2.

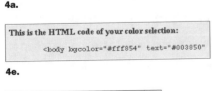

This is the HTML code of your color selection:

`<body bgcolor="#fff854">`

3e.

Text: *Default*

4a.

This is the HTML code of your color selection:

`<body bgcolor="#fff854" text="#003850"`

4e.

Link text: *Default*

5a.

2. Record the RGB value of your color(s).

The Color Picker dialog box will display RGB values of the color you choose. Record this information.

3. Find the hex code for background color.

a. On the BBS Color Editor Web page, make sure the radio button next to Background Color is selected.

b. Click to enter an "X" in the Input RGB value field.

c. Enter the RGB values you recorded from Photoshop.

d. Click on the Test It Now button *(Note: The BBS Color Editor is interactive, so you'll see a warning dialog box concerning security. Click on Don't Show Again.)*

e. The BBS Color Editor will change the background to your desired color, and the hexadecimal HTML code will be displayed at the top of the Editor (in this example, body bgcolor="#fff854").

4. Find the hex code for text.

a. On the BBS Color Editor Web page, make sure the radio button next to Text is selected.

b. Click to enter an "X" in the Input RGB value field.

c. Enter the RGB values you recorded from Photoshop.

d. Click on the Test It Now button.

e. The BBS Color Editor will change the text to your desired color, and the hexadecimal HTML code will be displayed at the top of the Editor (in this example, TEXT="#003850").

5. Find the hex code for link text.

(Note: Link text refers to highlighted hypertext that is activated with a mouse click.)

a. On the BBS Color Editor Web page, make sure the radio button next to Link Text is selected.

b. Click to enter an "X" in the Input RGB value field.

c. Enter the RGB values you recorded from Photoshop.

d. Click on the Test It Now button.

e. The BBS Color Editor will change the text to your desired color, and the hexadecimal HTML code will be displayed at the top of the Editor (in this example, LINK="#722916").

> **This is the HTML code of your color selection:**
>
>   <body bgcolor="#fff854" text="#003850" link="#722916">

5e.

6. Find the hex code for visited link text.

(Note: Visited link text refers to a link that has already been followed.)

a. On the BBS Color Editor Web page, make sure the radio button next to Visited Link Text is selected.

b. Click to enter an "X" in the Input RGB value field.

c. Enter the RGB values you recorded from Photoshop.

d. Click on the Test It Now button.

e. The BBS Color Editor will change the text to your desired color, and the hexadecimal HTML code will be displayed at the top of the Editor (in this example, VLINK="#f62500").

⊙ Visited link text: *Default*

6a.

> **This is the HTML code of your color selection:**
>
>   <body bgcolor="#fff854" text="#003850" link="#722916"
>   vlink="#f62500" alink="#008c3c">

6e.

7. Find the hex code for active link text.

(Note: Active link text refers to a link that's currently active or a link with a mouse button held down.)

a. On the BBS Color Editor Web page, make sure the radio button next to Active Link Text is selected.

b. Click to enter an "X" in the Input RGB value field.

c. Enter the RGB values you recorded from Photoshop.

d. Click on the Test It Now button.

e. The BBS Color Editor will change the text to your desired color, and the hexadecimal HTML code will be displayed at the top of the Editor (in this example, ALINK="#008c3c").

⊙ Active link text: *Default*

7a.

SimpleText

8. Try creating a new HTML document using color tags.

To test your color tags, create an HTML document on your hard drive, and open it in Netscape.

a. Open SimpleText.

b. Create a new document.

c. Begin a new document with the following markup tags

```
<HTML>
<HEAD>
<TITLE>New Colors</TITLE>
</HEAD>
```

9. Add the color tags.

```
<HTML>
<HEAD>
<TITLE>New Colors</TITLE>
</HEAD>
<BODY BGCOLOR="#fff854" TEXT="#003850"
     LINK="#722916" VLINK="#f62500" ALINK"=#008c3c">
</BODY>
```

10. Test a background picture.

The Color Editor can test any picture available on any server as a background image. All you need is the correct URL (Uniform Resource Locator). If the image is smaller than the Netscape window, Netscape will *tile,* or repeat, the image to form a wallpaper effect.

Netscape's server has background samples (Figure 10a) available to you for download (http://home.netscape.com/assist /net_sites/bg/backgrounds.html). The Color Editor can display a swatch as a test background.

a. Go to Netscape's *Background Samples* page at http://home.netscape.com/ assist/net_sites/bg/back-grounds.html.

b. Record the file names of any samples you'd like to test.

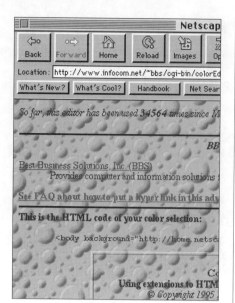

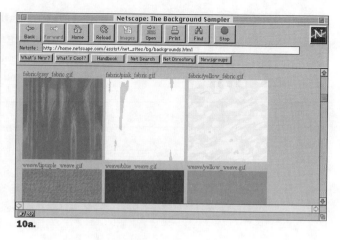

10a.

10c.

Tip: *To replace a file name in the URL field, click in the text and use the right arrow key to move the cursor all the way to the right. Press the Delete key until the file name is deleted, then re-type another name.*

c. Click on Yes in the Use Background Picture field on the Color Editor page.

d. Enter:

```
http://home.netscape.com/assist/net_sites/bg/fabric/
    yellow_fabric.gif
```

e. Try a few of your selections by substituting another file name in place of fabric/yellow_fabric.gif.

11. Create a new HTML document.

To test your background picture, create an HTML document on your hard drive, and open it in Netscape.

a. Open SimpleText.

b. Create a new document.

c. Add the following markup tags:

```
<HTML>
<HEAD>
<TITLE>Background Picture</TITLE>
</HEAD>
```

12. Add the BODY tag.

(Note: Step 12 requires that your PPP connection be open; however, you can test step 14 on your hard drive.)

```
<HTML>
<HEAD>
<TITLE>New Colors</TITLE>
</HEAD>
<BODY BACKGROUND="http://home.netscape
        .com/assist/net_sites/bg/fabric/yellow_fabric.gif">
</BODY>
```

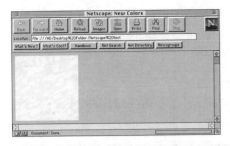

Tip: Try using the URL for a Netscape background sample in the <IMG> tag. Instead of tiling the swatch as a background, only one swatch will appear on the page.

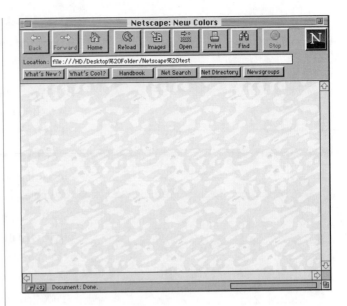

13. Copy a background sample (optional).

Copy a sample to your hard drive, and use the file name in your <BODY> tag.

a. Go to Netscape's *Background Samples* page at http://home.netscape.com/ assist/net_sites/bg /backgrounds.html.

b. Press and hold down the mouse pointer on a sample.

c. Select Save This Image As.

d. Use the default name, or type in a file name.

e. Click on Save.

14. Create a new <BODY> tag (optional).

(Note: the file name you create for your tag may vary depending on where the image is located. This example assumes the file yellow_fabric.gif is is in the same directory as the HTML document. The file name together with one or more directory names is referred to as the path.*)*

```
<HTML>
<HEAD>
<TITLE>New Colors</TITLE>
</HEAD>
<BODY BACKGROUND="yellow_fabric.gif">
</BODY>
```

15. Summary of HTML tags used in this section.

The tags you see in this list (in alphabetical order) reflect the HTML 3.2 specification.

<BODY>...</BODY>

A tag used to open and close the body of a document. This tag uses the following attributes:

BACKGROUND specifies a URL to point to a background image that will tile to the full document image area. For example:

```
<BODY BACKGROUND="yellow_fabric.gif">
```

BGCOLOR controls the color of the background. For example:

```
<BODY BGCOLOR="#fff854">
```

TEXT controls the color of normal text. For example:

```
<BODY TEXT="#003850">
```

LINK controls the color of link text. For example:

```
<BODY LINK="#722916">
```

VLINK controls the color of visited link text.

```
<BODY VLINK="#f62500">
```

ALINK controls the color of active link text.

```
<BODY ALINK="#008c3c">
```

<HEAD>...</HEAD>

A tag used to open and close the header portion of a document.

<HTML>...</HTML>

A tag used to open and close an HTML document.

<TITLE>...</TITLE>

Used inside the head, this tag describes the title of a document, which shows up inside a document's title bar.

Searching the Web on Yahoo! search

Summary: *Looking for links that compliment your page? Doing research? Just browsing the Web? Try using the search engine at http://www.yahoo.com.*

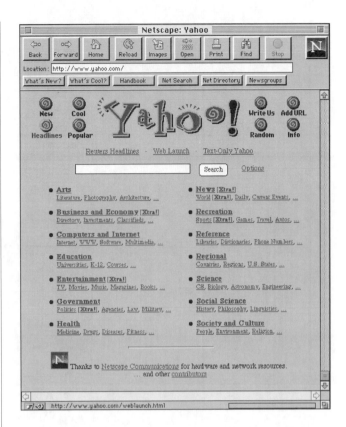

If you've never used a search engine, you'll be amazed at the power of this tool, which will search the Web for a topic of your choice. There are several such *search engines* or *robots* on the Web, and Yahoo! (http://www.yahoo.com) is one of the most popular.

Yahoo! was created by David Filo and Jerry Yang, both Electrical Engineering students at Stanford University, where this tool was housed for the first nine months of operation. Yahoo! is now off-campus. It's an independent company, and the robot runs on three Silicon Graphics Indy machines. For speed reasons, complex searches are not allowed. However, the engine supports a simple boolean *and* search, and an optional fill-in form allows a visitor to specify a number of matches through a popup box on the form.

1. Select a topic from Yahoo!'s top-level.

The simplest way to use Yahoo! is to select from among the categories organized on the home page. Each category has links that will lead you to related home pages.

a. Select one of the topics organized into top-level categories on the Yahoo! home page.

b. Click on a link.

1b.

c. The link will take you to pages of other links to related Web pages.

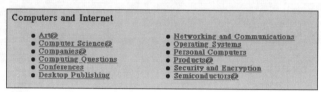

1c.

2. Use the Yahoo! search form.

a. Type in any topic on the Yahoo! home page.

b. Click on the Search button.

c. A page of related links will be displayed for you to explore.

2a, 2b.

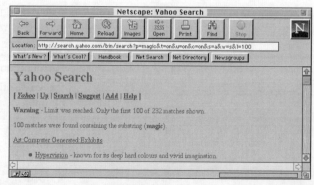

2c.

Extending your Yahoo! search to other search engines

Summary: *The Yahoo! search engine provides links to other search engines at the bottom of the pages that are returned. Use these links to extend your search without retyping your keyword(s).*

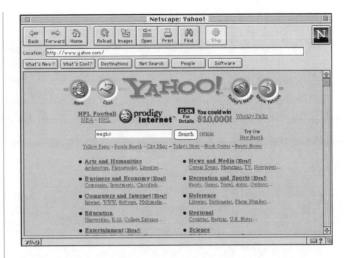

1b.

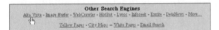

1c.

The page that returns the results of your Yahoo! search will have a group of links to other search engines at the bottom of the page. These links allow you to extend your search to one or more of the search engines listed without re-typing your search topic. (*Note: The search topic you typed is referred to as a* keyword.*)*

1. Steps to extend a search.

a. Follow the steps in the previous section to conduct a search on Yahoo!.

b. At the conclusion of your search, scroll to the bottom of the page that is returned.

c. Click on a link to another search engine.

d. A page of related links on the search engine you chose will be displayed in your browser window.

1d.

NetSite assistance from Netscape

Summary: Visit Netscape's home page to download Netscape plug-ins and updated reference material on changes in HTML.

Tip: If you're not currently online, it is possible to load Netscape on your hard drive and compose HTML documents locally. Create the HTML documents using TeachText, SimpleText, or your favorite word processor (be sure to save the document in your word processor as Text Only).

1a.

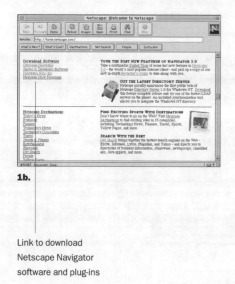

1b.

Link to download
Netscape Navigator
software and plug-ins

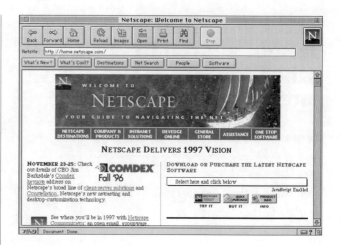

N etscape's Web site (http://home.netscape.com) is a valuable resource for downloading a current version of Netscape Navigator, plug-ins, and current reference materials on HTML.

1. Locating Navigator software and plug-ins.

a. Click on the Home button at the top of your Netscape browser window to go to the Netscape home page.

b. Scroll down the page to locate links to current Netscape Navigator software downloads and plug-ins. *(Note: Plug-ins add functionality to the Netscape Navigator software.)*

2. Steps to find Netscape's Web resources.

a. Click on the Assistance button in the Netscape splash screen at the top of the Netscape home page.

2a.

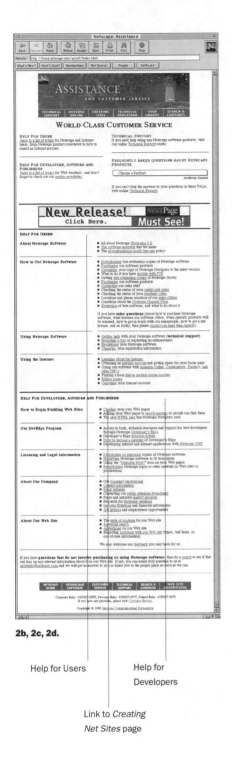

2b, 2c, 2d.

Help for Users

Help for Developers

Link to *Creating Net Sites* page

b. The Netscape Assistance and Customer Service page will appear.

c. Scroll down the page to view:

Help for Users

Help for Developers, Authors and Publishers

d. In the section labeled *Help for Developers, Authors and Publishers*, click on links in the *How to Begin Building Web Sites* section.

e. A *Creating Net Sites* page will be displayed, which includes the following sections:

Authoring Documents

Look for the latest reference materials on HTML. For example, this section provides *A Beginner's Guide to HTML, Composing Good HTML, Extensions to HTML,* and *Guides to Writing HTML Documents.*

Adding Functionality

Look for *Off the Web*, a monthly newsletter and additional directory listings of mailing lists and newsgroups to assist Web developers.

2e.

Add information about your site to Yahoo! and other search engines

Summary: *Promote your home page by adding your URL to one or more search engines.*

By adding your URL to a search engine, you're providing Web viewers with a way to find your page. Information may be added to each search engine individually or to several search engines at once by visiting the Submit It page at http://www.submit-it.com. *(Note: Changes to any of the search engine Web pages may affect the multiple submission functions on Submit It.)*

1. Steps to add your URL to Yahoo!.

a. Go to the Yahoo! home page at http://www.yahoo.com.

b. Use the Yahoo! search function to see if your page is already listed.

c. After you've run a search and you know your site is not listed, return to the Yahoo! home page at http://www.yahoo.com.

1a, 1b, 1c.

d. On the Yahoo! home page, click on the category where you'd like your site to appear.

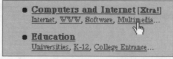

1d.

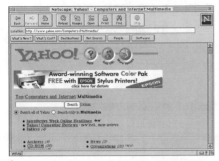

1e.

1f.

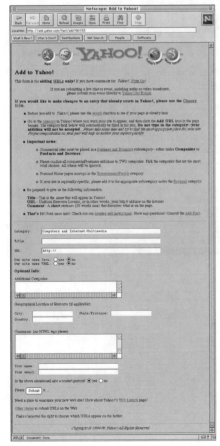

1g, 1h, 1i.

e. A page will be displayed that corresponds to the category you selected.

f. Click on the Add URL icon at the top of the page in the Yahoo! banner.

g. The Add to Yahoo! page will be displayed.

h. Scroll to the form at the bottom of the page and type your page title, your URL, and 20 words that describe your site.

i. Adding the following form information is optional:

- Geographic location of your site
- Your name and email address

j. When you have completed the form, click on the Submit button.

1j.

k. In the dialog box that follows, click on OK.

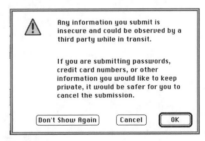

1k.

Locating, downloading, and decompressing shareware from the Web

Summary: *c\net's Shareware.com site is an excellent resource for shareware.*

Wondering if your software is outdated? Check c\net's Shareware.com site. The archive contains a very large collection of freeware and shareware programs that you can download.

1. Steps for locating and downloading software.

a. Go to the Shareware.com site at http://www .shareware.com.

b. Click on the Selections link.

c. A Selections page will be displayed.

1a.

1b.

1c.

1d.

1e, 1f.

StuffIt Expander™

2.

d. Click on a Mac or PC icon in a desired category.

e. A list of software in the category you chose will be displayed.

f. Click on a link to a desired software program.

g. A page displaying a download link will appear.

h. Click on a download link to begin downloading.

1g, 1h.

2. Notes on decompression.

Software available for downloading will often be encoded in a BinHex format with an .HQX file extension. If you have StuffIt Expander installed as a Netscape helper application, Netscape will automatically decompress the file at the conclusion of the download.

If you do not have StuffIt Expander installed as a Netscape helper application, you will be asked if you want to save the file on your hard drive at the conclusion of the file download. Save the file, locate StuffIt Expander on the CD-ROM in the back of this book, and decompress the file manually.

StuffIt Expander will also expand files that have been encoded in MacBinary (.BIN) format. If you have also installed DropStuff with Expander Enhancer, you will be able to expand files that were compressed or encoded on PCs and Unix systems with StuffIt Expander. These include: ZIP (.ZIP), ARC (.ARC) archives, gzip (.GZ), Unix Compress (.Z), UUencoded (.UU), and Tar (.TAR).

Artist featured in this chapter:

Mark Elbert *is a graphic artist and musician who graduated from Pratt Institute with a degree in industrial design.*

mother@interport.net

Artist featured in this chapter:

Jane Greenbaum *is vice president of New York's Graphic Artists' Guild and a new media artist specializing in 3D animation.*

IForward@aol.com

http://members.aol.com/ iforward/image1.html

Chapter 6

Photography

Images are the most popular multimedia elements on the Web. However, until browser software behaves like Quark XPress, there are many subtle details involved in placing images on a Web page. Because of bandwidth limitations—the objective is to keep graphics files to a minimum—image manipulation has more in common with the computer game industry than it does with print.

To introduce readers to these new concepts, Mark Elbert's notes on Web graphics summarize details such as Web page size, color scanning, bit depth, file naming conventions, and advice on testing a Web page before it's launched into cyberspace.

New media artist Jane Greenbaum introduces readers to Painter's Create Drop Shadow command, which provides a quick method of creating drop shadows. The command can be used for creating a drop shadow around text or an image. *(Note: Creating a drop shadow around type involves very few steps.)*

In remaining sections, Mark Elbert's Web projects will give readers clues about how to assemble their own pages, plus a section on creating a Super Palette with DeBabelizer, which offers color palette manipulation tricks from DeBabelizer's author and game industry expert, David Theurer.

Mark Elbert's notes on Web graphics

Summary: *Mark Elbert relays tips on Web page size, color palettes, dithering, and file formats.*

Graphic designers can leverage everything they know about print and often reuse graphics that have been created for print. In this section, Mark Elbert's notes on graphics will help graphic designers make a transition from print to Web graphics.

1. Plan the size of your images.

Because most microcomputer color monitors are 14-inch color screens, you should plan your graphics to fit this average-sized window. When Netscape launches, the browser window does not fill a 14-inch screen, but the Web visitor can resize the window to see wider images. The available space in a single Netscape window (resized to fill the screen) on an average monitor is as follows:

Dimension	Pixels (or pts)	Picas	Inches
Horizontal measure	604	50.33	8.38
Vertical measure	304	25.33	4.22

Although Netscape's default window has an inside horizontal dimension of 486 pixels on a Macintosh monitor, images are always offset 8 pixels from the edge of the browser window by default. As a result, the banner graphic should be no more than 604 pixels. *(Note:* Pixels *are dots, or screen elements.)*

When planning the height of your graphic, decide whether you'd like the average visitor to experience the graphic in "pages," or if you want the graphic to fit within the first viewable window. Set a graphic's height to 304 pixels to limit the graphic to one screen. Although Netscape's default window has an inside vertical dimension of 320 pixels, there will be an offset of 8 pixels along the top of the browser window by default.

Tip: Before resampling or changing the bit depth in your image, make a duplicate of the image. Select Duplicate from the Image pull-down menu in Photoshop, and give the file an alternate name.

2. Color scanning: The transition from print.

The 24- and 30-bit scanners that graphic designers use for print provide information for the printed page, far in excess of what you'll need or want for Web graphics.

The 24-bit image you edit in Photoshop should be reduced to a second, smaller image of 8 bits or fewer. Half of your image manipulation steps will be to reduce file size because file size is critical on a Web page. Look for examples in this chapter that demonstrate how to reduce bit depth in Photoshop or DeBabelizer.

a. Scan to a particular size. Most scanning software programs allow you to scan to a particular size. Rather than resizing the image in Photoshop, it's best to scan to your desired size on the scanner, as resizing in Photoshop causes blurriness.

b. Scan to a larger resolution. In spite of the fact that you will ultimately not need more than 72 pixels per inch, graphic designers generally agree that the best images are those that are *oversampled*, or scanned at a higher resolution and then resampled.

3. Correct the color of your image.

Improve the color of an image by redistributing the color tones. This can be accomplished by setting the white point and black point or by manually selecting the lightest and darkest areas in a scanned photo. *(Note: See* Creating a banner graphic or splash screen *in this chapter for steps on how to set the white point and black point.)*

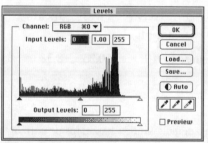

3a.

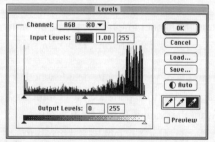

3b.

a. Histogram before color correction. A histogram from Photoshop reflects the tonal distibution in an image or the brightness and darkness values. Note that the x-axis reflects the colors from darkest (left) to brightest (right). The y-axis reflects the number of pixels with each value.

b. Histogram after color correction. After setting the white point and black point to color-correct the image, the color is more evenly distributed.

Tip: Set your monitor to 256 colors when you're working on images for the Web. Most computers on the Web have an 8-bit color depth, so this will give you a close idea of how your images will look. If you have a 24-bit monitor and you'd like to switch to 8-bit color, select Control Panels\Monitors from the Apple pull-down menu, and choose 256 colors (in System 7.5x, the Apple pull-down menu has a cascading pop-up menu that allows you to see and select any Control Panel).

Tip: Figure 5a, 5b, 5c, and 7 are available on the CD-ROM in the back of this book. Open the photos on a Macintosh with a color monitor to see the differences in bit depths.

5a.

4. Changing the bit depth.

By reducing bit depth, you reduce file size. Conversion to a smaller bit depth is accomplished through a mode change in Photoshop. When converting from RGB Mode to Indexed Color Mode, a dialog box will appear and allow you to select a bit depth and a dithering option.

By reducing the bit depth in an image, you also reduce the number of colors. When you convert an RGB image to Indexed color in Photoshop, the program builds a color table or palette for the image. Although an RGB image can contain 16.7 million colors, an indexed color image contains 256 colors. Photoshop simulates a larger RGB palette using the available 256 colors. *(Note: For more information and examples, see the secton on bit depth in this chapter.)*

Photoshop allows you to control the following palette types when you convert to Indexed Color Mode:

- *Exact Palette.* Photoshop uses the same 256 colors present in the original RGB image.

- *System Palette.* Photoshop uses the system's default color table. Dithering is an option.

- *Adaptive Palette.* Photoshop creates a color table of colors more commonly used in the image. *(Note: When converting to Indexed Color Mode in Photoshop, the Adaptive Palette is the best option.)*

- *Custom Palette.* Photoshop displays a Color Table dialog box, allowing you to edit the color table using the Color Picker. The palette can be saved for later use.

- *Previous Palette.* Photoshop makes this option available when you have already converted an image using the Custom or Adaptive Palette option.

5. Dithering.

Dithering adjusts the color of adjacent pixels to fool the eye into thinking there is a third color present. Greg Marr, a color manipulation expert at Equilibrium, recommends selecting dithering whenever it is an option.

- a. **24 bits, millions of colors, no dithering.** A 24-bit image on an 8-bit monitor has some dithering due to Color QuickDraw's intepretation of the color palette.

5b.

5c.

7.

b. 4 bits, 16 colors, dithering. Photoshop's dithering applied in a mode change from RGB to Index Color Mode camouflages a reduction in the number of colors.

c. 4 bits, 16 colors, no dithering. Without dithering, there are too few colors in a 4-bit image to approximate skin coloring.

6. Add type after reducing the bit depth.

Don't subject the type in your image to dithering. Add type after you have settled on a bit depth you like.

7. Color duotone and grayscale options.

Color duotone and grayscale images look better at smaller bit depths than do full color images. For instructions on how to create a duotone, see *Creating a duotone from a grayscale image* later in this chapter.

Image	Color	Duotone	Grayscale
8 bit, GIF	160 K	148 K	144 K
8 bit, JPEG (med.)	60 K	44 K	52 K
4 bit, GIF	92 K	100 K	80 K
4 bit, JPEG (med.)	32 K	15248 K	52 K

8. File naming conventions.

Your Web documents should have proper extensions, to help the Web server identify the file type.

Format	Extension
HTML	.html (Unix) .htm (DOS)
GIF	.gif
JPEG	.jpg .jpeg

Tip: Shortening a file name to eight characters can be a challenge for Macintosh users. Try removing the vowels from the file name. The file name can often be determined from the remaining consonants.

Tip: Browsers are constantly evolving like other software programs. Try to stay familiar with new developments by downloading new versions occasionally. Current information about updates to HTML can be obtained within Netscape's own system of Web pages at http://www .netscape.com.

Tip: Even though many users now have modems that operate at 28.8 Kbps or higher, it's often the case that users cannot connect to their Web sites at these optimum speeds. Always assume that average connection speeds are about 14.4 Kbps.

Use very short file names without spaces (eight characters or less), and avoid using the following characters in file names:

Character	Name
< >	angle brackets
\	back slash
|	vertical bar
[ ]	brackets
:	colon
,	comma
=	equal sign
/	forward slash
+	plus sign
"	quotation mark
;	semicolon

9. Test the download speed of your Web page.

HTML documents may be built on your hard drive using a text editor such as SimpleText or TeachText. Use Netscape off line to check your work. However, the download speed you'll experience when you load a file from your hard drive will be much faster than the average Web visitor's 14.4 or 28.8 Kbps modem.

As soon as you've developed a large graphic for your Web page, you should test the download speed over a 14.4 Kbps modem. If the graphics are slow to load, you'll have trouble attracting Web visitors. Web visitors will be reluctant to return if they have to wait several seconds for downloads.

10. Test your Web page on other browsers.

Images developed on a Macintosh may appear slightly stretched on an IBM PC browser window due to a difference in the aspect ratio. Pixels on an IBM PC are taller than pixels on a Macintosh.

In addition, different systems use different methods for ending a line. The text you've formatted with the <PRE>, or preformatted, tag on a Macintosh may change if you move your files to a Unix or IBM server.

If your firm does not own an IBM PC, consider getting on the Web through another platform at a public computer rental facility, which rents time on the Internet by the hour.

Pixel depth

Summary: Learn how pixel depth or bit depth, a critical color characteristic, will affect the performance of your Web pages with graphics.

Tip: Equilibrium, the company that created DeBabelizer, is continually adding functionality to their software. A recent addition includes a Windows edition of the DeBabelizer software. Look for further information at Equilibrium's Web site located at http://www.equil.com.

Graphic designers who have worked with Photoshop to produce artwork for print may not be acquainted with *pixel depth* or *bit depth*. *Bit depth* is defined as the number of bits used to make up a color pixel.

Bit Depth	Number of Colors
2 bits	4 colors
3 bits	8 colors
4 bits	16 colors
5 bits	32 colors
6 bits	64 colors
7 bits	128 colors
8 bits	256 colors
16 bits	65,536 colors
24 bits	16 million colors

For print graphics, the objective is to increase the bit depth; for Web graphics, as in game software development, the objective is to reduce bit depth.

The critical objective for a Web page artist is the same objective shared by game developers: combine what looks like the largest amount of color and the smallest possible file size. Web pages have a critical performance issue. Web visitors will grow impatient and won't want to return to a Web page if there's a long delay while images download.

1. Plan "target" size and physical dimensions.
Spend time traveling the Web, and get acquainted with the file sizes and physical dimensions of the graphics you see.

1b.

1c.

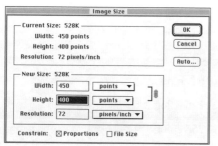

1d.

2a.

The images you see that download quickly will be the ones you'll want to examine closely. You can discover a file's format, the file size, and the physical dimensions by downloading the image to your hard drive, as follows:

a. Position your mouse pointer on a Web page graphic.

b. Hold down the mouse button, and select Save This Image As.

c. Let go of the mouse button, select a folder or your desktop for saving, enter the name of your file, and click on Save. The file name extension will tell you if the image is a GIF or a JPEG file.

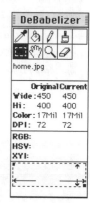

1e.

d. Open the image in Photoshop, and select Image Size from the Image pull-down menu. Note the image resolution and the physical dimensions.

e. DeBabelizer will display the number of colors beneath the tool box.

2. Compare image file sizes.

a. 40 K, JPEG. At 40 K, the Condé Nast image downloads very quickly.

b. 108 K, GIF. At 108 K, the Disney MoviePlex image downloads rather slowly.

2b.

4a.

4b.

4c.

3. Browsers have a 256 color per page total.

The palette you plan for one image may affect the palettes of other images on the page because browsers limit the total number of colors to 256 per page.

DeBabelizer's Super Palette feature selects the best 8-bit palette for a group of images by "polling" the images and determining the best colors for the images as a group. For instructions on how to create a Super Palette for a group of images, see *Creating a Super Palette with DeBabelizer* in this chapter.

4. Experiment with lower bit depths.

Images respond differently when you lower the bit depth. For example, an image with a large variety of colors will not respond well to a lower bit depth because palette colors get "used up" quickly.

a. **8 bits, 256 colors, dithered GIF.** This image of children waiting to climb into a school bus has a wide variety of colors. This image begins to look patchy even at 8 bits. (Note the little girl's back pack and the headlights of the bus.) As a 200 K GIF file, this image will download slowly.

b. **7 bits, 128 colors, dithered GIF.** The image of a teacher and student starts to look patchy at 7 bits. As a 112 K GIF file, this image will download slowly.

c. **4 bits, 16 colors, dithered GIF.** The image of the teacher and student holds up well in grayscale at a lower bit depth. As a 28 K GIF file, this image will download faster than the full-color version.

Both images look superior and download faster when saved as JPEG. However, there are tradeoffs. For a comparison of GIF versus JPEG, see the next section in this chapter. (*Note: Figure 4a, 4b, and 4c are available on the CD-ROM in the back of this book. Open the photos on a Macintosh with a color monitor to see the differences in bit depths.*)

Saving your image: GIF or JPEG?

Summary: Learn about the differences between GIF and JPEG, two popular graphics file formats found on the Web.

Tip: *Most HTML tags work in the Netscape browser as well as Microsoft's Internet Explorer browser. However, both browsers use a few unique HTML tags. Microsoft's Web Gallery at http://www .microsoft.com/gallery contains notes about Internet Explorer-specific tags and Netscape-specific tags.*

The decision to save an image as GIF or JPEG may depend on the image. Although GIF images are popular because of the special effects that can be used, detailed images and flesh tones often look better when saved as JPEGs.

1. GIFs are read by more browsers.

GIF is the predominant image file format used by Web page designers because it can be read by more browser programs as an inline image. *Inline images* appear on the browser page with text. *External images* are those that must be loaded and displayed with an add-on viewer program, referred to as a *helper application*.

Netscape and Internet Explorer can read JPEG images as inline graphics, but some other browser programs will ignore JPEGs tagged as inline images. A JPEG image referenced with a link will be displayed in a viewer application's floating window when the link launches the viewer software.

2. GIFs can be used for special effects.

GIF images are 8-bit images that may also be stored as *transparent GIFs*. This type of GIF is popular for special effects such as fading and silhouettes. *Interlaced GIFs* are another popular option because they appear to download faster than non-interlaced GIFs. The image is quickly drawn in low resolution and then gradually fills in with pixels as the image is downloaded.

3. GIF images sometimes have *banding*.

Because GIF images are 8 bit, the image may contain *banding*, or look posterized. This is due to the way the browser reads the image and usually occurs with blends and flesh tones. An image with a large amount of detail will look better if saved as a JPEG image. Banding, which will often be seen in an 8-bit

Tip: Equilibrium, the company that created DeBabelizer, also makes a DeBabelizer "Lite" product. Unlike the full package, which supports scripting and batch processing, DeBabelizer Lite is a translation tool that contains a large number of "readers and writers." (Note: Animation file formats, such as QuickTime, FLC, and FLI, are not supported in the Lite version of DeBabelizer.)

GIF, will be smoothed in the JPEG format with some dithering. A summary of file format characteristics follows:

Format	Plus/Minus
GIF	**Plus** GIF files can be read by a majority of browsers as an inline image.
	Plus GIF images can be saved as interlaced GIFs, a format that *appears* to download faster than non-interlaced GIFs. The image is quickly drawn in low resolution and is gradually filled in with pixels.
	Plus GIF images can be saved as transparent GIFs. This GIF drops out whatever color is assigned as transparent. This may be accomplished with Aaron Gile's Transparency software and DeBabelizer.
	Minus GIF images may appear posterized in some browsers. (See next page.)
JPEG	**Plus** Photographs do not appear posterized.
	Minus JPEG files look somewhat dithered and are not read as inline images by many browsers.

4. JPEG was designed for 24-bit color.

The JPEG compression algorithm (invented by the Joint Photographic Experts Group) is really intended for 24- or 32-bit color. When an image is compressed, this "lossy" algorithm throws information away.

Should a Web designer reduce an image to 8 bits and then save it as JPEG? Because most of the color monitors used on the Web are 8-bit color, 24-bit color images on Web pages are unnecessarily large and a waste of color information. An 8-bit JPEG image stores what appears to be a lot more than 8 bits of information and although the loss of data may be visible on a printed page, it is not visible on screen. *(Note: Do not save a JPEG image twice as JPEG, or your image will be noticeably pixelated.)* Reduce your Web graphic to 8 bit, save it as a JPEG, but store an original 24-bit RGB image for future editing.

Tip: Posterization *is a term that refers to a flattening of the brightness values in an image (Note: The image on this page is from the Pacific Coast Software collection of stock photography at http://www .pacific-coast.com.)*

The differences between GIF and JPEG images is most obvious in skin tones, where the posterization that occurs is very pronounced. Notice the difference in the two photos on this page. The top photo is a JPEG image, and the photo below is a GIF image.

GIF and the LZW compression patent

Summary: *Even though there have been rumors that the GIF file format may disappear due to the legal dispute between Unisys and CompuServe, the 8-bit file format, which may someday be upgraded to 24-bit, is not going away any time soon.*

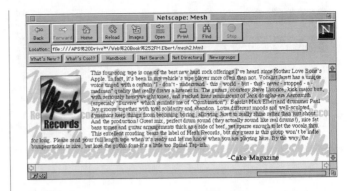

Graphic designers who develop Web pages appreciate the GIF file format for the transparent GIF, which makes silhouettes possible, and the interlaced GIF, which appear to download quickly to the browser screen in waves. Although the JPEG file format is superior to GIF for displaying color detail, a JPEG image can't be saved with a transparent background, nor can it be interlaced.

1. Unisys and the compression patent.

The GIF file format, owned by CompuServe, uses LZW compression. LZW (Lempel, Ziv, Welch) is a lossless, 8-bit compression-decompression scheme that was originally developed by the Lempel-Ziv team, but later improved by Terry Welch when he worked for the Sperry Corporation. Unisys took over the LZW patent when Sperry became part of Unisys in 1986. The LZW scheme, unlike a "lossy" compression schme, doesn't throw away information when it compresses. Ever since Unisys took over the patent, they have been licensing the compression algorithm to online services and modem manufacturers. They have also been quietly enforcing the patent in the software market, as the scheme is popular among companies who make image editing software programs.

2. Grandfathering the license.

In pursuing their right to the patent, Unisys *grandfathered* the license to any software product that used LZW compression prior to January 1995. However, as of January 1 1,996, any new product, or any software product update, requires a license.

HTML tags and page markup

Summary: *Understanding HTML, or the Hypertext Markup Language, is essential for Web page development.*

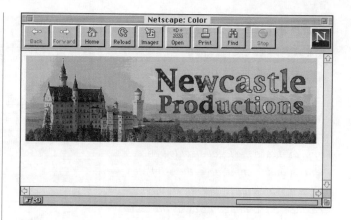

The term *markup* is a publishing term used to refer to a tradition in print. When pages are produced in publishing, typesetting instructions, known as *tags*, are added to a typewritten manuscript. In print, tags tell typesetting software how to display a page.

Unless a graphic designer works in book publishing, he or she may not be aware that Quark XPress, PageMaker, and other page layout programs can read and interpret plain text or ASCII text with tags containing style information. Quark's system of text tags are similar to HTML, the tagging system used on the Web.

Although Quark XPress is a powerful page layout program, its system of tags is not ideal. For example, Quark's tags can describe text very accurately, but the tagging system does not offer tags that describe images. Publishers who use XPress tags to assemble books or newsletters with pictures, use supplementary tagging software such as Xtags from Em Software.

In contrast to Quark's sophisticated text tagging system, the HTML tagging system has very crude tags for describing text. However, unlike XPress tags, HTML includes image tags as well as powerful tags that can create hypertext links across computer platforms and to multimedia resources such as sound, animation, and video.

The following chart shows how the Quark XPress tag system is similar to the HTML tag system. Xpress tags have been widely adopted in the book publishing industry.

HTML	Xpress	Meaning
<B>…</B>	<b>	Turn bold on/off
<I>…</I>	<i>	Turn italic on/off
<U>…</U>	<u>	Turn underline on/off
<P>	<\n>	New paragraph
 	<\d>	New line
<CENTER> …</CENTER>	</Center><*C>	Center a paragraph
<BODY TEXT='#rrggbb'> …</BODY>	<c"color">	Change text color
<FONT SIZE=value>	<z###.##>	Change font size
<NOBR>	<\!s>	No break

1. Special characters.

HTML and Xpress tags both have a set of special characters. For example, both need a method of indicating characters that would otherwise be interpreted as part of a tag, such as an angle bracket. In HTML, special characters are referred to as *character entities* or *numbered entities*.

HTML	Xpress	Meaning
&lt;	<\<>	<
&gt;	<\>>	>
&amp;	n/a	&
&quot;	n/a	"

Besides providing a means to generate characters that would otherwise be interpreted by a browser as a tag symbol, character entities also exist to generate characters from the ISO Latin-1 alphabet, which do not exist in the ASCII set of characters. These characters are generated with different key sequences on different computer platforms; making them special characters in HTML solves translation problems.

Tip: Although the <PRE>...</PRE> tag preserves preformatted text, a browser changes the font of preformatted text.

2. Starting tags and ending tags in HTML.

Most HTML markup tags require that a set of tags be used. The *starting tag* acts much like an on switch, and the *ending tag* acts like an off switch. Together, the set of markup tags act on the text that lies between the tags. *(Note: You can mix upper and lower case lettering when you create tags.)*

Meaning	Starting Tag	Ending Tag
Anchor	<A>	</A>
Bold style	<B>	</B>

3. Formatting inside <PRE>...</PRE> in HTML.

Although browsers usually ignore return characters and spacing, line breaks and blank spaces are left undisturbed inside the preformatted text tag.

4. Nesting tags in HTML.

Nested tags are tags inside of other tags. Most tags can be nested, except for anchors inside of other anchors or headings inside of preformatted text.

The moveable grid for pictures and text

Summary: *Can a graphic designer develop a grid for a Web page? Not really. HTML tags describe how elements should be placed in relationship to each other. Placement is not described in relationship to the page, because the page size can vary.*

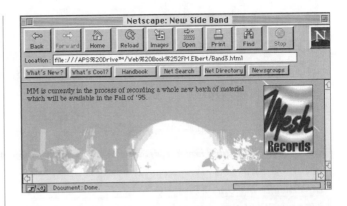

When a graphic designer uses Quark XPress for page layout, he or she has a tool that offers very precise page geometry for a printed page.

Because a Web page can be resized, page elements need to be described in relationship to each other, and not the page. In the sample shown on this page, the Mesh Records image has been tagged with an ALIGN=RIGHT attribute, which will align the image on the right side of the text regardless of how the browser window gets resized. Note there is a small amount of horizontal spacing on either side of the image to push the text away from the edge, which is the result of an HTML attribute called HSPACE shown later in this chapter.

If horizontal space gets added, you will only be able to control the space on both sides of the image, but not on one side or the other. This page offset around the edge appears to be 8 points or pixels.

Using HTML to move page elements horizontally

Summary: *In the absence of a grid, it's valuable to understand how HTML can be used to move elements horizontally or vertically. In Quark XPress or Microsoft Word, these commands would be referred to as paragraph-based.*

Tip: *Most HTML tags place images in relationship to the left margin. Very few tags are available that place images on the right or anywhere in between. The examples on the next few pages demonstrate a few tags that can be used like tabs to move elements varying distances across the page.*

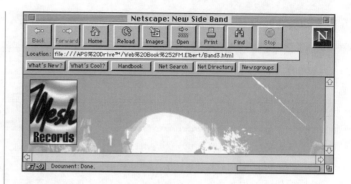

Images and text that are "tagged" into place horizontally on a Web page maintain their position relative to other elements when the page is resized.

1. Open SimpleText.

Use SimpleText or a word processor. If you use a word processor, be sure to save the document as Text Only.

2. Create a new HTML document.

Start a new document with the following markup tags:

```
<HTML>
<HEAD>
<TITLE>New Side Band</TITLE>
</HEAD>
<BODY>
```

3. Add the name of a GIF file to the <BODY> tag.

Background images can be used in Netscape. Add the name of the GIF file that you'd like to use as the background image to the <BODY> tag.

```
<HTML>
<HEAD>
<TITLE>New Side Band</TITLE>
</HEAD>
<BODY BACKGROUND ="New_Band.gif">
```

4.

4. Add an image tag.

The <IMG> tag contains a source, or SRC parameter, which contains the name of the image file.

```
<HTML>
<HEAD>
<TITLE>New Side Band</TITLE>
</HEAD>
<BODY BACKGROUND ="New_Band.gif">
<IMG SRC="Mesh Wave.gif">
</BODY>
</HTML>
```

The result is shown in Figure 4.

5. Add text after the image.

Unless the browser is instructed how to handle text, it will flow the text immediately after the image.

```
<HTML>
<HEAD>
<TITLE>New Side Band</TITLE>
</HEAD>
<BODY BACKGROUND="New_Band.gif">
<IMG SRC="Mesh Wave.gif">MM is currently in the process
of recording a whole new batch of material which will be
available in the Fall of '95.
</BODY>
</HTML>
```

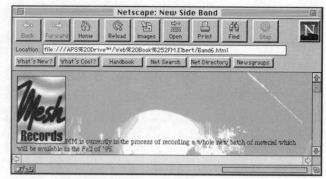

5.

6. Add a paragraph tag after the image (optional).

A paragraph tag <P> will flow the text on the line below the
image and open up paragraph spacing.

```
<HTML>
<HEAD>
<TITLE>New Side Band</TITLE>
</HEAD>
<BODY BACKGROUND ="New_Band.gif">
<IMG SRC="Mesh Wave.gif"><P>MM is currently in the
process of recording…
</BODY>
</HTML>
```

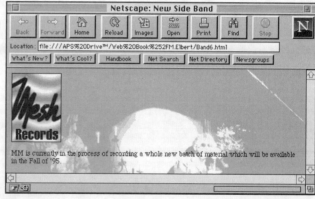

6.

7. Use the ALIGN attribute to move an image.

The ALIGN attribute, which is part of the <IMG> tag, is the simplest way to move an image across the page. Use the ALIGN=RIGHT attribute in an <IMG> tag.

```
<HTML>
<HEAD>
<TITLE>New Side Band</TITLE>
</HEAD>
<BODY BACKGROUND ="New_Band.gif">
<IMG SRC="Mesh Wave.gif"ALIGN=RIGHT>
</BODY>
</HTML>
```

7.

8. Use the <DL> tag to move an image or text.

Because the <DL> tag formats an indented list, nesting several <DL> tags works to further indent pictures, text, or both across the page.

a. Nest two <DL> tags with text and the ALIGN=LEFT attribute in the <IMG> tag. *(Note: The <DL> tag works to move an image.)*

```
<HTML>
<HEAD>
<TITLE>New Side Band</TITLE>
</HEAD>
<BODY BACKGROUND ="New_Band.gif">
<DL><DL><IMG SRC="Mesh Wave.gif"ALIGN=LEFT></DL></DL>
MM is currently in the process of recording a whole
new batch of material which will be available in the
Fall of '95.
</BODY>
</HTML>
```

8a.

b. **Nest four <DL> tags with text and the ALIGN=LEFT attribute in the IMG tag.**

```
<HTML>
<HEAD>
<TITLE>New Side Band</TITLE>
</HEAD>
<BODY BACKGROUND ="New_Band.gif">
<DL><DL><DL><DL><IMG SRC="Mesh
Wave.gif"ALIGN=LEFT></DL></DL></DL></DL> MM is cur-
rently in the process of recording a whole
new batch of material…
</BODY>
</HTML>
```

8b.

9. Add space around an image with HSPACE.

The HSPACE attribute added to the Image tag will push the text away from the image but it will add space on both sides of the image at once.

Using the HSPACE attribute may be a problem if you're trying to line up the left edge of the image with text further down the page. If this is the case, text offset may be created with extra Canvas in Photoshop which you can then make transparent with Transparency or DeBabelizer.

Tip: HSPACE adds space on both sides of an image, and VSPACE adds space above and below.

9.

Nest four <DL> tags (with text) and add HSPACE.

```
<HTML>
<HEAD>
<TITLE>New Side Band</TITLE>
</HEAD>
<BODY BACKGROUND ="New_Band.gif">
<DL><DL><DL><DL>
<IMG SRC="Mesh Wave.gif"ALIGN=LEFT HSPACE=20 >
</DL></DL></DL></DL>MM is currently…
</BODY>
</HTML>
```

10. Use <BLOCKQUOTE> to move page elements.

The <BLOCKQUOTE> tag will indent an image or text the same amount as two nested <DL> tags.

Use the <BLOCKQUOTE> tag.

```
<HTML>
<HEAD>
<TITLE>New Side Band</TITLE>
</HEAD>
<BODY BACKGROUND ="New_Band.gif">
<BLOCKQUOTE>
<IMG SRC="Mesh Wave.gif"ALIGN=LEFT>
MM is currently in the process of recording a whole new batch
of material which will be available in the Fall of '95.
</BLOCKQUOTE>
</BODY>
</HTML>
```

10.

Tip: The <CENTER>...</CENTER> tag can be used to move page elements horizontally. See the Image Map *chapter for an example of how to use this tag.*

11.

11. Use <BLOCKQUOTE> to move a column.

Depending on where you place the tag, the <BLOCK-QUOTE> tag will indent an image and several paragraphs.

Use the <BLOCKQUOTE> tag.

```
<HTML>
<HEAD>
<TITLE>New Side Band</TITLE>
</HEAD>
<BODY BACKGROUND ="New_Band.gif">
<BLOCKQUOTE>
<IMG SRC="Mesh Wave.gif"><P>
<FONT SIZE=+2>Clubs, New York</FONT><P>
<B>Chelsea</B><P>
Tramps<BR>
51 West 21st Street<BR>
727.7788<BR><P>
<B>East Village</B><P>
Brownies<BR>
169 Avenue A<BR>
420.8392<BR>
CBGBs<BR>
315 Bowery<BR>
982.4052<P></BLOCKQUOTE>
</BODY>
</HTML>
```

2. Use the <BR> tag to add line breaks.

In the example in Step 11, notice how the <BR> tag adds a line break.

Using HTML to move page elements vertically

Summary: *HTML tags that move page elements vertically are very few in number. (Note: For new developments in style sheets designed for the Web, see the* Style Sheets And New HTML Text Tags *chapter.)*

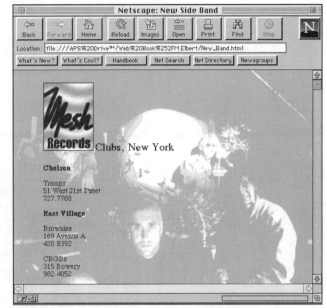

1.

Integrating inline pictures and text is challenging. For example, *align* does not refer to text alignment, as in word processing. Here, *align* refers to the position of an image.

1. ALIGN=BOTTOM.

In this example, ALIGN=BOTTOM lines the text up with the bottom of the image.

Use the ALIGN=BOTTOM attribute in an <IMG> tag. *(Note: The <FONT SIZE=+2> tag has been used to make the words* Clubs, New York *slightly larger than the body type. The value can be a number from 1 through 7. The number 3 is considered the* basefont, *or the default size).*

```
<HTML>
<HEAD>
<TITLE>New Side Band</TITLE>
</HEAD>
<BODY BACKGROUND ="New_Band.gif">
<BLOCKQUOTE>
<IMG SRC="Mesh Wave.gif" ALIGN=BOTTOM>
<FONT SIZE=+2>Clubs, New York</FONT><P>
<B>Chelsea</B><P>
Tramps <BR>
51 West 21st Street <BR>
727.7788 <P>
```

```
<B>East Village</B><P>
Brownies<BR>
169 Avenue A<BR>
420.8392<P>
CBGBs<BR>
315 Bowery<BR>
982.4052<P></BLOCKQUOTE>
```

2.

2. ALIGN=TOP.

In this example, ALIGN=TOP really doesn't line up the image with the top of the text.

Use the ALIGN=TOP attribute in an <IMG> tag.

```
<HTML>
<HEAD>
<TITLE>New Side Band</TITLE>
</HEAD>
<BODY BACKGROUND ="New_Band.gif">
<BR>
<BLOCKQUOTE>
<IMG SRC="Mesh Wave.gif" ALIGN=TOP>
<FONT SIZE=+2>Clubs, New York</FONT><P>
<B>Chelsea</B><P>
Tramps<BR>
51 West 21st Street<BR>
727.7788<P>
```

```
<B>East Village</B><P>
Brownies<BR>
169 Avenue A<BR>
420.8392<P>
CBGBs<BR>
315 Bowery<BR>
982.4052<P></BLOCKQUOTE>
```

3. The <BR> and <P> tags.

In the previous example, the break line tag, or <BR>, breaks the line but does not add extra line spacing.

The paragraph tag, or <P>, also breaks the line but adds paragraph or line spacing.

4. The VSPACE attribute.

The VSPACE attribute will immediately push the text further from the image but will add space on both sides of the image at once.

```
<HTML>
<HEAD>
<TITLE>New Side Band</TITLE>
</HEAD>
<BODY BACKGROUND ="New_Band.gif">
<BR>
<BLOCKQUOTE>
<IMG SRC="Mesh Wave.gif" ALIGN=BOTTOM VSPACE=25>
```

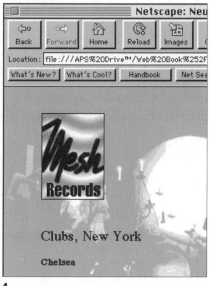

4.

Tip: For information and instructions on how to upload files to your Internet provider's server, see the Image Map *chapter.*

5. HTML tags used in the two previous sections.

The tags you see in this list (in alphabetical order) reflect the HTML 3.2 specification.

<B>...</B>

A tag used to apply boldfacing to text.

<BLOCKQUOTE>...</BLOCKQUOTE>

A tag used to create a paragraph indent on one or more paragraphs.

<BODY>...</BODY>

A tag used to open and close the body of a document. This tag can be used to refer to a background image in the form:

```
<BODY BACKGROUND=New_Band.gif">
```

**
**

A tag used to insert a line break.

<DL>...</DL>

The definition list tag is usually used for definitions or short paragraphs with no bullets or numbering. In this section, this tag is nested several times to indent the Mesh Records logo. For example:

```
<DL><DL><DL><DL><DL><DL><DL><IMG SRC="Mesh
Wave.gif"></DL>
</DL></DL></DL></DL></DL></DL>
```

<FONT SIZE=VALUE>...</FONT>

A tag used to change the default font size. The value can be any number from 1 through 7 or it can be represented +- any value from 1 through 7. The value 3 is considered the *basefont,* or the default font size.

<HTML>...</HTML>

A tag used to open and close an HTML document.

<HEAD>...</HEAD>

A tag used to open and close the header portion of a document.

*Tip: The SimpleText text processor sup-
plied with System 7.5x is more flexible
than the older TeachText supplied with
previous versions of the System.*

*For example, SimpleText allows you to
have multiple documents open at one
time.*

<IMG>

Used to refer to an inline image, this tag uses the SRC
attribute, which represents the the URL (location) of the
image. For example:

```
<IMG SRC="Mesh Wave.gif">
```

This tag uses the ALIGN attribute (or parameter) to indicate the placement of an inline image. Options include
TOP, BOTTOM, LEFT, and RIGHT. For example:

```
<IMG SRC="Mesh Wave.gif" ALIGN=LEFT>
```

This tag also uses the HSPACE attribute, which adds
space on both sides of an image. For example:

```
<IMG SRC="Mesh Wave.gif" ALIGN=LEFT HSPACE=20>
```

<P>

A tag used to indicate a new paragraph. This tag does not
require an ending tag.

<TITLE>...</TITLE>

A tag used to describes the title of a document, which
shows up inside a document's title bar.

Creating a banner graphic or splash screen

Summary: *Learn how to create a banner graphic or splash screen—the first image Web visitors will see when they visit your Web page.*

Tip: *When you capture a screen image with Command+Shift+3, the SimpleText file can be opened as a PICT image in Photoshop. The file size of this image will be small if the monitor is set to 256 colors and large if the monitor is set to millions of colors.*

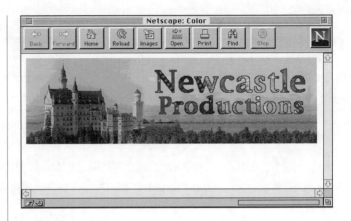

With the preparation of a banner graphic, Mark Elbert demonstrates how to size, scan, edit, and adjust the palette of a banner image. *(Note: See* Convert a Pantone RGB value to a Web page color with the BBS Color Editor *in the* Online Tools *chapter for steps on how to assign color to the browser background and text.)*

1. Plan the size of your banner.

To calculate the maximum width available for a banner graphic, Mark opened Netscape on a 14-inch monitor, resized the browser window to the width of the monitor, and captured the contents of the screen with Command+Shift+3. This command created a TeachText file, which could then be opened as a PICT document in Photoshop.

In Photoshop, Mark selected Window|Palettes|Show Info and dragged a rectangular marquee to select the inside browser area. The Show Info palette gave Mark a width measurement of 620 pixels and a height measurement of 320 pixels. Using the same technique, he also measured the offset distance between the edge of the browser window and the art on screens he captured as TeachText images. Mark discovered this offset is 8 pixels. These clues helped him determine the maximum width available for artwork.

Rather than fill the entire screen, Mark chose 504 pixels for the width of his banner, 100 pixels less than the maximum measurement. The height he chose was 144 pixels.

Tip: Browser software reads one palette of 256 colors per page. If you're building a page with more than one image, consider creating a Super Palette, or a palette that consists of the best 256 colors for a group of images.

If you need to transfer the image with this palette information via modem, always transfer it as binary information so this information is not lost. (Note: For information on how to create a Super Palette, see Creating a Super Palette with DeBabelizer in this chapter).

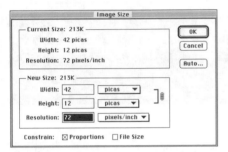

2b, 2c.

2d.

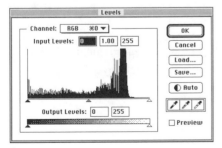

3a.

2. Scan your artwork.

Using a 24-bit flatbed scanner, Mark scanned more information than he needed (higher resolution) but to the exact dimensions. After opening the image in Photoshop, he resampled the image to 72 pixels per inch and used the Unsharp Mask filter to correct the slight fuzziness that results when Photoshop interpolates pixel information. To duplicate Mark's methods, follow these steps:

a. Select Image Size from the Image pull-down menu.

b. Type *72* in the pixels per inch field.

c. Click on OK.

d. Select Filter|Sharpen|Unsharp Mask.

e. With Preview selected, Photoshop will display what the filter will do to your image. Choose 25%, a Radius value of 1.0 pixels, and a Threshold value of 0.

2e.

Click on OK; the result is shown below.

3. Correct the color.

After color scanning, Mark checked to see how the brightness and darkness tones were distributed. By mapping the lightest and darkest parts of the image to a white target and a black target, Mark corrected the color, which made a significant visible difference in the image.

a. Select Adjust|Levels from the Image pull-down menu.

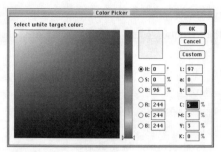

3b.

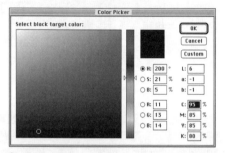

3c.

b. Set a white target by double clicking on the white eye dropper and typing 5, 3, 3 in the C, M, Y boxes. *(Note: Use 7, 3, 3 for images that have more dark values than light.)* Then click on OK.

c. Set a black target by double clicking on the black eye dropper and typing in 95, 85, 85, and 80 in the C, M, Y, K boxes. Click on OK.

d. Investigate which area of your image is the lightest. Remove the "X" from Preview in the Levels dialog box, hold down the Option key, and slowly drag the white triangle on the top slider to the left. The area that turns white first is the lightest portion of your image. Remember this location.

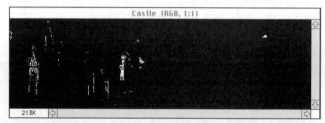

3d.

e. Investigate which area of your image is the darkest. Make sure the "X" is removed from Preview, hold down the Option key, and slowly drag the black triangle on the top slider to the right. The area that turns black first is the darkest area.

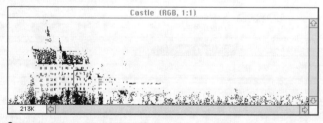

3e.

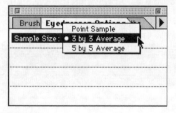

3f.

f. Set the eyedropper tool at a 3-pixel sample. Double-click the eyedropper, and select 3 by 3 Average from the pop-up menu.

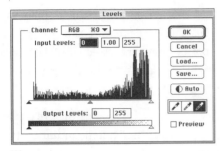

3i1.

g. Map the white target on the area that appeared as the lightest portion of your image by selecting the white eye dropper and clicking on that area.

h. Map the black target on the area that appeared as the darkest portion of your image by selecting the black eye dropper and clicking on that area.

i. You'll notice a change in most scanned images immediately. You'll also notice a change in the histogram (Figure 3i1). The x-axis reflects colors from darkest (left) to brightest (right), and the y-axis reflects the number of pixels with each value. The castle photo that results is shown in Figure 3i2.

3i2.

4. Create your type in Adobe Illustrator.

Type that originates in Illustrator and gets "rasterized" in Photoshop has neater, less jagged edges than type created in Photoshop. When you open an EPS file in Photoshop, you'll need to enter a desired resolution. Rasterized type will still look jagged unless this resolution is sufficiently high. For best results, open your EPS file at a resolution that is three to four times the screen resolution (288 ppi or 360 ppi).

Rather than place Illustrator type, open the type as an EPS image into another file, copy it, and paste it into your banner artwork. *(Note: If the resolution of the source artwork [type] and destination file [banner artwork] are not the same, the type will change size.)*

Either work at high resolution for both your image and your type, or rasterize a type size that is in proportion to the changes that you will know will occur when you paste the type into the image. If your banner artwork is already created, the size type you create in Illustrator will be a function of the

Tip: *In this example, Mark reduced pixel depth after he created type for his banner. If you use black type or some other solid color, add the type to your image after you reduce the pixel depth of your graphic. (Note: See Steps 9 and 10 for instructions on how to reduce pixel depth.)*

resolution you choose for rasterizing the type. In the following example, 10 point (Illustrator) type is opened as an EPS image in Photoshop at 360 ppi, or 5 times the resolution of the banner artwork file where it will be pasted. When the type gets pasted into the banner artwork, it will be five times as large.

Desired Type Size (Finished Graphic)	EPS Resolution/ Photoshop	Multiplication (or Division) Factor	Size To Create in Illustrator (To Paste into a 72 ppi Banner)
32	288 ppi	4	8 pt
40	288 ppi	4	10 pt
48	288 ppi	4	12 pt
40	360 ppi	5	8 pt
60	360 ppi	5	12 pt
70	360 ppi	5	14 pt

5a.

5b.

5c.

5d.

a. Mark's banner artwork was a 72 ppi image. He created 10 point type in Illustrator in order to open it into Photoshop (or rasterize) at five times the the resolution of his banner artwork. He did this to demonstrate how the type size would change if the type's resolution was different than the artwork's resolution.

b. After creating his type in Illustrator, Mark Elbert saved the type as an Illustrator file.

5. Rasterize the EPS type, then copy and paste it.

a. In Photoshop, Mark opened the Illustrator document and typed in 360 ppi as a resolution in the EPS rasterize dialog box.

b. To select the type for copying, Mark selected the white background with the Magic Wand tool.

c. He then selected Inverse from the Select pull-down menu.

d. Mark copied the type and pasted it into his banner artwork.

Tip: When you place type from an EPS file on a Photoshop page, it gets rasterized at the same resolution as your Photoshop image. If you're working on a 72 ppi file and you don't want "jaggies," rasterize the Illustrator file by opening the entire Illustrator document into Photoshop and typing in a resolution that is three to four times the screen resolution. Copy and paste your type into your Photoshop artwork, but plan ahead on a change in size (see chart on the previous page) if the resolutions are different.

6.

6a.

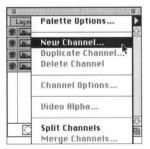

6c.

6. Create a channel.

Mark wanted a channel to have a record of the type's selection, because he planned to paste an image into the type selection and then add a stroke to outline the type. Before creating a channel, the opacity needed to be set to zero so the type's black pixels would not become part of the background.

a. With the type still selected, Mark selected Palettes|Show Layers from the Window pull-down menu.

b. When the palette appeared, he dragged the opacity slider to zero before creating a channel.

6b.

c. Mark clicked on the channels tab and selected New Channel from the options pull-down menu.

d. He labeled this channel *type*.

e. To return to the RGB layer, he clicked on the RGB channel.

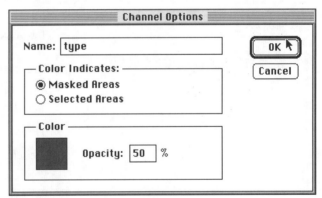

6d.

6e.

7b, 8a.

7d.

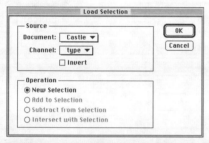

7c, 8b.

7e1.

7. Copy an image and paste it into the type.

a. Leaving the banner art open, Mark opened another image of film-strip art and copied the entire image to the clipboard.

7a.

b. Mark returned to the banner artwork, then loaded the selection of the type from the channel he had created by selecting Load Selection from the Select pull-down menu.

c. He chose Type from the pop-up menu that followed, and clicked on OK.

d. Next, he chose Paste Into from the Edit pull-down menu.

e. Mark positioned the filmstrip art inside the type by dragging the selection with the mouse. The filmstrip art moved inside the type each time he dragged the mouse. To drop the selection, he selected None from the Select pull-down menu (Command+D).

8. Add an outline to the type.

a. Mark reloaded the type selection by choosing Load Selection from the Select pull-down menu.

b. He chose Type from the pop-up menu that followed.

c. He selected Stroke from the Edit pull-down menu.

7e2.

8c.

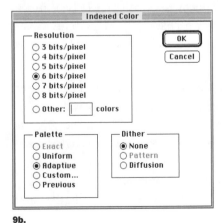

8d.

d. With black selected as a foreground color, he selected a width of 1 pixel, to be centered on the type selection at 100% Opacity and Normal Mode.

e. Mark found the combination of Stroke settings through trial and error. By selecting Undo from the Edit pull-down menu, he was able to try alternate paint colors in the outline and vary the location.

9. Reduce pixel depth (using Photoshop).

When Mark finished editing the image in RGB Mode, he experimented with Photoshop's Indexed Color Mode to see how far he could reduce the pixel depth without altering the color. (*Note: See the next section for instructions on how to reduce the bit depth in DeBabelizer.*)

a. Select Indexed Color from the Mode pull-down menu.

b. Experiment by selecting smaller bit depths with and without dithering to see how the color in your image holds up. Each time you try a selection, select Edit|Undo or press Command+Z if you do not like the color.

Mark was able to reduce the image to a 6-bit color depth (Figure 9b) without a noticeable change in the color. This made a significant change in the file size.

Bit Depth	File Size
24 bit	203 K
8 bit	71 K
6 bit	44 K
6 bit	33K (DeBabelizer)

9a.

9b.

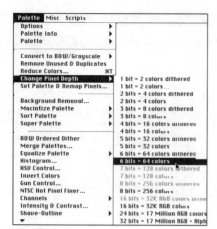

10b, 10c.

Tip: See the Online Tools *chapter for more information about how to download Macintosh shareware programs.*

Tip: The cost of this book doesn't include the use of the shareware programs on the CD-ROM. If you continue to use the software programs provided, please register those that you use.

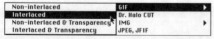

11c.

10. Reduce pixel depth (using DeBabelizer).

a. Open your RGB image in DeBabelizer.

b. Select Change Pixel Depth from the Palette pull-down menu. Equilibrium Technologies recommends that you always select dithering when you reduce the number of colors. Although you can change the amount of dithering by selecting Options|Dithering Options & Background Color from the Palette pull-down menu, DeBabelizer's default setting is the amount Equilibrium has determined to be the best amount.

c. Start by reducing your image to 128 colors and look at the image. If you don't like the change, select Undo from the Edit pull-down menu or press Command+Z. Keep stepping down to fewer colors to determine when the color change becomes visible. Mark was able to reduce the palette to 64 colors without a noticeable change in the image.

11. Save the image.

a. Select Save As from the File pull-down menu (in Photoshop or DeBabelizer).

b. Select CompuServe GIF or JPEG from the pop-up menu. *(Note: Photoshop 3.0 does not add interlacing to GIF images. Interlacing gives the Web visitor the impression of a faster download by quickly painting the image in low resolution and gradually filling it in.)*

To add interlacing to a Photoshop GIF image, you'll need GIFConverter by Kevin Mitchell. DeBabelizer has an option to save a file as an Interlaced GIF. *(Note: GIFConverter is available on the CD-ROM in the back of this book).*

c. Give your image a name. Try to keep your file name to a minimum of eight characters (no spaces) with a file extension such as .GIF, .JPG or .JPEG. *(Note: File extensions must be limited to three characters on the Windows 3.X platform.)* Removing vowels from the file name helps to reduce the number of characters. Mark used DeBabelizer and chose Interlaced GIF as the file format for saving.

12. Create an HTML file to test your image.

a. Open SimpleText. Use SimpleText or your word processor. If you use a word processor, be sure to save the document as Text Only.

b. Create a new HTML document. Start a new document with the following markup tags:

```
<HTML>
<HEAD>
<TITLE>Newcastle Productions</TITLE>
</HEAD>
<BODY>
```

c. Add the image tag. Reference your GIF (or JPEG) image with the addition of an <IMG> tag.

```
<HTML>
<HEAD>
<TITLE>Newcastle Productions</TITLE>
</HEAD>
<BODY>
<IMG SRC ="Newcstle.gif">
```

d. Close with an ending </BODY> and </HTML> tag and save the file. Save the document. If you're using a word processor, save the text as ASCII or Text Only. Give the file a name, and add an .HTML extension (.HTM if the Web server you're using is a DOS machine).

e. Test the HTML document in Netscape. Open Netscape, and then open your document by selecting Open File from the File pull-down menu. Make sure your GIF image and your HTML document are in the same directory.

To test a number of alternate images, create several HTML files and save them under different file names or open SimpleText and Netscape at the same time and vary between the two applications. Each time you edit your HTML document, save it, and click on Reload in Netscape's Toolbar to retest.

Linking a thumbnail GIF to an external JPEG

Summary: *By creating a small GIF thumbnail on your Web page, your image can be viewed with most browsers. The thumbnail loads quickly, and a larger, JPEG image download can be optional (a JPEG viewer helper application will be required with browsers other than Netscape).*

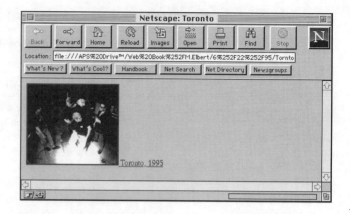

1.

By reducing an image to a thumbnail-size GIF and making the thumbnail a link to a larger, JPEG version of the same image, Mark Elbert created a Web page that can be viewed by most browsers. At the same time, he also provided an optional image format for a detailed photo.

1. Save an original image in Photoshop.

a. When you have finished editing your image in RGB Mode, select Indexed Color from the Mode pull-down menu. Select Adaptive Palette and Diffusion Dither. Try selecting smaller bit depths until you notice an unsatisfactory change in the image. (Select Undo from the Edit pull-down menu if you're unhappy with a selection.)

b. Select Save As from the File pull-down menu.

c. Choose JPEG from the Format pop-up box.

d. Choose an image quality.

e. Name the file using eight characters and no spaces. Add .JPG as a file extension at the end of the name.

2. Reduce your photo to thumbnail size.

a. Open your original RGB image (without the .JPEG extension) in Photoshop.

b. Select Image Size from the Image pull-down menu.

c. Type in a small number for the width value (such as 2 inches), and Photoshop will proportionally size the height for you. *(Note: Record what the height and width values are in pixels as you will need this information for your <IMG> tag.)* Click on OK.

Tip: *For information and instructions on how to upload files to your Internet provider's server, see the* Image Map *chapter.*

d. Select Filter|Sharpen|UnSharp Mask to correct the fuzziness that results when you resize an image. Use 25%, 1.0 Radius value, and a Threshold of 0.

3. Save the thumbnail.

a. Select Save As from the File pull-down menu.

b. Choose CompuServe GIF from the Format pop-up box.

c. Name the file using eight characters and no spaces. Add .GIF as a file extension at the end of the name.

4. Create an HTML document.

a. **Open SimpleText.** Use SimpleText or your word processor. If you use a word processor, be sure to save the document as Text Only.

b. **Create a new HTML document.** Start a new document with the following markup tags:

```
<HTML>
<HEAD>
<TITLE>Toronto</TITLE>
<BODY>
```

c. **Add an Image tag.** In this example, the thumbnail GIF image as well as the text, *Toronto, 1995,* will be a link to the external JPEG image listed inside the anchor tag <A HREF></A>:

```
<HTML>
<HEAD>
<TITLE>Toronto</TITLE>
</HEAD>
<BODY>
<A HREF = "toronto.jpg"><IMG SRC="Tor_sm.gif">
Toronto, 1995</A>
</BODY>
</HTML>
```

4d.

d. Add image sizing to your image tag (optional). Image sizing is a Netscape feature that adds speed to the downloading of images. When Netscape encounters an inline image, it builds a bounding box to display the image. With the height and width information in the <IMG> tag, the bounding box can be built without delay.

The height and width in pixels can be obtained from the Image Size dialog box in Photoshop. In this example, the width is 144 pixels, and the height is 123 pixels:

```
<A HREF = "toronto.jpg"><IMG SRC="Tor_sm.gif"
WIDTH=144 HEIGHT=123> Toronto, 1995</A>
```

e. Control the width of the image border (optional). When you make an image an anchor, or a link, the browser will display a colored border to act as a clue for visitors. For menu buttons that are obvious links, the border can be turned off by adding BORDER=0 to your <IMG> tag. In this example, this would be written:

```
<A HREF = "toronto.jpg"><IMG SRC="Tor_sm.gif"
WIDTH=144 HEIGHT=123 BORDER=0> Toronto, 1995</A>
```

(Note: For the formatting of this book, the lines are broken.)

f. Save the file. Save the document in SimpleText, TeachText, or your word processor. If you're using a word processor, save the text as ASCII or Text Only. Give the file a name and add an .HTML extension (.HTM if the Web server you're using is a DOS machine).

g. Test the HTML document in Netscape. Open Netscape, and then open your document by selecting Open File from the File pull-down menu. Make sure your GIF image, your JPEG image, and your HTML document are in the same directory.

h. Test the HTML document in other browsers. In browsers other than Netscape, a JPEG viewer will be launched when you click on either the thumbnail or the text link. The JPEG image will be displayed in a separate floating window.

4h.

5. Summary of HTML tags used in this section.

The tags you see in this list (in alphabetical order) reflect the HTML 3.2 specification.

<A>...</A>

Referred to as an *anchor,* this tag uses the HREF attribute to link to an external file or anchor. For example:

```
<A HREF="Toronto.jpg">Toronto, 1985</A>
```

(Note: The file name must include the path name if the file is located in another directory.)

<BODY>...</BODY>

A tag used to open and close the body of a document.

<HTML>...</HTML>

A tag used to open and close an HTML document.

<HEAD>...</HEAD>

A tag used to open and close the header portion of a document.

<IMG>

Used to refer to an inline image, this tag uses the SRC attribute that represents the the URL (location) of the image. For example:

```
<IMG SRC="Tor_sm.gif">
```

In this section, image sizing was added to the image tag with the WIDTH and HEIGHT attributes. For example:

```
<IMG SRC="Tor_sm.gif" WIDTH=144 HEIGHT=12>
```

To turn off the image border, the BORDER=0 attribute can be used in the image tag. For example:

```
<IMG SRC="Tor_sm.gif" WIDTH=144 HEIGHT=123
BORDER=0>
```

<TITLE>...</TITLE>

A tag used to describe the title of a document that shows up inside a document's title bar.

Wrapping text around a photo

Summary: *Prepare a Photoshop image with extra background to simulate a text offset for a text "runaround." Use an <IMG> tag in an HTML document with an ALIGN attribute to get the text to wrap.*

Transparency

Although space can be created around an image with the HSPACE attribute, which is used in the <IMG> tag, Mark didn't want the browser to add horizontal spacing on both sides of the image he planned for his Web page.

Mark created additional background and filled it with a gray that matches *most* browser backgrounds. He then used software that assigned the background a transparent value.

1. Create a text offset.

Text offset is the distance between an image and the text. Add a background equal to your desired offset distance with the Image|Canvas Size command in Photoshop. This "extra" edge around the photo can be assigned a transparent value using *Transparency,* by Aaron Giles (available on the CD-ROM in the back of this book), or *DeBabelizer,* a sophisticated color palette manipulation and file conversion tool from Equilibrium Technologies.

1a.

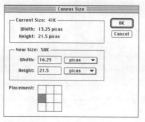

1b.

a. Working in RGB Mode, select Canvas Size from the Image pull-down menu.

b. In the Canvas size dialog box, click on the box-map to indicate where your image should go when you add canvas. Add background by increasing the values in the width or height box.

2b1.

2b2.

3a.

Tip: See the Page Layout Tools *chapter for instructions on using PhotoGIF, a Photoshop plug-in that will make GIF files transparent.*

c. Before you save, select Indexed Color from the Mode pull-down menu. Experiment to see how much you can reduce the bit depth without altering the image. Always select Adaptive Palette, and Diffusion Dither.

When you're satisfied with the dimensions of the background, choose Save As from the File menu, and select CompuServe GIF from the Format pop-up box.

d. Before you open your file in a program that can write a transparent GIF file, color the background a shade that is not in the photo.

Mark chose a blue-gray *(Note: Pick a shade that has a color and tonal value close to the background because both Transparency and DeBabelizer leave a tiny trail of pixels around the edge of the image.)*

2. Make the background transparent (Using Transparency).

a. Use the File|Open GIF command in the Transparency software to open the GIF file.

b. Press and hold the mouse pointer on the background shade. When you let go of the mouse, the background will change to a gray color. This shade is now transparent.

2a.

c. Choose Save As from the File menu, and select GIF89.

2c.

3. Make the background transparent (using **DeBabelizer**).

a. Use the File|Open command in DeBabilizer software to open the GIF file.

b. Select Options|Dithering & Background Color from the Palette pull-down menu.

3b.

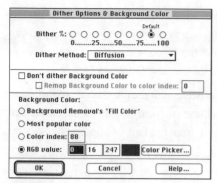

3c.

3d.

c. Click the RGB radio button at the bottom of the screen.

d. Use the Eyedropper tool to select the background shade you'd like to be transparent.

e. Choose Save As from the File pull-down menu.

f. Select GIF|Interlaced & Transparency from the pop-up box.

3f.

g. DeBabelizer will give your file name a .GIF extension. Save the file.

4. Use SimpleText to create an HTML file.

SimpleText from Apple Computer is a useful tool for creating HTML files. It's small (77 K), it's distributed with System 7.5, and it saves HTML text files in the ASCII form that's required by browser programs. Microsoft Word users can save a text file as Text Only or as ASCII.

a. Open SimpleText. Use SimpleText or a your word processor. If you use a word processor, be sure to save the document as Text Only.

b. Create a new HTML document. Start a new document with the following markup tags:

```
<HTML>
<HEAD>
<TITLE>Wrapping Text</TITLE>
</HEAD>
<BODY>
```

c. **Add an image tag.**

```
<HTML>
<HEAD>
<TITLE>Wrapping Text</TITLE>
</HEAD>
<BODY>
<IMG SRC = "MarkT.gif">
```

d. **Add an ALIGN attribute to your <IMG> tag.**
The ALIGN attribute in an <IMG> tag controls the way the image aligns with text. In this next example, ALIGN=LEFT moves the image to the left edge of the page and the text wraps around on the right.

```
<IMG SRC = "MarkT.gif" ALIGN=LEFT>
```

e. **Add headlines and HTML headline tags.** The HTML tags for headlines range from <H1>…</H1> through <H6>…</H6>. <H1> is the largest headline size available, and <H6> is the smallest. The actual size of this type will be relative to whatever the Web visitor has set as a default font size in his or her browser. For example, if a Web visitor has never altered the font size in Netscape's Preferences dialog box, the default size for body text will be 12 points.

All of the headline or title sizes will be relative to this basefont size. In this example, *Mark Elbert* and *Bassist* have been tagged with headline tags <H2> and <H3>.

```
<HTML>
<HEAD>
<TITLE>Wrapping Text</TITLE>
</HEAD>
<BODY>
<IMG SRC = "MarkT.gif" ALIGN=LEFT>
<H2>Mark Elbert></H2><P>
<H3>Bassist</H3><P>
```

Mark Elbert

Bassist

2f1.

Mark Elbert

Bassist

2f2.

f. Use the font size tag (optional). Font size can be controlled with the <FONT SIZE=value> tag where values range from 1 through 7. In this system, the basefont has a value of 3.

This tag can also be written with a preceding + or - to indicate a size that is relative to the basefont. The entire headline or just the initial capital can be controlled, depending on the placement of the tags.

Notice the tag is placed inside the headline tag and the ending </Font> tag is required.

```
<H2><FONT SIZE=+3>Mark Elbert</FONT></H2><P>
<H3><FONT SIZE=+3>Bassist</FONT></H3><P>
```

In this example, the font size tag is used to make the initial capital larger:

```
<H2><FONT SIZE=+3>M</FONT>ark
<FONT SIZE=+3>E</FONT>lbert</H2><P>
<H3><FONT SIZE=+3>B</FONT>assist</H3><P>
```

g. Add comment lines to your document (optional).
Comment lines are ignored by the browser and will never show up on your Web page. They provide a means of documenting the details of how the document was constructed. Use <!....--> to create comments. For example:

```
<!--This text changes the first week of each month.-->
```

(Note: Avoid using special characters such as <, >, &, and ! in comment lines.)

h. Add the body text and ending tags.

```
<HTML>
<HEAD>
<TITLE>Wrapping Text</TITLE>
<BODY>
</HEAD>
<IMG SRC = "MarkT.gif" ALIGN=LEFT>
<H2>Mark Elbert></H2><P>
<H3>Bassist</H3><P>
Mark, co-founder of Mother Mary, hails originally
from Bowie, Maryland…
</Body>
</HTML>
```

i. Test the HTML document in Netscape. Open your document in Netscape to test the appearance of your Web page.

3. Flip the image, and try an ALIGN attribute.

Text can wrap differently if you use the ALIGN attribute in the <IMG> tag. In this example, to get text to wrap on the left side of the image, Mark used the ALIGN=RIGHT in the <IMG> tag.

a. Open the image in Photoshop. If the image needs to be reversed, flip it in Photoshop (or DeBabelizer).

b. Flip the image. Select Flip|Horizontal from the Image pull-down menu.

c. Resave as a GIF image. Select Save As from the File pull-down menu, and give the image another name.

d. Make the background transparent. Use Transparency or DeBabelizer to make the image transparent. *(Note: Because Photoshop cannot write the transparent GIF information into the document header, this information is lost if you edit and save your document in Photoshop.)*

e. Add the ALIGN attribute to the HTML file.

```
<HTML>
<HEAD>
<TITLE>Wrapping Text</TITLE>
</HEAD>
<BODY>
<IMG SRC = "MarkT.gif"ALIGN=RIGHT>
<H2>Mark Elbert></H2><P>
<H3>Bassist</H3><P>
Mark, co-founder of Mother Mary, hails originally from
    Bowie, Maryland…
</BODY>
</HTML>
```

f. Resave the document, and test it in Netscape. Although the other ALIGN attributes (RIGHT, TOP, BOTTOM, and MIDDLE) are not appropriate for Mark's image, you may want to test others with smaller images.

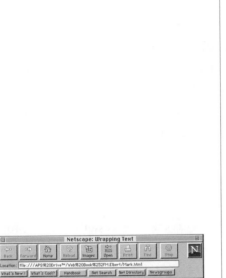

3f.

Controlling text wrap with HTML

Summary: *Use HTML <IMG> tag attributes VSPACE and HSPACE as a way to control text wrap around an image.*

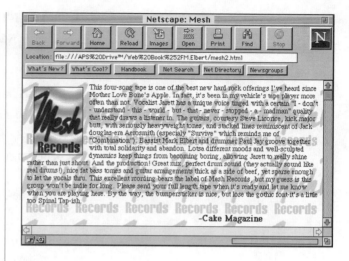

1a.

In this example, Mark used attributes HSPACE and VSPACE with an <IMG> tag. By assigning each a value in the HTML document, a text offset could be controlled.

1. An image with no extra background.

a. Open the image in Photoshop. Crop any extra background off the image that will have a text runaround.

b. Save as a GIF image. Select Save As from the File pull-down menu, and save the image as a CompuServe GIF file.

2. Use SimpleText to create an HTML file.

a. Open Simpletext. Use SimpleText or your word processor. If you use a word processor, be sure to save the document as Text Only.

b. Create a new HTML document. Start a new document with the following markup tags:

```
<HTML>
<HEAD>
<TITLE>Wrapping Text</TITLE>
</HEAD>
<BODY>
```

Tip: With Netscape and SimpleText both open, try varying the numbers assigned to VSPACE and HSPACE, re-save your text file, switch to Netscape, and reload the SimpleText file to see the results.

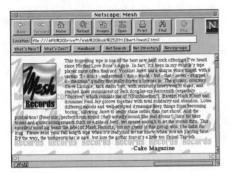

2f.

c. **Add an image tag.**

```
<HTML>
<HEAD>
<TITLE>Wrapping Text</TITLE>
</HEAD>
<BODY>
<IMG SRC = "Mesh Wave.gif">
```

d. **Add the alignment tags.**

```
<HTML>
<HEAD>
<TITLE>Wrapping Text</TITLE>
</HEAD>
<BODY>
<IMG SRC = "Mesh Wave.gif" ALIGN=LEFT VSPACE=5
    HSPACE=10>
```

e. **Add the body text and ending tags.**

```
<HTML>
<HEAD>
<TITLE>Wrapping Text</TITLE>
</HEAD>
<BODY>
<IMG SRC = "Mesh Wave.gif" ALIGN=LEFT VSPACE=5
    HSPACE=10>
This four-song tape is one of the best new hard rock
    offerings I've heard since Mother Love Bone's Apple…
</BODY>
</HTML>
```

f. **Test the HTML document in Netscape.** Open Netscape, and then open your document by selecting Open File from the File pull-down menu. Make sure your HTML document and your image are in the same directory.

Tip: For information and instructions on how to upload files to your Internet provider's server, see the Image Map *chapter.*

3. Summary of HTML tags used in this section.

The tags you see in this list (in alphabetical order) reflect the HTML 3.2 specification.

<BODY>…</BODY>

A tag used to open and close the body of a document.

<FONT SIZE=VALUE>…</FONT>

A tag used to change the default font size. Values range from 1 through 7. The tag can also be written with a preceding + or - to indicate a size that is relative to the basefont.

<H2>…</H2>
<H3>…</H3>

Tags used to enlarge text, as to indicate a heading. Lower numbers indicate larger type. The options range from <H1> through <H6>.

<HTML>…</HTML>

A tag used to open and close an HTML document.

<HEAD>…</HEAD>

A tag used to open and close the header portion of a document.

<IMG>

Used to refer to an inline image, this tag uses the SRC attribute that represents the URL (location) of the image. For example:

```
<IMG SRC = "clear.gif">
```

This tag uses the ALIGN attribute (or parameter) to indicate the placement of an inline image. Options include TOP, BOTTOM, LEFT, and RIGHT. For example:

```
<IMG SRC = "Mesh Wave.gif" ALIGN=LEFT>
```

Tip: *ClarisWorks includes an HTML import and export feature that is built into the software's XTND functions. The software also includes templates for creating Web documents. (http://www.claris .com/products/claris/clarispage20/clarispage20.html)*

The <IMG> tag also uses the HSPACE attribute, which adds space on both sides of an image. For example:

```
<IMG SRC = "Mesh Wave.gif" ALIGN=LEFT HSPACE=20>
```

<P>

A tag used to indicate a new paragraph. This tag does not require an ending tag.

<TITLE>…</TITLE>

A tag used to describe the title of a document that shows up inside a document's title bar.

Fading an image into the browser background

Summary: Photoshop's gradient tool and Quick Mask option can be used to "fade" an image to the gray that matches most browser backgrounds.

1a.

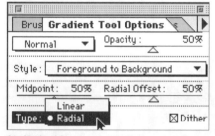

1a, 1b, 1c, 1d.

2b.

2c.

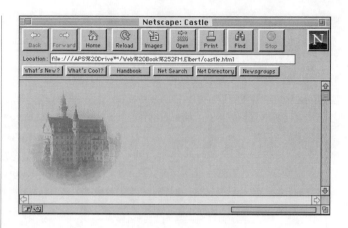

Photoshop's strength is image editing. In this example, Mark Elbert discovered a method to fade an image into the browser background. A similar technique can also be used to create a "fuzzy" drop shadow.

1. Adjust Photoshop's gradient tool.

Open your image in Photoshop, and adjust Photoshop's gradient tool setting.

a. Double click on the gradient tool (Figure 1a), and select Radial from the Type pop-up menu.

b. Drag the Opacity slider to 50%.

c. Drag the Radial Offset slider to 50%.

d. Drag the Midpoint slider to 50%.

2. Work in Quick Mask Mode.

a. Double click on the Quick Mask icon at the base of the Toolbox.

2a.

b. Select Color Indicates Masked Areas, and type 50% in the Color, Opacity field.

c. With the Quick Mask icon still selected, use the crosshair pointer provided in this mode, and draw a radius line from the center of your image outward and release the mouse button.

d. Switch to Selection Mode by clicking the icon to the left of the QuickMask Mode icon at the base of the Toolbox.

2d.

3a.

○ **R:** 201
○ **G:** 201
○ **B:** 201

3b.

3. Set the background color.

a. Double click on the background color swatch at the base of the Toolbox.

b. Type *201* into the R, G, and B fields. Click on OK.

4. Subtract the "unmasked" part of the image.

When you mask the middle of your image with a radial gradient mask, you protect the shaded area from further image manipulation in the Selection Mode.

With a background shade equivalent to the gray you find in most browser backgrounds, press the Delete key.

The image will appear to fade into the gray color. By varying the Midpoint setting in the Gradient Tool Options palette, you can make the mask stronger or weaker in the middle.

5. Create an HTML file to test your image.

a. Create an HTML document with an <IMG> tag.

```
<HTML>
<HEAD>
<TITLE>Castle</TITLE>
</HEAD>
<BODY>
<IMG SRC ="Castle.gif">
</BODY>
</HTML>
```

b. Save the file. Save the document in SimpleText, TeachText, or your word processor. If you're using a word processor, save the text as ASCII or Text Only. Give the file a name and add an .HTML extension.

c. Test the HTML document in Netscape. Open Netscape, and then open your document by selecting Open File from the File pull-down menu. Make sure your HTML document and your image are in the same directory.

Castle (RGB, 2:1)

213K/108K

4.

Create a tiled background

Summary: Using Netscape extensions to HTML, an image can be tiled in the browser window.

1a.

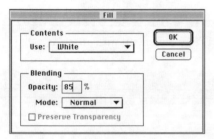

2a, 2b, 2c, 2d, 2e.

2f.

To create a wallpaper effect, Mark used a small photo and ghosted it with a white fill at an opacity level of 85%. By keeping the background very light, type can be loaded on top and still be readable. Using the Netscape extensions to HTML, he created an HTML document that tiled the image across the browser's background.

1. Create a tile.

When you're planning a tile pattern, any size image may be used. Netscape will repeat the image to fill the background. Working in RGB Mode, reduce the size of your image to the desired size of your tile.

2. Ghost the image.

a. Choose Select All from the Select pull-down menu.

b. Select Fill from the Edit pull-down menu.

c. Select White from the Use pop-up menu.

d. Type 85% in the Opacity field.

e. Select Normal from the Mode pop-up menu. Click on OK.

f. The resulting image is shown in Figure 2f.

3. Reduce the bit depth.

Before you save, select Indexed Color from the Mode pull-down menu. Experiment to see how much you can reduce the bit depth without altering the image. Always select Adaptive Palette, and Diffusion Dither.

4. Save this image as a GIF file.

Choose Save As from the File pull-down menu, and select CompuServe GIF from among the choices on the Format pop-up box.

4.

5. Create an HTML file to test your image.

a. Create an HTML document with an <IMG> tag.

```
<HTML>
<HEAD>
<TITLE>Mesh</TITLE>
</HEAD>
<BODY>
<IMG SRC ="Mesh.gif">
</BODY>
</HTML>
```

b. Save the file. Save the document in SimpleText, TeachText, or your word processor. If you're using a word processor, save the text as ASCII or Text Only. Give the file a name, and add an .HTML extension

c. Test the HTML document in Netscape. Open Netscape, and then open your document by selecting Open File from the File pull-down menu. Make sure your HTML document and your image are in the same directory.

5c.

Create a full-bleed photo background with larger tiles

Summary: *Netscape will tile any size image. Larger images will appear to be full-bleed images.*

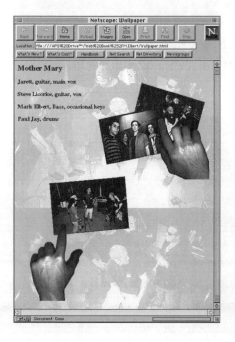

To create a full-bleed photo background, Mark filled in a black-and-white photo with white, in order to ghost the image. Using the Netscape extensions to HTML, he created an HTML document, which causes the full image to fill the browser's background.

1. Follow steps for creating a tiled background.
When you're planning a tile pattern, any size image may be used. Netscape will repeat the image to fill the background. Follow the steps for creating a tiled background, presented earlier in this chapter and shown here:

   a. Create a tile.

   b. Ghost the image.

   c. Reduce the bit depth.

   d. Save the image as a GIF file.

   e. Create an HTML file to test your image.

2. The background tiles as you add content.
You will not be able to scroll and look at the tiled background until you've added content to your HTML file.

Creating a silhouette on an image background

Summary: Silhouettes are created using a transparent GIF image. In this example, the background loads first when the Web page opens, and the silhouette can be loaded on top as an interlaced or non-interlaced image.

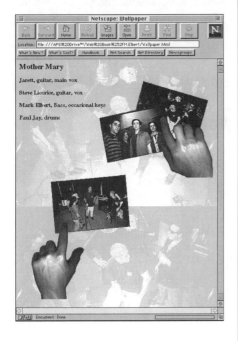

Tip: *See the* Page Layout Tools *chapter for instructions on how to use PhotoGIF, a Photoshop plug-in that will make GIF files transparent.*

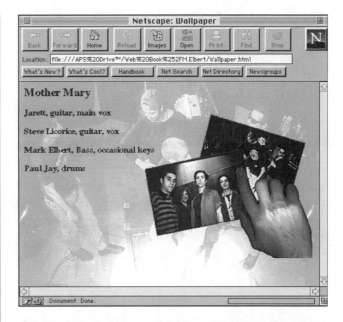

In this example, the positioning of the silhouette images was a greater challenge than the creation of the transparent GIF images. To position the transparent GIF images down the page, Mark Elbert experimented with the VSPACE attribute in the second image tag.

1. Make your image background transparent (using Transparency).

a. Use the File|Open GIF command in the Transparency software to open the GIF file.

b. Press and hold the mouse pointer on the background shade. When you let go of the mouse, the background will change to a gray color. This shade is now transparent.

c. Choose Save As from the File menu, and select GIF89.

2. Make your image background transparent (using DeBabelizer).

a. Use the File|Open command in DeBabelizer software to open the GIF file.

b. Select Options|Dithering & Background Color from the Palette pull-down menu.

c. Click the RGB radio button at the bottom of the screen.

Tip: *MacLink/Plus, a well-known trans-lation utility from Dataviz now converts Mac and Windows formats to and from HTML (http://www.dataviz.com/Upgrade/-upgmlp_home.html).*

d. Use the Eyedropper tool to select the background shade you'd like to be transparent.

e. Choose Save As from the File pull-down menu.

f. Select GIF|Interlaced Transparent from the pop-up box.

g. DeBabelizer will give your file name a GIF extension. Save the file.

3. Use SimpleText to create an HTML file.

a. Open SimpleText. Use SimpleText or your word processor. If you use a word processor, be sure to save the document as Text Only.

b. Create a new HTML document. Start a new document with the following markup tags:

```
<HTML>
<HEAD>
<TITLE>Wrapping Text</TITLE>
</HEAD>
```

c. Add a body background tag.

```
<HTML>
<HEAD>
<TITLE>Wrapping Text</TITLE>
</HEAD>
<IMG SRC = "MarkT.gif">
<BODY BACKGROUND="Toronto_Lg.gif">
```

d. Add an image tag.

```
<HTML>
<HEAD>
<TITLE>Wrapping text </TITLE>
<BODY BACKGROUND="Toronto_Lg.gif">
<IMG SRC="MarkT.gif">
```

e. Add a headline tag.

```
<HTML>
<HEAD>
<TITLE>Wrapping Text</TITLE>
</HEAD>
<BODY BACKGROUND="Toronto_Lg.gif">
<IMG SRC = "MarkT.gif">
<H2>Mother Mary</H2>
```

Tip: Microsoft provides free copies of their Internet Assistant software for Microsoft Word and Micosoft Excel users. The Assistant tools convert Word and Excel documents into HTML-equivalent documents. Visit http://www.microsoft.com/word/fs_wd .htm and http://www.microsoft.com /msexcel/internet/ia.

f. Add a group of nested definition list tags.

```
<HTML>
<HEAD>
<TITLE>Wrapping Text</TITLE>
</HEAD>
<BODY BACKGROUND="Toronto_Lg.gif">
<IMG SRC = "MarkT.gif">
<H2>Mother Mary</H2>
<DL><DL><DL><DL><DL><IMG
SRC="Hand50_bbT.gif"></DL></DL></DL></DL></DL>
```

g. Insert the ALIGN=RIGHT attribute in the image tag.

```
<HTML>
<HEAD>
<TITLE>Wrapping Text</TITLE>
</HEAD>
<BODY BACKGROUND="Toronto_Lg.gif">
<IMG SRC = "MarkT.gif">
<H2>Mother Mary</H2>
<DL><DL><DL><DL><DL><IMG
SRC="Hand50_bbT.gif"ALIGN=RIGHT></DL></DL></DL>
</DL></DL>
```

h. Add four more headlines.

```
<HTML>
<HEAD>
<TITLE>Wrapping Text</TITLE>
</HEAD>
<BODY BACKGROUND="Toronto_Lg.gif">
<IMG SRC = "MarkT.gif">
<H2>Mother Mary</H2>
<DL><DL><DL><DL><DL><IMG
SRC="Hand50_bbT.gif"ALIGN=RIGHT></DL>
</DL></DL></DL></DL>
<H3>Jarett, guitar, main vox</H3>
<H3>Steve Licorice, guitar, vox</H3>
<H3>Mark Elbert, bass, occasional keys</H3>
<H3>Paul Jay, drums</H3>
```

Tip: NetObjects Fusion is a hot new page layout software tool for graphic designers who want to create Web documents. Founded in November 1995 by Rae Technology Inc. and Studio Archetype (formerly Clement Mok Design), NetObjects, Inc, has introduced NetObjects Fusion for Windows 95/NT and the Power Macintosh.

Tip: Download a 30-day trial version of NetObjects Fusion from http://www .netobjects.com

i. Add a second image tag.

```
<HTML>
<HEAD>
<TITLE>Wrapping Text</TITLE>
</HEAD>
<BODY BACKGROUND="Toronto_Lg.gif">
<IMG SRC = "MarkT.gif">
<H2>Mother Mary</H2>
<DL><DL><DL><DL><DL><IMG
    SRC="Hand50_bbT.gif"ALIGN=RIGHT></DL>
    </DL></DL></DL></DL>
<H3>Jarett, guitar, main vox</H3>
<H3>Steve Licorice, guitar, vox</H3>
<H3>Mark Elbert, bass, occasional keys</H3>
<H3>Paul Jay, drums</H3>
<IMG SRC="BackT2.gif">
```

j. Add the VSPACE attribute to the second image tag.

```
<HTML>
<HEAD>
<TITLE>Wrapping Text</TITLE>
</HEAD>
<BODY BACKGROUND="Toronto_Lg.gif">
<IMG SRC = "MarkT.gif">
<H2>Mother Mary</H2>
<DL><DL><DL><DL><DL><IMG
    SRC="Hand50_bbT.gif"ALIGN=RIGHT></DL>
    </DL></DL></DL></DL>
<H3>Jarett, guitar, main vox</H3>
<H3>Steve Licorice, guitar, vox</H3>
<H3>Mark Elbert, bass, occasional keys</H3>
<H3>Paul Jay, drums</H3>
<IMG SRC="BackT2.gif" VSPACE=120>
```

k. Add ending tags.

```
</Body>
</HTML>
```

Tip: *For information and instructions on how to upload files to your Internet provider's server, see the* Image Map *chapter.*

4. HTML tags used in this section.

The tags you see in this list (in alphabetical order) reflect the HTML 3.2 specification.

<BODY>…</BODY>

A tag used to open and close the body of a document. This tag can be used to refer to a background image in the form:

```
<Body BACKGROUND="Toronto_Lg.gif">
```

<DL>…</DL>

The definition list tag is usually used for definitions or short paragraphs with no bullets or numbering. In this section, this tag is nested seven times in order to indent the Mesh Records logo. For example:

```
<DL><DL><DL><DL><DL><DL><DL><IMG
SRC="Hand50_bbT.gif"></DL>
</DL></DL></DL></DL></DL></DL>
```

<H2>…</H2>
<H3>…</H3>

Tags used to enlarge text, as to indicate a heading. Lower numbers indicate larger type, and the options range from <H1> through <H6>.

<HEAD>…</HEAD>

A tag used to open and close the header portion of a document.

<HTML>…</HTML>

A tag used to open and close an HTML document.

<IMG>

Used to refer to an inline image, this tag uses the SRC attribute that represents the URL (location) of the image. For example:

```
<IMG SRC="Mesh Wave.gif">
```

This tag uses the ALIGN attribute (or parameter) to indicate the placement of an inline image. Options include TOP, BOTTOM, LEFT, and RIGHT. For example:

```
<IMG SRC="Hand50_bbT.gif" ALIGN=RIGHT>
```

This tag also uses the VSPACE attribute, which adds space above and below an image. For example:

```
<IMG SRC="Mesh Wave.gif" VSPACE=120>
```

<TITLE>...</TITLE>

A tag used to describe the title of a document which shows up inside a document's title bar.

Creating a drop shadow in Photoshop

Summary: Use Photoshop's selection tools and channels to record the outline of an image. Next, create a drop shadow by blurring the edge of the shadow's channel image with the Gaussian Blur filter and filling the selection with 50% black.

1a.

⦿ R: 201
◯ G: 201
◯ B: 201

1b.

1c.

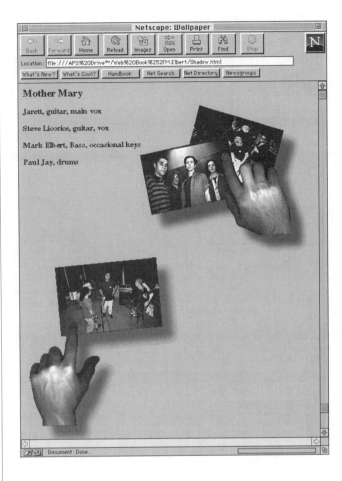

In this example, Mark created "fuzzy" drop shadows for photo silhouettes in Photoshop by using channels. Because he planned to make the background of each silhouette transparent, Mark minimized the amount of "fringe" from the fuzzy drop shadow by starting with a gray background that was very similar to the gray in the browser background.

1. Set the image background color to gray.

  a. With the Magic Wand tool, select the background of the object that will have a drop shadow.

  b. Double click the background color sample in the Toolbox and type *201, 201, 201* as an RGB value. This gray is very close to the browser background.

  c. With the background still selected, press the Select key to fill the background with the specified shade of gray.

2b.

2c.

2d.

2f.

2. Create two channels.

a. If it is not still selected, select the background of the object that will be shadowed.

b. Choose Inverse from the Select pull-down menu.

c. With the object selected, select Palettes|Show Channels from the Window pull-down menu.

d. Press on the Channels pop-up menu, and select New Channel

e. Give the channel the same name as your object.

```
Channel Options
Name: hand                          OK
Color Indicates:                    Cancel
  ● Masked Areas
  ○ Selected Areas
Color
  [  ]    Opacity: 50 %
```
2e.

f. To create the second channel, which will be the shadow channel, select Duplicate Channel from the Channel pop-up menu.

g. Name this channel *shadow*.

```
Duplicate Channel
Duplicate: hand                     OK
    As: shadow                      Cancel
Destination
Document: BackT2.gif ▼
    Name: [                    ]
          □ Invert
```
2g.

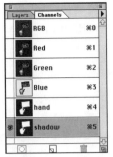

3a.

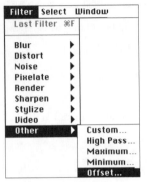

3b.

4a.

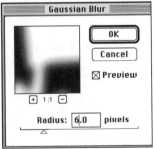

4b.

3. Use the Offset filter.

The shadow will need to be offset to the right and down at least 20 pixels in each direction. The offset filter will make this change.

a. Select the Shadow channel in the Channels palette.

b. Select Other|Offset from the Filter pull-down menu.

c. Select Repeat Edge Pixels. Fill in *20* for Horizontal Pixels Right and Vertical Pixels Down.

d. Click on OK.

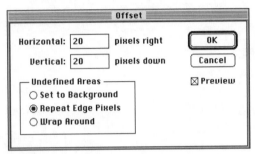

3c, 3d.

4. Gaussian Blur creates the "fuzziness."

a. With the Shadow channel still selected, choose Blur|Gaussian Blur from the Filter pull-down menu.

b. Type in *6* pixels, and click on OK.

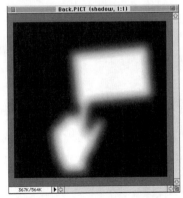

4.

5a, 6a, 7a.

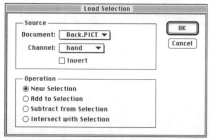

5b, 7b.

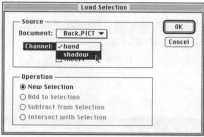

6b.

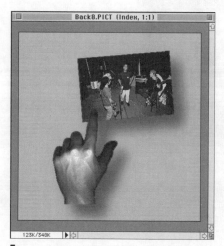

7c.

5. Copy the hand to the Clipboard.

Use the Hand channel to select the hand and copy it to the Clipboard.

a. Choose Load Selection from the Select pull-down menu.

b. Select Hand from the pop-up menu that follows.

c. Select Copy from the Edit pull-down menu.

6. Load the Shadow selection and do a fill.

a. Choose Load Selection from the Select pull-down menu.

b. Select Shadow from the pop-up menu that follows.

c. Choose Fill from the Edit pull-down menu.

d. Select Black from the Use pop-up box on the Fill dialog box.

e. Type 50% in the Opacity box, select Normal in the Mode pop-up, and click on OK.

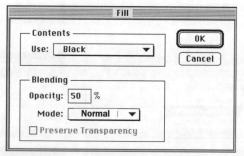

6c, 6d, 6e.

7. Paste an original of the hand on-top.

a. Reload the Hand channel by choosing Load Selection from the Select pull-down menu.

b. Select Hand from the pop-up menu that follows.

c. Choose Past from the Edit pull-down menu. The result is shown in Figure 7c.

8. Reduce the pixel depth (in Photoshop).

When Mark finished editing the image in RGB Mode, he experimented with Photoshop's Indexed Color Mode to see how far he could reduce the pixel depth without altering the color. *(Note: See the next section for instructions on how to reduce the bit depth in DeBabelizer.)*

8a.

a. Select Indexed Color from the Mode pull-down menu.

b. Experiment by selecting smaller bit depths with and without dithering to see how the color in your image holds up. If you don't like the color, select Edit|Undo or press Command+Z.

Mark was able to reduce the image to a 6-bit color depth without a noticeable change in the color. This made a significant change in the file size.

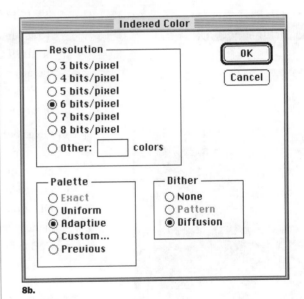

8b.

9. Reduce pixel depth (using DeBabelizer).

a. Open your RGB image in DeBabelizer.

b. Select Change Pixel Depth from the Palette pull-down menu. Equilibrium Technologies recommends that you always select dithering when you reduce the number of colors. Although you can change the amount of dithering by selecting Options|Dithering Options & Background Color from the Palette pull-down menu, DeBabelizer's default setting is the amount Equilibrium has determined is best.

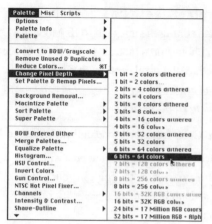

9b.

10b.

11a.

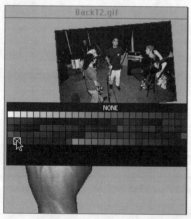

11b.

Start by reducing your image to 128 colors and look at the image. If you don't like the change, select Undo from the Edit pull-down menu or press Command+Z. Keep stepping down to fewer colors to determine when the color change becomes visible. Mark was able to reduce the palette to 64 colors (as shown in Figure 9b) without a noticeable change in the image.

10. Save the Image.

a. Select Save As from the File pull-down menu (in Photoshop or DeBabelizer).

b. Select CompuServe GIF or JPEG from the pop-up menu. *(Note: Photoshop 3.0 does not add interlacing to GIF images. Interlacing gives the Web visitor the impression of a faster download by quickly painting the image in low resolution and gradually filling it in.)*

To add interlacing to a Photoshop GIF image, you'll need GIFConverter by Kevin Mitchell. DeBabelizer also has an option to save a file as an Interlaced GIF. *(Note: GIFConverter is available on the CD-ROM in the back of this book.)*

c. Give your image a name, and try to keep your file name to a minimum of eight characters (no spaces) with a file extension such as .GIF, .JPG, or .JPEG. *(Note: File extensions must be limited to three characters on the DOS/IBM platform.)* Removing vowels from the file name helps reduce the number of characters. Mark used DeBabelizer and chose Interlaced GIF as the file format for saving.

11. Make the background transparent (using Transparency).

a. Use the File|Open GIF command in the Transparency software to open the GIF file.

b. Press and hold the mouse pointer on the background shade. When you let go of the mouse, the background will change to a gray color. This shade is now transparent.

c. Choose Save As from the File menu, and select GIF89.

11c.

12a.

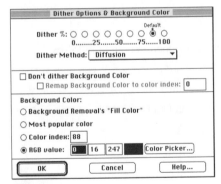

12c.

12d.

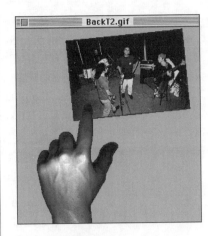

12. Make the background transparent (using DeBabelizer).

a. Use the File|Open command in DeBabelizer software to open the GIF file.

b. Select Options|Dithering & Background Color from the Palette pull-down menu.

12b.

c. Click the RGB radio button at the bottom of the screen.

d. Use the Eyedropper tool to select the background shade you'd like to be transparent.

e. Choose Save As from the File pull-down menu.

f. Select GIF|Interlaced & Transparency from the pop-up box.

12f.

g. DeBabelizer will give your file name a GIF extension. Save the file.

Tip: Visit the Submit It site and fill out a form that is part of a free service to list your site with 17 online directories—simultaneously (http://submit-it.perma-link.com/submit-it).

13. Use SimpleText to create an HTML file.

SimpleText from Apple Computer is a useful tool for creating HTML files. It's small (77 K), it's distributed with System 7.5, and it saves HTML text files in the ASCII form that's required by browser programs. Microsoft Word users can save a text file as Text Only or ASCII.

a. Open Simpletext. Use SimpleText or a your word processor. If you use a word processor, be sure to save the document as Text Only.

b. Create a new HTML document with an <IMG> tag. Start a new document with the following markup tags:

```
<HTML>
<HEAD>
<TITLE>Wrapping Text</TITLE>
</HEAD>
<BODY>
<IMG SRC="Back.gif">
</BODY>
</HTML>
```

c. Add an image tag.

```
<HTML>
<HEAD>
<TITLE>Wrapping Text</TITLE>
```

d. Save the file. Save the document in Simple Text, TeachText, or your word processor. If you're using a word processor, save the text as ASCII or Text Only. Give the file a name and add an .HTML extension.

```
<BODY>
```

e. Test the HTML document in Netscape. Open Netscape, and then open your document by selecting Open File from the File Pull down menu. Make sure your HTML document and your image aare in the same directory.

Jane Greenbaum's tips on creating a drop shadow in Painter 4.0

Summary: *Use the Create Drop Shadow command in Painter to create an automatic drop shadow.*

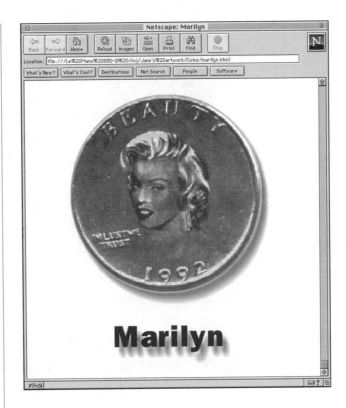

D rop shadows are a one-step procedure in Painter if an image is a floater. *Floaters* are elements created in a Painter document that behave like objects. They are discreet images that will not interfere with other design elements. Text elements created in Painter are considered to be vector-based objects or shapes and are therefore considered to be a type of floater. Image floaters behave like objects, but unlike shapes, they have pixel information stored as a mask instead of vector-based stroke and fill information.

In this section, Jane creates text with a drop shadow and then uses similar steps to create a drop shadow around an image that has been saved in a Photoshop layer. An image saved in a Photoshop layer will automatically be treated as a floater in Painter. (*Note: If you wish to follow the steps in this section, look for Jane's image on the companion CD-ROM.*)

Painter 4.0.3

1a.

1. Create text with a drop shadow.

a. Open Painter.

b. Select New from the File pull-down menu.

c. In the dialog box that follows, type *600 (pixels)* in the field labeled Width, *600 (pixels)* in the field labeled Height, and *72.0 (pixels per inch)* in the field labeled Resolution. Click on OK.

1b.

1c.

1d.

d. An untitled document will open.

e. Select the Text tool.

f. Select Controls from the Window pull-down menu.

g. In the Controls Text dialog box that follows, select Other Font from the Font pop-up menu.

1e.

1f.

1g.

1h.

h. In the Choose Font dialog box that follows, select a font, and click on OK.

i. Once you have selected a font in the Controls Text dialog box, use your mouse to move the Font Size slider to set the font size to 24 points.

j. Put the Controls Text dialog box away by clicking on the close box with your pointer arrow.

1i.   **1j.**

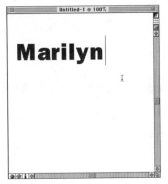

1k.

k. With the Text tool still selected, click on the untitled document, and type `Marilyn`.

l. As Painter creates individual text shapes in the untitled document, each letter will be represented as a separate floater in the Objects Floater List as shown.

m. Click on the Group button in the Objects Floater List.

n. The list will collapse to one Object Floater labeled Group 1. The object should be shaded, indicating that it is selected.

o. If the Group 1 object in the Object Floater List is not selected, click to the right of the object's name to select it in the list.

1m.

1l.   **1n.**

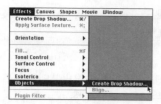

1p.

p. Select Objects|Create Drop Shadow from the Effects pull-down menu.

q. In the dialog box that follows, type *10* in the field labeled X-Offset, *15* in the field labeled Y-Offset, and *45* in the field labeled Opacity. Click on OK.

1q.

r. A drop shadow will appear.

1r.

2. Save your image.

a. Select Save As from the File pull-down menu.

b. In the dialog box that follows, select GIF from the Type pop-up menu.

c. Type a name in the field labeled Save Image As, and click on Save.

2a.

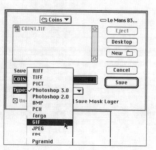

2b.

2c.

2d.

d. In the dialog box that follows, click on OK.

e. In the Save As GIF Options dialog box that follows, accept the default settings by clicking on OK.

2e.

3. Create an image with a drop shadow.

Images saved in a Photoshop layer are automatically treated as a floater in Painter. Although Painter has selection tools that may be used to create a floater, the selection tools are not as easy to use as the comparable tools in Photoshop.

Adobe Photoshop™

3a.

a. Open Photoshop

b. Select Open from the File pull-down menu.

c. Select a graphic in the dialog box that follows, and click on Open.

3b.

3c.

3d.

3e.

d. Your image will open in a Photoshop window.

e. Select the Magic Wand tool.

f. Click on the solid background.

g. The background will be enclosed with "marching ants," indicating that it is selected.

3f.

3g.

h. Select Inverse from the Select pull-down menu.

i. The image will be selected instead of the background.

3h.

3i.

j. Select Copy from the Edit pull-down menu.

k. Select Paste Layer from the Edit pull-down menu.

3j.

3k.

3l.

4a.

l. In the dialog box that follows, type a name for the new layer, and click on OK.

4. Save your image.

a. Select Save As from the File pull-down menu.

b. In the dialog box that follows, select Photoshop from the Format pop-up menu.

c. Type a name for your image, and click on Save.

d. In the dialog box that follows, click on Replace.

4b.

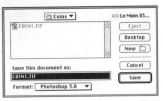

4c.

4d.

5. Quit Photoshop.

a. Select Quit from the File pull-down menu.

5a.

Painter 4.0.3

6a.

6. Open your image in Painter.

a. Open Painter

6b.

b. Select Open from the File pull-down menu.

c. Select your graphic in the dialog box that follows, and click on Open.

d. Your image will open in a Painter window.

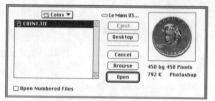

6c.

6d.

7. Enlarge the canvas size in Painter.

a. Select Canvas Size from the Canvas pull-down menu.

b. In the dialog box that follows, type *100* following the word *Add* in each of the fields used to increase the canvas size.

7a.

7b.

8. Zoom out.

a. Select the Magnifying Tool.

8a.

8b.

b. Hold down the Option key, and click on the image.

c. The image will be reduced from 100 percent to 50 percent.

9. Select the image in the Floater List.

a. If the Objects Floater List is not in view, select Objects from the Windows pull-down menu.

b. In the Objects Floater List, click on the image as shown.

c. A rectangular selection will appear around the image.

9a.

9b.

9c.

10a.

10. Create a drop shadow.

a. Select Objects|Create Drop Shadow from the Effects pull-down menu.

10b.

b. In the dialog box that follows, type *10* in the field labeled X-Offset, *15* in the field labeled Y-Offset, and *45* in the field labeled Opacity. Click on OK.

c. A drop shadow will appear.

10c.

11. Deselect the selection rectangle.

a. Select Deselect from the Edit pull-down menu.

b. The selection rectangle will disappear.

11a.

11b.

12a.

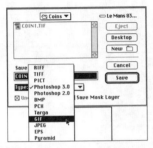

12b.

12. Save your image.

a. Select Save As from the File pull-down menu.

b. In the dialog box that follows, select GIF from the Type pop-up menu.

c. Type a name in the field labeled Save Image As, and click on Save.

d. In the dialog box that follows, click on OK.

e. In the Save As GIF Options dialog box that follows, accept the default settings by clicking on OK.

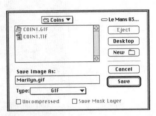

12c.

12d.

12e.

Creating a blue duotone with Photoshop

Summary: Use Photoshop's duotone presets to create a blue duotone.

1b.

1c.

In print, a color duotone is a print made from a mono-chrome original with a second color added for greater detail. The technique is a way to add color to an image without using full color. For the Web, this means a smaller file size and faster downloading.

1. Discard color from a color original.

a. Open your image in Photoshop.

b. Select Grayscale from the Mode pull-down menu.

c. Click on OK when a dialog appears that asks if you're sure you want to discard the color information.

2. Select a duotone.

a. Select Duotone from the Mode pull-down menu.

b. Select Duotone from the pop-up menu.

c. Click on Load to load the Photoshop duotone presets.

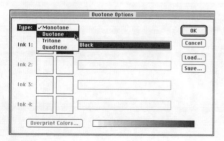

2a.

2b, 2c.

2d.

2f.

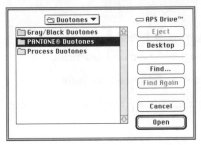

2g.

d. Find the Goodies folder inside the Photoshop software folder, and click it open.

e. Click open the Duotone Presets folder.

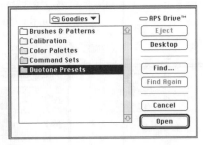

2e.

f. Click open the Duotones folder.

g. Click open the Pantone Duotone folder.

h. Mark selected Blue 286. When he applied this by clicking on the OK button on the Duotone Options dialog box, he decided he wanted the blue to look more saturated.

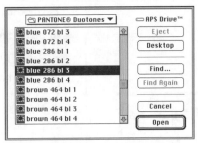

2h.

i. To adjust the amount of blue, Mark clicked opened the duotone curve.

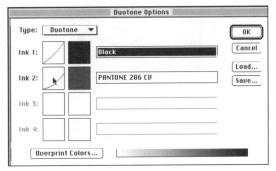

2i.

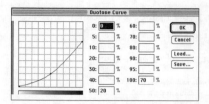

2j1.

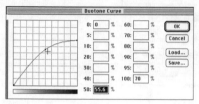

2j2.

3a.

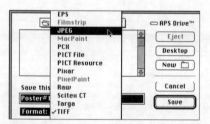

3c.

j. By pushing the curve up (shown at left) and to the left with the mouse, Mark altered the amount of blue in the duotone.

k. He reapplied the duotone information by clicking on OK in the Duotone options dialog box.

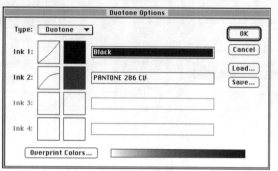

2k.

3. Save the image as a JPEG.

a. Choose RGB from the Mode pull-down menu.

b. Select Save As from the File pull-down menu.

c. Select JPEG from the Format pop-up menu in the Save dialog box.

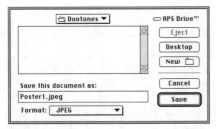

3d.

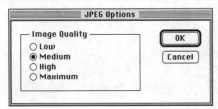

3e.

d. Type in a file name, and use a .JPEG or .JPG extension.

e. Select an image quality in the dialog box that follows.

4. Create an HTML file to test your image.

a. Open SimpleText. Use SimpleText or your word processor. If you use a word processor, be sure to save the document as Text Only.

b. Create a new HTML document. Start a new document with the following markup tags:

```
<HTML>
<HEAD>
<TITLE>Duotone</TITLE>
</HEAD>
<BODY>
```

c. Add the image tag. Reference your JPEG image with the addition of an <IMG> tag.

```
<HTML>
<HEAD>
<TITLE>Duotone</TITLE>
</HEAD>
<BODY>
<IMG SRC ="Poster1.jpeg">
</BODY>
</HTML>
```

d. Test the HTML document in Netscape. Open Netscape, and then open your document by selecting Open File from the File pull-down menu. Make sure your JPEG image and your HTML document are in the same directory.

Creating a Super Palette with DeBabelizer

Summary: *For 8-bit images that you plan to put on the same Web page, create a Super Palette in DeBabelizer because browsers can only read a total of 256 colors.*

DeBabelizer's Super Palette feature is designed to create the best palette of 256 colors for a group of images. Although Equilibrium didn't specifically design this feature for Web graphics, it helps Web artists find a palette that can be used for a group of photos because browsers will only read a total of 256 colors per page. *(Note: This sample demonstrates how to manually create a Super Palette. For information on how to use DeBabelizer's batch mode and scripting feature to process several images at once, see the steps in the* Video *chapter.)*

1. Organize your images.

   a. Create one folder for the images that have not had the Super Palette applied.

   b. Create another folder for images that have the Super Palette applied, and invent a naming convention that will remind you that the Super Palette has been applied.

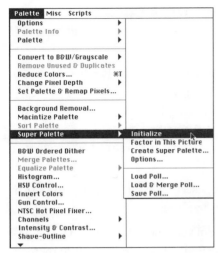

2.

2. Initialize the Super Palette.

To reset the Super Palette, select Super Palette|Initialize from the Palette pull-down menu.

3. Open the first image.

a. Select Open from the File pull-down menu, and open the first image.

b. Select Super Palette|Factor In This Picture from the Palette pull-down menu.

4. Create a Super Palette.

Select Super Palette|Create Super Palette from the Palette pull-down menu.

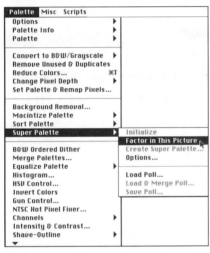

3b.

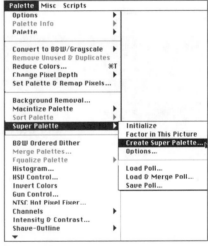

4.

5. Name the Super Palette.

a. Remove the "X" from the box labeled *On Creation Of Super Palette, Macintize It.*

b. Click on the radio button labeled *Call It,* and fill in a name.

c. Click on *Create It.*

5.

7b.

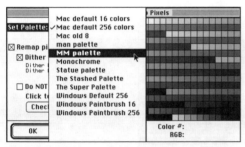

7c.

6. Factor in your other images.

a. Open each one of the other images that will be part of the Super Palette.

b. Select Super Palette|Factor In This Picture from the Palette pull-down menu.

7. Apply your Super Palette.

a. Open each one of the images to be part of the Super Palette.

b. For each image, select Set Palette & Remap Pixels from the Palette pull-down menu.

c. Select the name of your Super Palette from the pop-up menu on the Set Palette & Remap Pixels dialog box.

d. Click on OK.

8. Save your images.

a. Select Save As from the File pull-down menu.

b. Select GIF or JPEG from the Type pop-up menu.

c. Locate the folder designated for the completed images.

d. Click on Save.

Artist featured in this chapter:

Kleber Santos is a senior graphic designer with Straightline International, a New York-based firm specializing in strategic marketing communications. In addition to print, Kleber specializes in the development of electronic programs and multimedia.

santos@slinyc.com

Chapter 7

Client-Side Image Maps

Image maps have become an important feature in the Web interface allowing users to navigate a Web site by clicking different areas in an image. Up until recently, image maps required server transactions. The HTML code required to create the image map was difficult to write because it needed a reference to the image map script the provider had running on his/her Web server. Now, client-side image maps work entirely on the client side—or on the browser.

In this chapter, Kleber Santos sorts out the details related to image maps, including finding coordinates for clickable regions in a map file and creating a client-side image map HTML file.

If you're a Web traveler, you've probably used an image map to navigate. *Image maps* are inline images that have special regions "mapped" to URLs. Anyone who clicks on one of the predefined regions (or *hotspots*) will be taken to the page referenced in the URL. Well-known sites with image maps include: The Spot, a Web site of episodes (http://www.thespot.com); Sony (http://www.sony.com); IUMA or the Internet Underground Music Archive (http://www.iuma.com); and Hot Wired (http://www.hotwired.com).

If you're renting space on an Internet provider's server, this chapter will also lead you through the steps on how to upload your files from your studio or office to your provider's computer.

A virtual walking tour of NY's World Financial Center

Summary: *In this chapter, Kleber Santos provides thorough details on the steps required to create image maps. The first image map was invented by Kevin Hughes (kevinh@eit.com) while he was Webmaster at Honolulu Community College.*

Above: In the World Financial Center, 16 palm trees, each 45 feet high, line the glass-enclosed Winter Garden.

Kleber Santos, a graphic designer with Straightline International in New York City, likes to challenge himself with computer projects to satisfy a curiosity about how things work.

To learn how image maps work, Kleber created a "virtual walking tour" of New York's World Financial Center. Image maps are inline images with hotspots. Clicking on a hotspot links the user to another document with more hotspots. (*Note: If you want to work on this chapter's image map example step-by-step, look for Kleber's art on the companion CD-ROM.*)

Above: Ann Taylor is one of several retail tenants in the World Financial Center (WFC). Created on a landfill adjacent to New York's financial district, the WFC contains more than eight million square feet of office, retail, and recreational space.

Above: When a clickable image map exists on a Web page, the mouse pointer will turn into a hand.

Client-side vs. server-dependent image maps.

Client-side image maps are much easier to create than the original image-map implementation, which is server-dependent. The word *client* refers to the browser. As a result, a client-side image map means the browser processes, or *parses,* the map information, remembers the content, and links to a URL if a user clicks on an active area.

The components of Kleber's map project.

Although Kleber Santos' studio is relatively close to ECHO in New York City, he never had to physically go to the ECHO site because he uploaded his project components through a dial-up PPP connection. *(Note: Although you don't have to be in the same city as your provider, it is recommended that you and your provider be located on the same coast because cross-country Internet traffic can be unreliable.)* To complete his project, Kleber needed the items shown in the following table.

Item	Notes
An image	Kleber used Photoshop to create his photo montage of the shops and restaurants surrounding the World Financial Center's Winter Garden. This step will be familiar to designers. Photoshop is a popular image editor. For one of his image maps, Kleber needed transparent GIF images for silhouetted buttons (Sfuzzi). He used the PhotoGIF plug-in shareware software from BoxTop software. *(Note: PhotoGIF is available on the CD-ROM in the back of this book.)*
Space on an HTTP server	Kleber's image map project resides on ECHO's Web server in New York City. The services a designer can obtain from an Internet provider vary a great deal. Minimally, Kleber needed a dial-up PPP account, which provided access to the Internet and server space.

Curtis Eberhardt, New York, NY

Above: A 3D illustration containing Shockwave movies.

Above Right: Curtis' home page at http://www.new-kewl.com/curtiscape.

Above: A GIF animation from Curtis' Web site.

As an animator, Curtis Eberhardt (CurtisAE@aol.com) is very conscious of bit depth and related file sizes. He recommends that Web artists reduce bit depth as much as possible to maintain a reasonable bandwidth.

Curtis' design tips:

1. **GIF Wizard at http://www.raspberryhill.com/gifwizard.html** is an online tool that reduces the size of your GIF images either on a Web server or on your computer's hard drive.

2. **Use one-bit (black and white) cast members in Director movies.** Instead of importing color cast members into a Director movie, colorize one-bit cast members on Stage to make very small movies for downloading.

3. **GIFBuilder can be used to create individual GIF animation frames.** Use the GIFBuilder Grabber Hand tool, move your art, and save the frame.

Larry Rosenthal, New York, NY

Above: A VRML animation adventure.

Above Right: Larry's Starbase C3 page at http://www.cube3.com/starbase.

Above: A Java-based 3D chat area on Larry's Starbase site written by Dan and Matt O'Donnell of Cicada Web Development (http://www.cicadaweb .com). The 3D chat environment opens in a floating window. The top half is a VRML window containing Larry's 3D models. (Note: Look for Dan and Matt O'Donnell's VRML tips on the companion CD-ROM in the Windows edition.)

Larry Rosenthal (larryr@cube3.com) is an industrial designer, a new media artist, and chairman/founder of New York's VRMLSIG.

Larry's design tips:

1. **When creating VRML models, use 2D models whenever possible.** Use a plane instead of a box for representing walls, floors, bird wings, etc. If a VRML object is not meant to be examined up close and if your modeler can handle polygon-level manipulation, turn a solid object into a surface by removing any unneeded faces. This relieves the renderer from culling faces that are redundant or unnecessary.

2. **VRML 3D chat engines may be customized with your VRML models.** Cicada Web Development and Black Sun Interactive have both developed 3D chat engines that may be used to create your own chat environment.

3. **Web servers need to be configured with the proper MIME settings to display VRML models.** If you wish to display VRML models on your  site, check with your Internet service provider and inquire whether the MIME settings have been set to display VRML models.

Jane Greenbaum,
New York, NY

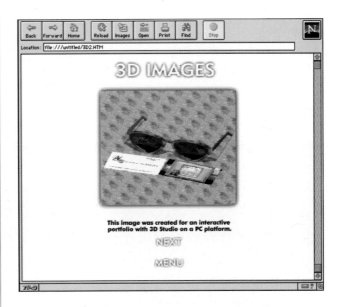

Above and Above Right: Sample pages from Jane's Web site at http://members .aol.com/iforward/image1.htm.

Jane Greenbaum (IForward@aol.com) is a new media artist and vice president of the New York Graphic Artists' Guild.

Jane's design tips:

1. **Using a Web site to display portfolio samples.** If you're using your Web site to display your portfolio, keep it organized and simple.

2. **Publish your Web site offline.** Consider publishing your Web site offline by writing the files to a CD-ROM. The CD-ROM may then be mailed or distributed as a self-promotion piece.

3. **Web visitors will expect fresh material.** Web designers will be expected to update their Web graphics at least once a month. As a result, try to think of ways to update your images without starting from scratch. For example, updating can be accomplished by rearranging the art or floating new objects on the same background.

Frank De Crescenzo, New York, NY

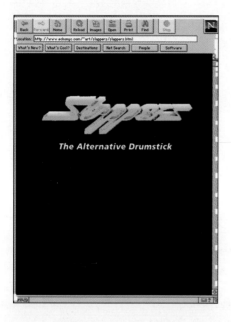

Above: A rotating 3D logo created as a GIF animation.

Above Right: The Slappers home page.

http://members.aol.com/flatsticks/
splash.html

Graphic designer Frank De Crescenzo (frank_decrescenzo@prenhall.com) designed the Slappers Web site for fellow percussionist Billy Amendola, who developed the Slappers flat drumsticks.

Frank's design tips:

1. **Client-side image maps are easy to create with NetObjects Fusion.** No HTML tagging is required when you use NetObjects Fusion to create a Web site. Download a 30-day trial copy from http://www.netobjects.com.

2. **Use a MAILTO command to route form data.** Avoid the use of difficult CGI scripts by using a MAILTO command to route form data to an email address.

Peju Alawusa,
New York, NY

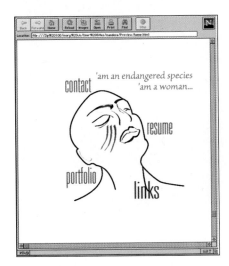

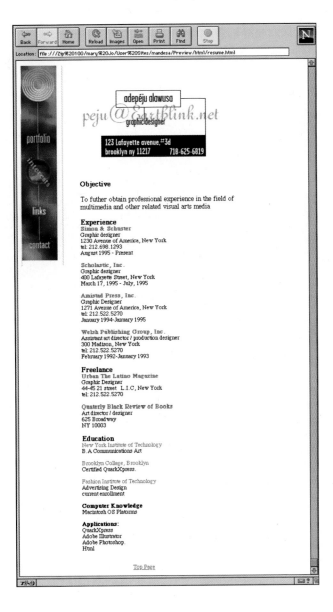

Above: *Peju's home page.*

Right: *Peju's resume page from her Web site.*

http://members.aol.com/alawusa/intro.html

Graphic designer Peju Alawusa (peju_alawusa @prenhall.com) designed her Web site using NetObjects Fusion.

Peju's design tip:

1. **Avoid HTML tagging.** Use NetObjects Fusion to create sophisticated Web pages with forms, frames, image maps, and multimedia elements.

Alex Shamson,
New York, NY

Above: *The Home Store from Alex's Virtual Mall.*

Above Right: *Alex Shamson's home page at http://www.vrmill.com.*

Above: *A wooden chair in the Home Store rotates and has an embedded link to another Web page containing manufacturer and price information.*

Industrial designer Alex Shamson (alex@vrmill.com) has created a Web site full of links to valuable VRML resources on the Web. Visit his site at http://www.vrmill.com for information about browser software, VRML tutorials, and updates on the VRML specification.

Alex's design tips:

1. **The rotating millstone at the upper-left corner of Alex's Web site is an example of VRML animation.** Simple animation can be added to VRML 1.0 models using a word processor.

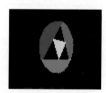

2. **The VRML models on Alex's site were created with Virtus WalkThrough Pro.** Virtus WalkThrough Pro is an inexpensive 3D visualization tool popular with architects and Hollywood directors. The software is available on both the Macintosh and Windows platforms and can export a VRML 1.0 model in the form of a WRL file.

Marc Thorner, New York, NY

Above and Below: Close-ups of the VivoActive digital video stream.

Right: Marc's VivoActive page on the PGI site at http://www.pgi.net/video .html.

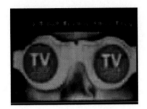

M arc Thorner (mthorner@pipeline.com) is a digital video specialist who is part of New York-based Premiere Graphics International.

Marc's design tips:

1. **VivoActive Producer software compresses a video file into a tiny video stream.** Compress your video files into video streams at a ratio of 200:1 using VivoActive Producer. A video stream starts playing immediately when a page loads into a Web browser.

2. **No extra hardware or software is necessary.** VivoActive requires no extra hardware or software on the Web server.

3. **Web servers need to be configured with the proper MIME settings to display VivoActive (VIV) files.** If you wish to display VivoActive streaming video models on your site, check with your Internet service provider and inquire whether the MIME settings have been set to display VIV files.

Diana DeLucia Design, New York, NY

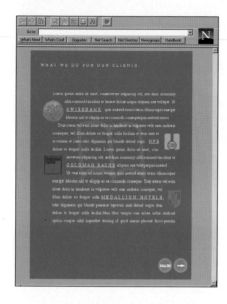

Above: A sample Web page from the Diana DeLucia Design Web site designed by Frauke Ebinger and art directed by Diana DeLucia.

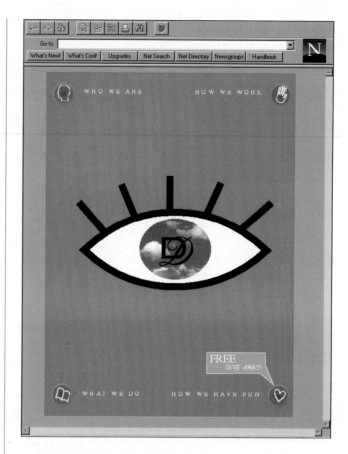

Diana DeLucia (dddnyc@interport.net) sees the role of the graphic designer changing, and the changes are being driven by technology. As Diana explains, "Today, a graphic designer is as much a marketing consultant as an artist. A graphic designer who is familiar with the Web is in a better position to help a client solve big-picture issues than a designer who limits himself/herself to print."

Diana's design tips:
1. **Don't forget your role as a marketer.** Create an incentive on a Web page for visitors to return. Examples include a flow of updated information and possibly art or multimedia files to download.

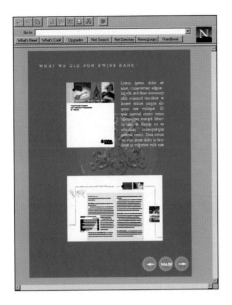

2. **Web pages should be easy to read.** Web visitors spend very little time reading pages. Make pages easy to read for quick scanning.

Frauke's design tips:

1. **Work out a schematic before creating pages.** Even if it's rough, a schematic helps to focus your ideas before you start designing Web pages (Figure 1).

2. **Watch for improvements in HTML.** HTML has already improved in just a few short months. Watch for new developments that will make Web page construction easier.

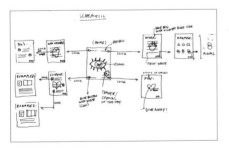

1.

Christina Sun,
New York, NY

*http://www.echonyc.com/~art/
sun_studio/sun_studio.html*

Christina Sun (chrissun@interport.net) is an illustrator who specializes in watercolor and collage for books, magazines, newsletters, posters, and fabric design.

Christina's design tips:

While working with Photoshop, Christina discovered that changes she made in a feature known as target gamma had a dramatic effect on the detail in her images. She noticed that a high (2.2) target gamma made her images look washed out. A target gamma of 2.2 is optimal for preparing images for transparencies, but too high for preparing images for the Web or print. Photoshop artists have the option of using curves to compensate for the decreased saturation (see Step 3).

Gamma is a measure of the amount of neutral midtone values displayed in an image. Although target gamma won't be written into the file, the value is significant because it will affect the adjustments an artist makes to a file when it's displayed.

1. Try to match the target gamma of the output device you intend to use. For example, the target gamma of IBM PC monitors that display Web graphics is 1.8, and the target gamma of Macintosh monitors that display Web graphics is 2.0.

2. To control the target gamma settings on the Macintosh, use the Knoll control panel that comes with Photoshop; for the PC, use the Monitor Setup dialog box under Preferences in Photoshop.

Gamma	Meaning
Low number	A narrow midtone range provides high contrast. Although a low target gamma will result in dramatic blacks and brilliant whites, it can mean a loss of detail in images that need a variation of tones (for instance, skin tones).
High number	A target gamma that is too high may result in images that look washed out.

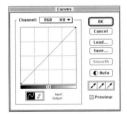

3a.

3b.

3. To increase the saturation in an image, use curves in Photoshop. Open the Curves dialog box by selecting Adjust|Curves from the Image pull-down menu. Instead of making the entire image darker by dragging the curve in the center, try dragging the handle on the curve from its starting point (Figure 3a) to the first gridline (Figure 3b). This technique causes darker areas to become more saturated, but doesn't affect the light areas.

Gail Garcia,
New York, NY

Above: Gail's Web catalog page was created for Elaine Arsenault, a handbag designer in New York City.

http://www.echonyc.com/~art/arsenault/ arsenault.html

Graphic designer Gail Garcia (gjgarcia@interport.net) specializes in product promotion and has a background in print. When Gail's clients approached her about designing Web pages, she experimented with software programs already familiar to her from her print work.

Gail's design tips:

1. **Use Quark XPress as a layout tool.** Use Quark XPress to build a layout, saving each page as a separate EPS file.

2. **Open the image in Photoshop.** A Quark XPress EPS image will open as an EPS Pict Preview image in Photoshop 3.0+ on the Macintosh or EPS TIFF Preview on the Windows platform.

3. **Reduce the bit depth.** If you're designing splash screens, be careful of file size. Reduce the bit depth by selecting Indexed Color from the Mode pull-down menu. (*Note: If you already have Indexed Color selected, select RGB, and reselect Indexed Color. Experiment with smaller bit depths for smaller file sizes.*)

Brandee Amber Selck, Santa Cruz, CA

Above and Above Right: *Brandee's sample Web pages from the IUMA site. Many of the IUMA pages provide Web visitors with a scrolling database window that they can use to access artists or labels.*

Above: *All of the Web graphics on the IUMA site have a 50s theme.*

Brandee Amber Selck's artwork is one of the most popular Web sites on the Internet. The IUMA (Internet Underground Music Archive) site at http://www.iuma.com is a home for over 500 independent, unsigned artists who want to reach people directly on the Internet.

Brandee's design tip:

Brandee (brandee@iuma.com) encourages Web artists to go "hog wild" with their scanners. When Brandee and artist David Beach began designing for the IUMA Web pages, they scavenged for everyday items around the office, at home, and at thrift stores. Brandee explains, "A lot of the best stuff came

from Beach's parents' kitchen and junk drawer: a cooking pot with a copper bottom, tin foil, a gas stove dial, a radio knob from a reproduction radio that David bought his dad at K Mart when he was a kid, and various knobs from an old Zenith television."

Shankweiler
Nestor Design,
New York, NY

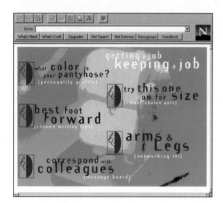

Above: *A sample Web page from a Shankweiler Nestor Web site, art directed by Okey Nestor and designed by Lindsey Payne.*

http://www.echonyc.com/~art/Nestor/Okey.html

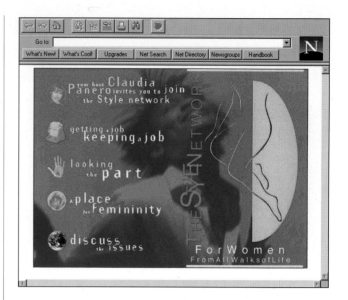

Okey Nestor (okey@interport.net), who taught corporate identity at Kent State University and owns Shankweiler Nestor Design in New York City, feels Web graphics offer a graphic designer broad new potentials in communication, with characteristics such as sound, video, and animation.

Okey's design tips:

1. **Integrate your Web site into your corporate identity program.** Instead of treating your Web site as a totally different entity, integrate it into your identity program and make it work with the goals and strategies of your company's marketing plans.

2. **Offer compelling content within your design.** Design is not the only part of the story. The Web is an interactive medium, so exploit the potential by offering your customers the ability to place orders, pose questions, or look up information in a database. Be creative with both design and content.

Merry Esparza, New York, NY

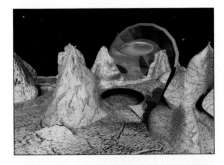

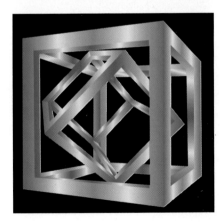

Above: *Sample images from the Mobius Gallery Web site.*

http://www.users.interport.net/~merry/mobius.html

2.

For her work on Web pages, Merry Esparza (merry @interport.net) uses Photoshop and Illustrator. Because these two programs have different properties, she likes to transfer graphics from one program to the other.

Merry's design tips:

1. Begin an illustration with a black and white line art drawing in Illustrator and import it into Photoshop.

2. Once the drawing is in Photoshop, create channels for all the distinct areas in your drawing. Do this before applying any color or textures. Channels provide a means to record selection areas and, with the various areas recorded, an artist can easily reselect an area and experiment with color (and textures) over and over.

For example, Merry created the tiled floor in the Mobius Gallery splash screen (Figure 2) with straight lines in Illustrator. When she imported her black and white line art drawing into Photoshop, she used the Magic Wand tool with the Shift key held down to select the tiles she wanted to fill with color. She made a channel to record the selection and then experimented with color fills.

Kleber Santos,
New York, NY

Above: Kleber's Sfuzzi Web page was created for his virtual tour of the World Financial Center.

Graphic designer Kleber Santos (santos@slinyc.com) recommends that Web designers watch the HTML 3.2 draft at http://www.w3.org/hypertext/WWW to keep up with changes in the Hypertext Markup Language.

Kleber's design tips:

1. **To conserve bandwidth, consider black and white images.** For his virtual tour of the World Financial Center, Kleber used black and white images instead of color. Because some of his images are large, black and white means smaller file sizes.

2. **Use Adobe Illustrator to create type, rasterize it in Photoshop, and save it as a GIF or JPEG.** Because HTML does not provide a large variation in type faces, Illustrator is the best tool to create original type. Save the file as EPS, open it in Photoshop, and save the type as a GIF or JPEG file.

Above: Outside view of the World
Financial Center designed by Cesar
Palli & Associates and built in 1981.

Above: The North Cove Harbor Marina
is tucked behind the World Financial
Center along the Hudson Riverfront.

A text processor	A text processor is required to build Web pages. On the Macintosh, SimpleText (which comes with the Mac) is a good choice because it automatically saves files in the required ASCII format. (*Note: See* Creating a client-side image map HTML file *later in this chapter.*)
A browser	Browser software is used to view the Web and is also a tool that can be used locally (without a modem connection) to view Web pages throughout the design process. Web documents are ASCII text files that can be opened by selecting Open File from the File pull-down menu.
Software to transfer files over a modem	Fetch is a popular Macintosh FTP software program used to transfer files over the Internet. Although files can also be transferred to your provider's server with popular communications programs, such as White Knight or MicroPhone, Fetch is useful because it has functions that allow you to create directories and delete files.

Finding coordinates for clickable regions with Photoshop

Summary: *Photoshop's Info palette can be used to find coordinates for your map file.*

Adobe
Photoshop

1. Plan the hotspot areas.

The hotspots on Kleber's image map are restaurant and retail store logos (Figure 1). Although image maps can have clickable regions shaped as circles, polygons, rectangles, or points, Kleber decided to use rectangular areas to cover the various store and restaurant names.

Photoshop's Info palette shows the coordinate position of the mouse pointer (measured from the upper-left corner of the image). Kleber recorded the palette's readings for a map text file. To obtain upper-left and lower-right coordinate readings for all the restaurant and store logos, he positioned the mouse pointer on the upper-left corners and the lower-right corners of each of the images.

1.

2. Open your image map in Photoshop.

a. Open Photoshop, and select Open from the File pull-down menu.

2a.

b. Select a graphic in the dialog box that follows, and click on Open.

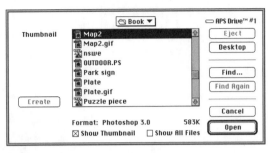

2b.

3. Open the Info palette.

a. Select Show Info from the Window|Palettes pull-down menu.

b. The Info palette will appear as a floating palette in the Photoshop work area. Press on the Info palette's pop-up menu, and select Palette Options.

c. Press on the Mouse Coordinates Ruler Units pop-up menu, and select Pixels. Click on OK.

Window
New Window
Zoom In   ⌘+
Zoom Out   ⌘–
Zoom Factor...
Show Rulers   ⌘R
Palettes ▶

Palettes submenu:
- Show Brushes
- Show Options
- Show Picker
- Show Swatches
- Show Scratch
- Hide Layers
- Show Channels
- Show Paths
- Show Info
- Show Commands

3a.

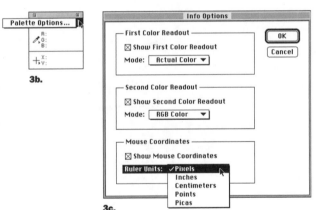

3b.

3c.

d. Select one of the rectangular areas on your image map and place the mouse pointer (in the shape of a crosshair) in the upper-left corner.

3d.

3e.

e. Look at the Info palette, and record the x and y readings (in a notebook) as follows:

```
x: 210
y: 257
```

f. Place the mouse pointer (in the shape of a crosshair) in the lower-right corner.

3f.

3g.

g. Look at the Info palette and record the x and y readings as follows:

```
x: 295
y: 305
```

h. You will need to repeat these steps for all of your planned hotspots.

4. Save the image as a GIF.

a. Select Save a Copy from the File pull-down menu.

b. Enter a file name for your image, and add GIF as the extension.

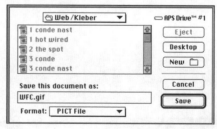

4a.

4b.

Tip: GIF and JPEG images can both be used in image maps. Although JPEG images cannot be seen by as many browsers, the file size is very small compared to GIFs. In this example, Kleber's montage was 70 K as a GIF and only 30 K as a JPEG.

c. Press on the Format pop-up menu, and select CompuServe GIF. Click on Save.

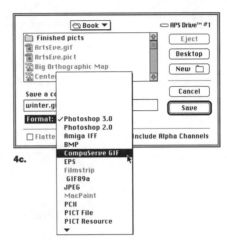

4c.

Creating a client-side image map HTML file

Summary: *Unlike server-dependent image maps, which rely on an HTML file and a separate map file, client-side image maps combine the HTML information and map in one document.*

1. Open SimpleText.

Use SimpleText or a word processor. If you use a word processor, be sure to save the document as Text Only.

SimpleText

2. Create a new HTML document.

Start a new document with the following markup tags:

```
<HTML>

<HEAD>

<TITLE>The World Financial Center</TITLE>

</HEAD>
```

3. Add a <BODY> tag.

Kleber wanted the browser background color to be white, which can be accomplished with a BGCOLOR attribute added to the <BODY> tag.

```
<HTML>

<HEAD>

<TITLE>The World Financial Center</TITLE>

</HEAD>

<BODY BGCOLOR=#FFFFFF>
```

4. Add a <CENTER> tag.

To center the remaining elements, Kleber added a <CENTER> tag.

```
<HTML>

<HEAD>

<TITLE>The World Financial Center</TITLE>

</HEAD>

<BODY BGCOLOR=#FFFFFF>

<CENTER>
```

5. Add an image tag for the banner graphic.

The <IMG> tag contains an SRC parameter that contains the name of an image file. In this case, the image is a banner graphic at the top of the page.

```
<HTML>

<HEAD>

<TITLE>The World Financial Center</TITLE>

</HEAD>

<BODY BGCOLOR=#FFFFFF>

<CENTER>

<IMG SRC="virtual.gif">

</CENTER>
```

6. Add an image tag for the map.

Add an <IMG> tag with an SRC attribute, a USEMAP attribute, and a BORDER=0 attribute. The USEMAP attribute indicates a client-side image map. It specifies which map to use with the image, followed by a #, followed by the name of the map.

In this example, Kleber's map image is called WFC.gif. This HTML document, which also contains the map information, will be saved as *map.htm,* and *WORLDTRADE* is the name of the map. BORDER=0 turns off the image border.

```
<HTML>

<HEAD>

<TITLE>The World Financial Center</TITLE>

</HEAD>

<BODY BGCOLOR=#FFFFFF>

<CENTER>

<IMG SRC="virtual.gif">

</CENTER>

<IMG SRC="WFC.gif" USEMAP="map.htm#WORLDTRADE"
BORDER=0>
```

7. Add a <MAP> tag.

Inside the <MAP> tag, add a NAME attribute, which specifies the name of the map so that it can be referenced by the
<IMG> tag.

After the opening <MAP> tag, add an <AREA> tag specifying a single clickable area of the image. Inside the <AREA>
tag, use a SHAPE attribute to give the shape of the area, a
COORDS attribute to describe an upper-left and a lower-
right set of coordinates, and an HREF attribute to specify
where a click in that area should lead. Any number of
<AREA> tags may be specified. This World Trade Center
example uses nine <AREA> tags.

```
<HTML>

<HEAD>

<TITLE>The World Financial Center</TITLE>

</HEAD>

<BODY BGCOLOR=#FFFFFF>

<CENTER>

<IMG SRC="virtual.gif">

</CENTER>

<IMG SRC="WFC.gif" USEMAP="map.htm#WORLDTRADE"
BORDER=0>

<MAP NAME="WORLDTRADE">

<AREA SHAPE=RECT COORDS="25,7,127,84"
HREF="yacht.htm">

<AREA SHAPE=RECT COORDS="151,8,217,84"
HREF="art.htm">

<AREA SHAPE=RECT COORDS="233,6,368,84"
HREF="river.htm">

<AREA SHAPE=RECT COORDS="166,132,218,171"
HREF="gap.htm">

<AREA SHAPE=RECT COORDS="22,224,132,246"
HREF="river.htm">

<AREA SHAPE=RECT COORDS="192,221,278,270"
HREF="sfuzzi.htm">
```

```
<AREA SHAPE=RECT COORDS="16,338,147,388"
HREF="ataylor.htm">

<AREA SHAPE=RECT COORDS="173,339,235,392"
HREF="jdavid.htm">

<AREA SHAPE=RECT COORDS="266,339,370,389"
HREF="rizzoli.htm">
```

8. Close the <MAP> tag.

Add a closing </MAP> tag after the last <AREA> tag.

```
<HTML>

<HEAD>

<TITLE>The World Financial Center</TITLE>

</HEAD>

<BODY BGCOLOR=#FFFFFF>

<CENTER>

<IMG SRC="virtual.gif">

</CENTER>

<IMG SRC="WFC.gif" USEMAP="map.htm#WORLDTRADE"
BORDER=0>

<MAP NAME="WORLDTRADE">

<AREA SHAPE=RECT COORDS="25,7,127,84"
HREF="yacht.htm">

<AREA SHAPE=RECT COORDS="151,8,217,84"
HREF="art.htm">

<AREA SHAPE=RECT COORDS="233,6,368,84"
HREF="river.htm">

<AREA SHAPE=RECT COORDS="166,132,218,171"
HREF="gap.htm">

<AREA SHAPE=RECT COORDS="22,224,132,246"
HREF="river.htm">

<AREA SHAPE=RECT COORDS="192,221,278,270"
HREF="sfuzzi.htm">

<AREA SHAPE=RECT COORDS="16,338,147,388"
HREF="ataylor.htm">
```

```
<AREA SHAPE=RECT COORDS="173,339,235,392"
HREF="jdavid.htm">

<AREA SHAPE=RECT COORDS="266,339,370,389"
HREF="rizzoli.htm">

</MAP>
```

9. Add line breaks.

Line breaks add space below the image map graphic. Add
two line breaks after the closing </MAP> tag.

```
<HTML>

<HEAD>

<TITLE>The World Financial Center</TITLE>

</HEAD>

<BODY BGCOLOR=#FFFFFF>

<CENTER>

<IMG SRC="virtual.gif">

<IMG SRC="WFC.gif" USEMAP="map.htm#WORLDTRADE"
BORDER=0>

<MAP NAME="WORLDTRADE">

<AREA SHAPE=RECT COORDS="25,7,127,84"
HREF="yacht.htm">

<AREA SHAPE=RECT COORDS="151,8,217,84"
HREF="art.htm">

<AREA SHAPE=RECT COORDS="233,6,368,84"
HREF="river.htm">

<AREA SHAPE=RECT COORDS="166,132,218,171"
HREF="gap.htm">

<AREA SHAPE=RECT COORDS="22,224,132,246"
HREF="river.htm">

<AREA SHAPE=RECT COORDS="192,221,278,270"
HREF="sfuzzi.htm">

<AREA SHAPE=RECT COORDS="16,338,147,388"
HREF="ataylor.htm">

<AREA SHAPE=RECT COORDS="173,339,235,392"
HREF="jdavid.htm">
```

```
<AREA SHAPE=RECT COORDS="266,339,370,389"
HREF="rizzoli.htm">

</MAP>

<BR>

<BR>
```

10. Add text.

Kleber added a line of text after the line breaks to give Web visitors directions.

```
<HTML>

<HEAD>

<TITLE>The World Financial Center</TITLE>

</HEAD>

<BODY BGCOLOR=#FFFFFF>

<CENTER>

<IMG SRC="virtual.gif">

<IMG SRC="WFC.gif" USEMAP="map.htm#WORLDTRADE"
BORDER=0>

<MAP NAME="WORLDTRADE">

<AREA SHAPE=RECT COORDS="25,7,127,84"
HREF="yacht.htm">

<AREA SHAPE=RECT COORDS="151,8,217,84"
HREF="art.htm">

<AREA SHAPE=RECT COORDS="233,6,368,84"
HREF="river.htm">

<AREA SHAPE=RECT COORDS="166,132,218,171"
HREF="gap.htm">

<AREA SHAPE=RECT COORDS="22,224,132,246"
HREF="river.htm">

<AREA SHAPE=RECT COORDS="192,221,278,270"
HREF="sfuzzi.htm">

<AREA SHAPE=RECT COORDS="16,338,147,388"
HREF="ataylor.htm">
```

Tip: Kleber's email address has a MAILTO URL added to the HREF attribute, which is part of an anchor link.

E-MAIL address: ksantos@echonyc.com

When a Web visitor clicks on the email link with a MAILTO URL, a blank email form appears with the address already filled out (Figure 11).

11.

```
<AREA SHAPE=RECT COORDS="173,339,235,392"
HREF="jdavid.htm">

<AREA SHAPE=RECT COORDS="266,339,370,389"
HREF="rizzoli.htm">

</MAP>

<BR>

<BR>

Select individual elements of the above image to go
on a virtual tour.
```

11. Add the signature area.

Although signature areas generally contain the <ADDRESS> tag, Kleber limited the signature area to an email address. He added a MAILTO URL to the HREF attribute so that viewers get a blank email form when they click on the email address (Figure 11).

```
<HTML>

<HEAD>

<TITLE>The World Financial Center</TITLE>

</HEAD>

<BODY BGCOLOR=#FFFFFF>

<CENTER>

<IMG SRC="virtual.gif">

<IMG SRC="WFC.gif" USEMAP="map.htm#WORLDTRADE"
BORDER=0>

<MAP NAME="WORLDTRADE">

<AREA SHAPE=RECT COORDS="25,7,127,84"
HREF="yacht.htm">

<AREA SHAPE=RECT COORDS="151,8,217,84"
HREF="art.htm">

<AREA SHAPE=RECT COORDS="233,6,368,84"
HREF="river.htm">

<AREA SHAPE=RECT COORDS="166,132,218,171"
HREF="gap.htm">

<AREA SHAPE=RECT COORDS="22,224,132,246"
HREF="river.htm">
```

```
<AREA SHAPE=RECT COORDS="192,221,278,270"
HREF="sfuzzi.htm">

<AREA SHAPE=RECT COORDS="16,338,147,388"
HREF="ataylor.htm">

<AREA SHAPE=RECT COORDS="173,339,235,392"
HREF="jdavid.htm">

<AREA SHAPE=RECT COORDS="266,339,370,389"
HREF="rizzoli.htm">

</MAP>

<BR>

<BR>

Select individual elements of the above image to go
on a virtual tour.

<ADDRESS>

<A HREF="Mail to: Ksantos@echonyc.com">

Ksantos@echonyc.com

</A>
```

12. Add the ending tags.

```
</BODY>

</HTML>
```

13. Summary of HTML tags used in this section.

The tags you see in this list (in alphabetical order) reflect the HTML 3.2 specification.

<B>...</B>

A tag used to apply boldfacing to text.

A tag used to add a line break. This tag does not require an ending tag.

<BODY>...</BODY>

A tag used to open and close the body of a document. This tag uses the BGCOLOR attribute, which adds color to a browser page. For example:

```
<BODY BGCOLOR="#FFFFFF">
```

\<CENTER>...\</CENTER>

A tag used to center elements on a page.

\<HEAD>...\</HEAD>

A tag used to open and close the header portion of a document.

\<HTML>...\</HTML>

A tag used to open and close an HTML document.

\<IMG>

Used to refer to an inline image, this tag uses the SRC attribute, which represents the URL (location) of the image. For example:

```
<IMG SRC="virtual.gif">
```

This tag also uses the USEMAP attribute, which indicates a client-side image map. It specifies which map to use with the image, followed by a #, followed by the name of the map. For example:

```
<IMG SRC="WFC.gif" USEMAP="map.htm#WORLDTRADE"
  BORDER=0>
```

MAILTO URL

The MAILTO URL is used in an email link inside the signature area of a document. Viewers who click on a link containing a MAILTO URL will get a blank email form with the address filled out.

\<MAP>...\</MAP>

A tag used to describe the regions in an image and where each region links.

This tag uses the NAME attribute, which specifies the name of the map so that it can be referenced by the \<IMG> tag. An \<AREA> tag is used between the \<MAP>...\</MAP> tags. \<AREA> tags specify a single

Tip: *Look for an example of a client-side image map at http://www.mis.nccu.edu.tw/ ~bibo/lab/client_side_image_map.html and http://www.learned.com/~apex/ imagemap.html.*

clickable area of the image. This tag uses the SHAPE attribute to give the shape of the area, a COORDS attribute to describe the coordinates of an area, and an HREF attribute to specify where a click in that area should lead.

<TITLE>...</TITLE>

A tag used to describes the title of a document, which shows up inside a browser's title bar.

Use PhotoGIF with Photoshop to create a transparent GIF

Summary: BoxTop Software's PhotoGIF plug-in added to your Photoshop folder gives you the ability to save transparent GIFs and interlaced GIFs.

PhotoGIF

When a Web visitor clicks on the Sfuzzi logo (top left), they branch to another HTML document with its own image map. On this page, the button choices are transparent GIF images, which Kleber created in Photoshop and saved using BoxTop Software's PhotoGIF plug-in. (*Note: PhotoGIF is a shareware software program available on the CD-ROM in the back of this book.*)

the boss

the menu

the bar

the extras

1c.

1. Open a Photoshop image.

Before opening Photoshop 3.0, Kleber placed the PhotoGIF plug-in into the File Format folder inside Photoshop's plug-in folder. *(Note: If you're using Photoshop 2.5, place the PhotoGIF plug-in into Photoshop's Plug-in folder.)*

a. Open Photoshop, and select Open from the File pull-down menu.

b. Select an image from the dialog box, and click on Open.

1a.

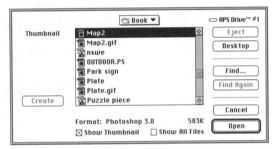

1b.

c. The image opens in a Photoshop window.

2. Open the Info palette.

a. Select Show Info from the Window|Palettes pull-down menu.

b. The Info palette will appear as a floating palette in the Photoshop work area.

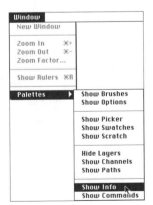

2a.

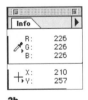

2b.

3. Test the RGB value of the background color.

Kleber's image is a set of oval buttons that float on a green background. Because the background will drop out as the transparent shade, he chose green because it's not in the image.

a. Select the Eyedropper tool from Photoshop's Toolbox.

b. Hold the Eyedropper over the background.

3a.

3b.

c. Note the RGB value in the Info palette.

d. When the image is saved as a transparent GIF, the green background will drop out.

4. Save the image as a transparent GIF.

a. With the image open, choose Save As from the File pull-down menu.

b. Select GIF89a from the Format pop-up menu. This is the extension for transparent GIFs.

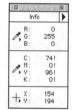

3c.

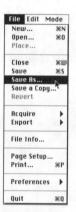

4a.

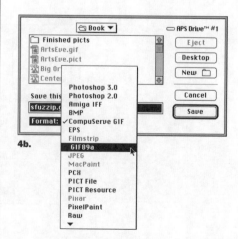

4b.

c. In the dialog box that follows, enter a file name and click on Save.

4c.

5. Make selections in the PhotoGIF dialog box.

a. In the BoxTop Software dialog box, select the radio button next to GIF89a.

b. Click on the color selection square to choose a transparent color.

c. In the dialog box that follows, choose a color, and click OK. (*Note: The PhotoGIF plug-in will assume that the background color drops out as transparent. The RGB value displayed should match the value you tested with the Eyedropper tool.*)

d. Click to put an X in the box labeled *Interlace Me, Baby!*

e. Click on Yeah Sure.

f. When the image is loaded into Netscape, the green background will be transparent.

5a, 5b, 5d, 5e.

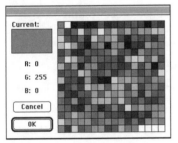

5c.

Use Fetch to upload files to a provider's server

Summary: *Jim Matthews' Fetch is a Macintosh shareware FTP utility that can be used to transfer files to and from file servers on the Internet. Look for Fetch on the CD-ROM in the back of this book.*

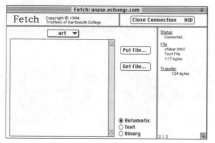

3a.

3b.

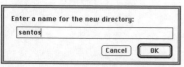

4a.

4b.

To use Fetch to transfer files to your provider's server, you'll need to obtain a host name (the name of the server), a user ID, and a password.

1. Open your Internet connection.
Click on the Open button in the ConfigPPP Control Panel to get on the Internet.

2. Open Fetch.
Open Fetch by double clicking on the Fetch icon.

3. Log in to your provider's server.
a. In the Open Connection dialog box, enter the host name, user ID, password, and directory name you obtained from your provider. This step is referred to as *logging in.* Click on OK.

b. You should be connected to your provider's server quickly. Look closely at Fetch's principal dialog box and notice the word *Connected* under *Status.*

c. Notice the name of the directory you obtained from your provider over the file list window (Figure 3c).

3c.

4. Create a directory.
a. Select Create New Directory from the Directories pull-down menu.

b. Enter a new directory name in the dialog box that follows.

5. Upload a text file to your directory.
a. Click on the Put File button.

5a.

b. Use the file list window in the dialog box that follows to select a text file that you would like to upload. Click on Open.

5b.

5c.

5d.

5e.

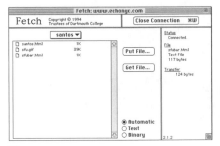

5f.

6b.

6c.

6d.

c. When you select a file, Fetch identifies the file format as Text. Notice the pop-up menu in the dialog box (Figure 5c).

d. If you're uploading map files or HTML files as text, only the .MAP and .HTML extensions are important. Delete the .TXT extension that Fetch adds to the end of the file name (Figure 5d). Click on OK.

e. Fetch's dog will run while your file is uploading.

f. When the file is uploaded, you will see the name displayed in the file list window in Fetch's principal dialog box.

6. Upload a graphic file to your directory.

a. Click on the Put File button.

Put File...

6a.

b. Use the file list window in the dialog box that follows to select a graphic file that you would like to upload.

c. When you select a file, Fetch identifies the file format as MacBinary II (Figure 6c).

d. It is important that you do not send a graphic file to a Unix server as a MacBinary file. Press on the pop-up menu next to Format, and select Raw Data. Click on OK.

e. When the file is uploaded, you will see the name displayed in the file list window in Fetch's principal dialog box.

6e.

7a.

7b.

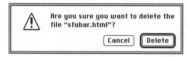
7c.

8a.

8b.

7. Delete a file.

a. Select a file in Fetch's principal dialog box.

b. Select Delete Directory or File from the Remote pull-down menu.

c. Click on Delete in the dialog box that follows to verify you want the file deleted.

8. Exit Fetch.

a. Click on the Close Connection button in Fetch's principal dialog box.

b. Select Quit from the File pull down menu.

Artist featured in this chapter:

Steven McGrew is a Senior Production Associate at the New Media Center/University of Oregon Computing Center. Steve has a B.S. from the University of Oregon in visual design/ computer graphics.

smcgrew@oregon .uoregon.edu

Artist featured in this chapter:

Marc Thorner is a new media artist specializing in 3D animation and digital video.

mthorner@pipeline.com

Chapter 8

Video

Streaming video is the latest technique for adding a video clip to your Web page. Streaming means there's no waiting for a video file to download. The file is instantly transferred for viewing on Power Macintosh and Windows 95/NT machines. Of the options available on the market, digital video expert Marc Thorner recommends VivoActive, which does not require special software or hardware on the Web server.

In this chapter, you'll learn how to compress a video file using a trial copy of VivoActive Producer software and learn facts about Apple's QuickTime Plug-in, which allows you to embed QuickTime movies on a Web page. You'll also learn how Premiere's Movie Analysis Tool can be used to examine movies you download, plus Steven McGrew offers tips on capturing and compressing.

Marc Thorner's tips on using VivoActive Producer to create streaming video

Summary: *Download a copy of VivoActive Producer to create a compressed video stream viewable with the VivoActive Player. Find both software programs at http://www.vivo.com.*

VivoActive Producer (Trial)

1a.

1d.

Tip: *The film clip image in this section was provided by Fabulous Footage at http://www.FOOTAGE.net:2900.*

Take advantage of Vivo Software's trial download to experiment with VivoActive Producer software, which compresses video at a ratio of 200:1. Build a streaming video file for Web visitors to see with the VivoActive Player.

1. Open a movie in VivoActive Producer.

a. Start VivoActive Producer.

b. The VivoActive software will be displayed.

c. Select Open Movie from the File pull-down menu.

d. In the dialog box that follows, select a movie to be compressed, and click on Open.

e. Your movie's file name will appear in a File List in the VivoActive Producer window.

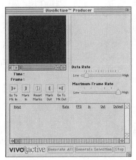

1b.

1c.

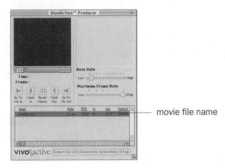

movie file name

1e.

1f.

VivoActive Guide

1g.

2a.

2b.

Tip: Follow the directions for using the <EMBED> tag in the next section as a guide for embedding a VIV file on a Web page.

statue.mov

3a.

statue.viv

3b.

f. Select Apply|Modem High Motion from the Settings pull-down menu. This will apply a data rate and a frame rate that is suitable for a modem transfer.

g. Documentation for VivoActive Producer is in the form of a VivoActive Guide. When you install the VivoActive software on a Power Macintosh, this document gets installed as an Apple Guide, which is accessible from the Guide pull-down menu in the Macintosh Finder.

2. Compress the movie.

a. Click on the Generate Selection button at the base of the VivoActive software window. *(Note: The Generate Selection button will only be available if your movie's file name is selected.)*

b. The software will display the original movie and the compressed version while it is being compressed. A VIV file will automatically be saved in the folder where your movie is located.

c. Should you decide to generate another compressed movie with an alternate setting from the Settings pull-down menu, a click on the Generate Selection button will display a Save As dialog box. You will need to save new movies under a different file name.

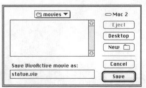

2c.

3. Compare file sizes.

a. The original compressed movie file (compressed with Cinepak) is 1.3 MB.

b. The VIV file following compression in VivoActive is 48 K. An Intranet High Motion setting produced a 204 K file.

Experiment with Apple's QuickTime Plug-in, and embed a QT movie on a Web page

Summary: *Build a page with an embedded QuickTime movie viewable with Apple's QuickTime plug-in. Download a copy of the plug-in from http://www.quicktime.apple.com.*

Also, look for details on how to configure your browser to work with the plug-in at http://www.quicktime.apple.com/sw/browserconfig.html.

Tip: *The film clip image on this page was provided by Fabulous Footage at http://www.FOOTAGE.net:2900.*

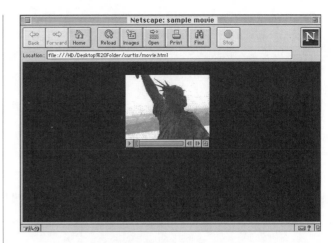

Follow these steps to experiment with Apple's QuickTime plug-in. Download the software, configure your browser, and create a Web page with an embedded QuickTime movie.

1. Download an all-in-one QuickTime bundle.

a. Visit http://www.quicktime.apple.com, and follow the links to Apple's "Easy Download" for Macintosh. One download includes QuickTime 2.5, MoviePlayer 2.5, and the QuickTime plug-in for Netscape.

b. (Optional) Download the MPEG Extension 1.0 for the Power Macintosh at the same location. When the QuickTime MPEG extension is installed in your Power Macintosh System folder, the MoviePlayer application will be able to play MPEG files.

2. Add the QT plug-in to the Plug-Ins folder.

Drag the new QuickTime plug-in to the Netscape Plug-Ins folder inside the Netscape Navigator folder. You will need to re-start the browser for the new plug-in to work, and you may need to visit http://www.quicktime.apple.com/sw/browserconfig.html for details on how to get your browser to recognize the new plug-in.

3. Embed a QuickTime movie in a Web page.

QuickTime movies, QuickTime VR Panoramas, and MPEG movies may all be embedded in a Web page using an <EMBED> tag.

Tip: If you do not know the width and height of your QuickTime movie, open the movie in the MoviePlayer 2.5 application, and select Get Info from the Movie pull-down menu. In the dialog box that follows, select Size from the File pop-up menu. The width and height will be displayed.

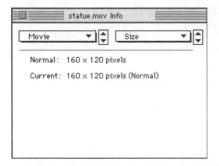

a. Open SimpleText. Use SimpleText or your word processor. If you use a word processor, be sure to save the document as Text only.

b. Create a new HTML document. Start a new document with the following markup tags:

```
<HTML>

<HEAD>

<TITLE>Sample Movie</TITLE>
```

c. Create a body tag, and add color attributes. *(Note: See the* Online Tools *chapter for details on how to select color for your Web page.)*

```
<HTML>

<HEAD>

<TITLE>Sample Movie</TITLE>

<BODY BGCOLOR="#000000">
```

d. Add a <CENTER> tag. The center tag will center the QuickTime movie on the page.

```
<HTML>

<HEAD>

<TITLE>Sample Movie</TITLE>

<BODY BGCOLOR="#000000">

<CENTER>
```

e. Add an <EMBED> tag. In this tag, the width and height of the embedded QuickTime window is defined in pixels. Add 24 pixels to the height of the movie for the default CONTROLLER. The width and height attributes are required for both QuickTime movies and QuickTime VR panoramas.

Optional attributes include:

- The CONTROLLER attribute, which may be set to TRUE or FALSE. The value controls its visibility. TRUE is the default setting for the CONTROLLER.

- The LOOP attribute makes the movie play in a loop. Optional values include TRUE, FALSE, or PALINDROME, which makes the movie play alternately forwards and backwards. PALINDROME should not be used with QuickTime VR panoramas. The default value for LOOP is FALSE.

- AUTOPLAY causes the movie to play as soon as the plug-in estimates it has enough data to play the entire movie. Optional values include TRUE and FALSE. The default value for AUTOPLAY is FALSE.

```
<HTML>

<HEAD>

<TITLE>Sample Movie</TITLE>

<BODY BGCOLOR="#000000">

<CENTER>

<EMBED SRC="statue.mov" HEIGHT=144 WIDTH=160
CONTROLLER=TRUE LOOP=TRUE AUTOPLAY=TRUE>
```

f. Add closing tags.

```
</CENTER>

</BODY>

</HTML>
```

g. Save your document, and test it in Netscape. Save your document. Open Netscape, and select Open File from the File pull-down menu. In the dialog box that follows, select your HTML document, and click on Open. Make sure your movie file is in the same directory as your HTML document. If you have the QuickTime plug-in installed, and you have the Netscape browser configured to identify the plug-in, the movie will load and play. *(Note: At the time of this writing, Apple Computer has not yet finished documenting and testing the Internet Explorer 3.x browser and the QuickTime plug-in.)*

Summary of HTML tags used in this section.

The tags you see in this list (in alphabetical order) reflect the HTML 3.2 specification.

\<B\>...\</B\>

A tag used to apply boldfacing to text.

\<BODY\>...\</BODY\>

A tag used to open and close the body of a document.This tag uses the BGCOLOR="#RRGGBB" or hexadecimal red-green-blue triplet attribute, which adds color to a browser page. For example:

```
<BODY BGCOLOR="#ffffff">
```

\<CENTER\>...\</CENTER\>

A tag used to center elements on a page.

\<EMBED\>

A tag used to embed elements on a page. In this example, the element is a movie file. This tag uses the SRC attribute to indicate the source of the movie file. The WIDTH and HEIGHT attributes are used to describe the size of the movie in pixels with 24 pixels added to the height to accomodate the movie controller bar beneath the movie. The CONTROLLER attribute controls the visibility of the controller and may be set to TRUE or FALSE. The LOOP attribute makes the movie play in a loop and may be set to TRUE, FALSE, or PALINDROME, which makes the movie alternately play forwards and backwards. The AUTOPLAY attribute makes the movie begin playing as soon as the plug-in has enough data and may be set to TRUE or FALSE. For example:

```
<EMBED SRC="statue.mov" HEIGHT=144 WIDTH=160
CONTROLLER=TRUE LOOP=TRUE AUTOPLAY=TRUE>
```

\<HTML\>...\</HTML\>

A tag used to open and close an HTML document.

\<HEAD\>...\</HEAD\>

A tag used to open and close the header portion of a document.

\<TITLE\>...\</TITLE\>

A tag used to describe the title of a document, which shows up inside the browser's title bar.

Use Premiere's Movie Analysis Tool to learn about data rate and compression settings

Summary: Familiarize yourself with the performance specs of movies you download from the Web.

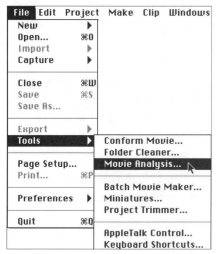

1.

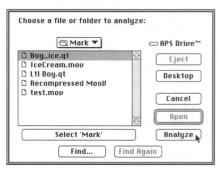

2.

Tip: The film clip image on this page was provided by The Image Bank, Inc., a source for still photographs, film footage, and illustrations (800-TIB-images).

Adobe Premiere's Movie Analysis Tool provides a valuable means to learn about movie specs, including average frame rate, data rate, compression settings, and audio quality.

Adobe Premiere™

1. Select the Movie Analysis Tool.
Select Tools|Movie Analysis from the File pull-down menu.

2. Select a movie to analyze.
Use the file list window in the dialog box to locate the movie you would like to analyze. Click on Analyze.

3. Print the specs.
Select Print from the File pull-down menu to print the specs.

The Web is considered "low bandwidth".
The World Wide Web is considered a "low-bandwidth" application for digital movies, considering that the average Web visitor uses a 14.4 Kbps modem to download movie files. Compare this to an average hard drive, which can transfer data at only 300 Kbps. If you want Web visitors to download movie files, special attention should be given to file size.

Capture settings.
Nearly every item in this movie analysis report (except for the file name) can be traced back to the capture settings.

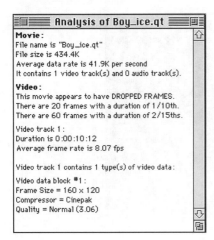

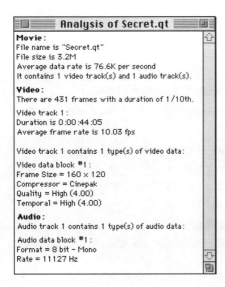

The choices you make when you digitize movie data will determine a movie's characteristics. Consider the following movie characteristics with respect to the World Wide Web:

Movie spec	If the movie is for the Web…
file size	File size will affect the amount of time a Web visitor will have to wait for a download to be completed.
	To calculate the amount of time it will take to download a movie at different modem speeds, divide the modem speed (14,400 or 28,800) by 8 because there are 8 bits to one byte of data in this situation. Divide the number that represents the size of your movie file by this number, then divide by 60 (60 seconds per minute). This will give the (theoretical) number of minutes required to download a movie file.
	(Note: When movie data is transferred over telephone wire, even if a Web visitor has a 28.8 Kbps modem, this bandwidth may not be available everywhere. Certain areas have a maximum bandwidth of 2.4 Kbps.)
average data rate	Data transfer inside a computer is measured in kilobytes per second. Because a Web visitor downloads movies and then plays them on a hard drive, your movie's data rate should not exceed 100 to 200 Kbps, because the data rate of an average hard drive is only 300 Kbps. If the movie data rate is too fast, the movie will drop frames.

average frame rate	When you capture a movie, frame rate is a function of the computer's processing power or the speed of the hard drive depending on whether the movie is captured to RAM or to the hard drive. Ideally, the frame rate should be a function of the playback requirement. However, download time is an important factor when you create movie files for the Web, and a higher frame rate implies larger files. *(Note: See* Steven McGrew's tips on capturing and compressing.*)*
frame size	Frame size affects file size, so Web movie frame size should be limited to 160×120.
compressor	QuickTime has seven software compressors built in: Animation, Cinepak, Component Video, Graphics, Photo-JPEG, None, and Video.
audio format	Three sound components affect sound data rate:
sample rate	the number of sound samples per second
sample size	8-bit or 16-bit
number of channels	mono or stereo; choose mono because stereo sound can only be heard on stereo-capable hardware

Steven McGrew's tips on capturing and compressing

Summary: When you're creating movies for the World Wide Web, the choices you make during capture and compression set the file characteristics. Learn about the variables that will affect the size and quality of your movies.

Tip: The film clip image on this page was provided by The Image Bank, Inc., a source for still photographs, film footage, and illustrations (800-TIB-images).

Little Girl

S teven McGrew, who is a digital media designer/ani–mator at the University of Oregon, offers the following advice on capturing and compressing.

1. Evaluate your material.

Before you capture a single frame, look at your material and think about issues such as frame size. Can the movie be captured at 320×240 or is 160×120 large enough? Is color necessary, or will black and white be good enough?

2. Uncompressed raw data.

If disk space is not a problem and your capturing hardware supports uncompressed capturing, this is the best choice. When you start with uncompressed footage, you'll always get superior results—especially if you post-produce your footage in a movie editor program such as Adobe Premiere. Compression adds artifacts such as jaggies and blurring, which are always compounded by effects, transitions, and filters in the editing software.

3. Post-production blues.

Limit the post-production process and remove as much material from the clip as possible. If the subject doesn't move, cut the frame!

4. Compression is about compromise.

For World Wide Web movies, use the lowest possible frame rate. You'll be able to get away with a very low

Tip: The MediaCity Web page at http://www.MediaCity.com/~erweb is a good place to sample a variety of QuickTime movies, QuickTime VR panoramas, and QuickTime sounds that have been embedded on the page.

frame rate if your subject is static or doesn't move very much. Fast action requires a much higher frame rate. Because compression involves a tradeoff between frame rate and image quality, use a "give-a-little, take-a-little" philosophy when determining the final compression /frames per second settings.

5. Selecting a type of compression.

QuickTime and MPEG are currently the most widely used compression standards. QuickTime is easy to use and gives good performance. It can include sound and can be played on both Macintosh and IBM PCs. Of the software compressors built into QuickTime, the Cinepak codec (compressor decompressor) is the best.

MPEG is difficult to use and is not well supported on Macs. However, MPEG can produce movies that are several times smaller than QuickTime movies. Use MPEG for longer movies that do not require audio; this format gives the maximum amount of compression and the best final product.

6. Apple's new MPEG extension.

Apple's QuickTime MPEG extension gets installed in a Power Macintosh computer's System folder and provides playback and control of MPEG movies. The MoviePlayer application can now be used to play QuickTime, QuickTime VR panoramas, and MPEG movies. Although the QuickTime MPEG extension provides playback, it does not provide a compressor component.

7. Conclusion.

When you're creating a movie for the World Wide Web, make it as small as possible. Try to design your material around the Web's bandwidth limitation and be aware of the time required to download your movie.

Each clip should be evaluated separately to determine the best compression method. When in doubt, use QuickTime Cinepak.

Creating a link to a movie on your Web page

Summary: Create HTML links to QuickTime movie files. Include the file type and file size to help Web visitors make a decision whether to download.

Tip: The film clip image on this page was provided by The Image Bank, Inc., a source for still photographs, film footage, and illustrations (800-TIB-images).

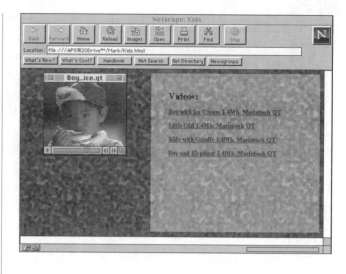

multicolor1_dots.gif

Nested definition list tags can be used to create a "paragraph indent" against a background GIF image that has been downloaded with the <BODY BACKGROUND> tag. To start the type down the page, begin with an <IMG> tag that references a small, clear GIF image.

Try this example, which contains four links to movie files.

1. Open SimpleText.
Use SimpleText or a word processor. If you use a word processor, be sure to save the document as a Text Only file.

SimpleText

2. Create a new HTML document.
Start a new document with the following markup tags:

```
<HTML>
<HEAD>
<TITLE>Kids</TITLE>
</HEAD>
```

3. Try the <BODY BACKGROUND> tag.
In this example, the multicolored background was downloaded as a small tile from the Netscape's Background Samples page (http://home.netscape.com/assist/net_sites/bg/backgrounds.html).

a. Open the tile called *multicolor1 _dots.gif* in Photoshop as a CompuServe GIF image.

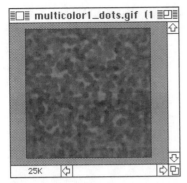

3a.

3d.

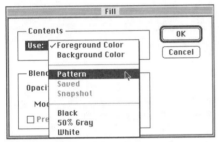

3f.

3j.

b. Select RGB from the Mode pull-down menu.

c. Choose All from the Select pull-down menu.

3c.

d. Choose Define Pattern from the Edit pull-down menu.

e. Open a New document, name it multi.gif, and make it 603×317 pixels and 72 dpi.

f. Choose Fill from the Edit pull-down menu. Select Pattern from the Use pop-up menu, 100% Opacity, and Normal Mode.

g. To create the "vellum" (to make the type readable against a busy background), drag to select an area of the background art, and choose Fill from the Edit pull-down menu.

h. Choose White from the Use pop-up menu, 50% Opacity, and Normal Mode.

i. Choose Indexed Color from the Mode pull-down menu, and click on OK.

j. Choose Save As from the File pull-down menu, and select CompuServe GIF from the choices on the Format pop-up menu. The result is shown in Figure 3j.

3i.

k. Refer to this image in the <BODY BACKGROUND> tag.

```
<HTML>
<HEAD>
<TITLE>Kids</TITLE>
</HEAD>
<BODY BACKGROUND="multi.gif">
```

Tip: The MoviePlayer application from Apple Computer can now be used to play QuickTime movies, QuickTime VR panoramas, and MPEG movies.

4. Start the type down the page.

To start the type down the page, use the <BR> tag to add line breaks.

```
<HTML>
<HEAD>
<TITLE>Kids</TITLE>
</HEAD>
<BODY BACKGROUND="multi.gif">
<BR>
<BR>
```

5. Add a group of nested definition list tags.

To create the equivalent of a paragraph indent, use the <DL> (definition list) tag. In this example, eight opening tags are used, and eight ending tags are used. Adding more than one is called *nesting* the tags.

```
<HTML>
<HEAD>
<TITLE>Kids</TITLE>
</HEAD>
<BODY BACKGROUND="multi.gif">
<BR>
<BR>
<DL><DL><DL><DL><DL><DL><DL><DL>
</DL></DL></DL></DL></DL></DL></DL></DL>
```

6. Add a headline between the <DL> tags.

Once the required number of <DL> tags are in place, add the text in between the opening and ending tags. *(Note: The <H2>...</H2> tag is for headline type.)*

```
<HTML>
<HEAD>
<TITLE>Kids</TITLE>
</HEAD>
<BODY BACKGROUND="multi.gif">
<BR>
<BR>
<DL><DL><DL><DL><DL><DL><DL><DL><H2>Videos:</H2></DL><
/DL></DL></DL></DL></DL></DL>
</BODY>
</HTML>
```

7. Add a paragraph tag.

The <P> tag will create a new paragraph.

```
<HTML>
<HEAD>
<TITLE>Kids</TITLE>
</HEAD>
<BODY BACKGROUND="multi.gif">
<BR>
<BR>
<DL><DL><DL><DL><DL><DL><DL><DL><H2>Videos:</H2><P></
DL>
</DL></DL></DL></DL></DL></DL></DL>
</BODY>
</HTML>
```

8. Add the links to movie files.

Create links to movie files by opening with the link tag <A> in conjunction with the HREF attribute, and placing text between the opening and closing tags. This text will serve as a clickable hotspot on the Web page and can be identified with an underline. (*Note: End each line with a paragraph tag,* <P>.)

```
<HTML>
<HEAD>
<TITLE>Kids</TITLE>
</HEAD>
<BODY BACKGROUND="multi.gif">
<BR>
<BR>
<DL><DL><DL><DL><DL><DL><DL><DL><H2>Videos:</H2><P>
<A HREF="Child1.mov">Boy with Ice Cream 1.4 MB,
Macintosh QT </A><P>
<A HREF="Child2.mov">Little Girl 1.4 MB, Macintosh QT
</A><P>
<A HREF="Child3.mov">Kids with Giraffe 1.4 MB,
Macintosh QT </A><P>
<A HREF="Child4.mov">Boy and Elephant 1.4 MB, Macintosh
QT </A><P>
</DL></DL></DL></DL></DL></DL></DL></DL>
</BODY>
</HTML>
```

Tip: QuickTime VR panoramas are usually much smaller than QuickTime movies.

Eric Chen, the computer scientist who developed QuickTime VR at Apple Computer, has formed his own company called RealSpace http://www.rlspace .com.

His Vistographer Lite is software that can be used to create a 360-degree panorama.

9. Add bolding to the underlined (link) text.

In this example, the <B> and </B> tags will bold the text that visitors will click on. The text will appear underlined and boldfaced.

```
<HTML>
<HEAD>
<TITLE>Kids</TITLE>
</HEAD>
<BODY BACKGROUND="multi.gif">
<BR>
<BR>
<DL><DL><DL><DL><DL><DL><DL><DL><H2>Videos:</H2><P>
<A HREF="Child1.mov"><B>Boy with Ice Cream 1.4 MB,
Macintosh QT </B></A><P>
<A HREF="Child2.mov"><B>Little Girl 1.4 MB, Macintosh
QT </B></A><P>
<A HREF="Child3.mov"><B>Kids with Giraffe 1.4 MB,
Macintosh QT </B></A><P>
<A HREF="Child4.mov"><B>Boy and Elephant 1.4 MB,
Macintosh QT </B></A><P>
</DL></DL></DL></DL></DL></DL></DL></DL>
</BODY>
</HTML>
```

Tip: One of the best ways to learn how to use HTML tags is to view the tags used in your favorite pages on the Web. To see the HTML tags that make up a page, select Source from Netscape's View pull-down menu.

Summary of HTML tags used in this section.

The tags you see in this list (in alphabetical order) reflect the HTML 3.2 specification.

<A>...</A>

Referred to as an *anchor*, this tag uses the HREF attribute to link to an external sound file or anchor. For example:

```
<A HREF="Child4.mov"><B>Boy and Elephant 1.4 MB,
Macintosh QT </B></A>
```

(Note: The movie file name must include the path name if the file is located in another directory).

<B>...</B>

A tag used to apply boldfacing to text.

<BODY>...</BODY>

A tag used to open and close the body of a document.

A tag used to insert a line break.

<DL>...</DL>

The definition list tag is usually used for definitions or short paragraphs with no bullets or numbering. In this chapter, this tag is nested eight times to indent the word *Video* at the bottom of each page. For example:

```
<DL><DL><DL><DL><DL><DL><DL><DL>Videos</DL>
</DL></DL></DL></DL></DL><DL></DL>
```

<HTML>...</HTML>

A tag used to open and close an HTML document.

<HEAD>...</HEAD>

A tag used to open and close the header portion of a document.

<IMG>

Used to refer to an inline image, this tag uses the SRC attribute, which represents the URL (location) of the image. For example:

```
<IMG SRC = "clear.gif">
```

<TITLE>...</TITLE>

A tag used to describe the title of a document, which appears inside a browser's title bar.

Pick the best palette for an 8-bit color QuickTime movie using DeBabelizer's Super Palette, and create a script to remap your movie

Summary: *Use this example to learn how to create a Super Palette in DeBabelizer, how to use DeBabelizer's functions in Batch mode, and how to create a script.*

DeBabelizer®

Tip: The film clip image on this page was provided by Fabulous Footage at http://www.FOOTAGE.net:2900.

DeBabelizer, by David Theurer, is a "graphics processing, manipulation, and translation tool" that can be used to alter QuickTime movie palettes. DeBabelizer's unique Super Palette feature is designed to create the best palette (of 256 or fewer colors) for a series of images or, in this case, frames.

1. The color tradeoff.

When a 16- or 24-bit movie is played on an 8-bit monitor, the Macintosh computer's Color QuickDraw will do the color mapping to approximate a larger color palette. In this case, DeBabelizer can be used to create a predictable 8-bit palette.

Although the custom, 8-bit Super Palette will look better than the approximate 8-bit palette drawn with Color QuickDraw, the only codecs that can save an 8-bit palette are Animation and None. Both of these compressors create much bigger movies than movies compressed with Cinepak, a codec that defaults to a 24-bit palette. As a result, you'll need to limit 8-bit QuickTime movies to very few frames to keep the file size small.

2. Creating a Super Palette.

You can create a Super Palette and manually remap a group of images with the new palette, but because a movie has so many frames, Greg Marr at Equilibrium recommends using DeBabelizer's Batch and Scripting features to automate the job. Try the example in this section to learn how DeBabelizer can automate your work.

3. Open DeBabelizer.

Click open DeBabelizer.

4. Begin a Super Palette in Batch mode.

Instead of manually factoring in a movie's frames as votes to form a Super Palette of the best 256 colors, DeBabelizer's Batch feature can be used to open the entire movie and look at color in every frame.

a. Select Batch|Super Palette from the File pull-down menu.

b. Click on the New button in the Batch Super Palette dialog box.

c. Use the file list window in the dialog box that follows to find your QuickTime movie.

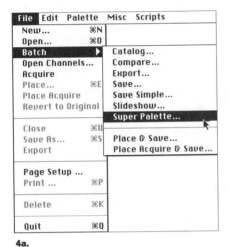

4a.

4b.

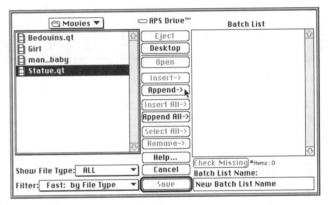

4c.

d. Click on the Append button.

e. Enter a name for this batch in the box labeled *Batch List Name*.

4e.

f. Click on the Save button.

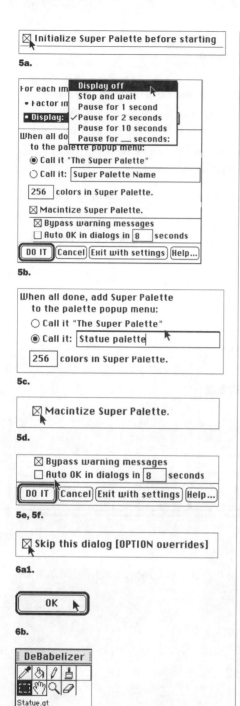

5a.

5b.

5c.

5d.

5e, 5f.

6a1.

6b.

6c.

5. Fill in the Batch Super Palette dialog box.

a. Click to put an X in the box labeled *Initialize Super Palette Before Starting*.

b. Select Display Off from the Display pop-up menu.

c. Click the radio button/box labeled *Call It,* and fill in your own palette name, replacing *Super Palette Name*.

d. Click to remove the X in the box labeled *Macintize Super Palette* because the movie will need to be seen on IBM PCs (on the Web).

e. Click to put an X in the box labeled *Bypass Warning Messages*.

f. Click to remove the X in the box labeled *Auto OK In Dialogs In 8 Seconds*.

g. Click the DO IT button. *(Note: The QuickTime Movie Open dialog box will be displayed.)*

6. Poll the frames.

a. Click to put an X in the box labeled *Skip This Dialog* at the bottom of the QuickTime Movie Open dialog box. (See Figures 6a1 and 6a2.)

b. Click on the OK button.

c. DeBabelizer will begin "polling" all the frames in your movie to make a choice of the best 256 colors.

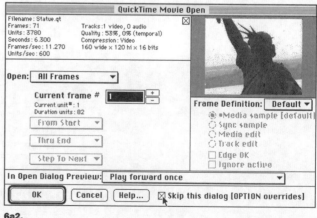

6a2.

7. Create the Super Palette.

Click on the Create It button in the corner of the Create Super Palette dialog box.

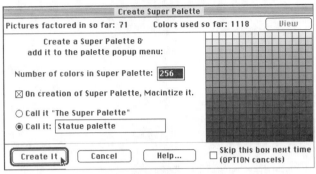

7.

8. Begin remapping by starting a script.

a. Select New from the Scripts pull-down menu.

b. With the Edit Script dialog box open, select Set Palette & Remap Pixels from the Palette pull-down menu.

8a.

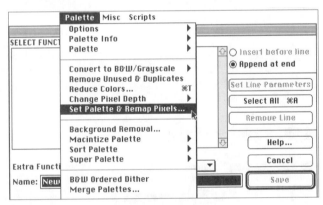

8b.

c. The function that you selected will appear in the Edit Scripts dialog box. A question mark will be visible because DeBabelizer does not yet have enough information to process your request.

8c, 8d.

d. Double-click on the question mark, and the Set Palette & Remap Pixels dialog box will appear.

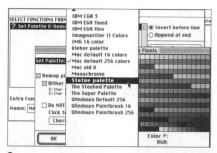

8e.

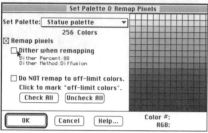

8f through 8i.

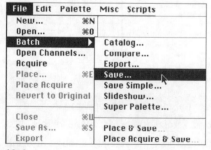

10a1.

e. Select the name you've given to your palette from the Set Palette pop-up menu.

f. Click to put an X in the box labeled *Remap Pixels*.

g. Click to remove the X from the box labeled *Dither When Remapping*.

h. Click to remove the X in the box labeled *Do NOT Remap To Off-Limit Colors*.

i. Click on OK. *(Note: The question mark has turned into an "OK" symbol.)*

9. Name and save your script.

a. Enter a name for your script in the box labeled *Name* at the bottom of the Edit Script dialog box.

b. Click on Save.

9a, 9b.

10. Save each frame in Batch mode.

When QuickTime movies are saved in DeBabelizer, individual frames are appended to the end of a movie. Like the polling required for creating a Super Palette, this is another job that should be batched.

a. Select Batch|Save (Figure 8a1) from the File pull-down menu. The dialog box shown in Figure 8a2 will appear.

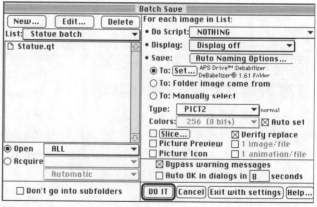

10a2.

For each image in List:
- **Do Script:** ✓ NOTHING
  - Bedouin set palette script
  - Dither to Stashed Palette
  - Dither to Super Palette
  - Drag&Drop To PICT
  - Mask Original with Alpha Channel
  - Print Best on 300 DPI B&W Printer
  - Print Best on 300 DPI Color Printer
  - Print Best on Color Imagewriter
  - **Statue script**
  - Trim to Solid Edges
- **Display:**
- **Save:**
  - ⦿ To: [Set.]
  - ○ To: Fold
  - ○ To: Man
  - Type: P
  - Colors:
  - □ [Slice...]
  - □ Picture Preview □ 1 image/file
  - □ Picture Icon □ 1 animation/file

10b.

b. Select the name of your script from the Do Script pop-up menu.

c. Select Display Off from the Display pop-up menu.

d. Click on the Auto Naming Options button.

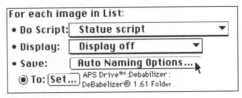

For each image in List:
- **Do Script:** **Statue script** ▼
- **Display:** **Display off** ▼
- **Save:** [**Auto Naming Options...**]
  - ⦿ To: [Set...] APS Drive™:Debabelizer : DeBabelizer® 1.61 Folder .

10c, 10d.

e. Click on the Original Name and the Extension For Save Type radio buttons. *(Note: Disregard the extension if it is incorrect; DeBabelizer will fill in the correct extension.)*

f. Click to put an X in the box labeled *Don't Duplicate Extension.*

Auto Namer

Save Filename =

○ Use this: [   ]
○ Use this & add 1 before .extension
○ Use this & add 1 at end

⦿ Original name +
  ⊠ Strip .extension first
  □ Add cell number
  ○ No extension
  ○ Extension: [mod] ⎫ ⊠ Don't duplicate extension
  ⦿ Extension for Save Type: PICT ⎭

[OK]   [Cancel]   [Help...]

10e, 10f.

11. Set the path.

DeBabelizer will need to know where it should save the new movie. Greg Marr at Equilibrium recommends that the movie be saved in a folder other than the folder that contains the original (to prevent accidental file overwrite).

a. Click on the Set button on the Batch Save dialog box.

11a.

b. Use the file list window in the dialog box that follows to select a destination folder. *(Note: As an option, create a New Folder to keep your new movie separate from your old movie.)*

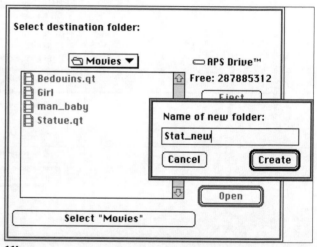

11b.

c. Click on the Select *(folder name here)* button. *(Note: DeBabelizer will display the path in small type next to the Set button, as shown in Figure 9c.)*

11c.

12. Indicate the file type.

a. Select QuickTime Movie|Movie from the Type pop-up menu in the Batch Save dialog box.

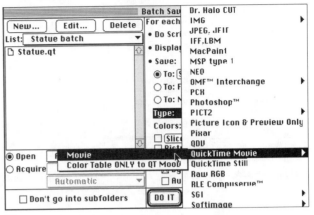

12a.

b. Click to put an X in the box labeled *Auto Set*.

c. Click to remove the X in each of the six checkboxes beneath the Auto Set box.

d. Click to put an X in the box labeled *Bypass Warning Messages*.

e. Click to remove the X in the box labeled *Auto OK In Dialogs In 8 Seconds*.

f. Click on the DO IT button.

12b.

12c.

12d, 12e, 12f.

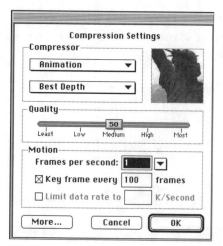

13a through 13d.

13e.

13. Select a compressor.

The only two codecs that support 256 colors are Animation and None. Selecting any other codec will create a 24-bit movie, not an 8-bit movie.

a. Select Animation and Best Depth from the Compressor pop-up menus in the Compression Settings dialog box.

b. Use the slider to select a compression quality.

c. Use the default setting of 1 frame per second and Key frame every 100 frames.

d. Click on OK.

e. DeBabelizer will display the progress of the batch operation in the toolbox window.

14. Test your movie.

Click to open your movie. If you have the MoviePlayer or some other QuickTime player on your hard drive, the movie will begin to play.

File conversion: Preparing QuickTime files for Windows

Summary: *Use Patrick Hennessey's flattenMooV utility to "flatten the forks" of a Macintosh QuickTime movie for playback on the Windows platform. Look for flattenMooV on the CD-ROM in the back of this book.*

2.

flattenMooV

On the Macintosh platform, all files have what are called a *data fork* and a *resource fork*. These must be rolled into one for playback on the Windows platform because Windows will not "see" two forks. Patrick Hennessey's flattenMooV is a utility that flattens a movie.

1. Open flattenMooV.

Double-click on the flattenMooV application to open it.

2. Select a movie.

Use the file list window to select a movie.

3. Run the movie.

Run the movie to review it.

4. Close the movie.

Close the movie window by clicking on the close box.

5. Save the movie.

When you close the movie window, you will be prompted to save the movie (with the extension .FLAT). Locate the folder where you would like the movie saved, and click on Save.

5.

File conversion: Converting QuickTime files to AVI

Summary: Use the Video for Windows Converter (developed by CoSA and Vital for Microsoft) to convert QuickTime movies to AVI movies.

VfW Converter

Windows Compressors

A VI (Audio/Video Interleave) is the Microsoft standard for digital video. This standard is also known as Video for Windows, although the movie files have an .AVI extension. Some Web sites offer QuickTime and AVI movie formats to accommodate Web visitors on both the Macintosh and IBM platforms; AVI is more common than QuickTime on the PC platform.

Before you convert a QuickTime movie to an AVI movie, install the Windows Compressors in the Extensions folder on your Macintosh.

1. Install the Windows Compressors.

a. Drag the Windows Compressors icon on top of your closed System folder.

b. Restart your computer.

2. Open the VfW converter.

Click to open the VfW converter utility.

3. Use the Video For Windows Converter dialog box.

a. Click on the Open Source button in the Video For Windows Converter dialog box.

b. Look through the Source Folder window, and click on a file to convert.

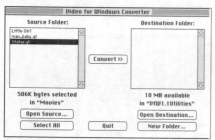

3a, 3c, 3d.

3b.

c. Click on the Open Destination button to select a destination folder for the converted files. Select New Folder if you'd like to create a New Folder.

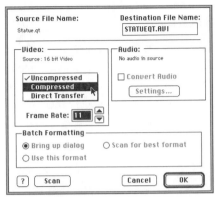

3e.

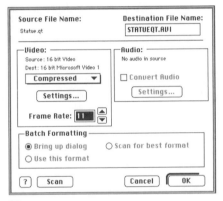

3g.

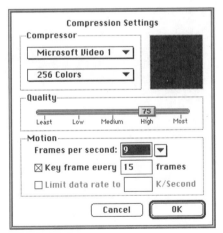

4a, 4b, 4c, 4d, 4e.

d. Click on the Convert button.

e. Click on the Compression Method pop-up menu and select Uncompressed, Compressed, or Direct Transfer. *(Note: You will want to select Compressed if the movie is a raw file or if the movie is already compressed with a non-IBM-compatible compressor. Select Direct Transfer if the movie is already compressed and the compressor is available on the IBM computer.)*

f. Selecting Uncompressed displays a video format pop-up menu, which allows you to specify the image depth of the converted QuickTime file. Choose 8-, 16-, or 24-bit.

g. Selecting Compressed displays a Settings button. Click on this button to display a Compression Settings dialog box.

4. Compression settings.

a. In the Settings dialog box, display the Compressor pop-up menu, and select an IBM-compatible compressor.

b. Drag the Quality slider to select an image quality.

c. Fill in a number in the Frame Rate field.

d. Fill in a number for Key frames. Key frames don't depend on previous frames to be drawn. Higher values for the Key frame field make the converted file smaller, but performance may suffer.

e. If the setting is available, specify a low data rate for Web movies. Playback will be on a hard drive, so make the data rate between 100 and 200 Kbps.

5. Audio options.

a. If audio is included in the QuickTime movie, the Convert Audio checkbox will be available. Click on the box to fill in an X if you want audio converted.

b. Click on the Settings button.

6. Audio settings.

a. Select the number of channels; either mono or stereo. *(Note: Stereo will only be heard on stereo-equipped hardware.)*

Tip: *The Animation, Graphics, Microsoft RLE, and None Compressors are lossless compression schemes. That is, no data is lost during compression. In contrast, data is thrown away during lossy compression. Be careful not to apply lossy compression more than once.*

When you run the Converter, you may need to increase the amount of RAM assigned to the program by increasing the minimum and preferred memory values in the Finder's Get Info dialog box.

Video for Windows interleaves audio with every frame of video. When you convert a QuickTime file to AVI with the Video for Windows Converter, the files are not interleaved. The authors suggest interleaving the files again with VidEdit.

b. Select the sample size. *(Note: 8-bit samples provide a range of 256 sound units, and 16-bit samples provide a range of 65,536 sound units.)*

c. Select the frequency. *(Note: Frequency is the number of audio samples per second. 44.1 kHz is CD-audio quality, 22.056 kHz is AM-radio quality, and 11.025 kHz is voice quality. Web developers should consider 11.025 for voice and 22.056 kHz for music.)*

File conversion: Converting AVI movies to QuickTime movies

Summary: *Use the AVI to QuickTime utility (developed by Vital and Media Vision for Microsoft) to convert AVI movies to QuickTime movies.*

Windows Compressors

AVI to QT Utility

The AVI to QT Utility creates a resource fork so an AVI file can be recognized by QuickTime.

Before you convert a QuickTime movie to an AVI movie, install the Windows Compressors in the Extensions folder on your Macintosh.

1. Install the Windows Compressors.

a. Drag the Windows Compressors icon on top of your closed System folder.

b. Restart your computer.

2. Open the AVI to QT utility.

Click to open the AVI to QT utility.

3. Use the Conversion window.

a. Use the file list window on the left half of the Conversion window to find the AVI file you would like to convert.

b. Select the AVI file, and click on the Add button.

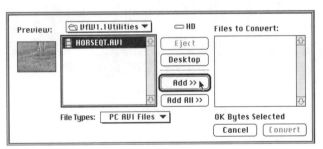

3b.

c. Click on the Convert button.

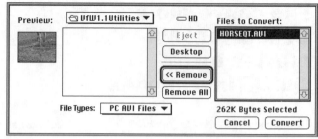

3c.

4. Select a destination folder.

a. Click on Save Self-Contained Movie.

b. Use the file list window in the next dialog box to select a destination folder.

c. Click on the Choose *(folder name here)* button to choose the folder you've selected and to start the conversion. *(Note: If you selected Save Self-Contained Movie, the movie may be opened by a QuickTime movie player such as the MoviePlayer.)*

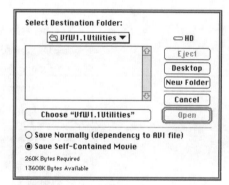

4a, 4b, 4c.

Artist featured in this chapter:

Tom Cipolla is a writer and producer of audio-visual educational materials. In this chapter, he teaches how to "hear with your mind."

cipolla@echonyc.com

Computer specialist featured in this chapter:

Greg Hess, a.k.a. "Red Dog," is a computer electronics instructor in Lakeland, Florida. The home page he created to support his Palace site opens with a background sound created with Netscape's new LiveAudio HTML syntax.

ghess@gte.net

Chapter 9

Sound

This chapter begins with a tour of some well-known Web sites that offer sound. You'll learn technical tips from the developers who created the sites, including Modem Media (Zima), Fry Multimedia (Ragu), and Robert Lord (IUMA). Tom Cipolla offers tips on selecting sound effects for your images. In this chapter, he works with clip sounds to create sound effects for photos from Pacific Coast Software (http://www.pacific-coast.com). Using Alberto Ricci's SoundEffects software (available on the CD-ROM in the back of this book), Tom alters, mixes, records, and reformats the sampled sound for use on other platforms. There's also a how-to section on using SoundApp to convert sound file formats (also available on the CD-ROM).

Now that Netscape's LiveAudio technology plays WAV, AU, and MIDI files, you'll no longer need a separate helper application to play sound. In fact, Greg Hess, a computer electronics instructor, demonstrates how to add a MIDI background sound to a Web page using Netscape's new LiveAudio HTML syntax. As electronic MIDI music continues to blend with computer technology, it makes sense to use this sound format on the Web because MIDI files are tiny. If you've never worked with MIDI sound files, you'll want to visit Heini Withagen's MIDI home page (http://www.eeb.tue.nl/midi/index.html). He has created links to articles and tech tips, MIDI sound archives, MIDI software utilities, and special interest group links.

Web sites with sound

Summary: Visit pages with sound to gather ideas for your own pages. The artists who have created the Web pages you see in this chapter are among the first to take advantage of the Web's multimedia characteristics.

Tip: Charles Marelli, the writer who created the Duncan character and Duncan's sound effects, uses clip sound effects from a variety of public domain sound archives, as well as a sound effects CD-ROM. (See Creating sound effects with clip media *for addresses of public sound archives.) Charles also creates sound effects from scratch using a 16-bit sound card and a microphone.*

The Zima site, developed by Modem Media in Westport, Connecticut, uses sound effects the same way sound was once used on radio. Visit http://www.zima.com and follow soap-opera-like installments about Duncan, the site's fictional Generation X character.

Weekly episodes contain inline audio links to sound effects. For example, in this segment, Duncan is dropping his date off at her door. He swings open an iron gate in front of her apartment, and the word *swung* has an audio link attached. A mouse click on the word *swung* will automatically play the sound of a gate swinging open.

```
"Duncan, I had a wonderful time."
Duncan's bountiful pool of clichés immediately evaporated.
"Um, .... me too," he stammered.
Duncan swung open the small iron gate in front of her
apartment.
```

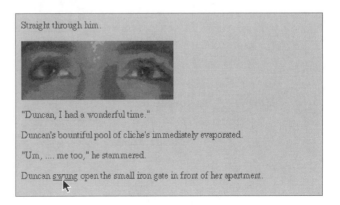

Tip: Download the latest version of Netscape to take advantage of the LiveAudio technology built into the browser (http://home.netscape.com /comprod/mirror/index.html).

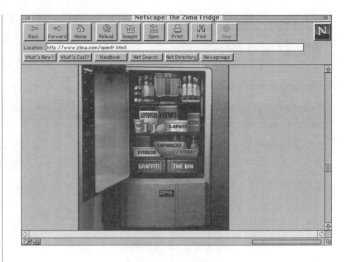

At the Zima site, you'll also find sound files in the "fridge." Click on the Earwacks bowl inside the refrigerator, and you'll visit a page of sound icons with links to AU files for Macintosh and Unix or WAV files for Windows, including:

 Smooch.date.au (18 K) | date.wav (36 K)

 Batter up! ball.au (21 K) | ball.wav (42 K)

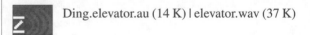 Ding.elevator.au (14 K) | elevator.wav (37 K)

A slight drizzle... rain.au (23 K) | rain.wav (62 K)

"I made a lasagna so good the other day, I swear it would have made Michelangelo cry from joy."

Tip: Fry Multimedia records Professor Antonio (8 bit at 22 kHz) on a Macintosh Quadra 650 using SoundEdit Pro and the Plaintalk microphone that Apple provides with some newer Macs. Using SoundEdit, the Fry team edits the sound bites into "right-sized" chunks. Files range from 16 K ("Hotel") to 95 K. ("I would like a hotel room facing the Grand Canal, please.") They estimate it takes about one second to download one kilobyte of data over a 14.4 Kbps modem. They prefer to hold file sizes under 40 K so that visitors never have to wait more than 40 seconds for sound to download.

To convert the sounds into AU, WAV, and AIFF file formats, Fry Web site developers use SoundApp, a shareware program for Macintosh. (SoundApp can be found on the CD-ROM in the back of this book. Note: SoundApp lists the AU format as the "NeXT format.")

Ragu's Web site (http://www.eat.com/index.html), produced by Fry Multimedia in Ann Arbor, Michigan, has a clever theme called Mama's Cucina (or Mama's kitchen). Included are Mama's Cookbook, Contests, Mama's Secrets, Italian Lessons, Cooking/Pasta Glossaries, Stories Around the Family Table, and Mama's Favorite Places.

Professor Antonio teaches Italian. A mouse click on the appropriate file type (AU, AIFF, or WAV) will play a phrase in Italian. The idea for the site came from David Fry (dfry@frymulti.com) and Michael Clemens. Writer Tom Cunniff creates much of the content for the site, and "Professor Antonio" is Antonio Antiochia, a software engineer with Fry Multimedia.

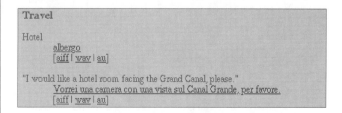

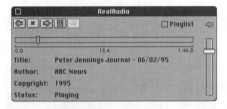

Tip: Visit Netscape's plug-in page to download a copy of the RealAudio plug-in (http://home.netscape.com/comprod/products/navigator/version_2.0/plugins/audio-video.html).

O ne of the most exciting developments on Web pages is RealAudio, by Progressive Networks, Inc. (http://www.realaudio.com). This interesting new technology allows you to simultaneously download and play sound. The Progressive Network Web site hosts pages that contain ABC, National Public Radio, and Radio Yesteryear radio programs.

Progressive Networks, Inc. sells RealAudio server software to sites that wish to offer *streaming* audio files or realtime playback. Web site visitors who have a RealAudio player installed will have only a two-second delay compared to the longer delays required for AU or WAV files.

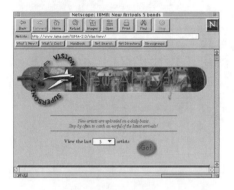

Tip: *Netscape and Internet Explorer both can guess at a Web site's protocol, which means you don't need to type* http://. *For example, try* www.iuma.com.

The IUMA site at http://iuma.com (Internet Underground Music Archive) is the epitome of organization, advanced sound technology, and beautiful graphics. Founders Robert Lord and Jeff Patterson are recent computer science graduates from the University of California at Santa Cruz. Created in 1993, the site is intended for independent, unsigned artists who want to reach the estimated 30 million people on the Internet. In 1994, IUMA was awarded "Best of the Web" by Internet book publisher O'Reilly & Associates for "contributions that have significantly improved the Internet."

For musicians, "base service" on IUMA is $120 per year and includes one song, one logo, two band or other images, up to two pages of text, and cross-indexing by artist, song title, location, and genre.

Songs submitted on DAT tape or CD are digitized and compressed to disk using MPEG2 audio compression techniques. MPEG (Motion Picture Experts Group) is a high-fidelity sound format (cassette quality) that offers better compression than AIFF or μ-law (pronounced *mu law*). On the Macintosh platform, Web site visitors will need the MPEG/CD player application to hear .MP2 files.

IUMA artists Brandee Amber Selck and David Beach create graphics with Macintosh computers, but create sound on Silicon Graphics Indys. Upon entering the site, the database of over 500 musicians can be viewed in five different ways.

1.

A Halo Called Fred
Abdirazak
Aboufadel, Edward
Action Figures
ADSR

2.

3.

4.

5.

1. New arrivals.

A list of the newest bands on IUMA.

2. By artist.

An alphabetical listing of all IUMA bands.

3. By genre.

A listing of musical genres or styles. Note that bands may be under multiple categories.

4. By location.

Bands can be sorted by country, state, and city.

5. By label (from the IUMA home page).

Several record labels have their own home page on IUMA. To access this section, click on the washing machine pictured on the IUMA home page.

Tip: When you discover a site you like, select Add Bookmark from the Bookmarks pull-down menu in Netscape. This will record the site address so you don't have to enter it the next time you want to visit. To view the list, select View Bookmarks from the Bookmarks pull-down menu. Click on the Export button if you want a copy of the list. Netscape will create a file, which you might email to a friend.

The Van Halen sound samples (http://vanhalen.warner-rcrds.com/Balance) are arranged on a beautiful page of wallpaper graphics and half buttons, which is the artist's clever scheme to use sound excerpts rather than full songs. Visitors have their choice of AIFF (Macintosh), WAV (Windows), or AU (Unix) files.

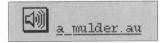

Enter *X-Files* on the Yahoo! search page (http://www.yahoo.com/search.html) and you'll get a list of several Web sites and several newsgroups. Charles McGrew's Web site has the best sound (http://www.rutgers.edu/x-files.html).

Tip: Although DigiPhone by Electric Magic does not have as high a profile as the new CoolTalk telephone tool developed by Apple Computer, it does not require as much hardware and software. CoolTalk requires a Power Macintosh running System 7.5.3 or later, Open Transport 1.1.1 or later, and QuickTime 2.5. These components may be downloaded from Apple at http://www .quickTime.apple.com/sw/qtmac.html.

Digiphone For Mac

DigiPhone (formerly NetPhone), introduced in 1995 by Electric Magic (http://www.emagic.com), provides realtime voice communication over the Internet on 68030-based Macintosh machines and Power Macs. *(Note: NetPhone was sold to Third Planet Publishing, makers of DigiPhone for the PC.)* Apple has introduced an Internet telephone tool called CoolTalk, which requires a Power Macintosh.

DigiPhone allows calls to be made between Macintosh Internet users over a minimum 14.4 Kbps phone connection, anywhere in the world. As Internet connections become more powerful in the next few years, Internet telephones could rival conventional phones.

Electric Magic, the maker of DigiPhone, provides a trial version of the software, which can be downloaded from their Web site (http://www.emagic.com). The demo is fully functional but terminates the call after 90 seconds.

Andrew Green, the British computer programmer who invented DigiPhone, compares the software—which uses a modem-based connection to send a maximum of 1,800 bytes of data per second—to telephone-quality speech (which consists of 8,000 bytes per second). To compensate, DigiPhone compresses the data before transmitting it over the Internet. At the receiving end, DigiPhone decompresses the data and sends it to the computer's speaker.

Although DigiPhone presents an interesting no-charge alternative to traditional fee-based long distance calling, America's Carriers Telecommunications Association, representing America's small- to medium-sized carriers, have filed a request with the FCC asking for a regulation of Internet phone products. Interestingly, the major carriers do not want regulation, and GATT (General Agreement of Trade and Tariffs) forbids individual governments from regulating computer networks.

CoolTalk for Mac™ OS Install

Tip: Although Apple has tried to make CoolTalk a video conferencing tool in addition to an Internet telephone tool, their product excludes non-Power Mac users.

CU-SeeMe from Cornell University is a free video conferencing software program for Macintosh/Windows machines and is not limited to Power Macintosh equipment. The software may be found at http://cu-seeme. edu/#GET. Multiple-party conferencing is also available with Cornell's Reflector program (Unix) or a Windows NT Reflector from White Pine Software. For more information, visit http://goliath.wpine.com/cu-seeme.html.

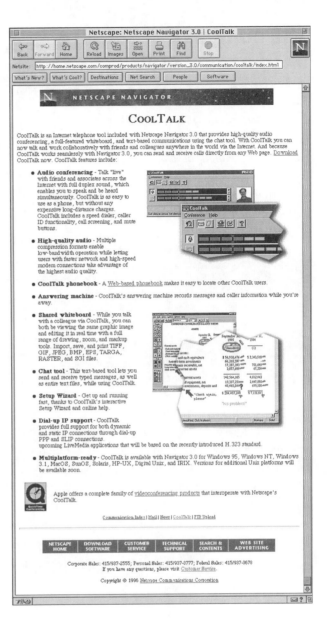

CoolTalk for Macintosh (http://home.netscape.com/comprod/products/navigator/version_3.0/communication/cooltalk/index.html) is an Internet telephone tool created by Apple Computer. Versions are available for Windows 3.1/3.11, Windows 95, Windows NT, and Unix machines.

The compact MIDI file format

Summary: *MIDI (Musical Instrument Digital Interface) was first developed in the 1980s. Although MIDI data transmission was originally developed for hardware sequencers, computer software sequencers and synthesizers have expanded MIDI's capabilities.*

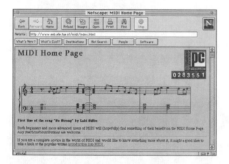

Tip: Heini Withagen's MIDI home page at http://www.eeb.tue.nl /midi/index.html has links to articles and tech tips, MIDI sound archives, MIDI software utilities, and special-interest group links.

Netscape's new LiveAudio technology plays WAV, AU, and MIDI files either through a floating sound controller or as background sound. *(Note: For details on background sounds, see* Greg Hess' tips on adding a background sound to your Web page.*)*

1. What is MIDI?

MIDI (Musical Instrument Digital Interface) refers to digital information passed between two MIDI-capable devices. The information is created with a music synthesizer. Although MIDI hardware sequencers predate computer-driven MIDI software, the transition to microcomputers has provided many more features. For example, not only can computers record and replay, but they can provide storage, editing capabilities, and elaborate synchronization, including MTC (MIDI Time Code) and SMPTE (Society of Motion Picture and Television Engineers).

2. MIDI file size is ideal for the Web.

MIDI music has been widely criticized by traditional instrumentalists. Some critics have described MIDI as having "little performance fire or flair, no musically sensitive timing, and lacking in subtlety."

In spite of this type of criticism, the format is ideal for the Web. File size is very small, and relative duration of play is very long compared to sampled sound.

File	Type	File Size	Duration
africa.mid	MIDI	50 K	2 minutes
seagull.au	AU	56 K	11 seconds

Set Netscape's Preferences to download music files

Summary: Once you've found free-of-rights MIDI or sampled sound on the Web, you'll need to adjust Netscape's Preferences to make the browser download a file and not play it.

1a.

2a.

When you click on a sound link in the Netscape browser window, Netscape's new sound controller will appear, and the sound will begin to play. If you want to save the file to your hard drive, alter the Preferences settings.

1. Open Preferences and select Helpers.

a. Choose Preferences from the Options pull-down menu.

b. In the dialog box that follows, click on the Helpers tab.

1b.

2. Edit MIDI file type handling.

a. In the Helpers dialog area, scroll to the LiveAudio section.

b. Click to select the audio/midi file type.

c. Click on the Edit button.

2b.

2c.

2d.

d. In the dialog box that follows, select the Save To Disk radio button.

e. Click on Ok. The next time you click on a sound link in the browser window, Netscape will save the file to your hard drive.

2e.

3. Rearrange where your files will be saved.

a. Choose Preferences from the Options pull-down menu to display the General Preferences dialog box.

b. Click on the Applications tab.

3a.

3b.

3c.

c. In the dialog box that follows, click on the Browse button.

d. Use the file list window to select a drive or folder where you would like Netscape to save your files.

e. Click on the Select… button at the bottom of the dialog box to select the drive or folder, and click on OK.

3d, 3e.

Greg Hess' tips on adding a background sound to a Web page

Summary: *Netscape's new LiveAudio HTML syntax added to the <EMBED> tag causes the browser to process a sound file and deliver it to your computer as a backgound sound.*

Above: *A room inside The Castle Red Dog.*

Above Right: *Greg Hess' The Castle Red Dog Web site, which provides support for his Palace site, is a virtual chat environment comprised of beautiful 3D images. To obtain Greg's Palace site address, go to the Palace directory at http://mansion.thepalace.com/ cgi-bin/directory.pl and look for "The Castle Red Dog."*

In this example, Greg Hess uses the <EMBED> tag and Netscape's new LiveAudio HTML syntax to add a background MIDI sound to his home page at http://www.geocities.com/~thecastle. *(Note: Look for Greg's MIDI files on the companion CD-ROM.)*

1. Open SimpleText.
Use SimpleText or your word processor. If you use a word processor, be sure to save the document as Text Only.

2. Create a new HTML document.
Start a new document with the following markup tags:

```
<HTML>

<HEAD>

<TITLE>The Castle</TITLE>

</HEAD>
```

3. Add an <EMBED> tag.
Use the SRC attribute to indicate the source of your sound file, the HIDDEN="TRUE" attribute to hide the sound controller, the AUTOSTART="TRUE" attribute to begin playing the sound automatically, the VOLUME="100"

Above: *A scene from The Castle Red Dog palace site. Visitors Jane and Les are represented as avatars against a 3D scene. Text entered in the Message box at the bottom of the screen causes a talk balloon to appear over an avatar's head. For more information on how to download a free palace client program or how to create your own palace site, visit http://www.thepalace.com.*

attribute to set the sound volume to the maximum level, and the LOOP="TRUE" attribute to play the sound continuously until the Stop button is pressed or the user goes to another page.

```
<HTML>

<HEAD>

<TITLE>The Castle</TITLE>

</HEAD>

<EMBED SRC="albinoni.mid" HIDDEN="TRUE"
AUTOSTART="TRUE" VOLUME="100" LOOP="TRUE">
```

4. Add a <BODY> tag.

Use the BACKGROUND attribute to add a background image, the BGCOLOR attribute to add a background color, and TEXT, LINK, VLINK, and ALINK attributes to add color to body text, link text, visited link text, and active link text. *(Note: See the* Online Tools *chapter for details on how to locate hexadecimal triplets to add color information to these attributes.)*

```
<HTML>

<HEAD>

<TITLE>The Castle</TITLE>

</HEAD>

<EMBED SRC="albinoni.mid" HIDDEN="TRUE"
AUTOSTART="TRUE" VOLUME="100" LOOP="TRUE">

<BODY BACKGROUND="a052.jpg" BGCOLOR="#00B9B9"
TEXT="#FFFFFF" LINK="#00FF00" VLINK="#01FFFF"
ALINK="#EE0000">
```

5. Add centered text.

```
<HTML>

<HEAD>

<TITLE>The Castle</TITLE>
```

Above: *A room inside The Castle Red Dog.*

```
</HEAD>

<EMBED SRC="albinoni.mid" HIDDEN="TRUE"
AUTOSTART="TRUE" VOLUME="100" LOOP="TRUE">

<BODY BACKGROUND="a052.jpg" BGCOLOR="#00B9B9"
TEXT="#FFFFFF" LINK="#00FF00" VLINK="#01FFFF"
ALINK="#EE0000">

<CENTER><B><FONT SIZE=+4>The Castle Red
Dog</FONT></B></CENTER>
```

6. Add a centered image.

```
<HTML>

<HEAD>

<TITLE>The Castle</TITLE>

</HEAD>

<EMBED SRC="albinoni.mid" HIDDEN="TRUE"
AUTOSTART="TRUE" VOLUME="100" LOOP="TRUE">

<BODY BACKGROUND="a052.jpg" BGCOLOR="#00B9B9"
TEXT="#FFFFFF" LINK="#00FF00" VLINK="#01FFFF"
ALINK="#EE0000">

<CENTER><B><FONT SIZE=+4>The Castle Red
Dog</FONT></B></CENTER>

<CENTER><A HREF="index2.htm"><IMG SRC="lothern.gif"
BORDER=0></A></CENTER>
```

7. Add additional centered text.

```
<HTML>

<HEAD>

<TITLE>The Castle</TITLE>

</HEAD>

<EMBED SRC="albinoni.mid" HIDDEN="TRUE"
AUTOSTART="TRUE" VOLUME="100" LOOP="TRUE">

<BODY BACKGROUND="a052.jpg" BGCOLOR="#00B9B9"
TEXT="#FFFFFF" LINK="#00FF00" VLINK="#01FFFF"
ALINK="#EE0000">

<CENTER><B><FONT SIZE=+4>The Castle Red
Dog</FONT></B></CENTER>
```

Above: *A room inside The Castle Red Dog.*

```
<CENTER><A HREF=index2.htm><IMG SRC="lothern.gif"
BORDER=0></A></CENTER>
```

```
<CENTER><FONT SIZE=+1>Out of the fog of night, comes
an oasis for the weary. Come and enjoy Castle Red Dog
- A Palace virtual chat site with no commercial
interests, just good art, good fun, and good people.
So if you are ready to enter, click on the Castle and
head inside to explore the many
delights.</FONT></CENTER>
```

Tip: MIDI Web at http://www.midiweb .com has an assortment of MIDI files to download.

8. Summary of HTML tags used in this section.

The tags you see in this list (in alphabetical order) reflect the HTML 3.2 specification.

<BODY>...</BODY>

This tag uses the BACKGROUND attribute to add an image to the background, and the BGCOLOR, TEXT, LINK, VLINK, and ALINK attributes to add color to the background and text. *(Note: See the* Online Tools *chapter for directions on how to add hexadecimal triplet values to these attributes.)*

<CENTER>...</CENTER>

A tag used to center an element on a page.

<EMBED>

This tag uses the SRC attribute to indicate the source of your sound file, the HIDDEN="TRUE" attribute to hide the sound controller, the AUTOSTART="TRUE" attribute to begin playing the sound automatically, the VOLUME="100" attribute to set the sound volume to the maxium level, and the LOOP="TRUE" attribute to play the sound continuously until the Stop button is pressed or the user goes to another page. For example:

```
<EMBED SRC="albinoni.mid" HIDDEN="TRUE"
AUTOSTART="TRUE" VOLUME="100" LOOP="TRUE">
```

<HTML>...</HTML>

A tag used to open and close an HTML document.

<HEAD>...</HEAD>

A tag used to open and close the header portion of a document.

<IMG>

Used to refer to an inline image, this tag uses the SRC attribute, which represents the URL (location) of the image. For example:

```
<IMG SRC = "lothern.gif">
```

<TITLE>...</TITLE>

Used under the <HEAD> tag, the <TITLE> tag describes the title of a document, which shows up inside a document's title bar.

Creating a link to sound files on your Web page

Summary: *Create HTML links to AIFF, AU (Mac and Unix µ-law, pronounced mu law), WAV (Windows), MP2 (MPEG audio), RA (RealAudio), and MIDI sound files.*

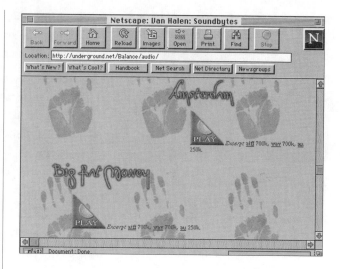

The Van Halen Soundbytes page offers AIFF, WAV, and AU files for downloading. To see the HTML tags that make up a page in Netscape, select Source from the View pull-down menu. This is a practical way to learn how to use HTML tags. For example, the HTML tags for the links to the Van Halen "Amsterdam" sound bytes include:

```
<DL><DL><DL><DL><DL>
<DD><IMG ALT="Amsterdam"
WIDTH=118 HEIGHT=50
SRC="/Balance/audio/balance-amsterdam.gif">
<BR>
<DL>
<DD><FONT SIZE=2>
<IMG ALT="" WIDTH=58 HEIGHT=58 ALIGN= BOTTOM
SRC="butt_play.gif"> <I>Excerpt</I>
<A HREF="/Balance/sounds/amstrdm.aiff">aiff</A> 700k,
<A HREF="/Balance/sounds/amstrdm.wav">wav</A> 700k,
<A HREF="/Balance/sounds/amstrdm.au">au</A> 250k.
</DL></FONT>
</DL></DL></DL></DL></DL>
<P>
```

Follow these steps to get an understanding of the effect these tags have on a Web page:

1. Open SimpleText.

Use SimpleText or your word processor. If you use a word processor, be sure to save the document as Text Only.

2. Create a new HTML document.

Start a new document with the following markup tags:

```
<HTML>
<HEAD>
<TITLE>Mother Mary:Soundbytes</TITLE>
</HEAD>
<BODY>
```

3. Try the definition list tag <DL>.

Add <DL>, followed by the word *Excerpt*. Add an ending </DL> tag .

```
<HTML>
<HEAD>
<TITLE>Mother Mary:Soundbytes</TITLE>
</HEAD>
<BODY>
<DL>Excerpt</DL>
```

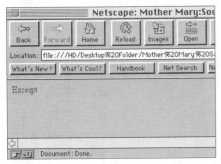

3.

Save this document as *Definition List Sample*, and open it in Netscape. Select Open File from the File pull-down menu to view your HTML document.

4. Try nesting two <DL> tags.

Add another <DL> and another </DL> tag around the word *Excerpt*.

```
<HTML>
<HEAD>
<TITLE>Mother Mary:Soundbytes</TITLE>
</HEAD>
<BODY>
<DL><DL>Excerpt</DL></DL>
```

4.

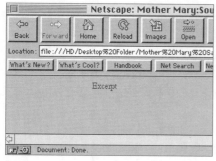

5.

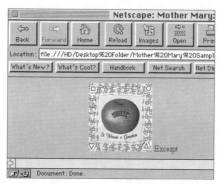

6.

5. Try nesting four <DL> tags.

Add two more <DL> and two more </DL> tags around the word *Excerpt*.

```
<HTML>
<HEAD>
<TITLE>Mother Mary:Soundbytes</TITLE>
</HEAD>
<BODY>
<DL><DL><DL><DL>Excerpt</DL></DL></DL></DL>
```

6. Add an inline image.

Insert an <IMG> tag after the opening definition list tags in the form <IMG SRC="apple.gif">. The SRC attribute indicates the file name of the image. (*Note: The file name alone, without a path name, indicates that the image file is in the same directory as the HTML document.*)

```
<HTML>
<HEAD>
<TITLE>Mother Mary:Soundbytes</TITLE>
</HEAD>
<BODY>
<DL><DL><DL><DL>
<IMG SRC = "apple.gif">
Excerpt
</DL></DL></DL></DL>
```

7. Add an ALT attribute to the image tag.

The ALT attribute in an <IMG> tag is an accommodation for people with text browsers. In this example, they see the word *Apple* instead of the GIF image.

```
<HTML>
<HEAD>
<TITLE>Mother Mary:Soundbytes</TITLE>
</HEAD>
<BODY>
<DL><DL><DL><DL>
<IMG ALT="Apple"
SRC = "apple.gif">
Excerpt
</DL></DL></DL></DL>
```

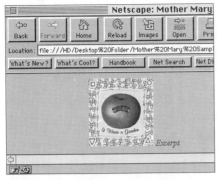

8.

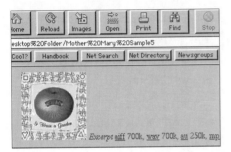

9.

8. Add an italic tag around *Excerpt*.

Add a set of italic tags around the word *Excerpt* with the pair
<I> and </I>.

```
<HTML>
<HEAD>
<TITLE>Mother Mary:Soundbytes</TITLE>
</HEAD>
<BODY>
<DL><DL><DL><DL>
<IMG ALT="Apple" WIDTH =100 HEIGHT = 102
SRC = "apple.gif">
<I>Excerpt</I>
</DL></DL></DL></DL>
```

9. Specify the height and width.

Insert WIDTH =100 and HEIGHT =102 in the <IMG> tag.
This information may be obtained from the Image Size dialog box in Photoshop. Specifying the HEIGHT and WIDTH
as attributes of the <IMG> tag speeds the loading of the
image on the Web page.

```
<HTML>
<HEAD>
<TITLE>Mother Mary:Soundbytes</TITLE>
</HEAD>
<BODY>
<DL><DL><DL><DL>
<IMG ALT="Apple" WIDTH = 100 HEIGHT = 102
SRC = "apple.gif">
<I>Excerpt</I>
</DL></DL></DL></DL>
```

10. Add links to sound files.

Create links to sound files by opening with the link tag <A>
and the HREF attribute, entering text, and then the closing
</A> tag. This text serves as the clickable hotspot on the
Web page and can be identified with an underline.

```
<HTML>
<HEAD>
<TITLE>Mother Mary:Soundbytes</TITLE>
</HEAD>
<BODY>
<DL><DL><DL><DL>
```

Tip: Keyboard Magazine's *Web site is a great resource for musicians who are interested in electronic sound. Visit http://www.keyboardmag.com.*

```
<IMG insert IMG attributes shown in previous steps
   (see Step 9)
SRC = "apple.gif">
<I>Excerpt</I>
<A HREF="/sounds/"garden.aiff">aiff</A> 700k,
<A HREF="/sounds/"garden.wav">wav</A> 700k,
<A HREF="/sounds/"garden.au">au</A> 250k,
<A HREF="/sounds/"garden.mp2">mp2</A> 250k,
<A HREF="/sounds/"garden.RA">RA</A> 250k.
</DL></DL></DL></DL>
```

File Format	Notes
AIFF	An audio file format used on the Macintosh platform.
WAV	An audio file format used on the Windows platform.
AU	An audio file format read by Sun Sparc, NeXT workstations, and Macintosh computers.
MP2	A hi-fidelity file format used on the Macintosh, Windows, and Unix platforms.
MIDI	A digital sound file format developed in the 1980s that has recently become popular on the Web because of its small file size and long play duration.
RA	An audio file format developed by Progressive Technology, Inc. for instant playback or *audio streaming.* Instant playback is only available from servers equipped with RealAudio server software, although the RA file will do a normal download to Macintosh, Windows, and Unix machines.

Tip: The ultimate band list at http://www.ubl.com is the Web's largest list of music links where a Web visitor can add music links for new bands. Browse the site alphabetically, by genre, by resource (newsgroups, mailing lists, FAQ files, lyrics, guitar tablatures, digitized songs, or Web pages), or view the complete list.

11. Summary of HTML tags used in this section.

The tags you see in this list (in alphabetical order) reflect the HTML 3.2 specification.

<A>...</A>

Referred to as an *anchor*, this tag uses the HREF attribute to link to an external sound file. For example:

```
<A HREF="/sounds/"garden.aiff">aiff</A>
```

(Note: The sound file name must include the path name if the file is located in another directory.)

<BODY>...</BODY>

A tag used to open and close the body of a document.

<DL>...</DL>

The definition list tag is usually used for definitions or short paragraphs with no bullets or numbering. In this section, this tag is nested four times to indent the word *Excerpt.* For example:

```
<DL><DL><DL><DL>Excerpt</DL></DL></DL></DL>
```

<HTML>...</HTML>

A tag used to open and close an HTML document.

<HEAD>...</HEAD>

A tag used to open and close the header portion of a document.

<I>...</I>

A tag used to format with italics.

<IMG>

Used to refer to an inline image, this tag uses the SRC attribute, which represents the URL (location) of the image. In this section, the <IMG> tag also uses the WIDTH and HEIGHT attributes, which speed up the downloading of the image, and the ALT attribute, which accommodates users limited to text browsers. For example:

```
<IMG ALT="Apple" WIDTH =100 HEIGHT = 102
SRC = "apple.gif">
```

<TITLE>...</TITLE>

Used under the <HEAD> tag, the <TITLE> tag describes the title of a document, which shows up inside a document's title bar.

Creating sound effects with clip media

Summary: By using free-of-rights clip media from public sound archives on the Web, you can add sound effects to photographic images.

Tip: Look for sound effects at http://info .fuw.edu.pl/multimedia/sounds/animals.

Tip: The images on this page are from Pacific Coast Software's collection of stock photography at http://www .pacific-coast.com.

Applying what he learned when working with an analog sound medium, Tom Cipolla selected electronic images from Pacific Coast Software's collection of stock photography, used Alberto Ricci's SoundEffects software to shape the sound, and converted files to formats for playback on Unix and Windows machines.

1. Select your photographs.

When selecting photographs to combine with sound effects, look for shots with elements that evoke sounds. Pictures with human content offer the greatest range of potential sounds.

2. How many sounds?

When sound waves are mixed in an 8-bit environment, there seems to be too little information for individual sounds to maintain their integrity. Clip sounds from the Web or sound effect CD-ROMs are usually 8-bit. Try to limit your selection to two sounds unless you start with 16-bit sound.

Short Country #2.AIFF

horse.aiff

3. "Listening" with your mind.

Put yourself in the picture, and try to imagine what you would hear. Look for sounds that are strong enough to convey what's happening in the photo. You cannot expect to hold a viewer's attention for long—15 or 20 seconds should be the maximum duration for your sound clips.

4. Compare clip sound format, sample rate, and other characteristics.

SoundMachine can be used to compare sound file characteristics such as file formats, number of channels, sample rate (Figure 4a), sample size, compression, and total time. SoundMachine displays each of these characteristics on the Control Panel as the choices are selected (Figure 4b). Tom Cipolla noted the following information about the file's short country.aiff and horse.aiff:

short country.aiff
Format: AIFF
Sample Size: 8 bits
Number of Channels: Stereo
Total Time: 7 seconds
Sample Rate: 22.3 kHz

horse.aiff
Format: AIFF
Sample Size: 8 bits
Number of Channels: Mono
Total Time: 1 second
Sample Rate: 22.3 kHz

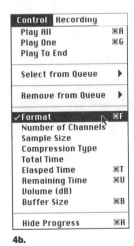

4b.

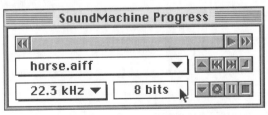

4a.

File conversion: AU to AIFF or WAV to AIFF

Summary: *Use SoundApp to convert AU files to AIFF. (Note: SoundEffects, the sound editor used in the next section, will be needed to read AIFF files.)*

1.

SoundApp

Tip: *When converting to AU, use the selection called NeXT on the SoundApp pull-down menu.*

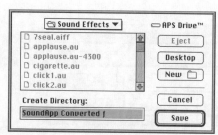

3.

The clip sound files found on numerous sites across the Web may need to be converted to a file format that your sound editor software can read. For example, Windows WAV files can be converted to AIFF with a Macintosh sound utility called SoundApp (look for SoundApp on the CD-ROM in the back of this book). SoundApp can also be used to convert edited files to WAV format for Windows visitors and AU for Unix visitors.

1. Select the file you'd like to convert.
Open the SoundApp software, and select Convert from the File pull-down menu.

2. Identify the file and format you need.
Use the convert dialog box to locate the file you need to convert. Choose the file format you need on the pop-up menu beneath the window.

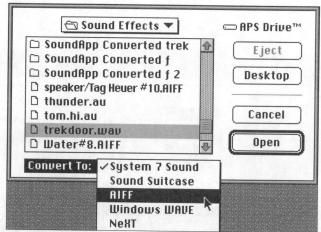

2.

3. Select a folder for the new file.
Either create a new destination folder for the converted file or select the default folder by clicking on Save.

Mixing clip music with sound effects in SoundEffects

Summary: *Use Alberto Ricci's SoundEffects software to alter and mix sounds.*

Tip: *Use Adobe Premiere to convert free-of-rights CD sounds to AIFF files. Open a new project, import, then open a CD sound, and export it as an AIFF file.*

Select Exactly

Select exactly

| 8 | Seconds ▼ |

of sound

○ Before
○ Centered on
◉ After

the selection.

[Cancel] [OK]

1.

Tip: *The Music Bakery Sound CD collection is royalty-free music available through a buy-out license. For more information, call 800-229-0312.*

Tom Cipolla gathered a country music clip from *The Music Bakery's* Sound CD, which contains a large selection of production-quality music sold with a royalty-free buy-out license. He also located the sound of a horse whinneying on a public domain archive on the Web. The sound sampling rates of the sounds Tom intended to mix were 8.8 kHz and 22.1 kHz. This discrepancy is not a problem easily straightened out in SoundEffects because the software identifies the differences and prompts the user about resampling sounds.

1. Clip a portion of a CD country music file.

Open a music file in SoundEffects, play the file, and determine the duration of the clip you'd like to use. Choose Select Exactly from the Selection pull-down menu to open the dialog box shown in Figure 1. Select minutes from the pop-up menu, and type in the number of minutes you'd like selected.

(Note: Sections of the wave pattern may also be altered with the Cut, Copy, and Paste commands. Start by drag-selecting a section of the wave pattern, and then use the Cut, Copy, or Paste commands.)

2. Save the music clip.

Select Save from the File pull-down menu, and save this music clip to your hard drive.

4b.   4c.

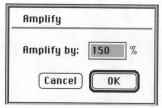

5.

Amplify

Amplify by: 150 %

        Cancel   OK

7.

3. Create more horse sound.

Open the horse sound in SoundEffects, select the wave pattern, copy it, and paste two more wave patterns at the end of the existing pattern.

4. Paste the horse sound into the music file.

Copy the new horse wave pattern to the clipboard. Open the music file, and paste the horse sound into channel 2. Click on Resample when the message in Figure 4a appears.

You are trying to paste a sound sampled at 8.000 kHz into a sound sampled at 22.050 kHz. Do you want me to resample the sound you are inserting at 22.050 kHz?

Cancel   Resample

4a.

(Note: If you need to create a second or third channel, drag the channel icon above or below the existing channel, as shown in Figure 4b. If you need to delete a channel, drag a channel icon to the trash, as shown in Figure 4c.)

5. Resampling.

According to Alberto Ricci, resampling sound from 8 to 22 kHz introduces a little distortion. To remove some of the distortion, select the wave pattern of the sound that was resampled, and then select Low Pass|FIR from the Effects|FIR|IIR pull-down menu.

6. Test the sound.

Click on the Play button to review the sound.

7. Amplify the music.

At this point, the horse's whinneying sound overwhelms the sound of the music. Select the music wave pattern, and select Amplify from the Effects pull-down menu. Enter *150* to increase the sound of the music.

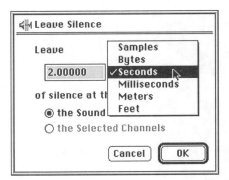

8a.

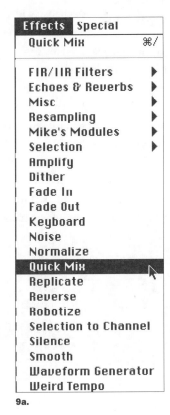

9a.

8. Leave two seconds of silence.

To balance the sound a little more (so that the horse doesn't overwhelm the music), select the horse wave pattern, then select Leave Silence from the Edit pull-down menu. Select seconds from the pop-up menu (shown in Figure 8a), enter *2*, and click on OK. The result is shown in Figure 8b.

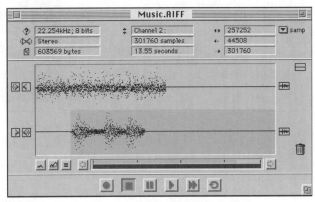

8b.

9. Mix the music and the horse sound.

Start by selecting both channels, then:

a. Choose Quick Mix from the Effects pull-down menu.

b. Choose New Document and Mono in the dialog box that follows. Click on OK.

(Note: When you mix sound, the respective proportions of each of the sounds are reduced. For example, if you have three channels and you mix the first two, then mix the output with a third channel, the proportions become .25, .25, and .50. If you mix all three together, the proportions will be .33, .33, and .33.)

10. Save the new sound file.

Select Save from the File pull-down menu, and name the file Music/horse.aiff.

9b.

Recording and mixing sound in SoundEffects

Summary: Use Alberto Ricci's SoundEffects software to record and mix sounds.

Occasionally, you'll want to record your own sound effects when clip sounds are not available. For the crowd photo, Tom used the sound of a crowd on a tape cassette he had recorded at a sports event. Your tape recorder can be hooked up to your Macintosh with a cable that runs from your tape recorder's output jack to the Macintosh microphone jack. You'll need a 1/8-inch plug on the Macintosh end. You should be able to find the proper cable at your local Radio Shack store. Buy a cable designed for a mono signal. Even if your Macintosh can handle stereo sound, your recording should be mono to keep file sizes small.

1. Open a new sound document.

Open SoundEffects. Use the default blank sound document or select New from the File pull-down menu.

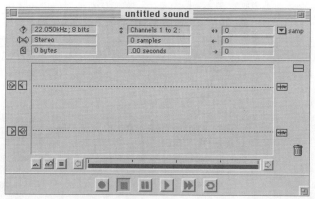

1.

2. Click the Record button.

Click on the circular red Record button at the bottom of the document. *(Note: This record button does not start the sound recording.)*

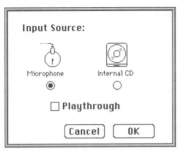

3b.

3. The Record dialog box.

To see more of the record dialog box:

a. Click on the small triangle to the left of General Settings.

b. Click on Device Settings to make sure the microphone is selected as your sound input source.

c. If your Macintosh can record at 16 bits, select this option from the Sampling Size pop-up box.

d. Set the the Play-Through Volume to Off if you're using a microphone hooked up to your Mac, otherwise feedback will occur. *(Note: If your external sound source is a CD player, you can turn up the Play-Through Volume to hear what is being recorded.)*

3c, 3d.

4. Click on the Record button.

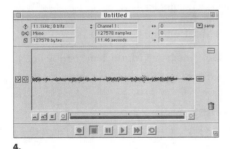

When your tape recorder is hooked up to your Macintosh, queue up your tape so that it is ready to play. When you're ready to begin, press Play on your tape recorder, and click on the circular record button at the top of the dialog box. When you're happy with the recording, click on Save. Figure 4 shows the result of Tom Cipolla's crowd recordings.

4.

5. Save the new sound file.

Select Save from the File pull-down menu, and name this file Crowd.aiff.

6. Create a new channel for a music sound.

Tom wanted to mix the sound of the National Anthem he found on a sound effects CD with the sound of the crowd. To do this, he dragged the existing channel icon to create a second channel.

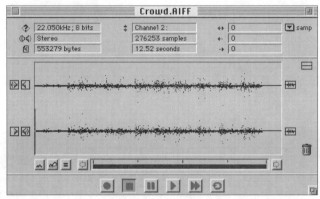

6.

7. Paste a music sound into the crowd file.

Tom opened the National Anthem file, selected the wave pattern, and copied it to the clipboard. He then pasted the music sound into channel 2.

8. Mix the two sounds.

Start be selecting both channels, then:

a. Choose Quick Mix from the Effects pull-down menu.

b. Choose New Document and Mono in the dialog box that follows. Click on OK.

9. Resave the new sound file.

Select Save from the File pull-down menu, and name this file crowd.aiff.

File optimization: Resample and downsample sound files for playback on the Web

Summary: *Take an inventory of file sizes, and use downsampling techniques to reduce them.*

After mixing sound for each of the photographs, Tom Cipolla took an account of the file components and total file sizes to see whether the files would be appropriate for the Web. File size is related to duration and sampling rate.

Larger files can be scaled down by resampling, although there is a loss of quality.

	File Size	Characteristics
Picture: Horse		
music (country)	330 K	Stereo, 8-bit, 22.254 kHz
horse	110 K	Mono, 8-bit, 22.050 kHz
Mix	605 K	Stereo, 8-bit, 22.3 kHz
Picture: Crowd		
crowd	286 K	Stereo, 8-bit, 22.3 kHz
National Anthem	100 K	Mono, 8-bit, 22.3 kHz
Mix	561 K	Stereo, 8-bit, 22.3 kHz
Picture: Cruise Ship		
steamship whistle	330 K	Mono, 8-bit, 22.3 kHz
Picture: Waterfall		
music (orchestral)	1276 K	Stereo, 8-bit, 22.3 kHz
waterfall	33 K	Stereo, 8-bit, 22.3 kHz
Mix	649 K	Stereo, 8-bit, 22.3 kHz

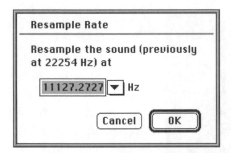

Resample Rate

Resample the sound (previously at 22254 Hz) at

11127.2727 ▼ Hz

Cancel   OK

Tip: Alberto explains that if you must halve the size of a 44 kHz, 16-bit sound, it is better to downsample it to 22 kHz, 16 bits, instead of 44 kHz, 8 bits. Depending on how small you need to make the file, you could downsample both the rate and the size.

If you downsample a 22 kHz, 16-bit sound to 22 kHz, 8 bit, only the Macs with 16-bit output (Power Macs and AV Macs) will notice the difference. If you downsample the sound to 11 kHz, 16 bit, it will sound better on the 16-bit Macs, but the 8-bit Macs will "hear" the sound as if it was 11 kHz, 8 bit.

For music, it is best to keep sound to 16 bits. However, for speech, 8 bit is suitable.

Alberto Ricci, the author of SoundEffects, recommends the following steps to reduce a sound's file size:

1. Remove trailing silence.

Remove any following silence parts. This often reduces the file as much as 100 K.

a. Drag-select the silence in the wave pattern.

b. Press Delete.

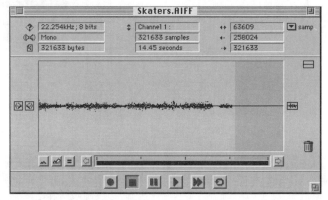

1a.

2. Resample the sound.

Downsample 16-bit sounds to 8 bit.

a. Select the sound wave.

b. Select Downsample from the Effects|Resampling pull-down menu.

3. Mix the channels to a mono sound.

If stereo sound is not essential, this step will reduce the file size.

a. Select the sound wave.

b. Choose Quick Mix from the Effects pull-down menu.

c. Choose New Document and Mono in the dialog box that follows. Click on OK.

Tip: Look for the commercial release of SoundEffects, which will be called SoundMaker.

4. Resample to 11 kHz or 8 kHz.

If the sound still sounds good, resampling to 11 kHz or 8 kHz will reduce the file size.

a. Select the sound wave.

b. Select Resample from the Effects|Resampling pull-down menu.

c. Select 11127.27 from the popup menu, or enter 8. Click on OK.

After trailing silence was removed, stereo sounds were mixed as mono, and the sounds were resampled to 11 kHz, the resulting sounds were substantially smaller. To reduce the sounds even further would require shortening the sound duration.

Picture	File Size (Mix)	New File Size
Horse	605 K	99 K
Crowd	561 K	154 K
Cruise ship	660 K	176 K
Waterfall	649 K	143 K

File conversion: Preparing sound files for other platforms

Summary: Use SoundApp to convert files for downloading on other platforms.

1.

File conversion comes at the end of your sound project when you're preparing files for your Web server. You'll need WAV files for Windows visitors and AU files for Unix visitors. Note that SoundApp refers to the AU format as NeXT.

1. Start SoundApp.

Start SoundApp, and select Convert from the File pull-down menu.

2. Identify the target file format.

Locate the file to be converted in the file list window. Press on the pop-up menu (Figure 2) beneath the window, and identify the target file format, which is Windows WAVE and NeXT (or AU).

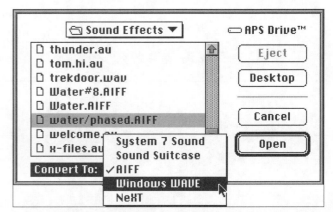

2.

3, 4.

3. Create a destination folder.

SoundApp will create a folder for your converted files. Accept the folder name or create a new one. Decide where you'd like the new folder to be saved. For example, click on Desktop if you'd like to see the folder saved to the desktop.

4. Save and convert.

Saving will start the conversion process. Look for your newly created folder; your new files will be inside.

Artist featured in this chapter:

Curtis Eberhardt has a B.A. from the Art Institute of Chicago and an M.A. from New York University. Curtis specializes in Macromedia Director, Strata Studio Pro, Softimage, Electric Image, FormZ, and Photoshop. His clients include Messner Advertising, Web TV/Philips Magnavox, and Young and Rubicam.

CurtisAE@aol.com

http://www.new-kewl .com/curtiscape

GIF Animation And Shockwave

GIF animation and Shockwave have become the two most popular forms of animation on the Web. This chapter opens with several examples of both and then covers tips on how to create your own animation projects. By following examples created by new media artist Curtis Eberhardt, you'll gather valuable infomation on how to use Photoshop to create animation stills, optimize color GIF images using GIF Wizard, assemble a GIF animation in GIFBuilder, assemble a Macromedia Director animation, and created a "Shocked" version of a Macromedia Director movie for the Web.

Curtis Eberhardt's GIF animation

Summary: *Follow the URLs mentioned in this section to view Curtis Eberhardt's GIF animations on the Web.*

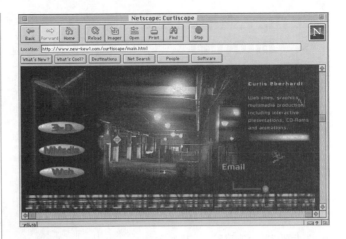

Above: *A close-up of the spaceship GIF animation.*
Above Right: *Curtis Eberhardt's portfolio page contains a tiny spaceship GIF animation in the lower-right corner (http://www.new-kewl .com/curtiscape/ main.html).*

Above: *Curtis Eberhardt's home page, containing a GIF animation (http://www.new-kewl.com/curtiscape).*

G IF animation is easy to implement because the animated image may be placed inline—or embedded in a Netscape page using the <IMG> tag. No scripting or plug-in is required.

This page and the next page contain GIF animation examples created by Curtis Eberhardt. For artists who are thinking about creating their own GIF animation, Curtis offers the following suggestions.

1. Create stills in Photoshop or GIFBuilder.

Use Photoshop to create animation stills for your "flip-book" animation, and save your animation stills as GIF or PICT images. GIFBuilder, by Yves Piguet, is an easy-to-use tool for building GIF animations. For simple animations that include only movement, start with one image in GIFBuilder, move the art, and save successive new stills.

2. Be conservative with GIF file sizes.

Try to limit the number of stills in your GIF animation as well as the physical size. Here are some examples:

Animation File	File Size
Curtis Spaceship (this page)	9 K
Bumpy Head (next page)	18 K
Bumpy Arrows (next page)	5 K

Bumpy, king of the Internet

Above: *Curtis Eberhardt's rotating cartoon head created with GIFBuilder. To see Bumpy, visit http://www.new-kewl.com/curtiscape/ bump.html.*
Right: *Curtis created his Bumpy character using 3D software.*

Above: *Curtis Eberhardt's animated arrows, created with GIFBuilder.*

3. Use GIF Wizard to reduce GIF file size.

GIF Wizard on the Raspberry Hill Web site (http://www
.raspberryhill.com/gifwizard.html) is an online tool that can
be used to reduce the size of your GIF images. (*Note: For
step-by-step instructions on how to use GIF Wizard, see* GIF
Wizard at Raspberry Hill *in this chapter.*)

Animation and interactive Web games that use Shockwave, Java, live video, and QTVR

Summary: Visit Web sites with Shockwave and Java to gather ideas for your own pages.

Above: *Web visitors who want to contact "the spirits of the Dominion" can play a WeeJee board game written in Java.*

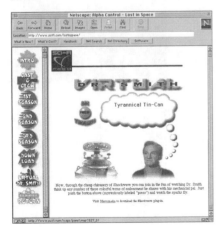

Above: *The SciFi Channel's Lost in Space pages contain a Virtual Dr. Smith Shockwave movie.*

The SciFi Channel's Dominion site (USA Network) at http://www.scifi.com is one of the most technically advanced sites on the Web. Visitors will find games and interactive pages created with Shockwave, Java, and CGI scripts. A live video feed accessed through a link on this site's home page displays what is currently being shown on the SciFi Channel. (*Note: Visitors can see video frames update every 30 seconds. To see new frames, they must click on the Netscape Reload button.*)

The SciFi Channel's Web site is produced by the following creative team: Creative Director Sharleen Smith, Senior Internet Producer Gary Markowitz, Online Projects Manager Sean Redlitz, and Lead Programmer Jamie Biggar.

"No designers were harmed in the production of this Web site."

Above: *Visitors who explore the links on The Arrival site discover an interactive console. It opens in an extra window over the Netscape browser.*

Above: *The content of the console's largest frame changes in response to mouse clicks on folder tabs.*

The Arrival site was created for the Live Entertainment's movie starring Charlie Sheen. This site has an interactive "console" created with Shockwave and Livescript. The button panel is a Shockwave movie with flickering lights and machine sound effects. The folder tabs are clickable hotspots that branch to pages with movie stills, movie clips, and a movie synopsis. You can reach The Arrival site at http://www.thearrival.com.

Movie fans interested in movie stills can use Netscape's built-in downloading image feature. To download a JPEG image:

- Position your mouse over an image. Then press and hold the mouse button until a pop-up menu appears.

- Select Save This Image in the pop-up menu.

- In the dialog box that follows, click on Save.

- The JPEG image will be saved to your hard drive.

Shockwave movies with moveable parts

Above: *The Ben & Jerry's Hair Game imitates a real-life game that uses a magnet and iron filings to move hair around.*

Above: *The Disguise-O-Rama game from Marlow Publications imitates a real-life paper cut-out game.*

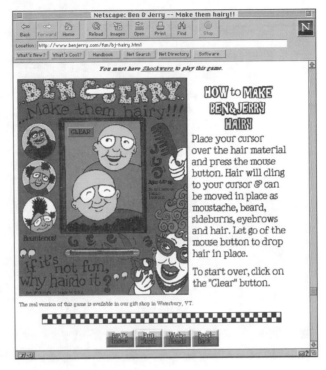

The Disguise-O-Rama game, the Ben & Jerry's Hair game, and the Build Your Own Bug game make innovative use of Director's moveable sprite option. This feature, which can be implemented in the Score or through Lingo, allows viewers to slide cast members around while a movie is playing. Visit the following sites to see Shockwave movies with moveable parts:

- **Disguise-O-Rama** (http://www.marlowpub.com/ Marlowe/disguise2.html) is based on Marlow Publication's cartoon characters Sam and Max. The Shockwave game was art directed by Pauline Neuwirth

Above: *To build a bug, players select bug parts from a collection at the bottom of the screen and drag them to the bug "stage."*

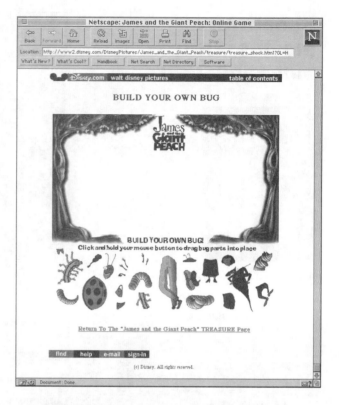

(redkit@aol.com) and created by Chris Kingsley (webmaster@romdog.com).

- **Ben & Jerry's Hair Game** (http://www.benjerry.com/fun/bj-hairy.html) is based on a magnet hair game available in the Ben & Jerry's gift shop in Waterbury, Vermont.

- **Build Your Own Bug** (http://www.benjerry.com/fun/bj-hairy.html) was created for Disney's movie *James and the Giant Peach.*

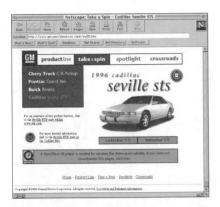

Tip: QuickTime VR authoring tools are available from the Apple Developer's Association (APDA) at apda@applelink .apple.com.

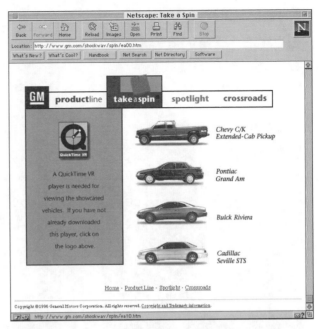

General Motor's Product Line Web page has a small Shockwave movie and interesting QuickTime VR movie downloads of car exteriors and interiors. You can reach General Motor's Web site at http://www.gm.com/ shock-wav/spin/ea00.htm.

QuickTime VR is Apple's cross platform movie format that offers a virtual reality experience in the form of a 320 by 240 (or full-screen size), 360 degree panoramic image. The movie can be played on a Macintosh or a Windows computer using the QuickTime VR Player. To download the QTVR Player, visit Apple Computer's Web site at http://qtvr.quick-time.apple.com/archive/index.html. Viewers can rotate the scene by positioning the mouse pointer to the left or right edge of the movie and pressing down on the mouse button. To Zoom in, press the mouse button and hold down the Option key. To Zoom out, press the mouse button and hold down the Control key.

QuickTime VR movies may be formed from either still photographs or computer generated images. The movie corrects the distortion ordinarily associated with a panoramic image by incorporating a distortion correction algorithm. The distortion correction occurs on the fly while a viewer is panning a scene.

Promotional game previews— created with Shockwave

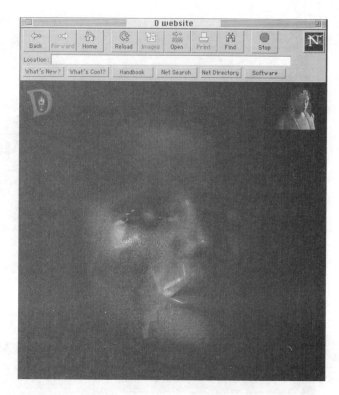

A Shockwave preview of D, a CD-ROM game created by Acclaim Entertainment can be found at http://www. acclaimnation.com/D. The D site was created by Engine.RDA, a multimedia start-up inside RDA International. Engine.RDA is a 20-year old New York City advertising agency owned by Michael Racz and Gail Dessimoz. Engine.RDA's client, Acclaim Entertainment, is well-known for their Mortal Kombat game, the most successful CD-ROM game ever produced.

Part of the nine-member Engine.RDA team, Web artist, animator, and pro-grammer Curtis Eberhardt can be reached at CurtisAE@aol.com.

"Until all digital media blends into one medium, design professionals must adapt their skills to several different formats."

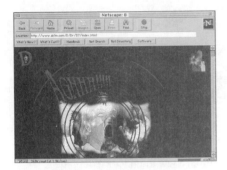

Above: A QuickTime movie preview of D is available on Acclaim Entertainment's Web site as a movie.

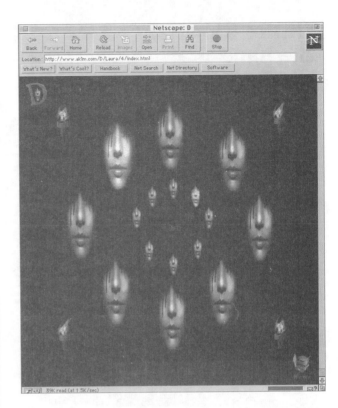

He created most of the art and Shockwave movies on the Web site. The Engine.RDA team is led by digital media creative director, Regina Joseph. Regina is a multimedia content developer who frequently speaks at design and entertainment conferences. She is well-known for her creation of *Blender*, the pop-culture digizine launched in 1994.

Regina's other team members include: 3D and animation artist Alex Ostroy, digital designer Chris Capuozzo, digital designer and recordable media artist John Hill, digital video specialists Claude Borenzweig and Damien Clayton, programmer Vineel Shah, Webmaster Rob Keenan, and online media technical director Rob Molchon. When asked about the rapid changes in digital design, Regina explains that multimedia artists must constantly reorient themselves to the changes in digital media. Until all digital media blend into one medium, creative design professionals must adapt their skills to several different formats such as CD-ROM, enhanced CD, and the World Wide Web. A fourth, digital versatile disc (DVD) is expected to be available soon.

"Killer Klowns, the band that produced the game's sound track, reports the song goes over very well in New York's downtown clubs."

Above: *Razorsnails pokes fun at drag racing and California skateboard art. You can reach the Thunk site at http://www .thunk.com (Note: look for Razorsnails and other Shockwave samples on the companion CD-ROM in the back of this book).*

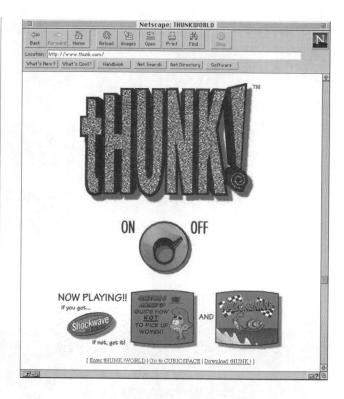

The Thunk site (http://www.thunk.com) contains a humorous digital game prototype called Razorsnails. The Shockwave movie was art directed by Larry Rosenthal and created by artist/animator Jason Fruchter. When the green light goes on, the snail runs over a razorblade. During the race, "snailjumps" include obstacles such as thumb tacks, a ginzu knife, salt, and broken glass. A teflon patch and a gasoline slick makes the snail feel good. The objective is to get the snail to the finish line with a minimal amount of damage.

Killer Klowns, the heavy metal band that produced the "Razorsnails" sound track, reports that the song is very popular in New York's downtown clubs.

Curtis Eberhardt's tips on creating GIF animation frames in Photoshop

Summary: *Flip-book animation can be created from a series of frames containing 2D images.*

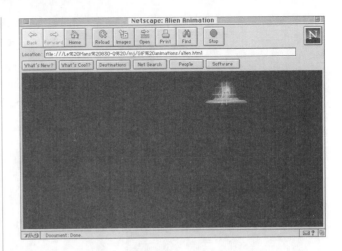

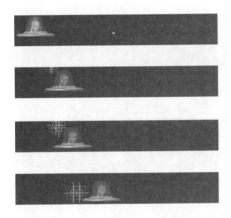

Two-dimensional images with implied motion can be adapted to form a flip-book type of animation known as GIF animation. In this example, Curtis Eberhardt staggers the position of an alien spaceship and a viewfinder that tracks the alien ship. Once the individual GIF frames are created in Photoshop, the GIF animation can be built in GIFBuilder. (*Note: Readers who wish to follow the steps in this section may look for Curtis' images on the companion CD-ROM.*)

1. Create a flip-book image in Photoshop.

a. Open Photoshop.

b. Select Open from the File pull-down menu.

c. In the dialog box that follows, select curtis_1.gif, and click on Open.

d. The alien image will open in a Photoshop window.

Adobe Photoshop™

1a.

1b.

1c.

1d.

2. Make changes to imply movement.

2a.

2b.

a. Select the Rectangle Marquee tool.

b. Click on the double-headed arrow in Photoshop's Foreground/Background color box to make the background color black, as shown.

c. Drag-select the alien ship.

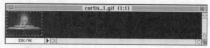

2c.

2d.

d. Reposition the alien ship slightly to the right.

e. Deselect the "marching ants" by selecting None from the Select pull-down menu.

2e.

3. Place the viewfinder image.

(*Note: Use the Place command in Photoshop to add the viewfinder. The Place command will only work if you have RGB Color Mode selected.*)

a. Select RGB Color from the Mode pull-down menu.

3a.

3b.

b. Select Place from the File pull-down menu.

c. In the dialog box that follows, select view.eps, and click on Open.

3c.

d. The viewfinder image will appear in the center of the Photoshop window surrounded by selection handles.

e. Move your mouse over the placed image until your pointer arrow turns into a mallet. When you see the mallet, click your mouse.

f. The selection handles will disappear, leaving a selection surrounded by marching ants.

3d.

3e.

3f.

4a.

4. Adjust the color of the viewfinder image.

Make the viewfinder image less bright by using Photoshop's Curves.

a. Select Hide Edges from the Select pull-down menu. This will make the marching ants disappear but the image will still be selected.

4b.

b. Select Adjust|Curves from the Image pull-down menu.

c. A Curves dialog box will appear.

d. Make sure the Preview box on the Curves dialog box has an "X" in it. Use your mouse to drag the curve downward, as shown.

e. With the marching ants hidden, you will see the viewfinder image become darker when you move the curve.

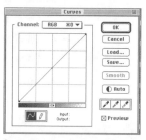

4c.   **4d.**

4e.

5a.

5. Move the viewfinder image.

Curtis made the viewfinder first appear in the extreme upper-left corner. Only a small portion of it appears in the slide where it is introduced.

a. Select Show Edges from the Select pull-down menu.

b. With the viewfinder image still selected, position your mouse over the marching ants until you see your selection arrow.

5b.

5c.

c. Drag the image up and to the left as shown.

d. Select Hide Edges from the Select pull-down menu.

5d.

6. Duplicate the viewfinder image.

(Note: Two viewfinders slightly off center give the impression of movement. An Option-drag will make a duplicate.)

a. Hold down the Option key, and drag the viewfinder image slightly to the left and down.

b. A new duplicate will appear.

7. Save the image as a GIF file.

(Note: Indexed Color Mode must be selected in order to save the image as a GIF file.)

a. Select Indexed Color from the Mode pull-down menu.

b. In the Indexed Color dialog box that follows, click on OK.

c. Select Save As from the File pull-down menu.

6a, 6b.

7a.

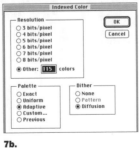

7b.

7c.

7d.

8.

9.

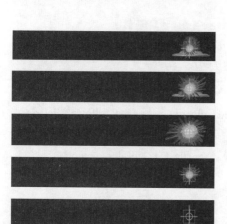

10.

d. In the Save As dialog box that follows, select CompuServe GIF from the Format pop-up menu.

e. Edit the file name so that it reads curtis_2.gif instead of curtis_1.gif, and then click on Save.

7e.

8. Make the viewfinder chase the alien ship.

Repeat Steps 2 through 7, and create screens to make the viewfinder chase the alien ship across the screen.

9. Make the viewfinder "lock on" its target.

At the far right of the screen, create an image showing the viewfinder superimposed on the alien ship.

10. Create an explosion.

To create the effect of an explosion, Curtis painted a ball of fire behind the viewfinder using yellow, orange, and red. (*Note: To see Curtis' explosion, open Netscape, and then open alien.html from the CD to view Curtis' completed animation in color.*)

The ball of fire grows over four to five slides and then subsides. The viewfinder is shown in the final slide, and the alien ship is missing.

Curtis Eberhardt's tips on assembling a GIF animation in GIFBuilder

Summary: *GIFBuilder, by Yves Piguet, is a program that combines several PICT or GIF images into one multiple image GIF file.*

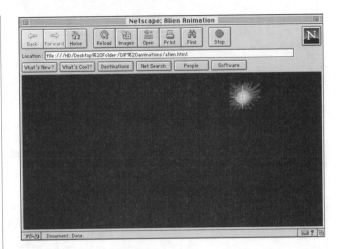

Assembling the GIF animation in GIFBuilder involves very few steps. In this example, Curtis creates a flicker effect by adding a black slide between images.

1. Open GIFBuilder and add frames.

a. Open GIFBuilder.

b. The Frames window will appear.

c. Select Add Frame from the File pull-down menu.

d. In the dialog box that follows, select the first of your animation frames, and click on Open.

GifBuilder

1a.

1b.

1c.

1d.

1e.

e. Re-select Add Frame from the File pull-down menu.

f. In the dialog box that follows, select curtis_black.gif, and click on Open.

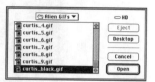

1f.

g. Repeat Steps c through f until you have added all of your images. *(Note: Remember to alternate the black slide between images.)*

2. Add a loop to the animation (optional).

(Note: Adding a loop to your animation will cause it to play over and over on the Netscape page.)

a. Select Loop from the Options pull-down menu.

2a.

b. Click on the radio button next to the field labeled *times,* and enter a number to indicate the number of times you would like the animation to loop.

2b.

3. Build the GIF89a file.

a. Select Save As from the File pull-down menu.

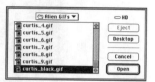

3a.

3b.

b. In the dialog box that follows, name the animation alien.gif, and click on Save.

4. Quit GIFBuilder and locate the GIF89a file.

a. Select Quit from the File pull-down menu.

b. Locate the GIF89a image in the Macintosh Finder. You'll need to drag the image to the directory where you plan to store your HTML document. *(Note: See* Curtis Eberhardt's tips on creating an HTML file to test your GIF animation.*)*

4a.

alien.gif

4b.

Curtis Eberhardt's tips on creating an HTML file to test your GIF animation

Summary: *Use the <IMG> tag in an HTML document to test your GIF animation.*

SimpleText

Use SimpleText or your word processor to create an HTML document. If you use a word processor, be sure to save the document as Text Only.

1. Create an HTML document.

a. Open SimpleText.

b. Start a new document. Use the following markup tags:

```
<HTML>

<HEAD>

<TITLE> GIF Animation</TITLE>

</HEAD>

<BODY>
```

c. Add an image tag. The image tag contains a SRC parameter, which contains the name of the image file.

```
<HTML>

<HEAD>

<TITLE> GIF Animation</TITLE>

</HEAD>

<BODY>

<IMG SRC="alien.gif">
```

d. Add ending tags.

```
<HTML>

<HEAD>

<TITLE> GIF Animation</TITLE>

</HEAD>

<BODY>

<IMG SRC="alien.gif">

</BODY>

</HTML>
```

2a.

2. Save the file.

a. Select Save As from the File pull-down menu.

b. In the dialog box that follows, name the document and add an .HTM extension.

2b.

3. Test the HTML file in Netscape.

(Note: Make sure your GIF image and your HTML document are in the same directory.)

a. Open Netscape.

3b.

b. Select Open File from the File pull-down menu.

c. In the dialog box that follows, select your HTML document, and click on Open.

3c.

d. Your GIF animation will load and begin to play.

GIF Wizard at Raspberry Hill

Summary: Use GIF Wizard at the Raspberry Hill Web site to reduce a GIF file size up to 90 percent.

GIF Wizard at http://www.raspberryhill.com/gifwizard.html is an online tool that reduces the size of your GIF images either on a Web server or on your computer hard drive. Curtis Eberhardt learned about the tool and gave me the URL just before this second edition went to press. Here's how it works.

1. Go to the Raspberry Hill Web site.

a. Open Netscape or the Internet Explorer browser.

b. Go to http://www.raspberryhill.com/gifwizard.html.

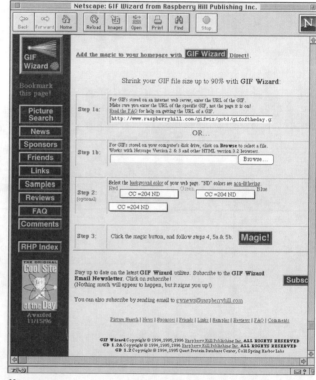

1b.

2. Identify your GIF image.

a. Type the URL of your GIF image if it resides on a Web server.

2a.

2b.

b. Alternatively, you can click on the Browse button to locate the file on your hard drive.

c. If the image is on your hard drive and you've clicked on the Browse button, use the File List window in the dialog box that follows to locate your file, and click on Open.

2c.

d. The file name will appear in the field to the left of the Browse button, as shown.

2d.

2e.

e. Click on the Magic button

f. Click OK in the warning dialog box that follows.

> ⚠ Any information you submit is insecure and could be observed by a third party while in transit.
>
> If you are submitting passwords, credit card numbers, or other information you would like to keep private, it would be safer for you to cancel the submission.
>
> [Don't Show Again] [Cancel] [OK]

2f.

g. A status page will appear, notifying you that the file reduction is in process.

> **COIN1SHD.GIF**
>
> Your request is being processed and the results should be ready in a few moments.
>
> This page will refresh automatically in 5 seconds if your browser supports that feature. If the page does not refresh automatically, press reload.
>
> **Processing Status:**
>
> Retrieving "COIN1SHD.GIF"
> Searching file for GIF
> Processing GIF Header
> Processing Global Color Table
> Processing Image Frame <1>
> Processing GIF Trailer
> Creating Clean GIF Format

2g.

2h.

h. When the image has been processed, it will appear on a Web page containing the original image and optimized versions.

i. Scroll down the page, and click on the link that reads *Optimized versions with modified colors.*

2i.

j. A page will be displayed, containing images made up of several different palette combinations. In this example, artist Jane Greenbaum's Marilyn Monroe icon is displayed with palettes ranging from 96 colors to 2 colors.

2j.

3b.

3c, 3d.

3. Save one or more GIF images.

a. When you see an image you like, press and hold down the mouse button on the image.

b. Select Save This Image As in the pop-up menu that appears.

c. Select a folder on your hard drive in the dialog box that follows.

d. Either accept the default file name of the new GIF image or type a new name and click on Save.

4. Process a new image.

a. To process another image, click on the link that says *New GIF Wizard Request*.

4a.

b. The GIF Wizard home page will be returned, and you can process another GIF image.

Create an interactive animation with Macromedia Director

Summary: *A self-running Macromedia Director Player movie can be added to your Web pages for downloading to Macintosh or Windows machines.*

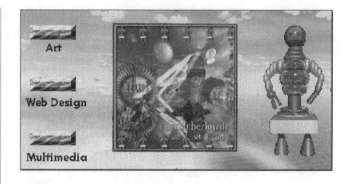

In this example, Curtis Eberhardt creates an animated, interactive resume in Macromedia Director. (*Note: A more advanced version of the interactive movie is on the CD-ROM in the back of this book.*) By creating a small stage and limiting the color palette, Curtis was able to keep the movie to a reasonable size for Web downloading.

1. Plan your animation.

a. Type of art. Director is a powerful authoring program that has limited art tools. Expect to create the art for your movie in programs such as Photoshop or KPT Bryce, known for their advanced graphics.

For this interactive self-promotion, Curtis created his background and Helios logo in KPT Bryce. He wanted an ethereal atmospheric effect, which he was able to create with *shaders* in KPT Bryce. Shaders are used to configure atmospheric conditions, such as the amount of sun and the amount of cloud cover. His goal was to create a Lady-in-the-Lake Arthurian legend-type feeling with a logo emerging out of clouds.

b. Animation. Director can be used to create 2D animations and to assemble 3D animations created in other software programs.

Curtis' movie begins with a 3D "camera fly-through" animation, which zooms in on the Helios logo. This animation effect has its origins in cinematography and can be achieved in KPT Bryce by starting with a long shot and stepping the software to render each new scene.

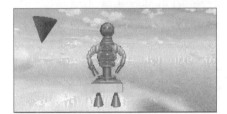

Director requires that art elements be imported in the form of PICT images; therefore, each rendered frame would be a separate PICT image for the Director cast. To conserve on memory, Curtis kept the total number of frames to a minimum.

Curtis' robot and cone animations were created in Strata Studio. He used the robot to add a retro, high-tech look to the movie and chose gold, chrome, and silver colors to coordinate with the purple shades in the background. The cone was rendered against a black background in Strata Studio because he needed the solid color background to drop out in Director.

Artists who create 3D animations in Strata Studio save their files as QuickTime movies and then use Adobe Premiere to save the animation as single frame PICT images required for importing into Macromedia Director.

c. Interactivity. The hypertext scripting feature in Macromedia Director (called *Lingo*) is an optional tool for creating highly interactive presentations. When you're planning your presentation, decide how much interactivity or how much scripting you would like built in.

Curtis has an unusual combination of skills—he's a painter and a Lingo programmer. He can use both skills to design and build an entire Director project. Artists who don't know Lingo should team up with a programmer who does because Lingo is the key to creating interactive elements. Working in tandem with a programmer, an artist can work on a visual interface while a programmer develops Lingo scripts with minimal graphics. The interface and Lingo scripts can then be stitched together when both are complete.

Most of Curtis' larger projects require more Lingo programming than the scripts he built for his self-promotion. Interactivity in this chapter's movie sample is limited to button scripts, which display his portfolio elements on screen.

Scripts can often make a movie more efficient and more interesting. As Curtis explains, "Lingo can be used to extend animation. For example, instead of building linear, pre-described motion using Director's Score, Lingo scripts can be used to create random motion."

2. Begin by collecting your art.

a. Create a folder, and name it Cast Members.

b. Move your art and sound files into the folder.

3. Define a movie stage size in pixels.

a. Select Preferences from the Edit pull-down menu.

b. In the Stage size section of the preferences dialog box, enter the width and height for your stage. Curtis chose a 400 pixel by 200 pixel stage area. You can also position the stage size onscreen by entering a number in the Centered and Left boxes.

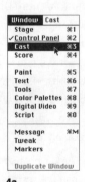

3a.

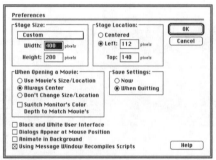

3b.

4. Import the cast into the Cast window.

a. Select Cast from the Window pull-down menu. This will open the Cast window.

b. Click on the Cast window to select it.

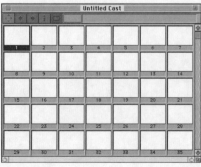

4b.

4a.

4c.

c. Select Import from the File pull-down menu. Director will display PICT files in a file list window.

d. You can either import each cast member one at a time, or click on the Import All button to import several cast members at once.

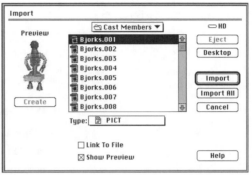

4d.

e. To select files other than PICT, select a file format from the Type pop-up menu. Each file format may be imported separately into the Cast window as single cast members or in groups.

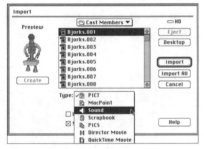

4e.

f. Curtis imported single frames from 3D animations he created in Strata Studio Pro. Next, he imported sound files he created using a Korg X-5 music synthesizer. With the cast members imported, Curtis was ready to begin the process of authoring the movie in the Cast window.

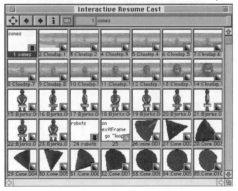

4f.

5a.

5. Save and compact your Director file.

a. Select Save And Compact from the File pull-down menu.

b. Name your Director file, and click on Save.

5b.

6. Plan the construction of the Score.

The Director Score window is where a Director movie is assembled. It consists of 48 rows and hundreds of columns. To assemble a movie, cast members are dragged from the Cast window into various positions in the Score. *(Note: See Step 7 for instructions on how to move cast members into the Score window.)* Note the elements of the Score window, below:

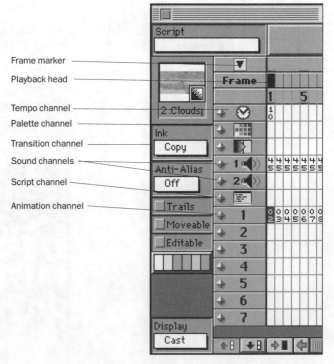

Frame marker
Playback head
Tempo channel
Palette channel
Transition channel
Sound channels
Script channel
Animation channel

6.

Review the elements of Curtis' movie to understand how to construct your own. His plan for the Score window included:

a. Background single frame elements that comprise a fly-through animation produced in KPT Bryce. These cast members occupy cells 1 through 24 in channel 1 in the Score window. In the Score window, low numbered channels contain background images. Elements in higher-number channels "layer" up in front of elements in lower-number channels.

Curtis placed the frame he produced with the long shot in cell 1 and the other images that "stepped" in cells 2 through 24. Because Director is based on a movie metaphor, animation occurs when the playback head moves from left to right, and frames are presented on stage in this time-based medium. (*Note: The* playback head *is the black cell-shaped object to the right of the word* Frame *in the figure below.*)

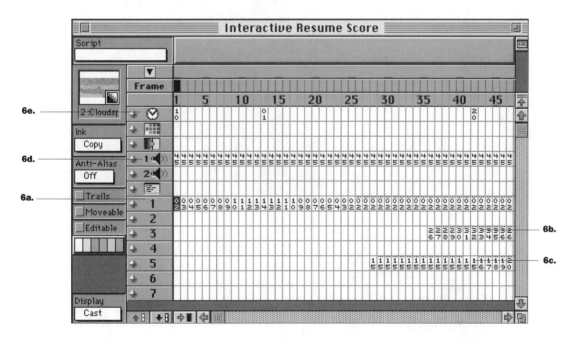

b. Curtis chose channel 3 for the cone animation so it would be in front of the background. He started the cone at cell 36, eight cells after the conclusion of the fly-through animation. Similar to the fly-through animation, the cone animation consists of single frame "stepped" images, created in Strata Studio and occupying cells 36 through 139.

c. Channel 5 holds the robot animation, which occupies cells 28 through 139.

d. The music files that Curtis created with his music synthesizer occupy cells 1 through 139 in the Sound channel.

e. Director is a time-based medium. The Tempo channel contains instructions that Curtis added to control the movie's timing. (*Note: See Step 12 for instructions on how to adjust a movie's tempo.*)

7. Move cast members to the Score window.

a. Click on a cast member in the Cast window to select the cast member.

b. Press and drag the cast member to a desired cell position in the Score window (the mouse pointer will turn into a hand while you drag). When the cast member is positioned over the desired cell position, release the mouse button.

7a.

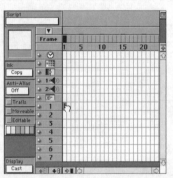

7b.

c. The cell where you dropped the cast member will contain an abbreviated number representing the cast member's number from the Cast window. (*Note: Cast members that occupy a cell position are no longer referred to as* cast members. *When you drag a cast member to the Score, it becomes a* sprite.)

7c.

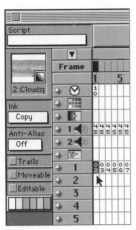

7d.

d. To see more information about a particular sprite than what can be seen in a cell, click on a cell to select it. Director will display the contents in the upper-left corner of the Score window.

8. Use In-Between Linear to duplicate a sprite.

To copy a sprite into a group of contiguous cells, use Director's In-Between command.

a. Click on the cell in the Score window that contains a sprite you would like to duplicate. This will select the cell and its contents.

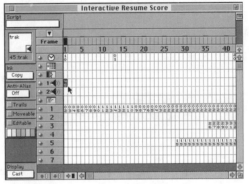

8a.

b. Drag to select the contiguous group of cells where you would like the sprite to be repeated.

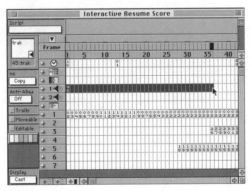

8b.

8c1.

c. Select In-Between Linear from the Score pull-down menu (Figure 8c1) to fill the group of contiguous cells with the sprite (Figure 8c2).

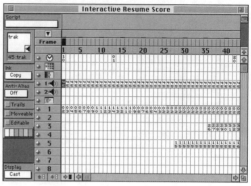

8c2.

9. Try playing your movie.

Once you have moved cast members to the Score and used In-Between Linear to duplicate sprites into channels, play your movie. Move the Score window to one side of the screen so you can see Director's stage, where the movie is played. When you press Play, notice the playback head move from left to right.

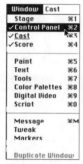

9a1.

a. Select Control Panel from the Window pull-down menu (Figure 9a1) and the Director's Control Panel (Figure 9a2) window will appear.

9a2.

b. Click on the Rewind button to rewind the movie.

9b.

c. Click on the Play button to play your movie.

9c.

10. Plan interactive areas in the Score.

When you played your movie, you probably noticed that the playback head moved straight across the Score from left to right and then kept on going. When you plan an interactive movie, you'll need to get the playback head to loop in sections, or move past a group of frames over and over, so the movie will appear to stop for viewer interaction. To create this section, you will need:

a. **A main interactive area.** Sometimes referred to as a *menu area,* this section can provide a viewer with choices concerning where to branch in a movie. The action is usually a mouse click on a button.

b. **Interactive areas where viewers branch.** These are areas in the Score where the viewer can branch to see something new. In this sample, the viewer branches to areas of the Score containing artwork.

c. **Frame markers to label areas in the Score.** Interactivity requires Lingo scripts. Frame markers help make scripting clear and easy to understand. (*Note: The frame markers are labeled* Art, Web, *and* Multimedia *in the figure below.*)

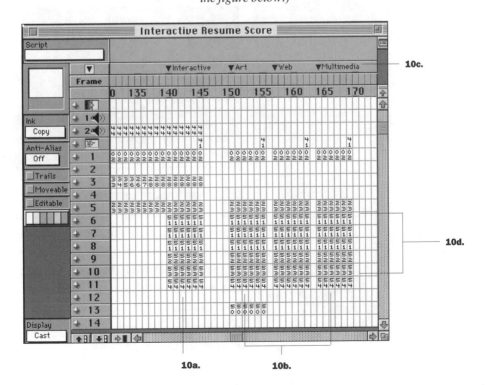

10a.   10b.

d. Navigation buttons. Buttons were not required when the movie opened; they don't show up in the Score window until frame 140. Rows 6 through 11 contain button sprites and their labels.

Buttons have Lingo "button scripts" attached that will cause Director to branch to a predesignated area in the Score. *(Note: See Step 14 for instructions on how to create button scripts.)* In the figure on the previous page, Curtis has added *go loop* commands in the Scripting channel in frame positions 145, 155, 162, and 169. *(Note: See Step 15 for instructions on how to create loops with Lingo's* go loop *command.)*

Curtis also added an image of a CD-ROM cover he designed as an item to branch to in the *Art* category. Notice the sprite for the CD-ROM cover occupies frames 150 through 155 in row 13 (see figure on previous page). Other art will be added to the Web and Multimedia sections, which are adjacent to the Art section. Notice these sections can be identified by their frame markers at the top of the Score window. (See figure on previous page.)

11. Position buttons in the Score.

Drag your button cast members (Figure 11a) into high-numbered channels (Figure 11b) in the areas you've planned for viewer interaction. Curtis designed Art, Web Design, and Multimedia buttons to branch to parts of the Score containing his portfolio pieces, and moved them into rows 6 through 11. *(Note: See the figure on the previous page and Step 7 for instructions on how to move cast members to the Score window.)*

11a.

11b.

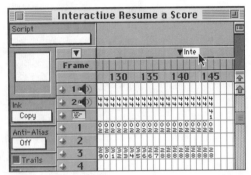

12a.

12. Create frame markers.

a. Drag markers from the marker well, and place them above the first frame in each of your interactive areas. (*Note: The marker well is the triangle above the row numbers over the word* Frame.)

b. After you have positioned a frame marker, let go of the mouse and enter a label.

12b.

Tip: The simplest way to make buttons interactive is to add a Lingo button script to button cast members and direct Lingo to branch to an alternate part of the Score. Although more elaborate schemes can be used, this method is the easiest for beginners. (Note: See Step 14 for instructions on how to create Lingo button scripts.)

13. Resave your movie.

a. Select Save And Compact from the File pull-down menu.

13a.

b. Notice Director does not display a Save dialog box the second time you save.

14. Add button scripts.

a. Click to select a button cast member in the Cast window.

14a.

14b.

b. Select Cast Member Info from the Cast pull-down menu.

c. Click on the Script button in the Bitmap Cast Member Info dialog box.

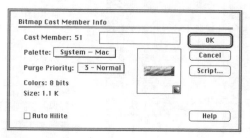

14c.

d. Clicking on the Script button will open a Script window. Button scripts are so common that Lingo will provide you with *on mouseUp* and *end*. (*Note:* end *is just* end MouseUp *abbreviated as* end.)

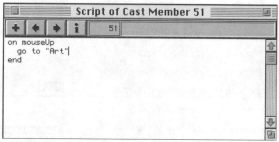

14e.

e. Type

```
on mouseUp
   go to "Art"
end
```

(*Note: Use Director's frame markers to label cell positions. This makes scripting easier, and Director will remember the cell position even if rows are inserted into the Score. For every unique button script, you will need a unique cast member. Cast members may be duplicated in the cast window and will have a unique cast member number.*)

Tip: *To learn Lingo, the hypertext scripting language that comes with Macromedia Director, John "J. T." Thompson and Sam Gottlieb's* Macromedia Director Lingo Workshop *is an excellent book. John Thompson wrote Lingo, so the information is right from the source. John Thompson teaches at New York University. His book is published by Hayden Books.*

Lingo is a hypertext computer language that comes with Director. The language is comprised of English-like sentences, called *scripts*, which may be placed in a sprite, a cast member, a frame, or a movie. As a result, scripts are described as *sprite scripts, cast member scripts, frame scripts,* or *movie scripts.*

An *event handler* is the most common Lingo script. It is used to tell Director what to do when an event occurs. Events are mouse and key actions, described below:

mouseDown mouse button is pressed

mouseUp mouse button is released

keyDown a key is pressed

keyUp a key is released

Event handlers, like all Lingo scripts, must be written with a required structure known as *syntax*. For example, in the following *go to* command, it is customary to put the name of the frame marker in quotation marks:

```
on mouseUp
    go to "Art"
end
```

15. Create loops with Lingo's *go loop* command.

Notice in the figure below that each of the cells at the end of each interactive section has an element in the script channel. These cells contain the Lingo command *go loop*. When the playback head reaches a *go loop* command as it travels from left to right, the playback head will loop to the previous marker and keep looping until Director receives some other command, such as directions in a button script.

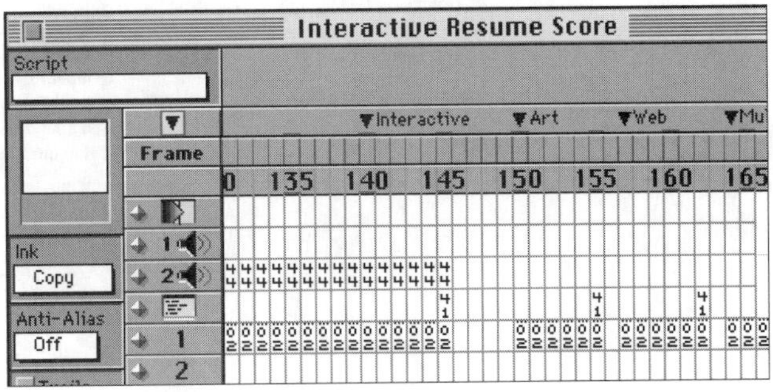

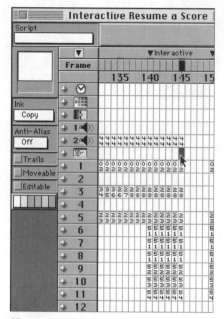

15a.

a. Position your mouse in the Script channel on the last cell in an interactive section.

b. Double-click your mouse to open a Script window.

c. Type `go loop`.

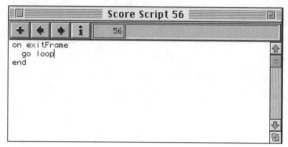

15c.

d. Click on the Close box in the Script window.

e. Repeat this or copy and paste the contents of this cell into other cells at the end of any other interactive sections.

16. Adjust the tempo of your movie.

When you play your movie for the first time, you'll notice that some sections play too fast. To adjust the timing of the movie, timing elements can be added to the Tempo channel.

a. To set the tempo of his movie, Curtis opened the Tempo dialog box in frame one. This can be done by double-clicking cell 1 in the Tempo channel.

b. To set the tempo, move the Tempo slider (Curtis used 10 fps—frames per second), and click on OK.

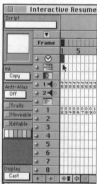

16a.

16b.

c. You can also use Tempo commands to pause a movie while a sound or video finishes playing.

17a.

17. Resave and create a movie projector.

When you have completed your movie, save it as a self-running projector.

a. Select Create Projector from the File pull-down menu.

b. Director will warn you that creating a projector will close the movie file you're working on. Click on Save to save any changes.

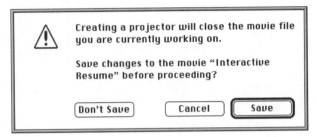

17b.

c. In the dialog box that follows, locate your movie file in the file list window on the left.

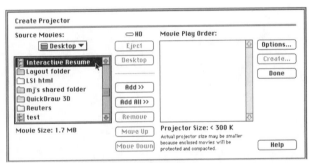

17c.

d. Click on Add.

17d.

e. Click on Create.

17e.

f. Select a location for your movie in the dialog box that follows.

g. Click on Save.

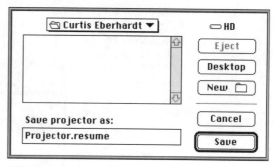

17f, 17g.

h. The projector that you create will be a self-running Director movie playable on any Macintosh computer.

Projector.resume

Creating a Director movie for use with the Shockwave Director Internet Player

Summary: *Macromedia's new tool for playing Director movies on the Internet includes a new Player technology that will be integrated into the next release of the Netscape browser.*

The Director Internet Player described in this section is one step on the way to integrating Director's multimedia authoring with Netscape. As a helper application, the new player technology provides sound, animation, and interactivity. When the Director Player is integrated into Netscape, movies can be played from the Web.

Director movies for the Web are created with Macromedia Director's software, but the size should be limited to 200 K. "Preprocessing" a movie with Macromedia's Afterburner software compresses a movie, and the Director Internet Player decompresses the file contents. *(Note: See* Compressing a Director movie with Afterburner *later in this chapter.)* In this section, Curtis Eberhardt offers tips on how to limit the size of your Director movies.

1. Colorize one-bit cast members.

Limiting the bit depth of cast members substantially reduces the file size. One-bit cast members, which are black and white, can be colorized on the Director stage to conserve on file size.

1a.

   a. Import one-bit images (black and white) into the Cast window. *(Note: See* Create an interactive animation with Macromedia Director, *earlier in this chapter, for instructions on how to import the cast into the Cast window.)*

1c.

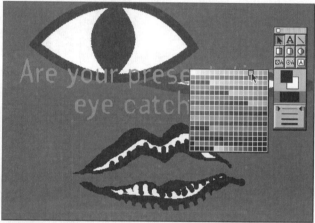

1d.

b. Move the cast member to the stage. *(Note: See* Create an interactive animation with Macromedia Director *for instructions on how to move cast members from the Cast window to the Score.)*

c. Click on an onstage cast member to select it. A bounding box will signify that the cast member is selected.

d. Select Tools from the Window pull-down menu.

e. With the cast member (or sprite) selected, click on the foreground color in the Tools window to open the palette. Drag to select a color.

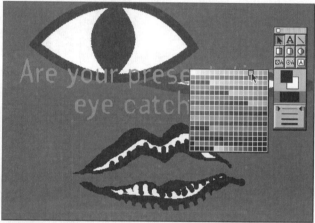

1e.

f. When you release the mouse button, the cast member will take on the color you selected.

1f.

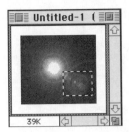

2a.

2b.

2e.

2f.

2. Use tiles to fill a background or other shape.

Tiles can be used to create a wallpaper effect on the Director stage. Because they are based on one small cast member, tiling is a way to conserve on file size. Use the Fill|Pattern command in Photoshop to experiment with the tile pattern.

a. Start by selecting an area of a Photoshop document you would like to see tiled. In Photoshop, this is referred to as a *pattern*.

b. Select Define Pattern from the Edit menu.

c. To test the pattern, open a new document by selecting New from the File pull-down menu.

d. Enter 200 pixels in the Width box and 200 pixels in the Height box.

2c.

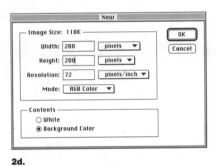

2d.

e. With the new test document open, select All from the Select pull-down menu.

f. You'll notice the document is selected when you see a trail of marching ants around the perimeter.

g. Select Fill from the Edit pull-down menu.

2g.

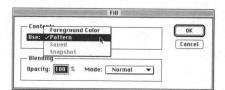

2h.

h. Select Pattern from the pop-up menu in the Fill dialog box.

i. Your document will be filled with the pattern you're testing.

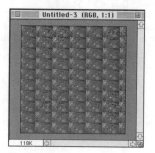

2i.

j. If you're satisfied with the tile and would like it to be available in Director, import the tile into Director's Cast window. *(Note: See* Create an interactive animation with Macromedia Director *for instructions on how to import the cast into the Cast window.)*

k. Open Director's Paint window by selecting Paint from the Window pull-down menu.

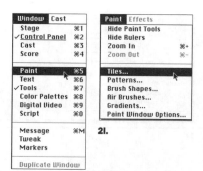

2k. **2l.**

l. With the Paint window open, select Tiles from the Paint menu.

m. Click on the Cast Member radio button, and click on the right and left arrows to locate the cast member you wish to tile.

n. Use the Width and Height pop-up menus to pick a size for the tile.

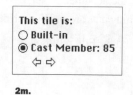

2m.

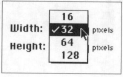

2n.

2o.

o. A small dotted rectangle will reflect the size of your tile in the Tile window. Drag the small dotted outline to the area you would like to use as your tile.

p. Click on OK.

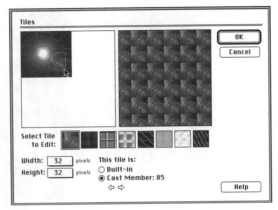

2p.

q. Your tile will become a pattern on the pattern selector chip at the base of the Tools window.

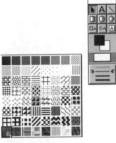

2q.

r. To create a tiled background, select the shaded half of rectangle tool from the Tools window.

s. Then use the tool's crosshair to drag a rectangle large enough to cover the stage.

2r.

2s.

2t.

t. With the rectangle selected, select the pattern selector chip, and drag-select the new pattern.

u. When you let go of the mouse, the new pattern will fill the rectangle.

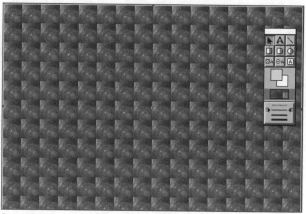

2u.

3. Check on cast member size.

The Bitmap Cast Member Info dialog box will provide valuable information about cast member sizes as you are building your movie.

a. Click on a cast member in the Cast window.

b. Select Cast Member Info from the Cast pull-down menu.

c. Notice the size is indicated in the dialog box that opens.

3a.

3b.

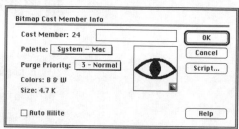

3c.

Tip: For information and instructions on how to upload files to your Internet provider's server, see the Image Map *chapter.*

4a.

4. Try remapping a color cast member.

Director's Transform Bitmap command allows you to alter the bit depth of a color cast member and, as a result, reduce the file size. This command cannot be undone, so always test the remap on a copy of the cast member.

a. Click on a color cast member in the Cast window to select it.

b. Select Copy Cast Members from the Edit pull-down menu.

c. Click on an empty cast member position in the Cast window.

4b.

4c.

d. Select Paste Bitmap from the Edit pull-down menu.

4d.

4e.

e. With the cast member copy still selected, select Transform Bitmap from the Cast pull-down menu to display the Transform Bitmap dialog box.

f. Select a smaller bit depth from the Color Depth pop-up menu. Click on OK to remap the cast member to a smaller bit depth.

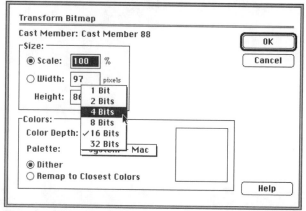

4f.

4g.

g. Double-click on the cast member to examine the color in Director's Paint window.

h. Sometimes the color is acceptable at a smaller bit depth; other times, it is not.

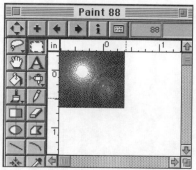

4h.

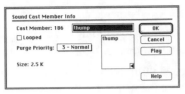

5a.

5b.

5c.

Tip: To conserve on file size, try to use sound sampled at 11 kHz rather than 22 kHz.

5. Use small sound snips and loop one or two.

a. Curtis used several small 2 K to 4 K sound snips throughout his movie (Figure 5a).

b. To loop a sound, start by selecting a sound in the Cast window.

c. Select Cast Member Info from the Cast pull-down menu to display the Cast Info dialog box.

d. Click to put an "X" in the box labeled *Loop*. This will extend a sound without adding to the file size.

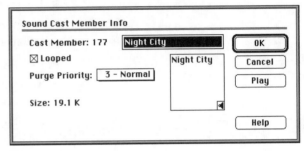

5d.

Compressing a Director movie with Afterburner

Summary: *Preprocess a Director movie with Macromedia's Afterburner before placing it on a Web server. This compression step makes the movie small and compact, so that it moves quickly over the Web.*

Macromedia's Afterburner adds a compression step to building movies for the Web. Afterburner is an easy-to-use drag-and-drop application that will create a file with a .DCR extension. The compressed movie will be decompressed by the Director Internet Player as it is received over the Web.

Afterburner

1. Drag and drop your Director movie.

a. Locate your Afterburner software.

b. Drag and drop the Director movie on top of the Afterburner icon.

c. Release the mouse button. This step automatically launches the Afterburner application. When the software is launched, you'll see an Output dialog box.

1b.

d. Use the default file name or type in some other name, but keep the .DCR extension.

1e.

1c, 1d.

e. You'll see a progress box as the movie is processed.

f. The compressed file is the file you will place on a Web server.

Sideshow.dcr

1f.

The "Father of VRML"

Mark Pesce initiated the development of VRML (Virtual Reality Modeling Language), the language that describes 3D space on the Internet. Look for a chapter from his book published by New Riders, VRML Browsing and Building Cyberspace, *at* http://www.mcp.com/general/news7/chap2.html.

Artist featured in this chapter:

Alex Shamson has a B.S. in Industrial Design from the Philadelphia University of Art.

alex@vrmill.com

http://www.vrmill.com

Chapter 11

VRML World Building

VRML or, Virtual Reality Modeling Language, is the language that describes 3D space on the Internet. Designers who are interested in creating VRML discover there are three ways to create these new 3D files. Traditional 3D modeling manufacturers have added VRML file writing features to 3D software programs, and several new, low-cost world-building tools have emerged. Hand coding VRML in a text processor is also an option.

In this chapter, industrial designer Alex Shamson shares tips on how to create a dinosaur head in Virtus WalkThrough Pro, a 3D visualization tool popular with architects and Hollywood film directors. Virtus Corporation, founded by David Smith, was the first 3D software manufacturer to add a VRML file-writing feature to their software. Also included in this chapter are tips on how to navigate your VRML file in the Virtus Voyager VRML browser, how to open your VRML file in a word processor and adjust the VRML code, and how to use the <EMBED> tag to add a VRML window to a Web page.

VRML on the Internet

Summary: Highly creative and far-sighted 3D world builders have taken Mark Pesce's vision and created imaginative new VRML worlds on the Internet.

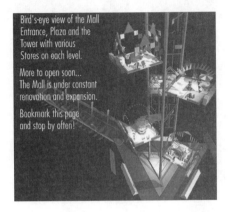

Bird's-eye view of the Mall Entrance, Plaza and the Tower with various Stores on each level.

More to open soon... The Mall is under constant renovation and expansion.

Bookmark this page and stop by often!

Above: A Virtual Reality Shopping Mall is the centerpiece of Alex's VRML portfolio.

Above Right: Alex Shamson's home page contains numerous links for world builders interested in VRML.

Above: A "scooter" from Alex's traditional 3D portfolio.

Alex Shamson (alex@vrmill.com), who teaches 3D design at New York's Pratt Manhattan, is a painter and an industrial designer. Industrial Design is the specialty that teaches the design of everyday objects and 3D space.

Although his industrial design background has given Alex a broad background in 3D design, Alex has aggressively pursued 3D world building on the Internet. Like a handful of design professionals nationwide, Alex feels the Internet holds enormous opportunities for 3D world builders.

Although Alex has used Virtus WalkThrough Pro and has built most of his models on the Macintosh, recent developments in VRML have required him to make changes. For example, he recently bought a Windows NT machine because of Apple Computer's failure to embrace VRML as a file standard. Although aspects of Apple's alternative 3DMF format have been added to VRML 2.0, their less-than-enthusiastic support of VRML has made it impossible to develop VRML worlds on a Macintosh because there are so few tools.

Even though there are many more VRML tools available on the Windows platform, Alex has also started to add VRML to his models by hand in a word processor.

Above: Auto showroom display from Alex's traditional 3D portfolio.
Above Right: Alex's "Metatown" from his traditional 3D portfolio.

At this time, no 3D applications support the multimedia features available in VRML 2.0. As Alex explains, "3D artists who want to adjust lighting, or add camera perspectives or any other new feature will need to learn how to hand code VRML. Until 3D software programs can write the new features into a VRML file, I recommend that artists use resources on the Web to learn about hand coding." Alex has generously prepared a very large number of links on his Web site (http://www.vrmill.com). These links are helpful for his clients and students who are new to VRML.

1. Assistance to surfers.
Besides providing links to the latest versions of Netscape Navigator with Live3D and the Internet Explorer browser, Alex has created a concise overview of VRML and has answered such questions as:

- What is VRML?
- What can you do with VRML?
- What do you need to see VRML files?
- What is VRML 2.0?
- What are multiuser virtual worlds?
- What's an avatar?

2. Resources.

In this section, Alex has organized a set of links to such famous sites as VAG (VRML Architectural Group) and The VRML Repository. This section also contains numerous valuable links that Alex used to learn VRML, including links to:

- VRML Architectural Group
- The VRML Repository
- NYVRMLSIG
- ARTNETWEB
- VRML tutorials
- Authoring software
- VRML browsers
- Compression utilities
- Books on VRML and 3D design

3. Alex's design and training and services.

Alex is a self-employed creative director/design consultant specializing in multimedia and Web development. As a pioneer in the area of creating 3D virtual worlds on the Internet and as a founding member of New York's NYVRMLSIG, Alex built his Web site to promote his 3D design business and to share the knowledge he has acquired in 3D modeling and virtual world construction.

SERVICES
VRML Construction
Creative Design
WWW Services

3.

Visit Starbase C3 to see a VRML adventure, shop for VRML spaceships, and participate in 3D chat

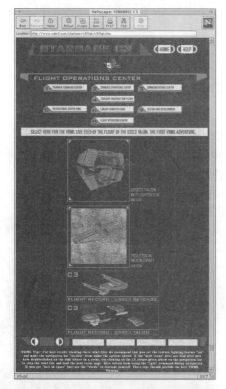

Above: *The Starbase C3 Flight Operations Center contains live VRML animations. In this VRML adventure, the USSC3 Talon leaves the flight dock, travels into an asteroid field, orbits a planet, and travels to another flight dock.*
Above Right: *Larry Rosenthal's Starbase C3 site.*

http://www.cube3.com/starbase.htm

Larry Rosenthal, industrial designer and founder of New York's NYVRMLSIG, has created Starbase C3 (http://www.cube3.com/starbase.htm), one of the most innovative new VRML sites on the Internet.

Larry has packaged his starship models as construction kits for interested VRML model builders who wish to assemble their own models. He's also built animated VRML adventures with the help of "Chief Engineer" Frederic Gontier and "Flightdock Engineer" Marc Thorner. For Web-initiated spaceship adventure fans, these animations represent a form of electronic entertainment that will soon be very popular among the computer gaming generation.

For his most devoted following, Larry has created a Starbase C3 Membership. For $29.95 per year, members receive monthly "extras," including a model that is not available on the Starbase C3 site, a custom "Conbot" avatar, extra model parts not offered on the site, about a half dozen high-resolution renderings of spaceships, and a monthly HTML newsletter containing VRML building tips. Larry will also launch the BlackSun CyberHub 3D chat engine, where he'll offer members private VRML chat that will be closed to the public.

In late 1996, Larry worked with New York developers Matt and Dan O'Donnell on his Starbase C3 3D chat site. Matt and Dan are identical twin brothers who are well known for

Above: *The USSC3 Talon entering the flightdock.*

their Web development skills. Nicknamed by their New York VRML and programmer colleagues as the "Cicada twins," Matt and Dan own Cicada Web Development and often get a room rumbling with energetic talk about new technology during Internet meetings in New York. When asked to demonstrate their latest project at the NYVRMLSIG meeting in January, the Cicada team unveiled their 3D chat engine written in Java. Working with Larry Rosenthal, who built the starbase model in VRML, the O'Donnell brothers developed their Java-based chat engine, which works in a Java-enabled Netscape Navigator window without any extra plug-ins or client software.

1. The CyberCash system.

Larry is a CyberCash merchant, which means customers who have a "CyberCash CyberCoin Wallet" can purchase a VRML model online and instantly download it to their computer's hard drive. CyberCoin wallets are programs that may be obtained free at the CyberCash site (http://www.cybercash.com). Once a Wallet program is downloaded, cash can be transferred from a consumer's credit card or checking account.

CyberCoin services are distributed through banks that offer online merchants the CyberCoin service and offer consumers co-branded wallets. Consumers and merchants each obtain free wallet software, and the merchants pay the bank a per-transaction fee to use CyberCoin. The bank pays CyberCash a transaction fee for providing the technology and processing service. Merchants find new revenue channels with CyberCoin because they can now offer services and goods at low and incremental costs that were previously prohibitive because the pricing models of credit cards were ineffective with low-cost items.

CyberCoin uses the most advanced security features for consumers, banks, and merchants. When consumers bind, or connect, their checking accounts to their wallets, CyberCash confirms three things: that the people are who they say they are, that the accounts are valid and are active accounts with

Above: *Close-up of a "Conbot" or Construction Robot.*

money in them, and that each person is connected legally to a specific account. After the account is confirmed, CyberCash protects the consumer through the use of 768-bit RSA encryption with the password-protected wallet. CyberCash is also working with VeriSign to incorporate Digital IDs for instantaneous validation of individuals' and merchants' identities. In addition, funds in the CyberCoin system are FDIC insured. This guarantees that, if the CyberCoin issuing bank goes out of business, the consumer's money is insured by the federal government.

CyberCash currently offers purchases made only with U.S. dollars and at online merchants who have a U.S. bank account. Eventually, CyberCoin will be able to be used outside the United States with any foreign or international bank that is a CyberCoin issuing bank. When a consumer buys a good or service on the Internet listed in foreign currency, the system will translate the currency on-the-fly with the exchange rate guaranteed by a bank, and the debit will occur in the consumer's domestic currency. Consumers will also be able to hold a number of different currencies in their wallet, similar to the way funds are held in the physical world.

2. Steps to order a construction kit online.

a. Visit the CyberCash site at http://www.cybercash.com and download a free CyberCoin wallet. (*Note: The Windows 95/NT platform is required at this time.*)

b. Add either credit card or checking account funds to your CyberCoin wallet.

c. Click on the New VRML Ships on the Starbase C3 home page to link to the Online Datakit Directory and Sales page.

2a, 2b.

2c.

2d.

d. On the Datakit Directory and Sales page that follows, scroll the page to find a model.

e. Click on a gold coin under the illustration of the spaceship you'd like to purchase.

2e.

f. The CyberCoin wallet launches a transaction, and a datakit in a compressed ZIP format is downloaded to your computer.

3. Steps to view the VRML adventures.

3a.

a. Click on the Fighter Flight VRML on the Starbase C3 home page to link to the Flight Operations Center.

b. On the Flight Operations Center Web page that follows, click on a VRML live feed.

c. If you have Netscape Navigator with Live3D, you'll see a VRML 3D animation.

3b.

3c.

4. Steps to become a Starbase C3 member.

a. Click on Membership Information on Larry's Starbase C3 home page.

MEMBERSHIP INFORMATION

4a.

OFFICIAL MEMBERSHIP FORM

4b.

4c.

Print

4f.

b. On the Starbase Command Center Web page that follows, click on the Official Membership Form link.

c. A Membership Form will appear on the Web page that follows.

d. Press and hold down your mouse button, and select Save This Image As from the pop-up menu.

4d.

e. In the dialog box that follows, save the form to your hard disk by clicking on Save.

4e.

f. Alternatively, you can click on the Print button at the top of your Netscape Navigator window to print the form.

g. If you have saved the form to your hard disk, open it in a paint software program, and print it on your printer.

5. Steps to visit the 3D chat area.

a. On the Flight Operations Center Web page, click on the Enter 3DVRML Flightdock Chat link.

ENTER 3DVRML FLIGHTDOCK CHAT

5a.

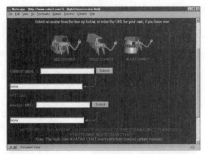

5b.

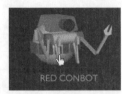

5c.

5d.

5e.

Live3D version
SELECT LIVE3D VERSION TO TRANSPORT

5f.

b. On the Web page that follows, scroll to the Avatar Selection area.

c. Select one of the available avatars by clicking on an avatar image. (*Note: The field labeled Avatar URL will fill in automatically when you select an avatar.*)

d. Enter a Conbot name in the field labeled *Conbot Name,* and click on Submit.

e. Enter an optional avatar URL in the field labeled *Avatar URL.* (*Note: This field is designed for people who want to add their own VRML avatars. If you've selected a Conbot, the field will already be filled in.*) Click on Submit.

f. To enter the 3D chat area, click on the Live 3D version link.

g. The Starbase C3 chat window will appear and float over your Web page. A VRML window will appear on the top half of the floating window, and a text-based chat area will appear in the bottom half. To participate, type a comment in the text window at the bottom of the floating screen, and press Return.

5g.

Live comedy in a VRML world— at Mom's Truck Stop

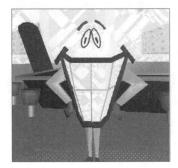

Above: *Argle, host of MetaPlay's Simprov.*
Above Right: *The MetaPlay Web site at http://www.metaplay.com.*

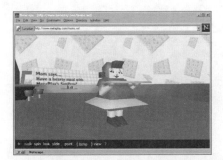

Above: *Waitress at Mom's Truck Stop.*

Tip: *The MetaPlay team has posted cartoons and logs of the live episodes at their Web site. The Web site is enhanced with MIDI tunes and QuickTime movies.*

Simprov. That's what the MetaPlay comedy team calls the multiuser improvisational comedy performance that Internet users experience at Mom's Truck Stop. The setting is a '50s diner, and the comedy team is Matt Dominianni (nose@echonyc.com), Paul Marino (havoc@interport.net), Frank Dellario, Matt Duhan, and Matt Hapke. Paul Marino is the 3D artist who created the VRML diner in 3D Studio Max.

Although you can access the VRML diner via Netscape Navigator with Live3D (http://www.metaplay.com), the MetaPlay comedy performances are performed live in a MOO. MOOs are social MUDs (multiuser domains), or places on the Internet where people interact and create their own worlds. MUDs have been traditionally text-based, but Chaco's Pueblo client software turns a text-based MOO into a multimedia experience.

Pueblo users who visit Mom's Truck Stop experience a split screen, with the 3D diner on one side and 3D chat or the performance on the other. There's also music and 2D images of the people who interact in the diner. At scheduled intervals, which are announced on the MetaPlay Web site (http://www.metaplay.com), visitors can arrive at Mom's and take part in a live performance.

"Don't be fooled by my cute smile, I'm actually planning to take over the world."

—Argle, host of MetaPlay's Simprov

Above: *Mom's Truck Stop through the Pueblo browser window.*
Above Right: *Mom's Truck Stop through Netscape's Live3D window.*

1. Getting to Mom's Truck Stop.

a. Download and install the Pueblo client from the Chaco Web site at http://www.chaco.com. (*Note: The Windows 95/NT platform is required. Alternatively, Mom's Truck Stop may be experienced with a Telnet client on a Macintosh computer, but this will be a text-only experience.*)

b. If you have the Pueblo client software installed on your hard drive, click on the Mom's Truck Stop link on the MetaPlay Web site at http://www.metaplay.com. This will launch Pueblo if it's available on your computer and take you directly to Mom's.

c. Alternatively, you can launch the Pueblo client software and select Quick Connect from the Worlds pull-down menu.

d. In the dialog box that follows, click in the field labeled *Host,* and type:

```
simprov.chaco.com
```

In the field labeled *Port*, type:

```
4444
```

Click on Connect.

e. The Mom's Truck Stop screen will appear.

f. Drag on the window pane that separates the VRML window from the chat screen, and make the VRML window occupy one-third of your screen.

Above: As you navigate a VRML browser window and come into Mom's Truck Stop, you discover the diner is located on the surface of a bowl of soup.

Above Right: The Pueblo window is an adjustable split screen. Users can drag the window pane to make the VRML window occupy one-third of the screen during show time.

Above: Emote buttons at the top of the Pueblo window provide a quick way to make your character smile, bow, wave, nod, wink, laugh, clap, or frown.

2. Participating in the improv.

Plan to arrive at Mom's Truck Stop 30 minutes before show time to explore the 3D diner through the VRML window in Pueblo's split screen or through the Netscape Navigator Live3D window at http://www.metaplay.com.

a. To participate as a character during a performance, click in the Message box at the bottom of the screen, and type:

    Connect Guest

This will generate a Guest character.

b. Click on an emote button at the top of the Pueblo screen to see what your face looks like.

c. To speak, type:

    "your comment here

and press Return.

d. At show time, you'll hear music if your computer is equipped with speakers, and the comedy team will fill the text half of the chat window, inviting you to participate via the Message box. For example, the MetaPlay cast will ask the audience for a suggestion to get the show started.

Argle, the show's host, may say, "Before we start today's show, would someone please suggest an important piece

Above: During a MetaPlay improv show, 2D images of guests and the characters at Mom's get added to the text chat.

of information the Cook finds out today…." Visitors are guests in the diner during the show and may jump in with a line or two at any time. For example, a guest might throw out, "The fryer is broken!" Another character might add, "Uh, oh…soggy fries." and the plot begins!

3. Why Pueblo?

MetaPlay chose a MOO for their performances because Moos are programmable. Although they have investigated other 3D chat environments, they've found that the programmable characteristics help during performances. For example, the performers can clear everyone's screen simultaneously and plant text, such as "Meanwhile…"

4. VRML design issues.

When you visit Mom's Truck Stop and experience the VRML 3D diner, you realize a traditional diner is built on the surface of a bowl of soup. The environment is much more enticing to explore than a classic room with four walls. VRML allows a 3D designer to let go of reality and build surprises into the surroundings—and you will find surprises navigating through Mom's.

Live3D's viewpoints provide a means to display camera shots that viewers can access with a right mouse button and a pop-up menu. A Control key and a right arrow take a viewer through the viewpoints in a slideshow fashion. Much like a filmmaker, 3D artist Paul Marino took advantage of Live3D's viewpoints and has set up several cinematic viewpoints that users can access through the Netscape Navigator Live3D window.

In VRML, camera shots are called PerspectiveCamera position views. Although 3D applications that write VRML files create an opening PerspectiveCamera view, several PerspectiveCamera views may be added to a VRML file. (*Note: See* Open a VRML file in a word processor and alter the PerspectiveCamera *in this chapter.*)

The NYVRMLSIG's Coney Island Project

Summary: *SIGs, or Special Interest Groups, have helped computer users accelerate learning for almost two decades.*

Tech tip from NYVRMLSIG member, Marc Thorner:

"A project like the Coney Island VRML site is historically significant since it represents a radical departure from the restraints imposed by 19th century ideas, and it provides a means for 3D designers to share technical information. As Mark Pesce has said, 'information shared is information squared.'"

You can reach Marc at: mthorner@pipeline.com.

Once a month, the New York VRML Special Interest Group (NYVRMLSIG) meets in the back room at Alt.Coffee to discuss the development of VRML and virtual worlds on the Web. The group was formed in February 1996 and attracts industrial designers, architects, and 3D graphics professionals who want to adapt their knowledge to fit the Web. There is no fee to attend the meetings and anyone can attend.

Larry Rosenthal and Alex Shamson, both industrial designers, are the most technically advanced members. Larry Rosenthal, who founded the SIG, is the unofficial chairman and the most aggressive user of 3D software. Shortly after Larry founded the NYVRMLSIG, he suggested a SIG group project. And in March, the members responded by creating Marc Thorner's suggestion of re-creating New York's Coney Island Amusement Park.

1. Coney Island at the turn of the century.

At the turn of the century, Coney Island, on the southwestern end of Long Island, was the largest amusement park in the United States. Amusement parks lured hundreds of thousands of visitors (some reports say millions) to Coney Island by ferry, railroad, electric trolley, subway, hackney carriage, automobile, and bicycle.

Above: *Luna Park Tower at the entrance to Luna Park.*

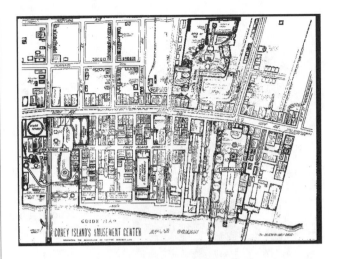

Much like a small city, the original Coney Island was arranged around a main promenade called the Bowery that was lined with carnival attractions. Canopied booths introduced elephants, camels, and "oriental beauties" to resort visitors.

- In 1897, George Tilyou opened Steeplechase Park, one of the three enclosed amusement parks to open at Coney Island. Occupying 15 acres, Steeplechase park was lined by a gravity-powered steeplechase ride.

- In 1902, Frederic Thompson and Skip Dundy, both employed by George Tilyou, planned what was to become the grandest enclosed park at Coney Island–Luna Park, which later opened in May 1903.

  Frederic Thompson was a former architectural student who indulged in ornaments, flags, towers, and turrets. At night, Luna park was illuminated with a quarter million electric lights. When it opened, Luna Park offered visitors a Venetian city with gondoliers, a Japanese garden, an Irish village, an Eskimo village, a Dutch windmill, and a Chinese theater. A rocket trip to the moon was the most popular attraction.

- In 1903, Coney Island's third enclosed park rivaled Luna Park with its massive proportions. Dreamland was planned and built by a group of politicians organized by William H. Reynolds, a former New York state Senator. The designers of Dreamland installed one million elec-

Above: *A statue called* The Creation *at the entrance to Dreamland.*

tric lights and an enormous nude sculpture called *The Creation* at its gates—both meant to overshadow Luna Park.

2. The Coney Island VRML Project.

Anyone can participate in the Coney Island project. Virtus WalkThrough Pro is the recommended software program because it is an inexpensive, easy-to-use 3D application that can write a VRML file with textures and links.

The project requires that participants build two models. The first model can be any ride, canopied side show, or building at Coney Island. The second model is a personal trailer that will be placed along Coney Island's Bowery, once the Amusement Park's main street. The trailer exteriors will be uniform because the NYVRMLSIG provides a template download on the NYVRML Web site at http://www.cube3.com/downloads/NYVRMLSIG. Inside, each trailer will have the model builder's own world or unique space with furniture, textures, or any objects of his/her choice. Here are a few recommended steps to get acquainted with the Coney Island project:

a. Visit Larry Rosenthal's extruded 3D map of Coney Island that contains existing models at http://www .cube3.com. This will give you an idea of what models have already been created.

b. Download one or more models from Larry's site and take them apart in Virtus WalkThrough Pro to see how they are constructed.

c. Look for photos and project tips on the NYVRMLSIG pages at Larry's Web site at http://www.cube3.com/ downloads/NYVRMLSIB.

d. Step through the construction of the Luna Park Tower in this section to learn about building, scaling, and adding texture maps.

e. Download the trailer template from http://www.cube3 .com/downloads/NYVRMLSIG to build your own room at Coney Island.

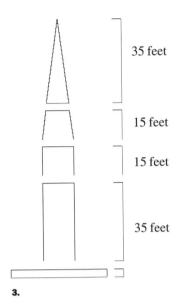

35 feet

15 feet

15 feet

35 feet

3.

3. Planning a model.

a. Make a rough sketch of your model on paper to plan components and their dimensions.

b. In this example, the Luna Park Tower is approximately 100 feet high. This is 100 inches in Virtus Walk-Through Pro.

4. Open an image or texture in Photoshop.

a. Open Photoshop. Then, select Open from the File pull-down menu.

b. Select a graphic in the dialog box that follows, and click on Open.

4a.

4b.

c. Your image will open in a Photoshop window.

4c.

5. Copy/paste a texture to a new document.

a. Select the Rectangle Marquee tool.

5a.

b. Drag-select an area of a photo you would like to use as a texture.

c. Select Copy from the Edit pull-down menu.

d. Select New from the File pull-down menu

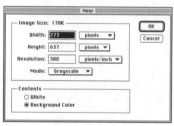
5b.

5c.

5d.

e. The dialog box that follows will display the dimensions of your selection. Click on OK.

f. An Untitled new document will be displayed.

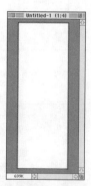
5e.

5f.

g. Select Paste from the Edit pull-down menu.

5g.

5h.

Above: Luna Park's venetian city.

7a.

h. Your selection will fill the Untitled new document.

6. Resize the texture.

a. Select Image Size from the Image pull-down menu.

b. Although 1 foot = 1 inch in Virtus WalkThrough Pro, you should be very conservative when you resize your texture. Large texture files will make your model difficult to download.

In this example, although the base of the Luna Park Tower will be 35 feet high, enter 15 or 20 in the field labeled *Height*. Photoshop will resize the width proportionally, and Virtus will resize the texture to fit your model. Enter 72 in the field labeled *Resolution*, and click on OK.

c. The texture will be resized in a Photoshop window.

6a.

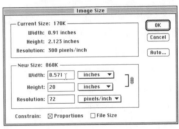

6b.

6c.

7. Save your texture.

a. Select Save As from the File pull-down menu.

7b.

Above: *Dreamland, the third enclosed park to open at Coney Island, was never as popular as Luna Park. Many feel the architecture was less successful. Frederick Thompson, the creator of Luna Park, thought the "park's architecture should be a departure from all that is traditional."*

b. In the dialog box that follows, name the texture *texture_1*, and click on Save.

8. Add the texture to WalkThrough Pro.

a. Open the WalkThrough Pro software.

b. Select Textures Window from the Windows pull-down menu.

c. A Textures palette will be displayed.

8b.

8c.

d. Select Add Textures from the pop-up menu on the Textures palette.

e. In the dialog box that follows, select texture_1, and click on Add.

f. The texture will be added to the Textures palette.

8d.

8e.

8f.

9. Building a model (the Luna Park Tower).

Work in a Left or Right View to make drawing easier.

a. Select New View|Left from the View pull-down menu.

9a.

9b.

9c.

b. Drag the Observer out of the way before you begin your drawing.

c. Select the Rectangle Tool.

d. Drag a rectangle to form the bottom portion of the Luna Park Tower.

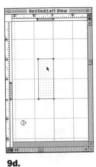

9d.

10. Applying textures.

a. In this example, you'll add the Luna Park Tower texture to the four sides of the tower base.

b. Select the Tumble Editor Tool.

c. Click on Luna Park Tower base in the Design View window.

d. A Tumble Editor window will open.

e. When the Tumble Editor window opens, the Grabber Hand Tool will be selected.

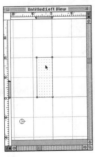

10b.

10c.

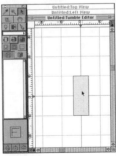

10d.

10e.

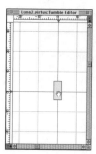

10f.

f. Refer to the Orientation Cube at the base of the Tools window and rotate the rectangle to display the four surfaces where textures are to be applied.

g. Select the Pointer Arrow Tool.

h. Click on a surface to select it.

i. Select Textures Window from the Windows pull-down menu.

j. Double-click on the texture labeled *texture_1* to apply the texture to any of the surfaces.

10g.

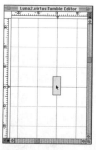

10h.

10i.

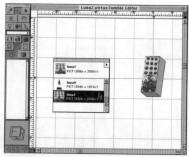

10j.

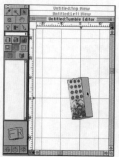

10k.

k. Repeat Steps f through j to apply the texture to four sides of the tower base. (*Note: You will need to re-select the Grabber Hand Tool to rotate the tower base.*)

l. Click on the Close Box in the Tumble Editor window.

10l.

11. View your room in the Walk View.

As you complete your model, navigate around each component in the Walk View to inspect the texture you applied.

a. Level the Observer by selecting Level Observer from the View pull-down menu.

11a.

b. The line of sight on the Observer will be aligned at a 3:00 position.

c. Select New View|Walk View from the View pull-down menu.

d. Navigate around your model.

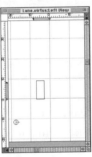

11b.

11c.

11d.

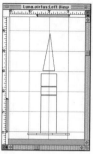

12b.

12. Complete your model.

Use the drawing techniques described in this section to complete the Luna Park Tower.

a. Plan each section of your model, and copy a texture map from a photograph to make your model look realistic.

b. Build each section separately.

c. As you're creating each section, access the Top View by selecting New View|Top from the View pull-down menu.

d. With the Top View selected, you can determine if the sections of your model are lined up.

12c.

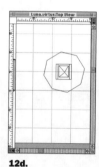

12d.

e. Check the Walk View as you complete each section to view the appearance of your model.

12e.

13a.

13. Save your model.

a. Select Save from the File pull-down menu.

b. In the dialog box that follows, name this model *Luna.virtus,* and click on Save.

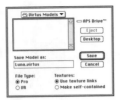

13b.

14. Exporting the model as a VRML file.

a. Select Export|VRML from the File pull-down menu.

b. In the dialog box that follows, click on the box labeled *Include Texture Links*. Then, click on OK.

c. In the dialog box that follows, name the file *Luna.wrl,* and click on Save. (*Note: VRML files must end in a .WRL file extension.*)

14a.

14b.

14c.

Alex Shamson's tips on creating a VRML model in Virtus WalkThrough Pro

Summary: Use Virtus WalkThrough Pro to create a 3D model, and then save it as a WRL file for viewing on the Web.

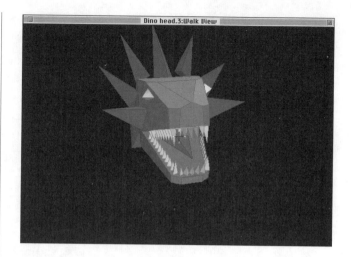

WalkThrough Pro

1a.

Alex Shamson's dinosaur ("Dino") is created with 2D polygons in the Virtus WalkThrough Pro Design View, which then get edited and colored as 3D objects in the software's Tumbler Editor.

1. Open Virtus WalkThrough Pro.

a. Open Virtus WalkThrough Pro.

b. An Untitled:Top View window and an Untitled:Walk View window will open. *(Note: Alex Shamson recommends saving the model immediately. See Steps 8a and 8b for details on how to save your model in Virtus WalkThrough Pro.)*

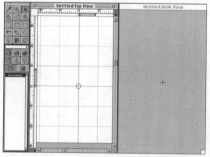

1b.

2a.

2. Change the Design View.

Design View is where you will draw a 2D image of the dinosaur's head.

a. Select Change View|Left from the View pull-down menu.

b. The Untitled:Top View window will change to an Untitled Design:Left View window.

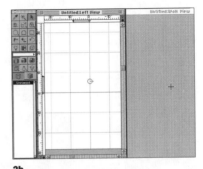

2b.

3. Begin a 2D drawing of the dino head.

a. Select the Irregular Object Tool. (*Note: The Irregular Object Tool is used to draw irregular-shaped polygons by clicking on each vertex.*)

b. Move left to right with three successive clicks to begin the irregular-shaped polygon, as shown in Figure 3b. Follow the grid marking in Figure 3b, and try to make your drawing approximately the same size.

c. Continue to create vertices by clicking to form the polygon shown in Figure 3b. Finish by clicking on your starting point to close the polygon. The polygon should look roughly like a dinosaur skull facing left.

3a.

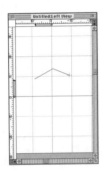

3b.

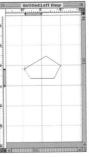

3c.

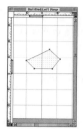

3d.

d. The closed polygon will display a black handle at each vertex. You may drag on any of these handles to alter the polygon's shape.

4. Change views, and alter the inflation.

a. In Virtus WalkThrough Pro, an artist draws in 2D, and the object is instantly rendered as a 3D object in the Walk View window.

b. Your ability to see a 3D object in the Walk View window is dependent on the position of the *Observer*. Details on how to control the Observer will be presented later. The Observer may be dragged out of the way if it's in the way while you're working with your 2D polygon.

4a.

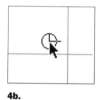

4b.

4c.

c. When you draw a 2D shape, you create two dimensions, and the missing "third dimension" is referred to as the *inflation distance*.

The inflation distance is represented as a gray bar in each of the rulers along the Design View Window.

The default value for the inflation distance is eight feet. This distance may be adjusted prior to drawing. Follow the next steps to check the front view of your object to see the model's proportions.

d. Select Change View|Front from the View pull-down menu.

e. The Untitled:Left View will change to an Untitled:Front View.

f. You may need to adjust the width of the dinosaur's head in the Front View by dragging on a handle as shown. I dragged a polygon handle in the Front View to make the model slightly wider.

4d.

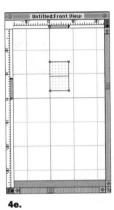

4e.

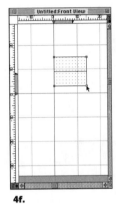

4f.

5. Open the object in the Tumbler Editor.

a. Select the Tumbler Editor Tool.

b. Double-click on the polygon in your Front View window.

5a.

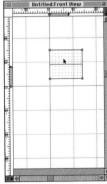

5b.

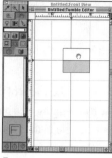

5c.

c. A Tumbler Editor window will open. This view will allow you to rotate an object in 3D and edit a surface.

d. When the Tumbler Editor window opens, the Grabber Hand Tool will be selected.

e. Use the Grabber Hand Tool, and try rotating the object in the Tumbler Editor window. Notice that, as you rotate the object, the orientation cube at the base of the Tools window will reflect the object's position in the Tumbler Editor window (T=Top, B=Bottom, F=Front, B=Back, L=Left, and R=Right).

5d.

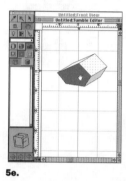

5e.

6a.   6b.   6c.

Tip: The Rotation Constraint Tools will help you control rotation when you edit objects in the Tumbler Editor window.

6. Try the Rotation Constraint Tools.

Rotation Constraint Tools affect how the object in the Tumbler Editor window can be rotated. Clicking on a tool will cause the tool to become activated.

You may turn on more than one tool at one time. You will know a particular tool is "on" because it will appear shaded. At least one tool must be selected at any time. The tools may be turned "off" with a second click, causing the shading to turn light.

a. X-Y Motion Tool. This tool allows rotation in an X-Y plane.

b. X-Z Motion Tool. This tool allows rotation in an X-Z plane.

c. Y-Z Motion Tool. This tool allows rotation in a Y-Z plane.

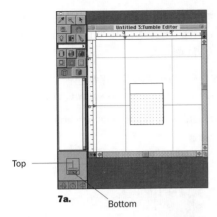

7a.

Top

Bottom

7b.

Tip: Alex Shamson recommends that you always slice in a clockwise direction. By doing this, you always lose the left side of the slice.

7. Reshape the head with the Slice Tool.

Alex used the Slice tool in the Tumbler Editor window to taper the front of the dinosaur's nose. You'll need to work on the model looking down at the dinosaur's head from a Top View. In this position, the nose will be pointing to the bottom of your screen.

a. Rotate your model in the Tumbler Editor window so that it is oriented with the top and bottom sides, as shown in Figure 7a. Refer to the orientation cube at the base of the Tools palette for help.

b. Select the Slice Tool.

c. Using the Slice Tool, drag a slice down the right side of the model, as shown in Figure 7c.

d. When you release your mouse button, a triangular segment will have been "sliced" off, leaving a set of handles where you placed the slice. These handles allow you to edit the slice if necessary. To edit a slice, drag on one of the handles. *(Note: To edit a slice by its handles, you need the Selection Tool.)*

7c.

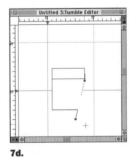

7d.

e. Using the Slice Tool, drag a slice up the left side of the model, as shown in Figure 7e.

7e.

7f.

f. When you release your mouse button, a triangular segment will have been sliced off, leaving a set of handles where you placed the slice.

g. Taper the nose even further by dragging a slice down the right side of the front snout area, as shown in Figure 7g.

h. Again, a set of handles will remain when you release your mouse button.

7g.

7h.

i. Drag a similar slice down the left side of the front snout area, as shown in Figure 7i.

j. Again, a set of handles will remain when you release your mouse button.

7i.

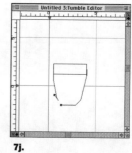

7j.

7k.

k. Your slices have been recorded in the Tool palette. If you wish to see where the slices have been placed or if you wish to further edit one of the slices, you may select a slice by name in the Tool palette window. The respective set of handles will then appear in the Tumble Editor window.

l. To taper the end of the dinosaur's snout even further, position your model in the Tumbler Editor window, as shown in Figure 7l. Use the Orientation Cube as a guide.

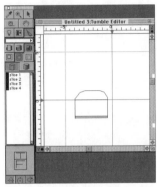

7l.

m. With the front of the dinosaur's snout facing away from you, drag another slice off the right front of his snout, as shown in Figure 7m.

n. Drag a similar slice off the left front of his snout.

7m.

7n.

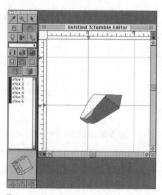

7o.

o. When you've completed your slices, rotate your dinosaur's head to see how the slices have tapered the snout. Notice the slices will be listed in the Tool palette.

p. Put the Tumbler Editor away by clicking on the close box in the upper-left corner.

7p.

8. Save your model.

If you have not yet saved your model, save it as a Virtus WalkThrough Pro file. Later, you will be saving it as a WRL file to be viewed on the Web.

a. Select Save from the File pull-down menu.

b. In the dialog box that follows, type a file name, and click on Save.

8a.

8b.

9a.

9. Create the lower jaw from a duplicate.

Return to the Left View to create the lower jaw, create a duplicate, and then open the Tumbler Editor to remove the top portion of the head. A remaining lower section will form the lower jaw.

a. Select Change View|Left from the View pull-down menu.

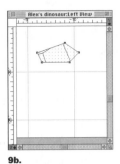

9b.

9c.

b. A Left View window will be displayed.

c. Select Duplicate from the Edit pull-down menu.

d. A duplicate of your model will appear.

e. Drag the duplicate polygon away from the original, as shown in Figure 9e.

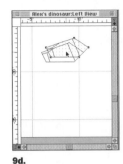

9d.

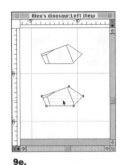

9e.

9f.

f. Select the Tumbler Editor Tool.

g. Double-click on the duplicate polygon in your Left View window.

h. A Tumbler Editor window will open.

9g.

9h.

9i.

i. When the Tumbler Editor window opens, the Grabber Hand Tool will be selected.

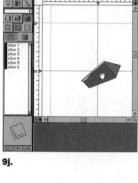

9j.

9k.

j. Use the Grabber Hand Tool to orient your model, as shown in Figure 9j. Use the orientation cube at the base of the Tools palette as a reference.

k. Select the Slice Tool.

l. Using the Slice Tool, drag the head from left to right, as shown in Figure 9l.

m. When you release the mouse button, the upper portion of the head will have been sliced off, leaving a set of handles where you placed the slice.

n. You may want to rotate the new lower jaw in the Tumbler Editor window using the Grabber Hand Tool.

o. Put the Tumbler Editor window away by clicking on the close box in the upper-left corner.

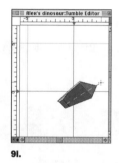

9l.

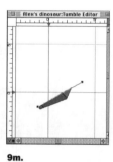

9m.

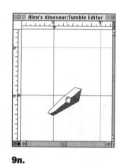

9n.

9o.

10. Create a neck.

Create a neck by drawing a new polygon in the Left View window.

a. Select the Irregular Object Tool.

10a.

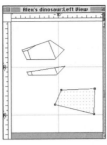

10b.

b. Draw a four-sided polygon to form a neck, as shown in Figure 10b.

c. Drag the completed neck polygon to line up with the head, as shown in Figure 10c. You may need to drag on one of the neck polygon handles so that it lines up properly with the dinosaur head.

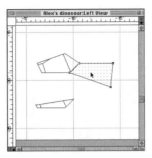

10c.

11. Rotate the jaw.

Alex's dinosaur has a lower jaw that is open, showing a mouth full of teeth and a tongue. In order for the jaw to appear open, the lower jaw must be rotated.

11a.

a. Select the Rotate Tool.

b. Click inside the lower jaw polygon, and drag your mouse away from the polygon to the right as shown. As you move your mouse with the mouse button held down, you'll notice that the lower jaw segment can be rotated. When you are happy with the angle of rotation or, when the angle of rotation approximates what is shown in Figure 11b, let go of the mouse button.

c. Drag the lower jaw into position, as shown in Figure 11c.

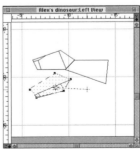

11b.

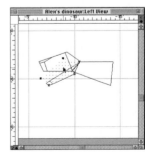

11c.

12. Color the dinosaur polygons.

The surfaces of your polygons may be colored in the Tumble Editor or the Surface Editor. Alex chose a bright green shade for the dinosaur head and a pink shade for the inside of the mouth.

Start by coloring the dinosaur's neck. However, before you go into the Tumble Editor, check the Front View to see if the head and neck are approximately the same width.

a. Select Change View|Front from the View pull-down menu.

b. The Front View window will be displayed.

c. Adjust the neck polygon width so that it matches the width of the dinosaur head in this view.

12a.

12b, 12c.

d. Select Change View|Left from the View pull-down menu.

e. The Left View window will be displayed.

f. Select the Tumbler Editor Tool shown in Figure 12f1. *(Note: Alternatively, you may select the Surface Editor Tool shown in Figure 12f2 and follow similar directions to color an object in the Surface Editor.)*

12d.

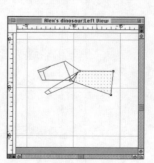

12e.

12f1.

12f2.

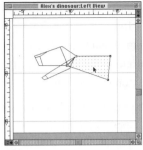

12g.

12h.

12l.

g. Click on the neck polygon in the Left View window.

h. A Tumbler Editor window will open.

i. When the Tumbler Editor window opens, the Grabber Hand Tool will be selected.

j. Select the Pointer Arrow Tool as shown.

k. Click one of the polygon surfaces to select it.

12i.

12j.

12k.

l. Press and hold down the color bar, drag the pointer to select a green, and release the mouse button.

m. The green you selected will be applied to the surface you selected.

n. Follow Steps j through m to apply green to all of the neck surfaces.

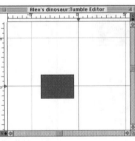

12m.

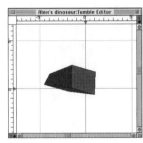

12n.

o. Open the remaining polygons you've created and the lower jaw in the Tumbler Editor. Follow Steps g through l to apply green to all but the underside surface of the dinosaur's head and the upper surface of the dinosaur's lower jaw. Apply pink to these two surfaces.

p. Close the Tumbler Editor window by clicking on the close box in the upper-left corner.

12p.

13. Create horns.

Alex gave the dinosaur a crown of horns, which he colored red.

a. Select Irregular Object Tool.

b. Select the Inflate Pointed Modifier Tool. This tool will inflate an object with sides that converge to a point.

c. Draw a three-sided polygon to form a horn polygon, as shown in Figure 13c.

d. Before duplicating the horn, check on the horn's proportions in the Front View window. Select Change View|Front from the View pull-down menu.

13a.

13b.

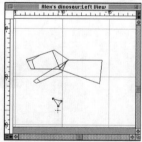

13c.

13d.

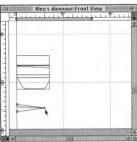
13e, 13f.

e. The Front View window will be displayed.

f. Adjust the horn polygon so that its width is almost as wide as the dinosaur's head.

g. Drag the horn into position on the right side of the head, as shown in Figure 13g.

13g.

h. With the horn still selected, select Duplicate from the Edit pull-down menu.

i. A duplicate horn will appear.

j. Select the Rotate Tool.

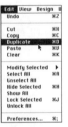
13h.

13i.

13j.

k. Click inside the horn polygon, and drag your mouse away from the polygon to the right. As you move your mouse with the mouse button held down, you'll notice the horn can be rotated. Rotate the horn slightly and let go of the mouse button.

l. Drag the duplicate into position on the right side of the head.

m. Repeat Steps h through k to create five more horns, as shown in Figure 13m.

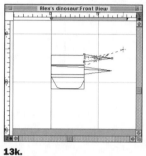
13k.

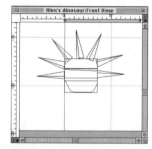
13l, 13m.

14. Create eyes.

Alex gave the dinosaur small yellow pyramids for eyes.

a. Select Change View|Left from the View pull-down menu.

b. The Left View window will be displayed.

c. Select the Irregular Object Tool.

d. Select the Inflate Pointed Modifier Tool. This tool will inflate an object with sides that converge to a point.

14a.

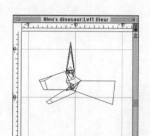
14b.

14c.

14d.

e. Draw a three-sided polygon to form an eye, as shown in Figure 14e.

f. Select Change View|Front from the View pull-down menu.

g. The Front View window will be displayed.

h. Adjust the width of the eye, as shown in Figure 14h.

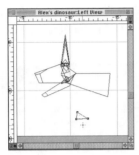

14e.

14f.

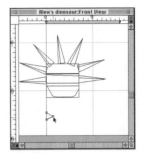

14g, 14h.

14i.

i. Select Change View|Left from the View pull-down menu.

j. The Left View window will be displayed.

k. Drag the left eye into position on the dinosaur's head.

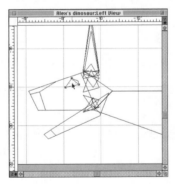

14j, 14k.

l. Follow Steps 14i and 14j to duplicate the eye.

m. Change to the Front View, and position the right eye on the right side of the dinosaur's head.

15a.

15. Create a tongue.

Give the dinosaur a dark red tongue.

a. Select Change View|Left from the View pull-down menu.

b. The Left View window will be displayed.

c. Select the Irregular Object Tool.

d. Select the Inflate Pointed Modifier Tool. This tool will inflate an object with sides that converge to a point.

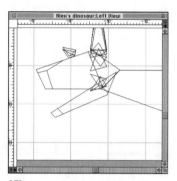

15b.

15c.   **15d.**

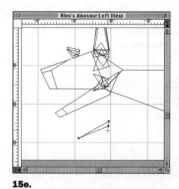

15e.

e. Draw a three-sided polygon to form a tongue, as shown in Figure 15e.

f. Select Change View|Front from the View pull-down menu.

g. The Front View window will be displayed.

h. Adjust the width of the tongue, as shown in Figure 15h.

15f.

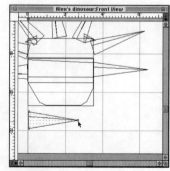

15g, 15h.

15i.

i. Select Change View|Left from the View pull-down menu.

j. The Left View window will be displayed.

k. Drag the tongue into position inside the dinosaur's mouth, as shown in Figure 15k.

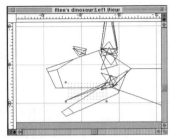
15j, 15k.

16. View the model in the Walk View.

a. Drag the Observer in front of your model, as shown in Figure 16a.

b. The black line in the middle of the Observer should be pointing toward the dinosaur. This represents the direction of the Observer or the line of sight.

To manually change the line of sight, position the tip of the mouse pointer arrow in the center of the Observer, hold down the Option key, and click and drag in a new direction. A dotted line will appear. Release the mouse button, and the line of sight will be repositioned.

c. Select New View|Walk View from the View pull-down menu.

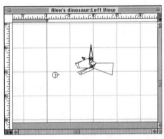
16a.

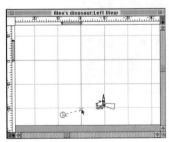
16b.

16c.

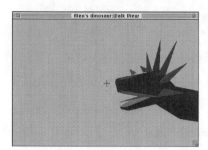

16d, 16e, 16f.

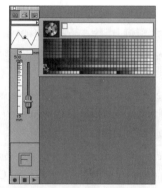

16g.

d. The Walk View will be displayed.

e. Position your mouse on either side of the center crosshair, and click on the mouse button a few times. This action causes you to navigate in the Walk View window to the right or to the left.

(Note: If you position your mouse to the left of the center crosshair and click, you will turn left. You will turn right if you position your mouse to the right of the center crosshair and click. If you position your mouse above the center crosshair and click, you will move forward. You will move backward if you position your mouse button below the center crosshair and click.)

f. In the Walk View window, you can see if your model needs adjustment.

g. The background color of the Walk View window may be changed by pressing on the Color bar in the Tool palette and selecting an alternate color, as shown in Figure 16g.

h. Alex Shamson changed the background color from the default light blue to black. *(Note: The dinosaur you see in the step-by-step examples is the dinosaur I created for this section. Figure 16h is is the dinosaur Alex created.)*

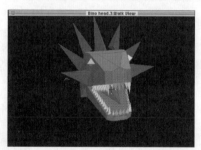

16h.

17. Repositioning the dinosaur's eyes.

The Walk View revealed that my dinosaur's eyes needed to be moved toward the head. The Front View is the best view to do this.

17a.

a. Select Change View|Front from the View pull-down menu.

b. The Front View window will be displayed.

c. Click on one of the eye polygons, and press the down arrow on your keyboard to move the eye down.

d. Repeat this step to move the other eye polygon to line it up with the first eye polygon you moved.

e. Follow Steps 16c and 16d to change to the Walk View and check on this adjustment.

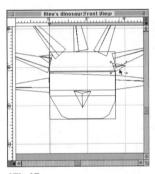

17b, 17c.

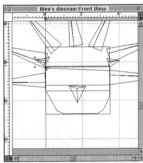

17d.

17e.

18a.

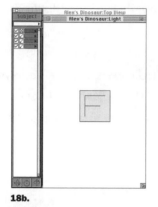

18b.

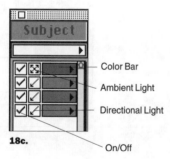

Color Bar

Ambient Light

Directional Light

On/Off

18c.

18. Adjust the World Lighting.

The World Lighting Editor may be used to adjust the lighting on or around your model. The objects you create in Virtus WalkThrough Pro have four default light sources. One of these is an ambient light source (light from all directions simultaneously) and three are directional light sources (light from a single direction).

All of the default light sources have a neutral gray color, which may be changed. Lights may be added or deleted, turned on or off, and designated as either ambient or directional.

To add brighter light to the dinosaur, change the color of the lights from gray to white.

a. Select New View|World Lighting from the View pull-down menu.

b. The World Lighting Editor will be opened.

c. A Lights list, containing the four default light sources, will appear in the Tools palette. Each light has a(n):

- **On/Off switch.** Click to turn a light source on or off.

- **Ambient/Directional icon.** Click to toggle between these two types of light sources.

- **Color bar.** Press and hold down the Color Bar to select a light color.

d. To change the light color from gray to white, press and hold down the Color bar, drag the pointer to select white, and release the mouse button.

18d.

18e.

e. Repeat this step to change the light color of the remaining lights from gray to white.

f. To observe the effects of the change in the light color, open the Walk View. Select New View|Walk View from the View pull-down menu.

g. Note the change in the model. Besides the change in the background color, the light is brighter.

18f.

18g.

19. Create a duplicate jaw to hold teeth.

a. Select Change View|Left from the View pull-down menu.

b. The Left View window will be displayed.

c. Click on the lower jaw to select it.

d. Select Duplicate from the Edit pull-down menu.

19a.

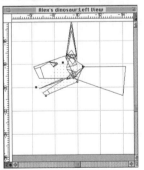

19b.

19d.

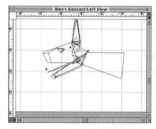

19e.

e. A duplicate lower jaw will appear.

f. Use the down arrow key on your keyboard to move the duplicate away from your model.

g. When you've moved the duplicate away from your model, use your mouse pointer arrow to move the jaw in front of your model.

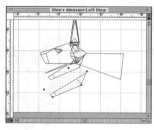

19f.

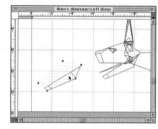

19g.

19h.

19i.

h. Select the Irregular Object Tool.

i. Select the Inflate Pointed Modifier Tool.

j. Draw a three-sided polygon to form a tooth, as shown in Figure 19j.

k. Select Change View|Front from the View pull-down menu.

l. The Front View window will be displayed.

m. Adjust the width of the tongue, as shown in Figure 19m.

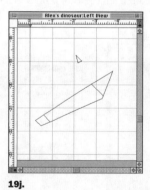

19j.

19k.

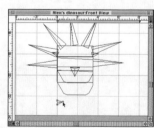

19l, 19m.

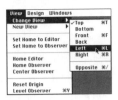

19n.

n. Select Change View|Left from the View pull-down menu.

o. The Left View window will be displayed.

p. Drag the tooth and line it up on the jaw, as shown in Figure 19p.

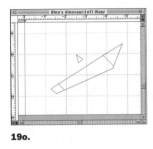

19o.

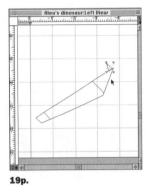

19p.

19q.

q. With the tooth still selected, select Duplicate from the Edit pull-down menu.

r. A duplicate tooth will appear.

s. Move the duplicate tooth and line it up on the jaw, as shown in Figure 19s.

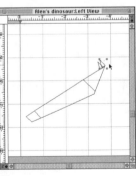

19r.

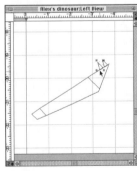

19s.

19t.

t. Reselect Duplicate from the Edit pull-down menu.

u. A new duplicate will appear and Virtus WalkThrough Pro will remember where you moved the original.

v. Continue to select Duplicate from the Edit pull-down menu until you have filled in the jaw with teeth, as shown in Figure 19v.

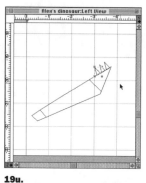

19u.

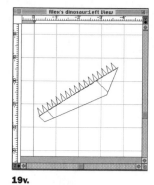

19v.

20a.

20. Adjust the teeth in the Top View.

a. Select Change View|Top from the View pull-down menu.

b. The Top View will be displayed.

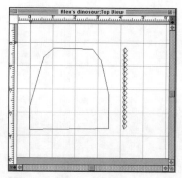

20b.

c. Drag a selection marquee around the teeth, as shown in Figure 20c, and then let go of the mouse.

d. When you release the mouse, the teeth will display selection handles, indicating that they are selected.

e. Drag the teeth inside the jaw, as shown in Figure 20e.

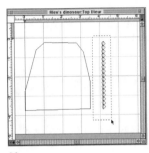

20c.

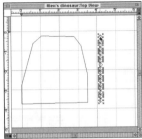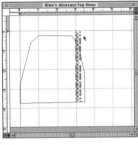

20d.   20e.

f. Move the front teeth around to the front of the jaw, one at a time. To do this, click on a tooth, and move it to the left using the left arrow key on your keyboard.

g. Use the drag-select and duplicate techniques presented in this section to create a row of teeth on the right side of the jaw.

h. When you have completed a full set of teeth using the jaw as a guide, move the jaw away from the teeth, as shown in Figure 20h.

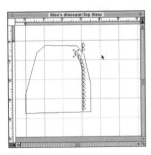

20f.

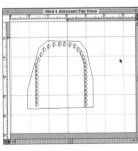

20g.

20h.

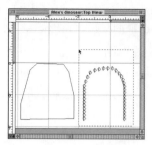
21a.

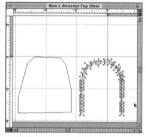
21b.

21c.

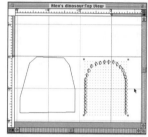
21d.

21e.

21. Group the teeth.

a. Drag a selection marquee around the teeth, and then let go of the mouse.

b. When you release the mouse, the teeth will display selection handles, indicating that they are selected.

c. Select Group from the Design pull-down menu.

d. The teeth will become one object, and the new object will be surrounded with a new set of selection handles.

e. Select Change View|Left from the View pull-down menu.

f. The Left View will be displayed.

g. Select the duplicate jaw.

h. Press the Delete key on your keyboard to delete the duplicate jaw. The jaw was used as a guide to create teeth and is no longer needed.

21f.

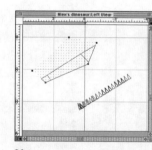
21g.

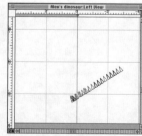
21h.

i. Select the teeth, which are now one object.

j. Select Duplicate from the Edit pull-down menu.

k. A duplicate set of teeth will appear superimposed on the original.

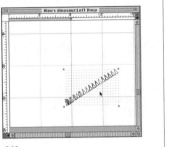

21i.

21j.

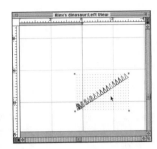

21k.

l. Move the new duplicate set of teeth away from the original.

m. Drag the duplicate set of teeth into the dinosaur's mouth, as shown in Figure 21m.

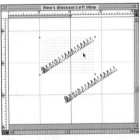

21l.

21m.

22. Rotate the original set of teeth.

22a.

a. Select the Rotate Tool.

b. Click inside the grouped object, and drag your mouse down and to the left. As you move your mouse with the button held down, you'll notice that the teeth can be rotated.

c. Rotate the teeth so they are facing down, as shown in Figure 22b. You may need to rotate the teeth a few times to get them to line up horizontally.

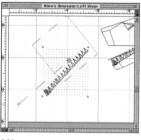
22b.

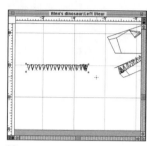
22c.

d. Select Change View|Top from the View pull-down menu.

e. The Top View will be displayed.

f. Select the Rotate Tool.

g. You've rotated the teeth in the Left View so that they point down. Now, rotate the teeth so that the set faces in the same direction as the top row. Click inside the remaining set of teeth, drag your mouse to the right, and rotate the row so that it faces the opposite direction.

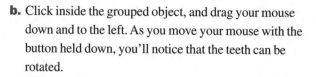
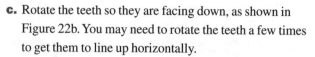
22d.

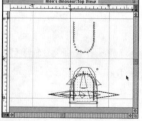
22e.

22f.

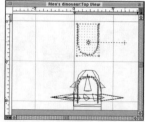
22g.

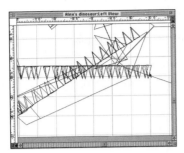

23a.

23. Drag the upper teeth inside the mouth.

a. Drag the duplicate row of teeth inside the dinosaur's mouth, as shown in Figure 23a.

b. Select New View|Walk View from the View pull-down menu. (*Note: See Steps 16a and 16b in this section for details on how to position the Observer.*)

c. The Walk View will be displayed. Both rows of teeth have extra teeth that need to be deleted.

23b.

23c.

24. Delete extra teeth.

a. Select Change View|Left from the View pull-down menu.

b. The Left View will be displayed.

c. With the upper row of teeth selected, select Ungroup from the Design pull-down menu.

d. Although individual handles may not appear around each tooth, you'll discover that the teeth are no longer one object by clicking on one of the rear teeth.

24a.

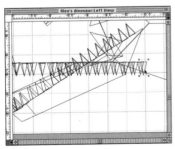

24b.

24c.

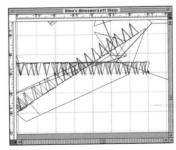

24d.

e. Click to select individual teeth, and press the Delete key on the keyboard to remove the extra teeth.

f. Repeat Step 24c to ungroup the lower set of teeth.

g. Click to select individual teeth along the lower jaw, and press the Delete key on the keyboard to remove extra teeth.

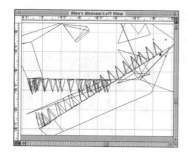

24f.

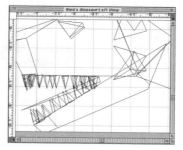

24g.

h. Select New View|Walk View from the View pull-down menu.

i. The Walk View will be displayed.

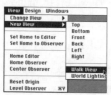

24h.

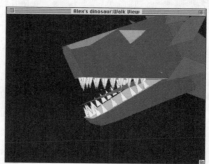

24i.

25. Resave your model.

a. Select Save from the File pull-down menu.

25a.

b. Your file will be updated.

26. Export the model as a VRML file.

a. Select Export|VRML from the File pull-down menu.

b. In the dialog box that follows, click OK. (*Note: The dinosaur has no textures.*)

c. In the dialog box that follows, type a name with a WRL extension, and click on Save.

d. A file-writing status bar will appear as the .WRL file is written to your hard drive.

26a.

26b.

26c.

26d.

Open your WRL file in a VRML browser

Summary: Use the Virtus Voyager VRML browser to open your WRL file.

dino.wrl

Open your WRL file in a browser that can see VRML files. Examples include Netscape Navigator with Live3D plug-in, the Virtus Voyager browser, or Brad Anderson's ExpressVR browser. SGI has announced that they intend to provide a version of their Cosmo browser for the Macintosh. *(Note: The dino.wrl model in this example is available on the book's companion CD-ROM. The model was created by Alex Shamson of VRmill, Inc. Look for his site at http://www.vrmill.com.)*

1. Open a VRML file in Virtus Voyager.

a. Open the Voyager software that corresponds to your hardware (Macintosh PowerPC or 68 K Macintosh).

b. The Voyager browser window will open. *(Note: Look for the Virtus Voyager browser on the companion CD-ROM. The Voyager browser may be used as a standalone application, or it may be configured as a Netscape helper appplication.)*

c. Select Open File from the File pull-down menu.

Voyager B2 68k

1a.

1b.

1c.

1d.

d. In the dialog box that follows, open a WRL file and click on Open.

e. The VRML model will open in the browser window.

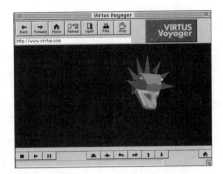
1e.

2. Navigate your VRML file.

a. Press on the Forward navigation button to move forward.

b. Press on the Backward navigation button to move backward.

c. Press on the Left navigation button to move left.

d. Press on the Right navigation button to move right.

e. Press on the Up navigation button to move up.

f. Press on the Down navigation button to move down.

g. Press on the Home navigation button to reposition the model to its opening position.

2a.   2b.

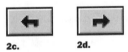
2c.   2d.

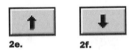
2e.   2f.

2g.

Open a VRML file in a word processor and alter the Perspective-Camera

Summary: Follow this example to change the PerspectiveCamera node's parameters by making changes to a WRL file in a word processor.

dino.wrl

Many people who create VRML models use a word processor to create "hand coded" VRML. These files and the files you export from a 3D application program are text files that may be opened and modified in a word processor.

As VRML changes, hand coding provides a means to make changes in a VRML model that applications may not be able to add. In this example, changes in XYZ position values in the PerspectiveCamera node parameters will alter the position of the dinosaur head when the model opens.

1. Open a VRML file in a word processor.

a. Open Microsoft Word or some other word processor. *(Note: SimpleText may be used, although the software's document size is limited, and some VRML models may not open.)*

b. Select Open from the File pull-down menu.

c. In the dialog box that follows, select a WRL file, and click on Open.

Microsoft Word

1a.

1b.

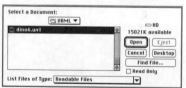

1c.

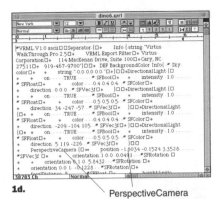

1d.

PerspectiveCamera positions

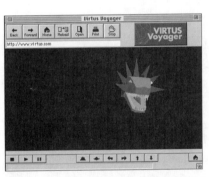

2b.

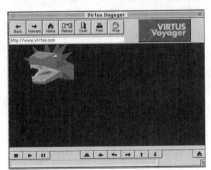

2d.

d. The WRL file will open in a document window.

e. The file may not have a neat column of VRML code that you'd expect it to have. For example, the VRML code you're looking for is most readable in the column format:

```
PerspectiveCamera {

position -14.7574 -5.9690 -1.3716      #SFVec3f

orientation 0 1 0  4.4438      #SFRotation

focalDistance  2            #SFFloat

heightAngle 1.0486

}
```

Although the text file looks scrambled in a Microsoft Word window, it does not need to be cleaned up or formatted.

2. Change the XYZ position values.

a. The XYZ position values in the file that opens are:

```
-1.8034
-0.1524
 3.3528
```

b. These values correspond to the location of the camera. See Figure 2b.

c. To reposition the cameras entry view, change these values to:

```
1.2034
-.5524
3.3528
```

(Note: The Netscape Navigator browser window with Live3D has a pop-up menu that accomodates several PerspectiveCamera position views. These extra camera position views are an example of VRML that needs to be hand coded.)

d. The new XYZ values correspond to the position of the camera view. See Figure 2d. *(Note: The dinosaur's head does not move; the camera does.)*

3. Save your WRL file and view changes.

3a.

a. Select Save As from the File pull-down menu.

b. In the dialog box that follows, select Text Only from the Save File As Type pop-up menu.

3b.

c. Alter the file name by adding an alphanumeric character, make sure the file has a WRL extension, and click on Save.

3c.

d. Follows Steps 1a through 1e in the previous section to view the position changes.

4. Create a Camera Switch (a Live3D option).

Live3D's viewpoints provide a means to display several camera shots that you can access through the View pop-up menu in the Netscape Navigator window. To write these extra viewpoints into a VRML file, you'll need to create a Camera Switch node. You can then add as many viewpoints as you'd like.

a. The following example is from Alex Shamson's Plaza.wrl file, which can be viewed at his Web site (http://www.vrmill .com). Each new viewpoint's

Bird's-eye view of the Mall Entrance, Plaza and the Tower with various Stores on each level.

More to open soon... The Mall is under constant renovation and expansion.

Bookmark this page and stop by often!

4a.

description follows each line, beginning with DEF. *(Note: Viewpoint descriptions appear in the Live3D pop-up.)* Alex Shamson warns that spaces between words in a description are not allowed. For example, notice he has closed the space in EntryView and LeftRear:

```
DEF Cameras Switch {
    whichChild -1
DEF EntryView PerspectiveCamera {
    position 0 3.6 159        #SFVec3f
    orientation 1 0 0  0.2      #SFRotation
    focalDistance  678.69      #SFFloat
    heightAngle 1.3
}

DEF LeftRear PerspectiveCamera {
    position -80 5.5 25
    orientation 0 1 0 4.5  #SFRotation
    focalDistance 678.69
    heightAngle 1.3
}

DEF Bird'sEyeView PerspectiveCamera {
    position 70 50 15
    orientation 0 1 0 -4  #SFRotation
    focalDistance 500
    heightAngle -3
}

DEF DirectoryPanel PerspectiveCamera {
    position -10 4 45
    orientation 0 1 0 -6  #SFRotation
    focalDistance 500
    heightAngle -3
}
```

Embed a VRML window in a Web page

Summary: *Use the <EMBED> tag to add a VRML file to a Web page.*

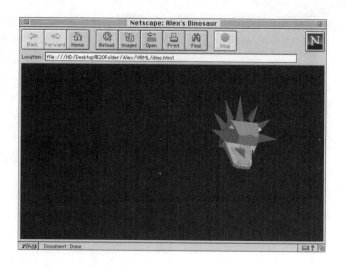

VRML files can be added to a Web page using the <EMBED> tag. This tag defines an inline window that is part of the page.

1. Create an HTML document.

a. Open SimpleText or your word processor. If you use a word processor, be sure to save the text as Text Only.

b. Create a new HTML document. Start a new document with the following markup tags:

```
<HTML>

<HEAD>

<TITLE> Alex's dinosaur

</TITLE>

</HEAD>
```

Tip: The BBS ColorEditor has moved a few times. If you have trouble finding the site, visit the Alta Vista search engine at http://www.altavista.digital.com. Do a search on ColorEditor for HTML. Do not include a space between Color and Editor.

c. Create a body tag, and add color attributes. Adding color to a Netscape background requires placing a hexa-decimal red-green-blue triplet in the body tag. Best Business Solutions' Color Editor provides an online tool to locate a hexadecimal triplet for your page at http://uccnitk.edu.tw/html.courses/colorEditor.html.

```
<HTML>

<HEAD>

<TITLE> Alex's dinosaur

</TITLE>
```

```
</HEAD>

<BODY BGCOLOR="#000000">
```

d. Add a <CENTER> tag

```
<HTML>

<HEAD>

<TITLE> Alex's dinosaur

</TITLE>

</HEAD>

<BODY BGCOLOR="#000000">

<CENTER>
```

e. Add an <EMBED> tag. In this tag, the width and height of the embedded VRML window is defined in pixels. In this example, the width is 400, and the height is 300.

```
<HTML>

<HEAD>

<TITLE> Alex's dinosaur

</TITLE>

</HEAD>

<BODY BGCOLOR="#000000">

<CENTER>

<EMBED SRC="dino.wrl" WIDTH=400 HEIGHT=300>

</CENTER>
```

f. Add the ending tags.

```
</BODY>
</HTML>
```

g. Save the file. Save the document in SimpleText or your word processor. If you're working in a word processor, save the text as Text Only. Give the file an .HTM extension.

h. Test the frame document. Open Netscape or Microsoft's Internet Explorer browser. Open your document by selecting Open File from the File pull-down menu.

2. Summary of HTML tags used in this section.

The tags you see in this list (in alphabetical order) reflect the HTML 3.2 specification.

<BODY>...</BODY>

A tag used to open and close the body of a document. This tag uses the BGCOLOR=#RRGGBB or hexadecimal red-green-blue triplet attribute, which adds color to a browser page. For example:

```
<BODY BGCOLOR=#000000>
```

<CENTER>...</CENTER>

A tag used to center elements on a page.

<EMBED>

A tag used to add an embedded object to a Web page. This tag uses the SRC attribute, which represents the name of the source data. This tag also uses the WIDTH and HEIGHT attributes to indicate the width and height of an object in pixels. For example:

```
<EMBED SRC="dino.wrl" WIDTH=400 HEIGHT=300>
```

<HEAD>...</HEAD>

A tag used to open and close the header portion of a document.

<HTML>...</HTML>

A tag used to open and close an HTML document.

<TITLE>...</TITLE>

A tag used to describes the title of a document, which shows up inside a browser's title bar.

Artist featured in this chapter:

Frank DeCrescenzo is a graphic designer at Simon & Schuster in New York City and a new media artist specializing in Web site design, 3D animation, and digital video. He is also a musician with the band Mantus.

frank_decrescenzo@ prenhall.com

http://members.aol.com/ flatsticks/splash.html

Chapter 12

Forms

A Web page form is an advanced feature because it requires a user to type data into the form's fields, select from multiple-choice-type data fields using radio buttons, or drag-select from multiple-choice-type data in pop-up menus. These responses must then be routed from the Web page to some destination on the Internet. The designer who builds the form must either create a strategy for routing the data or turn this task over to a programmer. Typically, data is routed from a form to some destination with a CGI script (Common Gateway Interface) written in a computer language such as PERL, Java, or C++.

In this chapter, new media artist Frank DeCrescenzo demonstrates how to design a form using NetObjects Fusion. The routing of data is handled with a simple MAILTO command and avoids the use of CGI scripts. By using a MAILTO, the designer who creates the form may have the form data mailed to an email address. Even though this method is the least sophisticated technique for routing form data, it's generic enough for any Web server. *(Note: For details on CGI directory access, see* Before you design a form for your Web site....*)* Special thanks to Web specialist Peter Chowka for his tips on how to use a MAILTO to route form data.

The Slappers
Web site

Summary: *Learn how to design a Web site with a form by following Frank DeCrescenzo's step-by-step example.*

Above: *The site's Where page contains a form.*

Above Right: *The Slappers home page.*

S lappers are flat drumsticks created by percussionist Billy Amendola. Billy and Frank DeCrescenzo are both members of a New York City-based band called *Mantus*. *(Note: Readers who wish to follow Frank's sample step-by-step may look for both art and text files on the companion CD-ROM.)*

1. Overview.

This chapter presents readers with the techniques used to create a form with NetObjects Fusion. Visit http://www .netobjects.com to download a 30-day trial copy of the software.

2a.

2b.

2c.

2. The site's structure.

The structure Frank designed for the Slappers site is a simple hierarchy.

a. Splash page. When visitors load the first Slappers page into their browser, the first thing that appears is a GIF animation of a rotating 3D logo.

b. Home page. Frank's home page contains a transparent GIF image of the Slappers drumsticks and an image map panel.

c. Who. Frank's Who page includes background information about Billy Amendola, who developed the Slappers drumsticks. Included are endorsements from fellow artists and magazines, such as *Drum!, Modern Drummer,* and *Rip Magazine.* The Who branch contains another branch to a Mantus page, which in turn contains details about Frank's band.

d. How. The How page explains how to use Slappers drumsticks. The links on this page load QuickTime video demonstration clips.

e. Where. This page answers the question, "Where can I get them?" Frank's form is included on this page.

2d.

2e.

2f.

3a.

3b.

f. Hot Links. This page contains links to related percussion pages on the Web.

3. Image maps as a navigation device.

Frank chose image maps as a navigation device. He designed image map panels containing percussion instrument icons for each of the pages. These include a full drum set, a set of cow bells, a timbale, and a set of bongos.

a. Home page. Frank's icons on the home page are all visible, and they're clickable hotspots that branch to related Web pages.

b. Branch pages. On a branch page, a related icon is a ghosted representation of the original. This is a visual device meant to confirm that the user is on the right page.

4. Data collection with forms.

Frank's form on the Where page collects personal data such as name, address, city, state, ZIP, country, and email. He has also created fields for a business transaction for visitors who wish to purchase a set of "Slappers."

Customer Information
Name
Street Address
City
State
Zip Code
Country
E-mail Address
Alternate way to verify order: Phone number
Home
Work

4.

Using NetObjects Fusion to create a client-side image map

Summary: Form design in NetObjects Fusion couldn't be simpler. To download a 30-day trial version of the software, visit http://www.netobjects.com.

NetObjects

FUSION™

Version 1.0

©1996 NetObjects, Inc. All Rights Reserved

NET**objects**

NetObjects Fusion is a wonderful tool for designers who do not want to write HTML tags. This simple introduction uses single-line text fields for data entry. For details on how to add multiple-line text fields, radio dials, checkboxes, and combo boxes, visit the NetObjects Web site at http://www.netobjects.com and download the software's documentation. To follow this step-by-step sample, look for related art and text files on the companion CD-ROM.

1. Start NetObjects Fusion.

The step-by-step sample in this section assumes you have learned the basic Web page techniques using NetObjects Fusion presented in Chapter 3.

a. Start NetObjects Fusion.

b. A New site dialog box will appear on your screen. *(Note: If the New Site dialog box did not appear, select New Site from the File pull-down menu.)*

c. Type a name for your site in the field labeled *Site Name* at the top of the New Site dialog box, and click on OK. The site name will serve as a file name, which is given an .NOD extension. The site name will also be used as the subfolder name that stores the NOD file and the site's assets. (*Note: See Chapter 3 for details on how to create a path to your project folder if you do not want your file to be stored in the NetObjects Fusion folder.*)

NetObjects Fusion
1a.

1b, 1c.

New page button

Home page icon

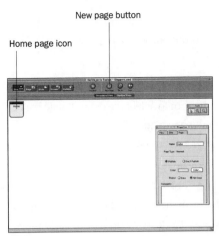

1d, 2a.

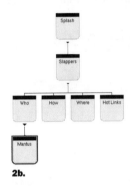

2b.

d. A NetObjects Fusion Site view will be displayed. *(Note: The Site view will be where you create pages and a structure for your site.)*

e. (Option) Review Chapter 3 to learn about NetObject Fusion's preferences and selecting a browser to preview your Web pages.

2. Create Web pages and label them.

a. In NetObjects Fusion's Site view, locate the New Page button at the top of the screen. Notice the Home Page icon is highlighted, indicating that it is selected.

b. For the Slappers site, Frank created a preliminary splash page that contains a small GIF animation, a home page, and four principal branches named *Who, How, Where,* and *Hot Links*. The Mantus page, which branches from the Who page, is devoted to Frank's band.

Follow Figure 2b to create these pages. *(Note: Review Chapter 3 for details on how to create pages and label them.)*

3. Change views and add art to a page.

The NetObjects Fusion Page view is the layout area where Web pages are created.

a. Double-click the Slappers page in the Site view to go to the Slappers Page view.

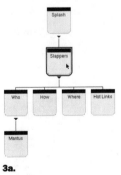

3a.

Default page banner

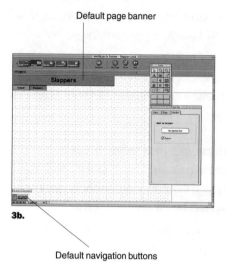

3b.

Default navigation buttons

3c.

3f.

b. NetObjects Fusion's Page view will be displayed. Notice the screen contains a default page banner labeled *Slappers*.

c. Select the Selection Tool.

d. Use the Selection Tool to select the default page banner. Delete the default page banner by pressing the Delete key. Also, delete the default navigation buttons in the page footer.

e. Use the Selection Tool to drag the page divider that separates the header from the body and move it up to make more room. Also, drag the page divider that separates the footer from the body and move it down.

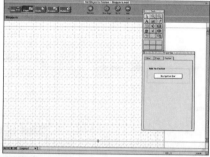

3d, 3e.

f. Select the Picture Tool.

g. Draw picture boxes on the Slappers page, as shown in Figure 3g. Import Frank's art into these boxes. *(Note: Review Chapter 3 for details on how to import art into picture boxes.)*

File name: Slapper_logo.gif

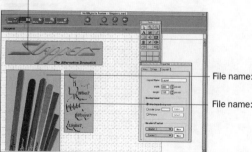

File name: Home_sticks.gif

File name: instruments.gif

3g.

4a.

4. Add text to a page.

a. Select the Text Tool.

b. Draw a text box, as shown in Figure 4b.

c. Launch SimpleText.

d. Open the text file named *Welcome.txt* in SimpleText.

e. Copy the text, and paste it into the NetObjects Fusion text box, as shown in Figure 4e.

f. Add boldfacing and center the text, as shown in Figure 4f. *(Note: Review Chapter 3 for details on how to center text and add boldfacing.)*

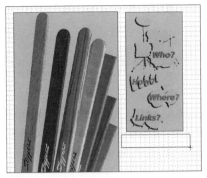

4b.

SimpleText

4c.

4d.

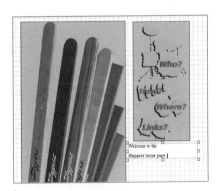

4e.

4f.

File name: Welcome.txt

4g, 4h.

First text box
File name: Welcome.txt

Second text box
File name: the only place.txt

g. Create a second text box, open a text file named *the only place.txt* in SimpleText, copy the text, and paste it into the NetObjects Fusion text box.

h. Center the text, as shown in Figure 4h.

5. Lengthen the page.

a. Click on the Layout tab in the Properties dialog box to select the Layout page.

b. In the field labeled *Width,* type:

800

In the field labeled *Height,* type:

800

Press Return.

Layout tab

5a, 5b.

c. The page will be lengthened, giving you more space to create another text box.

6. Add more text.

a. Create a third text box, open a text file named *text links.txt* in SimpleText, copy the text, and paste it into the NetObjects Fusion text box.

b. Insert a line break after the words *Hot Links,* and center the text, as shown in Figure 6b. *(Note: Review Chapter 3 for details about line breaks.)*

First text box   Second text box

6a, 6b.

Third text box
File name: text links.txt

7.

7. Add a tiled background.

Frank created embossed tiles in Photoshop using the instrument shapes he used to create the image map panel. He duplicated the tiles and added colors to match the page color schemes.

a. Click on the Picture radio dial on the Layout page of the Properties dialog box.

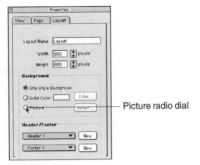

Picture radio dial

7a.

b. In the dialog box that follows, select the file named *Purple_bkgrd.gif,* and click on Open.

c. Your tile will fill the back of the page in the Page view to form a wallpaper pattern.

7b.

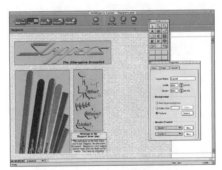

7c.

8a.

8b.

8. Create an image map.

a. Double-click the Picture Tool.

b. A set of secondary Picture tools will appear at the base of the Toolbox.

c. Click to select the Rectangle Hotspot tool.

d. Drag a rectangle over the drum set in Frank's image map panel.

e. When you release the mouse button, a Link dialog box will be displayed. Type the name of the page you would like to link to in the field labeled *Page Name,* and click on Find. *(Note: Review Chapter 3 for details on page links, smart links, and external links.)*

8c.

8d.

8e.

f. A dialog box will appear with the message *Successfully linked to Who Page.* Click on OK.

g. Repeat Steps 8a through 8f to create hotspot boxes around the remaining percussion icons in Frank's image map panel. A set of rectangles will be visible when you have completed the set of rectangular hotspots.

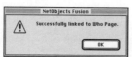

8f.

8g.

Before you design a form for your Web site...

Summary: Before you design a form, determine where the form data will be sent.

Before you design a form for your Web site, develop a strategy for routing the data from the form to some destination on the Internet.

1. Options for routing data.

a. A CGI script to route data to a text file. Several different types of CGI scripts may be used to route the data that's entered on your form to some destination on the Internet. Many scripts write form data to a text file on the Web server. These scripts may be custom-written in computer languages such as Perl, Java, or C++.

Alternatively, you may consider using a CGI script that exists in the public domain. For example, visit the Dreamcatchers site at http://dreamcatchersweb .com/scripts to download a form script. Most CGI scripts are created for Unix Web servers, and this strategy also assumes that you have access to the CGI-BIN or the CGI folder on the Web server you're using.

Contact your Internet service provider and inquire whether you have access to the server's CGI directory. Access may be allowed to commercial account users and not users with personal accounts.

b. A CGI script to route data to a database. If you run your own server or you rent from an ISP that is willing to allow you to run software on the server, consider setting up a database software program that will store the form data. For Macintosh users, FileMaker from Claris Corporation is an easy-to-use option. Everyware Development Corporation's Tango for FileMaker will create a CGI script to route form data from your Web page into FileMaker. *(Note: Claris is planning to add increased Web functionality to FileMaker in the next release. Watch for this development.)*

c. MAILTO. Using a MAILTO command to route data allows you to avoid the use of a CGI script. Use the following tags if you are creating your own HTML tags:

```
<FORM METHOD=POST ACTION="MAILTO:
your_e-mail@address.com">

<P>
```

```
Name <INPUT TYPE="TEXT" NAME="NAME">

<P>

Address <INPUT TYPE="TEXT" NAME="ADDRESS">

<P>

City <INPUT TYPE="TEXT" NAME="CITY">

<P>

State <INPUT TYPE="TEXT" NAME="STATE">

<P>

Zip <INPUT TYPE="TEXT" NAME="ZIP">

<P>

Country <INPUT TYPE="TEXT" NAME="COUNTRY">

<P>

E-mail <INPUT TYPE="TEXT" NAME="EMAIL">

<P>

<INPUT TYPE="SUBMIT" VALUE="SUBMIT FORM">

<P>

<INPUT TYPE="RESET" VALUE="CLEAR FORM">

</FORM>
```

(Note: Format the form as a table to create even columns.)

2. Examples of commercial ISP service in NYC.

a. alt.coffee. This Internet café in New York's East Village is also an Internet provider. Owner John Scott is the Webmaster and offers commercial Web accounts (no personal PPP accounts). Included in a commercial account is a private CGI directory (CGI-BIN) where customers can place a CGI script. The alt.coffee commercial services include:

Single Commercial Web Account:

- $100 per month, $100 setup fee

- 1 virtual domain (IP address on host machine)

- 1 email account with multiple aliases ($10 each additional per month)

- 20 MB of storage space ($.50 each additional per month)
- 1 FTP account ($10 each additional per month)
- 1 private CGI-BIN directory
- 500 MB of data transfer per month ($.10 each additional per month)
- 1 monthly statistics report ($10 each additional per month)
- Weekly tape backup
- SSL secure server (must provide own certificate)
- Full T1 direct to Netcom's T3 backbone
- ISDN redundant backup line

Developer's Discount:

- 4 Commercial Web accounts for $300 per month, $300 setup fee

Contact: John Scott, 212.529.2233,
jetsam@flotsam.com

b. **The Internet Channel.** The Internet Channel is one of New York's larger Internet providers, offering personal PPP accounts and commercial Web accounts. A small library of CGI scripts is available to users with personal PPP accounts, but users cannot upload their own CGI scripts to the server. A commercial Web account does include a private CGI directory (CGI-BIN). Call for current prices.

Contact: Beth Haviland, Director of Technical Support,
212.243.5200, support@inch.com

Using NetObjects Fusion to design a form (with a MAILTO for routing data)

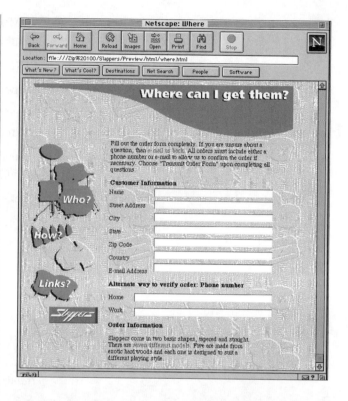

Follow this step-by-step sample if you have completed the previous section. Review basic NetObjects Fusion Web page creation techniques in Chapter 3 before starting this section. Readers who wish to follow this example should look for Frank DeCrescenzo's art and text files on the companion CD-ROM.

1. Change views.

a. If you have completed the previous sample, switch to the Site view by clicking on the Site button.

1a.

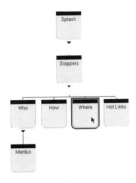

1b.

b. In the NetObjects Fusion Site view that follows, double-click the Where page to go to the Where Page view.

c. (Option) Alternately, you may select Go To from the Go pull-down menu.

d. (Option) If you selected Go To from the Go pull-down menu, type *Where* in the field labeled *Go To,* and click on OK.

e. The Where Page view will be displayed.

1c.

1d.

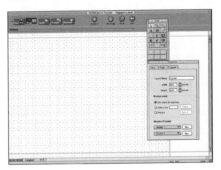

1e.

2a, 2b.

2. Change the page size.

a. Click in the Width field on the Layout page of the Properties dialog box, and type:

1066

b. Click in the Height field on the Layout page of the Properties dialog box, and type:

1066

3a.

3. Add art to the page.

a. Select the Picture Tool.

b. Draw picture boxes on the Web page, as shown in Figure 3b. Import Frank's art files into these boxes.

File name: Silver_head.gif

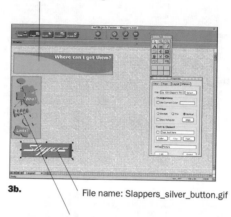

3b.

File name: Slappers_silver_button.gif

File name: Where_imagemap.gif

Picture tab

Stretch radio dial

4a, 4b.

4c.

4. Scale an image.

The Slappers button needs to be scaled proportionately so that it is a smaller button.

a. Because you have been working with picture boxes, the Picture page on the Properties dialog box should be selected. If it is not selected, click the Picture tab at the top of the dialog box to select the Picture page in the Properties dialog box.

b. Click to select the Stretch radio dial.

c. Hold down the Shift key and drag the lower-right handle on the Slappers button. Move your mouse up and to the left to scale the Slappers button. This will create a smaller button.

5a.

5b.

5. Add text.

a. Select the Text Tool.

b. Draw a text box, as shown in Figure 5b.

c. Launch SimpleText.

SimpleText
5c.

d. Open a text file named *Where_intro.text*, copy the text, and paste it into the NetObjects Fusion text box, as shown in Figure 5d.

e. Create a second text box, open a text file named *fields.txt* in SimpleText, copy the text, and paste it into the NetObjects Fusion text box, as shown in Figure 5e.

5d.

File name: Where_intro.text

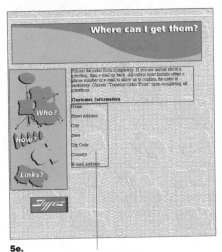

5e.

File name: fields.txt

6. Create single-line text fields.

a. Double-click the Form Tool.

6a.

6b.

6c.

b. A set of secondary form tools will appear at the base of the Toolbox.

c. Click to select the Single-line Form Tool.

d. Draw a form text box, as shown in Figure 6d. (*Note: Although you'll need a long text box for this field, the length will need to be controlled from the Properties dialog box.*)

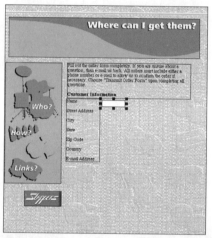
6d.

6e, 6f.

e. When you draw a single-line text field, the Single Line page on the Properties dialog box is displayed. Label each of the single-line text fields numerically. In the field labeled *Name*, type:

1

f. Drag-select the number in the field labeled *Visible Length*, and type:

38

Drag-select the the number in the field labeled *Max Length*, and type:

38

Press Return.

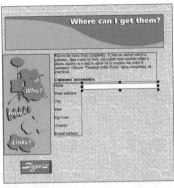

6g.

Tip: Use the arrow keys on your keyboard to position a single-line text field. To align the fields, select the Selection Tool, drag a marquee around the fields, and select Align Elements/Left from the Page pull-down menu.

7a.

7b.

7c.

g. The length of the text box will change in response to the new field length numbers you entered in the Properties dialog box.

h. Repeat Steps 6a through 6e to create six more single-line text fields, as shown in Figure 6h. Label them 2, 3, 4, 5, 6, and 7.

6h.

7. Create a Submit button.

A Submit button functions to submit form data. Although Frank's form contains several more fields, the Submit button will be added here for the purpose of this example.

a. Double-click the Form Tool.

b. A set of secondary Form tools will appear at the base of the Toolbox.

c. Select the Button tool.

d. Draw a Button box.

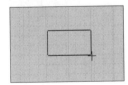

7d.

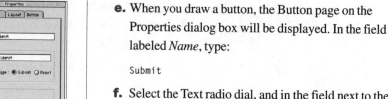

7e, 7f, 7h.

e. When you draw a button, the Button page on the Properties dialog box will be displayed. In the field labeled *Name*, type:

Submit

f. Select the Text radio dial, and in the field next to the radio dial, type:

Submit

g. The button you create will contain the word *Submit* in response to your typing. *(Note: You can use your own button image by selecting the Image radio dial, clicking on the Select button, and selecting an image from your hard drive.)*

7g.

h. Select the Submit radio dial.

8. Create a Reset button.

a. Double-click the Form Tool.

b. A set of secondary Form tools will appear at the base of the Toolbox.

c. Select the Button Tool.

d. Draw a Button box.

8a.

8b.

8c.

8d.

8e, 8f, 8h.

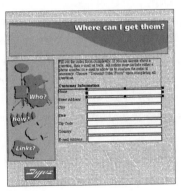

9a.

e. When you draw a button, the Button page on the Properties dialog box will be displayed. In the field labeled *Name*, type:

```
Reset
```

f. Select the Text radio dial, and in the field next to the radio dial, type:

```
Reset
```

g. The button you create will contain the word *Reset* in response to your typing. *(Note: You can use your own button image by selecting the Image radio dial, clicking on the Select button, and selecting an image from your hard drive.)*

8g.

h. Select the Reset radio dial.

9. Assign a MAILTO action to the form.

A NetObjects Fusion page can contain one form. You may have noticed a Form Settings option each time you accessed the Properties dialog box while you were building the form's fields. Even though you have access to the Settings option each time you build a field, you only need to fill it in once for the entire form.

a. Select the first text field you created for your form.

9b.

b. When you select any single-line text fields on your form, the Single Line page on the Properties dialog box will be displayed.

c. Click on the Settings button.

d. In the Form Settings dialog box that follows, click in the field labeled *Action,* and type:

`mailto:<your_email@address.com>`

Click on OK.

9c.

9d.

10. Publish your site.

Follow the directions for publishing a site in Chapter 3.

11. Test your form.

Your form will need to be tested online. Move your newly published pages to your Web site with the FTP client that is built into NetObjects Fusion or use Jim Matthews' Fetch. Fetch is a Macintosh FTP shareware utility. (*Note: For details on how to use Fetch, see* Use Fetch to upload your files to a provider's server *in the* Client-Side Image Maps *chapter.*)

Using a MAILTO command to route form data provides a simple solution for designers who do not want to get involved with CGI scripts. However, you'll find that the data that is mailed to an email address will need to be cleaned up in a word processor (Figure 11 and following).

```
1=Mary+Jo+Fahey&2=233+Lexington+Avenue+%23603&3=New+York&
  4=NY&5=10021&6=USA&7=mjfahey
@interport.net&Submit=Submit
```

11.

Index

2D graphics, 34-35, 37-39
2D images, 349
2D navigation, 39
3D animation, 364
3D browsers, 27, 35
3D Chat, 396, 397, 400-401
3D graphics, 30-32, 35, 40. *See also* VRML.
3DMF, 30-31, 35, 393

A

Active link, changing color of, 132
ActiveX, 1
Adobe Illustrator, creating type in, 181-182
Adobe Systems, OpenType initiative, 95, 99, 106, 107, 113, 125
Afterburner (software), 381, 390
AIFF files, 307, 322, 326
Alawusa, Peju, 69, 72, 88
alt.coffee commercial service, 474-475
alt.coffee Web site, 54-68
Amendola, Billy, 463, 464
America Online, 195
Anchors, 31, 35, 40, 52, 60, 66, 283, 323
Animation, 337-390
  flip-book animation, 349-354
  games, 341
  GIF animation, 337, 339-340, 349-363
  interactive, 341, 364-380
  loops, 356, 377-378
  reducing file size, 340, 360-363
  Shockwave, 337, 341-348, 381
Antiochia, Antonio, 303
Apple Computer
  PC enabling hardware, 5
  VRML, 393
Applets, 35
Arizona Macintosh Users Group, 37
The Arrival Web site, 342
Arrows, 39
Art. *See* Graphics, Images.
Associative indexing, 34
Audio. *See* Sound.
Audio streaming, 322
AU files, 299, 302, 307, 322, 326, 336

AVI files, 294-298

B

Background, 133
  color, 63, 101, 109-110, 203, 213, 260
  fading an image into the browser background, 202-203
  full-bleed images, 13, 206
  HTML coding, 13, 45-51, 136, 166, 208-211, 278-273, 314, 317
  Internet Explorer style sheet, 101
  in Netscape, 45, 133-135, 202-212
  samples, 133-135
  sound, 313-323
  tiled, 204-206, 383-386, 471
BackWeb (software), 9
Banding, GIF images, 158-159
Banner graphics, 178-187
BBS Color Editor. *See* Online Color Editor.
Beach, David, 305
Ben & Jerry's Hair Game, 343, 344
Berners-Lee, Tim, 33
Best Business Solutions (BBS), 127, 129
Biggar, Jamie, 341
BIN files, 145
Bin-Hex format, 19
Bit depth, 151, 155, 157, 182, 185-186, 217-218
BlackSun International
  CyberHub, 30, 396
  virtual scavenger hunt, 63
Blender (digizine), 347
Bookmarks, 307
Borders, 39
Borenzweig, Claude, 347
Browsers
  3D, 27, 35, 243
  cascading style sheets, 95
  client-side image maps, 253
  color palette, 157, 179
  Fetch, 36, 94, 243, 262-264, 484
  image quality on, 153-154
  Internet Explorer, 95
  NetObjects Fusion Web page preview, 75, 90-92
  offline browsers, 1, 9

style sheets, 98
for VRML files, 452-453
Build Your Own Bug (game), 344
Bush, Vannevar, 34
Buttons
animated, 342
borders, 39
cropping graphics, 42-44
HTML table to hold, 42-53
interactive movies, 344
Lingo buttons, 374-377
outline turned off, 14
Reset button, 482-483
Submit button, 481-482

C

Cameron, Ewan, 99
Capuozzo, Chris, 347
Cascading style sheets (CSS1), 95, 98
Castle Red Dog Web site, 313-316
CD-ROMs, 7-8
CGI script, 461, 473, 474
Character entities, 163
Chat, 8, 31, 396, 397, 400-401
Chen, Eric, 282
Chowka, Peter B., 95, 97, 461
Cicada Web Development, 397
Cinepak (software), 277
Cipolla, Tom, 299, 324, 325, 333
ClarisWorks (software), 201
Classes, in HTML tags, 103
Clayton, Damien, 347
Clemens, Michael, 303
Client-side image maps, 239, 242
components, 242-243
creating, 241-257, 466-473
planning, 244-247
Clip media, sound effects, 324-325, 327-329
clnet, Shareware.com site, 144
Color
background, 63, 101, 109-110, 203, 213, 260
dithering, 151-152
of font, 101, 122-123
grayscale, 152
images, 150, 151, 157, 179-181
Internet Explorer style sheet, 101

movies, 284-292, 381-382
Super Palette, 236-238, 284-292
text, 63
text links, 39
Color codes
adding, 129-136
hex code for, 127, 129-131
Pantone color, 129, 130
RGB color, 123, 129-136
Color duotone, 152, 232-234
Comment tags, to embed style sheet, 99, 105-108
Compression. *See* File compression.
CompuServe, GIF file format patent, 161
Coney Island Project Web site, 406-417
Conferencing software, 309
CoolTalk (Apple), 308, 309
Cosmo browser, 452
CSS file, 100
Cunniff, Tom, 303
CU-SeeMe (software), 309
CyberCash CyberCoin Wallet (software), 397-398
CyberHub (BlackSun Interactive), 30

D

Data, forms and, 461, 465, 473-475
Data fork, 293
Data transfer, video, 274-275
DeBabelizer (Equilibrium Technologies), 284
bit depth, 150
number of colors, 156
pixel depth, 186
Super Palette, 147, 157, 236-238, 284-282
text offset, 170, 192, 193
transparent GIF, 197, 207, 219
DeBabelizer Lite (Equilibrium Technologies),
159
Decompression, of shareware from the Web, 145
DeCrescenzo, Frank, 53, 69, 461, 476
Dellario, Frank, 402
Dessimoz, Gail, 346
DigiPhone (Electric Magic), 308
Digital media, 347
Digital versatile disc (DVD), 347
Director (Macromedia), 337, 381
Director Internet Player (Macromedia), 32, 35,
381-390

Director Player (Macromedia), 364-380
Disguise-O-Rama game, 343-344
Dithering, 151-152
Domain names, 36-37
Domain Name Service (DNS), 36
Dominianni, Matt, 402
Download speed, 153, 157-158
Drop shadow, 147, 213-220
Duhan, Matt, 402
Duotones, 152, 232-235
DVD, 347
D Web site, 346

E

Eberhardt, Curtis, 338, 339-341, 346, 364-366
Elbert, Mark, 147, 175, 178, 188, 202
Email addresses
  Alawusa, Peju, 69
  Apple Developer's Association, 345
  Chowka, Peter B., 95
  Cipolla, Tom, 249, 299
  DeCrescenzo, Frank, 461
  Dominianni, Matt, 402
  Eberhardt, Curtis, 337, 346
  Elbert, Mark, 142
  Esparza, Mary, 27, 29
  Greenbaum, Jane, 147
  Haviland, Beth, 475
  Hess, Greg, 299
  Hughes, Kevin, 241
  Kingsley, Chris, 344
  Marino, Paul, 402
  McGrew, Steven, 265
  Neuwirth, Pauline, 343-344
  Reinfurt, David, 1
  Santos, Kleber, 239
  Scott, John L., 27, 475
  Shamson, Alex, 391, 393
  Tekserve, 6
  Thorner, Marc, 265, 406
Embedded fonts, 95, 125
Embedded style sheet, 99, 102
Empyrean (game), 30, 41
The Engine.RDA, 346-347
Environmental designers, 11
EPS file, 181
Esparza, Guillermo, 29, 31

Esparza, Merry, 27, 29, 31, 32, 39, 41
Event handlers (script), 377
Express VR browser, 452
External images, 158
External links, NetObjects Fusion, 87

F

Fetch (software), 36, 94, 243, 262-264, 484
File compression
  audio, 295-296
  formats, 145
  GIF files, 157-160
  GIF patent, 161
  JPEG files, 157-160, 161
  movies, 381, 390
  video, 267, 276-277, 295-296
File compression algorithms, JPEG, 159
File compression formats, 145
File conversion, sound files, 326, 336
FileMaker (Claris), 473
Filo, David, 127, 137
FLAT files, 293
FlattenMooV (software), 293
Flowcharting, 41
Fonts. *See also* Typography.
  boldface, 163
  changing in a headline, 116-117
  color, 101, 122-123
  embedded fonts, 95, 125
  family, 100, 122-123
  HTML, 63, 67
  Internet Explorer style sheet, 100
  italic, 163
  OpenType initiative, 95, 97, 99, 106, 107, 113, 125
  style sheets, 99
  TrueType fonts, 102, 105, 108-112, 124-125
  underline, 163
Forms, 461
  client-side image map, 466-472
  data and, 461, 465, 473-475
  designing, 467-484
  MAILTO URL, 461, 473-474, 483-484
  Reset button, 482-483
  Submit button, 481-482
Frame layout, 54-68
Freeloader (software), 9

Frequency, 296
Fruchter, Jason, 348
Fry, David, 303
FTP, 36
Full bleed images, 13, 206

G

Games, 30, 341, 343-344, 348
General Motor's Product Line Web page, 345
Ghosting image, 204
GIF animation, 337, 339-340, 349-363
GIFBuilder (software), 339, 340, 349, 355-357
GIFConverter (software), 186
GIF files, 31, 157-161, 198
  download speed, 157-158
  interlaced GIF, 158-161, 186, 218
  reducing size, 360
  transparent GIF, 158-161, 258-261
GIF images, 158-159, 247
  animation, 337, 339-340, 349-363
  banding, 158-159
  directory for, 190, 359
  linking to, 188-191, 278
  NetObjects Fusion software, 80
  posterization, 160
  transparent GIF, 207
GIF Wizard (software), 340, 360-363
Giles, Aaron, 192
Gontier, Frederic, 396
Gottlieb, Sam, 377
Graphics, 147-238. *See also* Buttons, Images.
  animation, 337-390
  arrows, 39
  banner graphics, 178-187
  color duotone, 232-235
  drop shadow, 147, 213-231
  fading an image into the browser background, 202
  linking thumbnail GIF to external JPEG, 188-191
  silhouettes, 207-212
  tiled background, 204-206, 383-386, 471
  uploading file to server, 263
  VRML, 391-460
  wrapping text around a photo, 192-197
Grayscale, 152
Green, Andrew, 308

Greenbaum, Jane, 147, 221
Grouped formatting, text, 102-103

H

Hale, Tom, 8
Hapke, Matt, 402
Haviland, Beth, 475
Hennessey, Patrick, 293
Hess, Greg, 299, 313
Hexadecimal codes, for color, 39, 123, 127, 129-131
Hill, John, 347
Histograms, Photoshop, 150
Home page, 33, 35
HotJava, 35
Hotspots, 31, 35, 239, 241
.HTM extension, 190
HTML. *See also* HTML attributes, HTML documents, HTML tags.
  acronym, 162
  creating 2D navigation controls with, 39
  locating images on Web page, 165-177
  NetObjects Fusion and, 69, 88
  Netscape Navigator reference material, 140-141
  typographic controls, 47
  updates posted to Netscape, 153
  World Wide Web Consortium, 95
HTML attributes
  align=, 14, 64, 169, 173-175, 177, 192, 195, 197
  alink=, 61, 132, 133, 136, 314, 317
  alt=, 60, 61, 62
  area=, 250-254
  autoplay=, 271, 272
  autostart=, 313, 317
  background=, 13, 45-51, 136, 166, 208-211, 278-283, 314, 317
  base=, 60
  base target=, 64, 66, 67
  bgcolor=, 60-64, 67, 120, 123, 129, 131, 133-136, 248-254, 255, 272, 314, 317, 460
  border=, 49-51, 60, 62, 249
  color=, 122-123
  cols=, 56, 58, 68, 120, 257
  controller=, 270, 272
  coords=, 250-254, 257
  face=, 122-123
  height=, 321

hidden, 313, 317
href=, 39, 47-51, 60, 61, 64, 67, 123, 190, 191,
   250-254, 281, 318, 321-323
hspace=, 165, 170-171, 177, 198-199
link=, 132, 133, 136, 314, 317
loop=, 270, 272, 314, 317
marginheight=, 57, 58
marginwidth=, 57, 58, 67
method=, 473
name=, 57, 58, 250-254, 256-257
noresize=, 57, 58
rows=, 56
scroll=, 57, 58
shape=, 250-254, 257
size=, 163, 173, 196, 200
src=, 46-51, 57, 60, 62, 64, 68, 113, 167, 177,
   187, 191, 199-200, 208-212, 249-254, 256,
   313, 317, 320, 460
style=, 101-104, 114
target=, 57, 60, 61
text=, 131, 136, 314, 317
type=, 102-104, 474
usemap=, 249
vlink=, 60, 61, 132, 133, 136, 314, 317
volume=, 313-314, 317
vspace=, 171, 175, 198-199
width=, 48-51, 321
HTML documents
   borders, 39
   buttons, 14, 39, 42-44
   client-side image map, 242-257
   column format, 119-121
   comment lines, 196
   completing, 59
   creating, 45, 59-60, 105, 166, 187, 189, 194, 198
   ending link tag, 39, 164
   fading an image into browser background,
      202-203
   GIF animation testing, 360-361
   linking thumbnail GIF to exernal JPEG, 188-191
   link text, 38-39
   margins, 97, 100
   paragraph, 168
   style block, 105-107, 108-109
   style sheets, 98-102
   styling, 98-118
   subheads, 68, 102, 104
   table for buttons and text links, 42-53

text wrap, 198-200
type size, 195-196
typography, 98-103, 162
VRML window, 458-460
wrapping text around a photo, 192-197
HTML files, 19, 187, 190
   cross-platform, 8
   save as SimpleText, 45, 55, 62, 63, 66, 105, 114
   testing an image, 187
   uploading to server, 262-264
   viewed online or offline, 7
HTML tags, 34, 162, 163
   <A>, 39-40, 52, 60-61, 67, 123, 189, 282, 318,
      322, 323
   <ADDRESS>, 52, 254
   <AMG>, 195, 197
   <AREA>, 250-254
   <B>, 163, 176, 255, 272, 282, 283
   <BASE>, 57
   <BLOCKQUOTE>, 97, 100, 171-172, 176
   <BODY>, 13, 39, 45-51, 52, 61-64, 66, 67,
      103-104, 120, 123, 129, 131, 133-136, 163,
      166, 176, 187, 189, 198-201, 208-212,
      248-256, 272, 278-283, 314, 315, 317,
      458-460

, 50-52, 61, 62, 67, 104, 113, 123, 163,
      172, 175, 176, 255, 280-283
   <CENTER>, 60, 61, 163, 172, 248-254, 256,
      270, 272, 317, 459, 460
   <DL>, 97, 169-170, 171, 176, 209, 278-283,
      319-321, 323
   <EMBED>, 268-272, 313-314, 317, 458-461
   <FONT>, 63, 67, 95, 122-123, 163, 173, 176,
      196, 198-200, 200
   <FONTFACE>, 99
   <FORM>, 473-474
   <FRAME>, 55, 57, 67
   <FRAMESET>, 55-56, 58, 68
   <H1>, 113, 120, 123, 195
   <H2>, 68, 102, 104, 113, 120, 195, 196,
      198-200, 209-211
   <H3>, 68, 102, 104, 198-200, 211
   <H6>, 195
   <HEAD>, 45-51, 52, 56, 58, 60-64, 68,
      105-106, 120, 123, 133-136, 176, 187, 189,
      198-200, 208-211, 248-254, 256, 272,
      278-283, 317, 319-321, 323, 458-460
   <HR>, 51, 52

<HTML>, 45-51, 52, 56, 58-63, 68, 105-106, 120, 123, 133-136, 176, 187, 189, 198-200, 208-211, 248-254, 256, 272, 278-283, 317, 319-321, 323, 458-460
<I>, 163, 321, 323
<IMG>, 14, 39, 46-51, 53, 60, 61, 64, 113, 135, 167, 169, 177, 187, 188, 195, 197, 198-201, 208-211, 249-254, 256, 278-283, 317, 318, 320-323, 358, 399
<INPUT>, 474
<MAILTO>, 254, 256, 473-474
<MAP>, 250-254, 256-257
<MULTICOL>, 95, 119-121
<NOBR>, 163
<NOFRAMES>, 55, 58, 68
<P>, 68, 104, 163, 168, 175, 177, 198-199, 201, 281
<PRE>, 154, 164
<STYLE>, 102-104, 106-111
<TABLE>, 46-51, 53
<TD>, 47, 53
<TH>, 47-51, 53
<TITLE>, 45-51, 53, 56, 58, 60, 61, 63, 64, 68, 105-106, 120, 123, 133-136, 177, 187, 189, 201, 208-210, 208-211, 212, 248-254, 256, 257, 272, 278-283, 317, 458-460
<TR>, 46-51, 53
<U>, 163
with classes, 103
nesting, 164, 319-320
NetObjects Fusion and, 69, 88
Quark XPress tags compared to, 162, 163
special characters, 163, 196
starting and ending tags, 164
viewing on a Web site, 318
HTTP, 36
Hughes, Kevin, 241
Hybrid CD-ROM, 8
HyperCard, 34
Hyperlinking, 27, 33, 40
Hypermedia, 33-34

I

Image maps, 32, 239, 465. *See also* Client-side image maps.
Images, 147
  animation, 337-390
  bit depth, 151, 155, 157, 182, 185-186
  color, 150, 157, 179-181
  color duotone, 232-235
  dithering, 151-152
  download speed, 153
  drop shadow, 147, 213-231
  duotones, 152, 232-235
  external images, 158
  fading an image into browser background, 202-203
  file format, 158-161, 186
  file naming, 152-153
  file size, 150, 156
  full bleed images, 13
  ghosting, 204
  GIF files, 157-161
  grayscale, 152
  inline images, 158
  JPEG files, 157-161
  linking thumbnail GIF to external JPEG, 188-191
  locating on Web pages, 165-177
  resizing, 411
  scaling, 478
  scanning, 150, 179
  silhouettes, 207-212
  size of, 149, 155-156, 178
  wrapping text around a photo, 192-197
Images GIF, 158-159
Inflation distance, 420
Inline graphics links, 27, 39
Inline images, 158
Inline style tags, 99, 101, 115
Insignia Solutions, Win95 emulation program, 6
Interactive movie, 364-380
Interlaced GIF, 158-161, 186, 218
Internet Assistant (Microsoft), 209
Internet Channel, 475
Internet Explorer (Microsoft), 95
  client-side image maps, 253
  HTML tags specific for, 158
  style sheets, 95, 97, 99-101
Internet Phone (Vocaltec), 31
Internet Protocol (Microsoft), 35
Internet service providers (ISPs), 474-475
Internet telephone, 31, 308
InterNIC, 36-37
Inverted perspective, 30

IUMA site, 305-306

J

Joseph, Regina, 347
JPEG, 31, 157-160, 161
  downloading, 342
  images, 159, 190, 247, 342
  linking thumbnail GIF to JPEG file, 188-191
  saving, 159

K

Keenan, Rob, 347
Keyboard Magazine Web site, 322
KPT Bryce (software), 364

L

Lerner, David, 6
Linear perspective, 30
Linear slide shows, 37-38
Line-height, Internet Explorer style sheet, 101
Lingo (software), 365, 373-377
Linked style sheet, 99
Linking. *See* Hyperlinking.
Links
  to movie, 278-282
  to sound files, 318-323
Link text, 38-39
Live3D (software), 402, 405, 456-467
LiveAudio, Netscape, 299, 302, 310, 313
Livescript (software), 342
Long distance calling, 31, 308
Loops, animation, 356, 377-378
Lord, Robert, 305
LZW patent, 161

M

Mac, PC cards for, 5-6
MacBinary file, 145, 263
MacLink/Plus (Dataviz), 208
Macromedia, 30, 32
Macromedia Directory Lingo Workshop
  (Thompson and Gottlieb), 377
MAILTO URL, 52, 64
  forms, 461, 473-474, 483-484

HTML tags, 254, 256
Marelli, Charles, 301
Margins, 97, 100, 101
Marino, Paul, 402
Markowitz, Gary, 341
Marr, Greg, 151, 284, 290
Matthews, Jim, 36, 484
McGrew, Charles, 307
McGrew, Steven, 265, 276
Memex system, 34
MetaPlay Web site, 402
Microsoft
  browser "war" with Netscape, 1
  OpenType initiative, 95, 99, 106, 107, 113, 125
  TrueType fonts, 102, 105, 108-112, 124-125
MIDI files, 310, 322
  acronym, 310
  for downloading, 317
Milktruck (Traveling Software), 9
Mitchell, Kevin, 186
Mobius Gallery site, 29-32, 42
Molchon, Rob, 347
Mom's Truck Stop Web site, 402-405
Moos, 402, 405
Mortal Kombat (game), 346
Mosaic (Spyglass), client-side image map, 253
Motion Picture Experts Group. *See* MPEG.
Movie Analysis Tool (Adobe Premiere), 265,
  273-275
Movies
  animation, 345-348, 364-380
  characteristics, 274-275
  color, 284-292, 381-382
  create a movie projector, 379-381
  performance specs, 273-274
  photography, 267-298
  video compressor, 292
MP2 files, 305, 322
MPEG files, 269, 277, 305
MUDs (multiuser domains), 402
Multi-party conferencing, 309
Music. See also Sound.
  clip music mixed with sound effects, 327
  downloading on Netscape, 311-312
  interesting links, 322-323
  MIDI files, 310
  royalty-free, 327

N

Navigation, 27-68
  2D, 27, 34-35, 37-39
  3D, 27, 30-32, 35, 40
  buttons, HTML table to hold, 42-53
  flowcharting, 41
  frame layout, 54-68
  hypermedia, 33-34
  image maps, 32
  interactive movies, 374
  storyboarding, 41
  textlinks, HTML table to hold, 42-53
  URLs, 35-37
  VRML file, 453
Nelson, Ted, 34
Nesting tags, 164, 319-320
Net Attache Light (Tympani Software), 9
NetObjects Fusion (software), 69, 71, 210, 466
  <MULTICOL> tag, 95, 119-121
  creating client-side image map, 466-473
  creating Web pages with, 76-88
  design a form, 476-484
  hardware and software requirements, 71
  HTML and, 69, 88
  publishing the site, 92-94
  selecting browser for, 75
  staging the site, 88-90
  starting, 72-75
  testing the site, 90-91
NetPhone, 308
Netscape, 307
  background, 45, 202-212
  background samples, 133-135
  bookmark, 307
  browser "war" with Microsoft, 1
  client-side image map, 253
  Director Internet Player and, 381
  HTML tags viewed, 318
  HTML updates posted, 153
  images, 149
  LiveAudio, 299, 302, 310, 313
  music files, 311-312
  text wrap, 198-200
  tips, 13, 14
  using, 305
Netscape features
  active link, 39
  Body Background tag, 45
  inline images as links, 39
  link text, 38-39
  tables, 42
  visited link, 39
Netscape Navigator, 140-141
  HTML tags specific for, 158
  style sheets, 95, 97, 99
Network anchors. See Anchors.
Neuwirth, Pauline, 343
Node pointers, 40
NOD files, 73
Number entities, 163
NYVRMLSIG, 61, 395, 396, 406, 408

O

O'Donnell, Dan, 396-397
O'Donnell, Matt, 396-397
Offline browsers, 1, 9
Online Color Editor (BBS), 122, 123, 129-136, 458
Online publications, 3
OpenType initiative, 95, 99, 106, 107, 113, 125
Optical illusion art, 30
Orange Micro, PC enabling hardware, 5-6
Ostroy, Alex, 347

P

Page links, NetObjects Fusion software, 87
Painter 4.0, drop shadow, 147, 221-231
Pantone color, 39, 129, 130
Paradigm, for Web site, 17
Patterson, Jeff, 305
Pauling, Linus, 95, 97-100
PC cards, for Macs, 5-6
Pesce, Mark, 391, 393, 406
Phone links, 31, 308
PhotoGIF (BoxTop Software), 193, 258, 261
Photographs. See Images.
Photoshop (software), 364, 409
  animation, 337, 339
  banner graphics, 178-185
  blue duotone with, 232-235
  color codes, 129-130
  cropping button graphics, 42-44
  drop shadow, 213-220, 225
  GIF animation, 349-354

gradient tool, 202
histograms, 150
image quality, 150
Info palette, 244
palettes, 151, 244
PICT image, 178
pixel depth, 217-218
saving image, 188
text offset, 170, 192-193
text wrap, 192-197, 198
tiled background, 471
transparent GIF, 258
wrapping text around photo, 192-197
Piguet, Yves, 339, 355
Pixels, 149, 155
Planning Web pages, 26
concept development, 17
development team, 16-17
flowcharting, 41
graphic design, 21
Reuters Web site as model, 11-15, 23-25
schematic development, 18-19
schematic prototype, 20-21
storyboarding, 41
wayfinding, 11, 22-25
Plug-ins, 140, 265, 269-271
Posterization, 160
Print publications, 3
augmented by CD-ROMs, 7-8
PC Novice, 3
The Net, 3, 7-8
Web Techniques, 3
Webweek, 3
Pueblo (Chaco), 402-404

Q

Quark XPress (software), 162-163, 165
QuickTime (Apple), 277, 297
files, 293, 294-296
plug-ins, 265, 269-271
QuickTime VR (Apple), 31-32, 40, 282, 345
QuickTime VR Player, 345

R

Racz, Michael, 346
RA files, 322

Ragu Web site, 303
Rasterized type, 182
Razorsnails (game), 348
RealAudio (Progressive Technologies), 304, 322
Realtime voice communication, 31
Redlitz, Sean, 341
Redundancy, in wayfinding, 25
Reflector (software), 309
Reinfurt, David, 1, 11-12
Reply Corp., PC cards, 6
Resampling, sound files, 333-335
Resource fork, 293, 297
Reuters
Business Alert, 13
Business Briefing, 13
Business Information Products site, 13-15, 17, 19, 23, 25
News Machine site, 12-13, 17-19, 23-25
RGB color, 123, 129-136, 151
Ricci, Alberto, 299, 328, 330
Rosenthal, Larry, 61, 62, 65, 348, 396, 397, 406, 408
Rubber bands, 40

S

Santos, Kleber, 239, 241
Scaling, images, 478
Scanning, 150, 179
Schematic prototype, 20-21
SciFi Channel Web site, 341
Scott, John L., 27, 54, 55, 474, 475
Search engines, 127
extending the search beyond Yahoo!, 139
Yahoo!, 127, 137-139
Selamohlu, Handan, 98-99
Selck, Brandee Amber, 305
Shaders, 364
Shah, Vineel, 347
Shamson, Alex, 64, 391, 406, 418, 423, 438, 452, 456, 457
Shareware, 144-145
Shockwave (software), 337, 341-348, 381
Silhouettes, 207-220
SimpleText, 45, 55, 62, 63, 66, 105, 114, 166, 177, 194, 208, 243
Simprov, 402-405
Site Mill (Adobe), 10

Slappers, 53
Slappers Web site, 463-465
Smart links, NetObjects Fusion, 87
Smith, David, 391
Smith, Derrick, 53
Smith, Sharleen, 341
SoftWindows (Insignia), 6
Sound
  background sound, 313-323
  clip media, 324-326, 327-329
  data rate, 275
  file conversion, 326, 336
  file formats, 322
  file optimization, 333
  Internet telephone, 31, 308-309
  links to, 318-323
  MIDI files, 310
  recording and mixing, 330-332
  resampling and downsampling, 333-335
  sample Web sites, 301-307
  streaming, 322
  video conferencing, 309
SoundApp (software), 303, 326, 336
SoundEdit (software), 303
SoundEffects (software), 299, 324, 327-332
Sound files, 322
  compression, 295-296
  optimization, 333
  resampling, 333-335
SoundMachine (software), 325
SoundMaker (software), 335
Spatial problem solving, in wayfinding, 23
Special characters, 163, 196
Spike Lee's Web site, 4
Splash screen, 30, 178
Starbase C3 Web site, 396-401
Storyboarding, 41
Strata Studio (software), 365
Strata Studio Pro (software), 31, 367
Streaming audio, 304, 322
Streaming video, 265, 267-268
StuffIt Expander (software), 145
Style sheets
  adding style sheet properties to a tag, 101-102
  comment tag, 99, 105-108
  defined, 98
  embedded, 99, 102
  FAQ, 98-100

fonts, 99
  inline style tags, 99, 101, 115
  Internet Explorer, 95, 97, 99-101
  linked, 99
  Netscape Navigator, 95, 97, 99
  properties, 100-101
  W3C proposal, 95, 98, 107
Sumex-Aim mirror sites
  ftp://ftp.amug.org/pub/mirrors/info-mac, 37
  ftp://mirror.apple.com/mirrors/
    Info-Mac.Archive/, 36
  gopher;//gopher.cnuce.cnr.it/11/pub/info-mac,
    36
  http://mirror.apple.com, 36
Surfbot 3.0 (Surflogic LLC), 9

T

Tables, formatting form as, 474
Tango for FileMaker (Everyware Development),
  473
Tekserve, 6
Telephone links, 31, 308
Text
  adding to Web page, 469, 479
  in client-side image maps, 253-254
  color, 63
  formatting in columns, 119-121
  grouped formatting, 102-103
  Internet Explorer style sheet properties, 100-101
  styling, 98-118
  wrapping text around a photo, 192-197
Text links, 27, 38-39
  color, 39
  HTML table to hold, 42-53
  NetObjects Fusion software, 85-88
Text offset, 170, 192-193
Text processor, 243
Text wrap, 198-200
Theurer, David, 284
Thompson, John (J.T.), 377
Thorner, Marc, 265, 396, 406
tHUNK, 61, 348
tHUNKWORLD VRML, 65
Tiled background, 204-206, 383-386, 471
Transparency (software), 192, 193, 207, 218
Transparent GIF, 158-161, 197, 207, 258-261
Traveling Software, Milktruck, 9

TrueType fonts, 102, 105, 108-112, 124-125
TrueType Open Version 2, 106
Two-dimensional HTML, 34-35
Two Twelve Associates, 11
Typography. *See also* Fonts.
  adding to Web pages, 103
  HTML font sizes, 195, 196
  rasterized, 182
  style sheets, 98-102
TrueType fonts, 102, 105, 108-112, 124-125

U

Unisys, 161
URL, 133
  defined, 35
  directory and file name information, 37
  domain name information, 36-37
  function, 35, 40
  protocol information, 35-36
  replacing file name in Netscape URL field, 134
  submitting to Yahoo!, 142-143
URLs
  ftp://ftp.amug.org/pub/mirrors/info-mac, 37
  ftp://ftp.microsoft.com/developr/drg/truetype, 112
  http://cu-seeme.edu/#GET, 309
  http://dreamcatchersweb.com/scripts, 473
  http://goliath.wpine.com/cu-seeme.html, 309
  http://home.netscape.com/assist/net_sites/bg/backgrounds.html, 133, 135
  http://home.netscape.com/comprod/mirror/index.html, 302
  http://home.netscape.com/comprod/products/navigator/version_2.0/plugins/audio-video.html, 304
  http://home.netscape.com/comprod/products/navigator/version_3.0/communication/cooltalk/index.html, 309
  http://info.fuw.edu.pl/multimedia/sounds/animals, 324
  http://mansion.thepalace.com/cgi-bin/directory.pl, 313
  http://members.aol.com/alawusa/intro.html, 69, 88
  http://members.aol.com/flatsticks/splash.html, 461
  http://members.aol.com/iforward/image1.html, 147
  http://members.aol.com/mediumcool, 95, 98
  http://qtvr.quicktime.apple.com/archive/index.html, 345
  http://uccnitk.edu.tw/html.courses/colorEditor.html, 458
  http://www.acclaimnation.com/D, 346
  http://www.adobe.com, 10
  http://www.altavista.digital.com, 458
  http://www.altdotcoffee.com, 27
  http://www.backweb.com, 9
  http://www.bbsinc.com, 123
  http://www.bbsinc.com/bbs-cgi-bin/colorEditor.cgi, 129
  http://www.benjerry.com/fun/bj-hairy.html, 344
  http://www.blackamericaonline.com/bus/index.html, 4
  http://www.blacksun.com, 30
  http://www.cetobjects.com, 210
  http://www.chaco.com, 403
  http://www.claris.com/products/claris/clarispage20/clarispage20.html), 201
  http://www.cube3.com/downloads/NYVRMLSIG, 408
  http://www.cube3.com/starbase.htm, 396
  http://www.cybercash.com, 397, 398
  http://www.dataviz.com, 9
  http://www.dataviz.com/Upgrade/upgmlp_home.html, 208
  http://www.eat.com/index.html, 303
  http://www.eeb.tue.nl/midi/index.html, 299, 310
  http://www.emagic.com, 31, 308
  http://www.equil.com., 155
  http://www.ffg.com, 9
  http://www.firstfloor.com, 9
  http://www.FOOTAGE.net:2900, 267, 269, 284
  http://www.freeloader.com, 9
  http://www.geocities.com/~thecastle, 313
  http://www.gm.com/shockwav/spin/ea00.htm, 345
  http://www.hotwired.com, 239
  http://www.incontext.com, 10
  http://www.insignia.com, 9
  http://www.internic.net/ds, 36, 37
  http://www.iuma.com, 35, 239, 305
  http://www.iworld.com, 3
  http://www.keyboardmag.com, 322

http://www.learned.com/~apex/imagemap.html, 257

http://www.marlowpub.com/Marlowe/disguise2.html, 343

http://www.mcp.com/general/news7/chap2.html, 391

http://www/MediaCity.com/~erweb, 277

http://www.metaplay.com, 402

http://www.microsoft.com/gallery, 101, 158

http://www.microsoft.com/gallery/files/styles/default.htm, 99

http://www.microsoft.com/msexcel/internet/ia, 209

http://www.microsoft.com/truetype/faq/faq8.htm, 105

http://www.microsoft.com/truetype/fontpack/default.htm, 102

http://www.microsoft.com/truetype/iexplor/quick.htm, 103

http://www.microsoft.com/word/fs_wd.htm, 209

http://www.microsoft.com/workshop/author/howto/css-f.htm, 98-99, 100

http://www.microsoft.com/workshop/design/desgen/ss/css-des.htm, 100

http://www.midiweb.com, 317

http://www.mis.nccu.edu.tw/~bibo/lab/client_side_image_map.html, 210, 257

http://www.netobjects.com, 71, 463

http://www.netscape.com, 153

http://www.new-kewl.com/curtiscape, 337, 339

http://www.new-kewl.com/curtiscape/bump.html, 340

http://www.new-kewl.com/curtiscape/main.html, 339

http://www.orangemicro.inter.net, 6

http://www.pacific-coast.com, 160, 299, 324

http://www.quickTime.apple.com, 269

http://www.quickTime.apple.com/sw/browserconfig.html, 269

http://www.quickTime.apple.com/sw/qtmac.html, 308

http://www.raspberryhill.com/gifwizard.html, 340, 360

http://www.realaudio.com, 304

http://www.reply.com, 6

http://www.reuters.com, 12, 13

http://www.rlspace.com, 282

http://www.rutgers.edu/x-files.html, 307

http://www.scifi.com, 341

http://www.shareware.com, 144

http://www.sony.com, 239

http://www.submit-it.com, 142

http://www.submit-it.permalink.com/submit-it, 220

http://www.surflogic.com, 9

http://www.thearrival.com, 342

http://www.thenet-usa.com, 3, 7

http://www.thepalace.com, 314

http://www.thespot.com, 239

http://www.thunk.com, 348

http://www.travsoft.com, 9

http://www.tympani.com, 9

http://www.ubl.com, 323

http://www.users.interport.net/merry/mobius.html, 27, 29

http://www.vivo.com, 267

http://www.vrmill.com, 391, 394, 452, 456

http://www.vrmill.com/Shopping.htm, 64

http://www.w3.org/hypertext/WWW/Arena/style.html, 47

http://www.w3.org/pub/WWW/TR/WD-css1.html, 98

http://www.webtv.net, 4

http://www.webweek.com, 3

http://www.yahoo.com, 36, 137, 142, 307

http://www.zdnet.com/intweek, 3

http://www.zima.com, 301

User group SIGs, 4

User's Guide to Style Sheets, A (Selamohlu), 98

V

Van Halen Web site, 307, 318

VBScript, 1

Vellum, 279

VidEdit (software), 296

Video
data transfer, 274, 275
streaming video, 265, 267-268

Video compression, 267, 276-277, 292, 295-296

Video conferencing, 309

Video for Windows (software), 294

Video for Windows Converter (CoSA), 293

Virtual Reality Modeling Language. *See* VRML.

Virtual reality Web sites
Coney Island project, 406-417

Mom's Truck Stop, 402-405
Starbase C3, 396-401
Virtus Voyager browser, 391, 452
Virtus Walkthrough Pro (software), 31, 408-417, 418
Vistographer Lite (RealSpace), 282
VIV file, 268
VivoActive Player, 267
VivoActive Producer (software), 265, 267-268
Voice communication, 31, 308
VRML, 30-31, 35, 391-460
  creating VRML model, 418-451
  embedding a VRML window in a Web page, 458-460
  hand coding, 454
  network anchors, 40
  PerspectiveCamera, 405
  Web sites, 396-417
  WRL files, 418, 451-457
VRML Architectural Group, 395
VRML files, hand coding, 391
VRMSLIG, 65

W

W3C (World Wide Web Consortium), style sheet proposal, 95, 98, 107
Walkabout 3D World Browser (Duet Development Corp.), 30, 31, 40
Walkthrough environment, 31
Wallpaper effect, 133, 204-205
WAV files, 299, 302, 307, 322, 326, 336
Wayfinding
  cognitive mapping, 22
  color, 25
  conditions, 23-24
  decision making, 23, 24
  defined, 11, 22-23
  design process, 24-25
  graphic landmarks, 25
  iteration, 25
  redundancy, 25
  spatial problem solving, 23
WebAnalyzer (InContext), 10
Web Buddy (Dataviz), 9
Web pages
  banner graphics, 178-187
  color codes, 123, 129-136

drop shadow, 147, 213-231
fading an image into browser background, 202-203
forms, 461-484
home page, 33, 35
HTML for design. See Images.
MAILTO URL, 52, 64, 254
movies, 267-298
NetObjects Fusion for design. See NetObjects Fusion.
Pantone color, converting, 39
planning. See Planning Web pages.
signature area, 51, 52, 254
silhouettes, 207-212
sound, 313-323
style sheets, 98-102
text, 469-470, 479
text wrap, 198-200
tiled background, 204-206, 383-386, 471
type size, 195, 196
typography, 98-103
uploading to server, 262-264
video, 265-297
VRML windows, 458-460
Web site analysis software, 10
Web site development. See Planning.
Web sites
  browsers. See Browsers.
  flowcharting, 41
  frame layout, 54-68
  free submittal service, 220
  home page, 33, 35
  image maps, 32, 239-264
  images. See Images.
  navigation. See Navigation.
  with sound, 299, 301-336
  storyboarding, 41
  submitting, free service, 220
Web trends
  CD-ROMs augmenting a Web site, 7-8
  emulation software, 6
  games, 30
  Internet magazines for, 3
  offline browsing, 1, 9
  PC cards, 5-6
  PC-related, 1, 4
  user groups, 3
  Web site analysis software, 10

Webtv, 4

Webtv, 4
Web Whacker (Forefront), 9
Welch, Terry, 161
Windows95 software, use on Mac platform, 4, 5-6
Withagen, Heini, 299
World Wide Web Consortium (W3C), 95, 98, 107
WRL file, 418, 451-457
WSmart Bookmarks (First Floor), 9

Y

Yahoo!
  search techniques, 137-139
  URL submission process, 127, 142-143
Yang, Jerry, 127, 137

Z

Zima Web site, 301-302